THE MOUNTAIN TRAVEL® BOOK OF TREKS, OUTINGS & EXPEDITIONS

1⊖ TEN SPEED PRESS
BERKELEY, CALIFORNIA

River crossing, Pakistan/Dick McGowan

You may order single copies prepaid direct from the publisher.
$9.95 + $1.00 for postage and handling. (California residents add
6% state sales tax; Bay Area residents add 6½%.)

 TEN SPEED PRESS
P.O. Box 7123
Berkeley, California 94707

Library of Congress Catalog Number: 83-040079
ISBN: 0-89815-114-7

ASIA

& THE PACIFIC

The pioneer in Himalayan adventure travel in 1967, Mountain Travel, Inc., is still the acknowledged leader in adventuring, still the innovator, fielding the first-ever treks in China in 1980 and the first treks in Mongolia in 1982.

What is trekking? Simply walking, following age-old trails through valleys and villages. Anyone who leads an active life and is in good health will enjoy Himalayan trekking. We hire porters and/or pack animals to carry all the gear and employ a staff to do all cooking and camp chores.

The concept of "trekking" as a means of touring originated in Kashmir, favorite retreat of the British Raj, and in Nepal, a Himalayan kingdom with the largest variety of trekking routes in all Asia.

China continues to open more and more of its fascinating and remote provinces for trekking tourism, and we offer a wide selection of one-of-a-kind China and Tibet treks.

In India, we focus much of our attention on the Himalayan highlands of Ladakh, where Tibetan Buddhist monasteries preserve a treasury of ancient Buddhist art.

Trekking in northern Pakistan, where there are 17 mountains higher than 25,000 feet, is a particular specialty of Mountain Travel. We travel to K2, world's second highest peak, to legendary Hunza and to the mysterious Hindu Kush, beneath the great walls of the Karakorum Mountains.

There are many reasons why trekking is becoming such a popular form of travel—come to Asia with us in 1984 and you'll see why.

Front cover left to right:

Bangkok's floating market/Sara Steck
Below Mt. Annapurna, Nepal/Lanny Johnson
Balti woman, Pakistan/Pam Shandrick
Camping in the Karakorum/Dick McGowan
Mt. Dhaulagiri from Poon Hill/Skip Horner
Tibetan yak driver, China/John Thune
Kishtwar Himalayas, India/Leo Le Bon
Tibetan padlock, China/Jerry Coe
Terraced rice fields, Nepal/Bruce Klepinger
Potala Palace, Lhasa, Tibet/Leo Le Bon
Porters on the Baltoro Glacier/Dick McGowan
Dancer at Mani Rimdu/Stan Armington
Village headman, Ladakh/Gordon Wiltsie
Ghandrung village, Nepal/Gordon Wiltsie
Mani stone in the Khumbu region/Sara Steck
Bharatpur Bird Sanctuary/Bruce Klepinger

1984 CALENDAR INDEX

Most of our 1984 trips will be repeated in 1985 on approximately the same dates.

Joe Brennan

Jerry Coe

Nigel Dabby

LEADERSHIP

Trip leaders are an important part of what makes a Mountain Travel trip special. Our Asia leaders come to us with a wide variety of backgrounds. Some are chosen for their knowledge of the language or culture, some for their mountaineering experience, but above all, for their ability to assure a safe, enjoyable and successful trip.

STAN ARMINGTON, 40, American managing director of Himalayan Journeys in Kathmandu, has been organizing and leading Nepal treks since 1971 and is author of "Trekking In the Himalayas." A member of the Alpine Stomach Club, he is also founder and habitue of the Rum Doodle Bar & Restaurant in Kathmandu.

JOE BRENNAN, 37, is a photographer/lecturer, ocean sailor and long distance bicyclist who has led trips in such varied places as Chile, Hawaii, Peru, Ecuador, Pakistan, Nepal and China.

JEFF CAMPBELL, 30, is an American who was born and brought up in the Punjab of India. He is fluent in Hindi, Punjabi, Nepali and other regional languages, is an excellent naturalist and has guided many treks in India and Nepal.

JERRY COE, 33, is a mountaineer, woodworker and blacksmith. He speaks fluent Japanese, is studying Chinese, and has led trips in most of China's mountain regions.

DAKU TENZING NORGAY, 43, is a Sherpani, born in the Everest region of Nepal. Wife of Everest summiteer Tenzing Norgay, she is an experienced mountain guide and manages a trekking agency in Darjeeling.

NIGEL DABBY, 31, is Mountain Travel's Asian operations manager. He has lived in Nepal and led treks in Nepal, Sikkim, Bhutan, Pakistan, India and Mongolia.

CHARLES GAY, 35, lived in Nepal for several years as a Peace Corps volunteer, speaks fluent Nepali, and is an experienced trek leader.

Daku Tenzing Norgay

Peter Hackett

Linda Liscom

John Thune

Bruce Klepinger

Scott Macbeth

John Mueller

PETER HACKETT, M.D., 35, is Director of Medical Research for the Himalayan Rescue Association of Kathmandu, and Director of High Altitude Research in the Department of High Latitude Studies of the University of Alaska, Anchorage. He was medical officer of the 1981 American Medical Research Expedition to Everest, on which he became the fourth person (and first American) to climb to the summit of Mt. Everest alone.

DICK IRVIN, 53, is a graduate student in ecology at the University of California, Davis, and is a veteran of many mountain expeditions in the Himalayas, Andes and Alps.

Leo Le Bon (right) with China leaders

LANNY JOHNSON, 28, is a professional mountain guide, nordic ski instructor and ski patrolman. He has extensive experience in guiding treks and climbs in Nepal and India and was a member of an international expedition on Makalu in 1977.

BRUCE KLEPINGER, 42, has led more than 50 Mountain Travel treks in Asia and South America. His mountaineering background includes over 1,000 climbs, and he has led expeditions on Aconcagua (highest peak in the Western Hemisphere), Huascaran (highest peak in Peru), and several peaks in Nepal and India. He has also spent many years as a senior boatman on the Grand Canyon.

LEO LE BON, 49, president and founder of Mountain Travel, Inc., has more than 25 years of professional experience in all phases of the travel industry, both in his native Europe and in the U.S. His early interest in wilderness travel led him to the creation of Mountain Travel in 1967. An avid sailor, skier and mountaineer, he has made exploratory expeditions on five continents in search of unusual forms of adventure travel.

LINDA LISCOM, 43, is a professional photographer with twelve years of experience in leading Sierra Club and Mountain Travel trips in Asia and South America.

SCOT MACBETH, 52, is a field geologist by profession, mountaineer by avocation, and founder of the Alpine Stomach Club. He has spent years in Nepal, calls the Khumbu region his "second home," and was a member of the 1981 American Expedition to Tibet.

Dick McGowan

Hugh Swift

DICK MCGOWAN, 50, Mountain Travel's vice president, has climbed and trekked throughout the world. He led the first guided ascent of Mt. McKinley and was Chief Guide on Mt. Rainier from 1956 to 1965 (with 83 ascents of that mountain!). He has also been on ten major expeditions, including Everest-Lhotse in 1955 and Masherbrum in the Karakorum in 1960. Dick has a lengthy business background as administrator, consultant and manager of several equipment firms.

JOHN MUELLER, 28, is a professional climbing guide in the Pacific Northwest. He has spent most of the last three years leading treks and expeditions for Mountain Travel in the mountains of Nepal and Pakistan.

STEVE MCKINNEY, 30, is the world's fastest man on skis. A member of the U.S. Ski Team from 1970 to 1974, he won the International Speed Skiing Championship in 1974, 1977 and 1978 (at 124 m.p.h.). In 1982, he led Mountain Travel's successful ascent and ski descent of Muztagata (24,757') in China.

MUNEO NUKITA, 32, is a Japanese mountaineer who climbed to the summit of Dhaulagiri in 1979. He is a professional climbing guide with experience in the European Alps and Alaska.

MIKE PERRY, 27, a New Zealander, is a photographer by profession and has climbed extensively in the Southern Alps of New Zealand for the last ten years.

HUGH SWIFT, 40, author of *The Trekker's Guide To the Himalaya and Karakoram*, has visited just about every nook and cranny of the Himalaya and leads treks in Nepal, India and Pakistan. In 1981 and 1982, he and Arlene Blum walked from Bhutan to Pakistan, a nine-month foot journey called the "Great Himalayan Traverse."

RAJ SINGH, 28, is a Rajput from Bharatpur, India. He is a professional naturalist, an ornithologist of repute, and leads our wildlife and camel safaris in India.

JOHN THUNE, 66, is a mountain enthusiast, skier and runner. A former Park Ranger in Yellowstone, Survival Training Officer in Naval Aviation and a long-time member of the National Ski Patrol, he is a noted photo-lecturer and has trekked extensively in China and Nepal.

GORDON WILTSIE, 30, is a professional mountain guide and photographer. He has lived in Nepal and India, is fluent in Nepali and conversant in Bengali and Hindi-Urdu, and has been a member of several major climbing expeditions in the Himalayas.

JAN ZABINSKI, 34, is a ski instructor, mountaineer and teacher. He taught for three years at the American School in Lahore, Pakistan, and recently completed a walk from the southern tip of India to Kashmir in the north. He speaks Urdu and Hindi, and has traveled extensively in Asia.

Raj Singh

Gordon Wiltsie

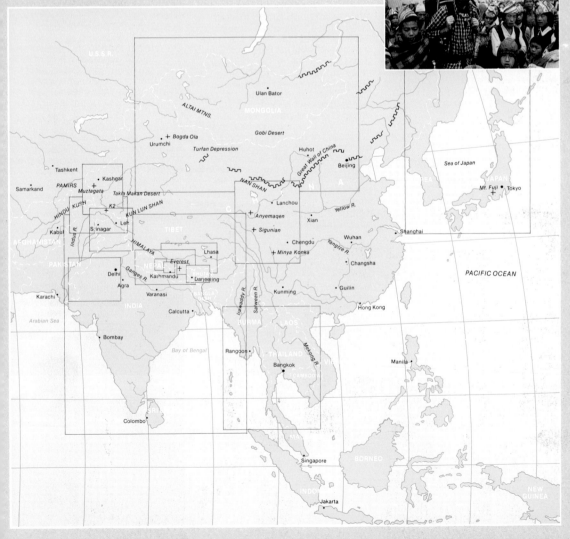

IT4PAISFMT1

K2 & THE CHINESE KARAKORUM

DATES: Sep 1–Oct 6 (36 days)
LEADER: John Thune
GRADE: C-2
LAND COST: $6900 (13–15 members)
$7400 (8–12)

The northern ramparts of the Karakorum Mountains of Asia, the second largest mountain chain in the world, have not been visited by Westerners since 1936, when mountaineer-explorer Eric Shipton visited the area. The objective of our expedition is the northern base of K2 (28,741'), 2nd highest peak in the world, and a majestic mountain site. Shipton wrote eloquently about this place in his classic book, *Blank On the Map.* "...Nothing interrupted my view of the great amphitheatre about me. The cliffs and ridges of K2 rose out of the glacier in one stupendous sweep to the summit of the mountain, 12,000 feet above. The sight was beyond my comprehension, and I sat gazing at it, with a kind of timid fascination, watching wreaths of mist creep in and out of corries utterly remote."

Shortly after Shipton's visit, the Chinese Karakorum, Sinkiang, and all of China became inaccessible to outsiders. The north faces of the other big peaks in the area —including Broad Peak (26,400'), Masherbrum (25,660') and Gasherbrum IV (26,180') are unknown, except for what has been glimpsed by mountaineers making ascents from the southern side (in Pakistan).

Our approach, via the Silk Road cities of Urumchi (3,000') and Kashgar (4,000'), takes us along the southern edge of the great Takla Makan Desert to Yarkand, an extremely remote Silk Road stopover. Driving from here to the town of Khudi (9,678'), we continue up across the western reaches of the Kunlun Mountains to Mahza (12,375') near the Yarkand River, where our camel caravan will be awaiting us for a ten-day round trip trek to K2 base camp.

We'll hike over the historic Aghil Pass (15,700'), first crossed by Sir Francis Younghusband on his epic journey from Beijing to India in 1887, ford the Shaksgam River by camel, and hike two more days to about 12,900 feet at the northern foot of K2. We'll have five days in the base camp area for exploration before retracing our route back through Kashgar and Beijing.

ITINERARY:

DAY 1 and 2: Leave U.S. Arrive Beijing. Transfer to hotel.

DAY 3 and 4: Sightseeing in Beijing and environs, including the Great Wall at Badaling, dating from the Ming Dynasty, with a short stop at a stone gate built in the Mongol period, beautifully carved with Buddhist images and inscriptions; drive through the 15th century Avenue of Animals on the way to the Ming Tombs, sepulchres built

CHINA
ABOUT TREKKING IN THE PEOPLE'S REPUBLIC

In addition to a Mountain Travel leader, our China trips are accompanied by a liaison officer from the Chinese Mountaineering Association who acts as overall head of the trip, as well as an interpreter (usually from Beijing) who has studied English at college level. A Chinese cook completes the team.

No camp assistants are available in China, so trip members will be expected to pitch their own tents and help with some of the kitchen chores. Our camp gear is transported by horses, camels or yaks (porters are not usually available).

Most of the camp food will be Chinese, supplemented by supplies from the U.S. (cheese, salami, granola, etc.). We supply all the tentage for trip members and Chinese personnel.

On mountaineering expeditions; and any excursions above base camp cooks do not accompany us and members will prepare meals from freeze-dried supplies.

Please note that trek itineraries in China are subject to change due to the complex nature of negotiations with the Chinese Mountaineering Association. Contact us for the latest information on each trek.

during the emperors' lifetimes; and tour Forbidden City, the elegant architectural masterpiece which was the Imperial Palace.

DAY 5 and 6: Fly to Urumchi. Day in Urumchi for sightseeing, visiting the local museum and tasting some of the melons and grapes which are grown by the local communes.

DAY 7: Fly to Kashgar, in far western Sinkiang, the westernmost city in China, untouched by the 20th century and actually closed to all tourism except expeditions.

DAY 8: Sightseeing in Kashgar, including the bazaar.

DAY 9: Drive southeast along the great Takla Makan desert, where Sir Aurel Stein and Sven Hedin carried out their great explorations at the turn of the century. We'll pass the cities of Yengishar and Soche and arrive at Yarkand.

> **"The sight was beyond my comprehension, and I sat gazing at it, with a kind of timid fascination, watching wreaths of mist creep in and out of corries utterly remote."**

DAY 10: Drive due south towards the Aghil Range and the Great Karakorum, over a 10,800-foot pass then descend into the small town of Khudi (9,678').

DAY 11: Drive over a 16,279-foot pass, descending to Mahza (12,375'), to meet our camel caravan and drivers who will carry the expedition equipment.

DAY 12: On foot or by camel along the Yarkand River, fording several

feeder streams then crossing the river with the camels.

DAY 13: Continue along the left bank of the Yarkand to the confluence of the river, and camp at a place known as Ilica (11,482')

DAY 14: Ford the Zug Shaksgam River which takes its source in the Gasherbrum peaks; cross Aghil Pass (15,682'), from where, according to Shipton's reports, we should enjoy a grand panorama of K2 and the Karakorum peaks, about 20 miles away. Shipton stood on this pass in 1936, and Younghusband 50 years before him! Our party will be only the third western expedition to reach this historic pass since that time.

DAY 15 to 17: Descend the pass into the wide Shaksgam River canyon, which drains the northeastern watershed of the great massifs of K2, Broad Peak, and Masherbrum. Trekking at about 12,800 feet, we follow the Shaksgam to a confluence with a number of small feeder streams coming off the north side of K2, which we follow to a base at about 12,900 feet, near Shipton's 1936 base.

DAY 18 to 22: Five days for exploration in the area.

DAY 23 to 31: Return journey back to Yarkand and Kashgar.

DAY 32: In Kashgar.

DAY 33: Fly to Urumchi.

DAY 34: Fly to Beijing.

DAY 35: In Beijing.

DAY 36: Depart Beijing and connect with homeward-bound flights.

IT4PAISFMT1

SINKIANG: THE MUZTAGATA & KONGUR TREK

DATES: Jul 1–Jul 28 (28 days)
LEADER: John Thune
GRADE: C-2
LAND COST: $4200 (13–15 members)
$4700 (8–12)

No part of China is more remote and isolated than the extreme western corner of Sinkiang Province. Indeed, this is the very heart of Central Asia, as far away as one can travel from Beijing (3,000 miles) and still be in China!

Here the landscape is a magnificent wide-open setting of high windswept plains dotted with the yurt dwellings of nomadic Kazakh shepherds, and dominated by huge brooding peaks of Mt. Kongur (25,320') and Mt. Muztagata (24,757'). Little has changed since the days of the "Silk Road," when camel caravans passed through here on the trade route between the Yellow River and the Mediterranean.

This journey undertakes short treks to the bases of both Mt. Muztagata and Mt. Kongur. Our pack animals will be Bactrian camels; local herdsmen will be our guides. Between treks, we'll sponsor a "bushkashi," a traditional polo-like event at Karakol Lake (12,000'). During our time in this region we'll see occasional nomadic herdsmen and their families in their portable "yurts", dome-shaped dwellings made of felt.

Before the treks, we visit Urumchi (3,000'), Sinkiang's capital, and historic Kashgar (4,000'), a fascinating oasis town in the Takla Makan Desert which was once a stopover on the Silk Road and just opened to Western visitors in 1980.

After the trek we tour Xian, an ancient town with a vast archaeological legacy.

ITINERARY:

DAY 1 and 2: Leave U.S. Arrive Beijing. Transfer to hotel.

B

D

A

DAY 3 and 4: Sightseeing including the Great Wall, dating from the Ming Dynasty, with a stop at a beautifully carved stone gate built in the Mongol period; drive through the 15th century Avenue of Animals, to visit the Ming Tombs, built during the emperors' lifetimes to be their underground palaces in the afterworld; tour the Forbidden City, a vast treasure-house begun in the Yuan Dynasty.

DAY 5: Fly to Urumchi. Afternoon sightseeing.

DAY 6: Fly to Kashgar.

DAY 7: Local sightseeing in Kashgar.

DAY 8 and 9: Drive to Karakol area. Camp at 12,000 feet. Rest day in area.

DAY 10 to 12: Trek by Bactrian camel to Muztagata Base Camp (14,500'). Optional hiking from base camp to Camp I.

DAY 13: Trek by camel down to valley, camp in meadow south of Subashi village (12,500')

DAY 14: Trek to Konsiver River gorge, northeast of Karakol. Camp near a yurt village on the river.

DAY 15: "Bushkashi" event at Big Karakol Lake. Travel by camel to and from our camp.

DAY 16: Trek up along the Konsiver River and camp in a fantastic grass valley.

Little has changed since the days of the "Silk Road," when camel caravans passed through here on the trade route between the Yellow River and the Mediterranean.

DAY 17 and 18: Trek to Muztagata-Mt. Kongur Narrows. Extra day in area to trek to a higher camp on Mt. Kongur.

DAY 19 and 20: Return to Ajaga village and camp at Big Karakol lakes for swimming and relaxation.

DAY 21: Drive back to Kashgar.

DAY 22: Sightseeing, feast and dancing in Kashgar.

DAY 23: Fly to Urumchi.

DAY 24: Fly to Xian.

DAY 25: Visit Xian's incredible archaeoolgical sites, such as the Qing Shi Huang Di Tomb, just discovered in 1974, where thousands of life-size terra cotta warriors and horses have been unearthed.

DAY 26: Fly to Beijing.

DAY 27: In Beijing.

DAY 28: Depart Beijing and connect with homeward-bound flights.

IT4PA1SFMT1

SINKIANG: THE MUZTAGATA SKI EXPEDITION

DATES: Jun 1–Jul 8 (38 days)
LEADER: Steve McKinney
GRADE: E-1
LAND COST: *$7300 (8–12 members)

The expedition will attempt an ascent and descent on skis of Mt. Muztagata (24,757'), "the father of ice mountains" in the western corner of Sinkiang Province. We hope to repeat the success of our first Muztaga ski expedition in 1982.

Muztagata is an isolated peak, king of Central Asiatic mountain giants. The great Swedish explorer Sven Hedin attempted to climb it in 1894, Shipton and Tilman tried it in the 1940's, but the first successful ascent was not until 1956 by a Sino-Russian team. The first Americans climbed it in 1980.

This will be a unique opportunity to climb a peak which is very high but does not have the objective dangers of other peaks its size.

At least three years of mountaineering experience is required for this expedition. Climbers wishing to make the ski descent must be

B

strong, advanced skiers. We may have to ski roped on certain sections due to possible crevasse danger.

Cultural highlights of the trip include contact with the Kazakh herdsmen of the Muztagata region, visits to the fascinating Silk Road towns of Urumchi and Kashgar and a two-day tour of Beijing.

ITINERARY:

DAY 1 and 2: Leave U.S. Arrive Beijing. Transfer to hotel.

DAY 3 and 4: Sightseeing in Beijing—the Forbidden City, the Summer Palace, excursion to Great Wall and Ming Tombs.

DAY 5: Fly to Urumchi, capital of Sinkiang Province.

DAY 6: Fly to Kashgar in far western China.

DAY 7: In Kashgar, touring this ancient and remote city.

DAY 8: Drive to Karakol Lake (12,000') and camp.

DAY 9 to 32: Establish base camp. Approximately 25 days will be spent on the mountain with Camp I at 17,000 feet, Camp II at 19,000 feet, Camp III at 21,000 feet and Camp IV at 23,000 feet.

The great Swedish explorer Sven Hedin attempted to climb it in 1894, Shipton and Tilman tried it in the 1940's, but the first successful ascent was not until 1956 by a Sino-Russian team.

DAY 33: Return to Karakol Lake and drive to Kashgar.

DAY 34: Fly to Urumchi.

DAY 35: In Urumchi.

DAY 36: Fly to Beijing.

DAY 37: In Beijing.

DAY 38: Depart Beijing and connect with homeward-bound flights.

100 Miles

MUZTAGATA TREK ....
K2 & THE CHINESE KARAKORUM _____

SINKIANG

• KASHGAR

+ Kongur   • Yarkand

+ Muztagata

PAMIR   TAKLA MAKAN DESERT

Yarkand R.
Shaskumba R. Aghil Pass
• GILGIT   KUNLUN RANGE
                    Shaksgam
        + K2   Khapalung
KARAKORUM   + Gasherbrum
RANGE
                    ✕ Karakorum Pass

A

IT4PA1SFMT1

SINKIANG: TREKKING IN THE TIEN SHAN RANGE

DATES: Jul 1–Jul 20 (20 days)
LEADER: Dick McGowan
GRADE: B-2
LAND COST: $2750 (13–15 members)
$3250 (8–12)

China's Tien Shan Range ("Celestial Mountains") comprises one of the longest mountain ranges in the world. It spans a distance of some 1,000 miles, rising in western Soviet Turkestan, forming the northern ramparts of the huge Takla Makan Desert, and finally ending 200 miles east of Urumchi, capital of Sinkiang Province.

The highest mountain in the eastern Tien Shan is Mt. Bogda Ola (17,900'), first attempted in 1946 by British explorers Shipton and Tilman. Surrounded by many smaller and as yet unexplored peaks, Bogda's beautifully shaped massif of rock and ice is reflected by Tien Schi (10,000'), the "heavenly lake" below it.

From this lake, we will take a five-day round trip trek to the base of Mt. Bogda, with the support of Kirghiz horsemen, pack horses and a camp staff. The walk to base is two days, with layover time at base camp to photograph, explore nearby glaciers, or hike up a 14,000-foot peak for great views. Cultural highlights will include visits to nomadic settlements in the area.

Before the trek we visit Urumchi, capital city of the desert province of Sinkiang, and inhabited by people of the Central Asian Uygur culture. After the trek, we will visit Xian, once a model of imperial splendor and capital of 11 dynasties, now known for its archaeological treasures.

ITINERARY:
DAY 1 to 3: Leave U.S. Arrive Beijing. Transfer to hotel.
DAY 4 and 5: Sightseeing including the Great Wall at Badaling, dating from the Ming Dynasty, with a stop at a beautifully carved stone gate built in the Mongol period; afternoon drive through the 15th century Avenue of Animals, with its huge stone sculptures, to visit the Ming Tombs, built during the emperors' lifetimes to be their underground palaces in the afterworld; tour the Forbidden City, once the Imperial Palace, a vast treasure-house begun in the Yuan Dynasty and enlarged over the centuries.

> **Surrounded by many smaller and as yet unexplored peaks, Bogda's beautifully shaped massif of rock and ice is reflected by Tien Schi (10,000'), the "heavenly lake" below it.**

DAY 6: Fly to Urumchi. Overnight in hotel.
DAY 7: In Urumchi. Sightseeing including museum, market and melon-growing commune.
DAY 8: Drive to Tien Schi at 10,000 feet in the Tien Shan Mountains. Overnight at forest lodge.
DAY 9 and 10: Hike in to Bogda base camp, arriving on Day 10. Pack horses will carry gear.
DAY 11 and 12: At base camp with a visit to the Bogda Glacier.
DAY 13 and 14: At Tien Schi with boat trip on lake.
DAY 14: Return to Tien Schi Lake in the afternoon.
DAY 15: Bus to Urumchi. Overnight in hotel.
DAY 16: Fly to Xian. Overnight in hotel.
DAY 17: In Xian. Visit the famous excavations and the Emperor's tomb.
DAY 18: Fly to Beijing.
DAY 19: In Beijing.
DAY 20: Depart Beijing and connect with homeward-bound flights.

IT4PA1SFMT1

QINGHAI/GANSU: ANYEMAQEN, HOLY MOUNTAIN OF TIBETANS

DATES: Aug 1–Aug 26 (26 days)
LEADER: Jerry Coe
GRADE: B-2
LAND COST: $3400 (13–15 members)
$3800 (8–12)

Mt. Anyemaqen (20,600'), in the untamed Qinghai Province of China's "wild west", is a McKinley-like peak of impressive bulk and one of the most sacred mountains in all China. It is said that at the turn of the century as many as 10,000 Tibetan Buddhist pilgrims each year would circumambulate this mountain to gain spiritual merit. We make a six-day trek in the foothills flanking the peak, walking on the pilgrimage route and possibly seeing some wildlife on our way to our 14,500-foot base camp at the foot of the snowy Anyemaqen Range.

The people of the Anyemaqen area are Goloks, Tibetan nomads once feared by travelers of old as "highway robbers," and now largely engaged in the peaceful occupation of sheep and yak herding on remote communes. Golok herdsmen and their yaks will carry our gear to base camp.

Visits are also included to the monastery of Kumbum and famous Buddhist rock carvings at Bingling, the archaeological site at Dun Huang, and the cities of Lanzhou and Beijing.

ITINERARY:
DAY 1 and 2: Depart U.S. Arrive Beijing. Transfer to hotel.
DAY 3 and 4: Sightseeing including the Great Wall at Badaling, dating from the Ming Dynasty; afternoon visit to the Ming Tombs; tour the Forbidden City, a vast treasure-house begun in the Yuan Dynasty and enlarged over the centuries.
DAY 5: Fly to Lanzhou (6,500'), capital of Gansu Province. Visit Lanzhou Museum, with its treasure of Buddhist art, including the "Flying Horse of Gansu." Overnight at hotel.

DAY 6: All-day tour along the Huang Ho ("Yellow River"), visiting the spectacular Buddhist temple of Bingling, housing hundreds of stone carvings including a 100-foot-high statue of Buddha carved out of a rock face overlooking the river. Transfer to smaller craft to land at the "Valley of the Buddhas."
DAY 7: By train to Xining, provincial capital of Qinghai. Overnight at hotel.
DAY 8: All-day visit to Kumbum Monastery (also known as Ta-er), a colorful Tibetan monastery in good condition and very active with about 200 monks in residence.
DAY 9: By bus to Hot Springs Station (10,000'), an all-day ride over a graded dirt road with great open vistas and snow-clad peaks. Nomad tents dot the grasslands. A truck will carry our gear, food and camping equipment.
DAY 10: By bus to Dawu, a remote village which we reach by another all-day ride on a dirt road, crossing a 16,000-foot pass. Overnight at guest house.
DAY 11: By truck for five hours over a primitive mountain road to the trailhead at the Snow Mountain Commune (10,000') near Mt. Anyemaqen. Camp nearby.
DAY 12 and 13: Two-day walk to Anyemaqen base camp (14,500') with yaks carrying our gear. Magnificent glaciers stretch out towards the camp, which is just about at snowline.

> **It is said that at the turn of the century as many as 10,000 Tibetan Buddhist pilgrims each year would circumambulate this mountain to gain spiritual merit.**

DAY 14 and 15: At base camp. Explore, photograph and take optional walks.
DAY 16: Walk back downhill to the Snow Mountain Commune. Camp.
DAY 17: By truck to Dongqingdu, then by bus to Hot Springs Station for overnight.

B

C

D   E

A

DAY 18: By bus to Gonghe, overnight at guest house.

DAY 19: Six-hour drive to Xining. Overnight in hotel.

DAY 20: By train to Lanzhou. Afternoon to explore city, then depart by sleeper train for Jiayuguan.

DAY 21: Arrive at Jiayuguan. Dinner and overnight at hotel.

DAY 22: Visit the westernmost section of the Great Wall and the "Jade Gate," last gate in the wall, through which early travelers entered into the lawless reaches of western Sinkiang. Continue by bus to Dun Huang. Overnight at hotel.

DAY 23: Explore the Dun Huang Caves known as the "Caves of 1000 Buddhas," one of China's finest treasures of Buddhist antiquity.

DAY 24: All-day excursion by bus to visit the mountain passes of Yang-guan and Hongshan, which served as China's gateways to the western world during the height of the Silk Trade. Buddhism came to China along this route, and beacon towers built during the Han Dynasty may still be seen here. Excellent views of the entire area, both pastureland and land newly reclaimed, and the seemingly endless Takla Makan Desert beyond.

DAY 25: Fly to Beijing via Lanzhou. Transfer to hotel.

DAY 26: Depart Beijing and connect with homeward-bound flights.

IT4PA1SFMT1

SICHUAN: THE MINYA KONKA TREK

DATES: Oct 1–Oct 25 (25 days)
LEADER: Bruce Klepinger
GRADE: C-3
LAND COST: $3600 (13–15 members)
$4100 (8–12)

Mt. Minya Konka is the most beautiful mountain in China, a mountain so awesome that "to behold the peak is worth ten years of meditation." This is written on an inscription in the now-ruined Konka Gompa ("Snow Monastery") at the foot of the peak.

Mt. Minya Konka—located in the Alps of Chinese Tibet—was truly unknown and unexplored until about 50 years ago. In the early part of this century, a few travellers reported the distant sight of a great mountain in western Sichuan, on the edge of the Tibetan Plateau. Some thought it might be higher than Mt. Everest. It wasn't until the epic National Geographic Society Expedition of 1927–30, led by Dr. Joseph Rock, that the stupendous range called Minya Konka was definitely located and explored. Its highest peak, Mt. Minya Konka (also called Mt. Minya Gongga) towers 24,950 feet, its base drained by the Tatu River at 3,000 feet, less than 20 miles away.

We'll make our own explorations in this region, completing a 13-day trek through remote "Greater Tibet," an autonomous district in western Sichuan, with a visit to the base camp below Minya Konka, and an optional hike up to "Rock's Ridge" at 17,000 feet for spectacular views.

Before the trek, we visit Kanding, a small town nestled in the mountain valleys of western Sichuan, and Chengdu, capital of Sichuan Province.

ITINERARY:

DAY 1 and 2: Leave San Francisco. Arrive Beijing. Transfer to hotel.

> **In the early part of this century, a few travellers reported the distant sight of a great mountain in western Sichuan, on the edge of the Tibetan Plateau. Some thought it might be higher than Mt. Everest.**

DAY 3: Sightseeing including the Great Wall at Badaling, dating from the Ming Dynasty, with a stop at a beautifully carved stone gate built in the Mongol period; afternoon drive through the 15th century Avenue of Animals, with its huge stone sculptures, to visit the Ming Tombs.

B

DAY 4: Fly to Chengdu. Afternoon tour of city.

DAY 5 to 7: Drive to Kanding via Ya'an and Luding, and on to starting point of trek at Yue Ling at 10,000 feet.

DAY 8 and 9: With horses carrying equipment, walk through a landscape dotted with Tibetan houses and tents and striking mountain scenery. Camp at about 13,000 feet.

DAY 10 and 11: Trek over Sam Pan San Pass (also called Djezi La) at 15,685 feet, then walk down Yulong-shi Valley through wild country.

DAY 12 and 13: Walk through small Tibetan villages where there has been little contact with foreigners. Rest day in area.

DAY 14 and 15: Up and over the Tsumei La (15,288') and on to Minya Konka base camp and the site of Konka Gompa at 12,300 feet. Magnificent views of Minya Konka

DAY 16 and 17: Layover days to photograph, explore, hike to Rock's Ridge and advance base camp for the standard route on Minya Konka.

DAY 18 to 20: Walk back down to Tsumei, once again cross over the Tsumei La to the Yulongshi Valley. Continue past the Sorbu Gompa to Tibetan village of Liuba at the roadhead.

DAY 21: Drive to Kanding.

DAY 22 and 23: Drive to Chengdu via Ya'an.

DAY 24: Fly to Beijing.

DAY 25: Depart Beijing and connect with homeward-bound flights.

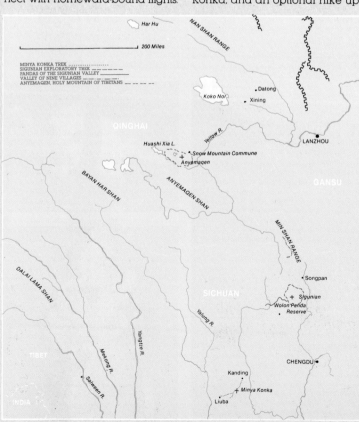

C

IT4PA1SFMT1

SICHUAN: THE VALLEY OF NINE VILLAGES

DATES: *Aug 24–Sep 14 (22 days)
LEADER: Jerry Coe
GRADE: B-1
LAND COST: $3100 (13–15 members)
$3600 (8–12)
*Note date change from 1984 Trip Schedule.

This trip features two short treks in northwestern Sichuan. The first takes us on foot (or by Tibetan pony, if one prefers) for three days into the mountains of the Min Range. This is a remote area which has seldom had foreign visitors (except for a few explorers and botanists during the 1920's). En route, we'll pass Tibetan villages of the Awa people, yak herders who cultivate high pastures.

The second three-day trek explores an untouched mountain valley in northern Sichuan called Jiu Zhai Gou ("The Valley of Nine Villages"), replete with Tibetan hamlets and enchanting waterfalls. The valley is prime panda habitat, dense with bamboo. Many Chinese consider the Jiu Zhai Gou Valley to be one of the most scenic in all China.

In between treks, we visit the Huang Long Shi ("Yellow Dragon Monastery") which we reach by hiking along a three-mile ridge of travertine pools.

Visits are also included to Chengdu, Beijing, and the ancient walled village of Son Pan.

ITINERARY:

DAY 1 and 2: Leave U.S. Arrive Beijing. Transfer to hotel.

DAY 3 and 4: Sightseeing including the Great Wall at Badaling, dating from the Ming Dynasty, with a stop at a beautifully carved stone gate built in the Mongol period; afternoon drive through the 15th century Avenue of Animals, with its huge stone sculptures, to visit the Ming Tombs, built during the emperors' lifetimes to be their underground palaces in the afterworld; tour the Forbidden City, once the Imperial Palace, a vast treasure-house begun in the Yuan Dynasty and enlarged over the centuries.

DAY 5: Fly to Chengdu.

DAY 6: Tour Chengdu.

DAY 7: Begin three-day bus ride to Jiu Zhai Gou, a journey of about 400 miles. The first day we enter the mountains of northwestern Sichuan and follow the course of the Min River to its source. The Min is one of the four major Sichuan rivers (Sichuan means "Four Rivers"). Overnight in guest house in Monwen, a town inhabited mostly by Hui Moslems, one of China's national minority people. Our group will be the first party of Westerners into this region since the 1920's.

DAY 8: Continue by bus for about six hours to Son Pan, a village

whose ancient city walls can still be seen in places. Overnight in government guest house.

DAY 9 to 11: Three-day excursion on foot or with Tibetan pony into the Min Range, whose highest peak is Mt. Shue Baoding ("Precious Snow Peak"—18,234'), an ice-clad Matterhorn-like spire. Along the trek route, we pass Tibetan villages, with their cultivated pastures and yak herds. Return to Son Pan at the end of the trek.

> **The valley is prime panda habitat, dense with bamboo. Many Chinese consider the Jiu Zhai Gou Valley to be one of the most scenic in all China.**

DAY 12: By bus, crossing Sueshan Pass (14,300'), to visit Huang Long Shi, an ancient Buddhist monastery, which we reach by a three-mile walk along a beautiful ridge of yellow rock filled with deep azure pools. Camp nearby.

DAY 13: Return to the main road via the Sueshan Pass, then over Konkalin Pass (9,500') into the northern watershed of Sichuan Province. Arrive at Jiu Zhai Gou in the late afternoon. Overnight at government guest house.

DAY 14 to 16: Three days exploring the valley, during which we will either camp in a secluded glen and make day hikes, or stay at a lodge and visit the park by bus.

DAY 17: Drive to Son Pan.

DAY 18: Drive to Mon Wen.

DAY 19: Drive to Chengdu.

DAY 20: In Chengdu.

DAY 21: Fly to Beijing.

DAY 22: Depart Beijing and connect with homeward-bound flights.

IT4PA1SFMT1

SICHUAN: PANDAS OF THE SIGUNIAN VALLEY

DATES: Oct 1–Oct 20 (20 days)
LEADER: John Thune
GRADE: B-2
LAND COST: $2800 (13–15 members)
$3300 (8–12)

In Sichuan Province, Wolon Panda Research Station was established in 1960 to provide sanctuary for the giant panda and other species including golden-faced monkeys, wild yaks, snow leopards, bharal sheep and several types of Himalayan pheasant. We'll visit this wildlife refuge where naturalist and author George Schaller has done much research, and have a chance to walk in the reserve amid picturesque grottos that inspired some of the finest Chinese landscape painting.

From Wolon, we drive over Palung Pass (14,500') into country that is both geographically and ethnically akin to Tibet. Approaching the foothills of the Sigunian Alps, a very beautiful group of granite peaks which rise out of heavily forested valleys, we make a leisurely six-day natural history trek. The highest peak in the area, formidable Mt. Sigunian, soars to 21,600 feet. With its sheer granite walls, it may be one of the world's most difficult rock peaks and is certainly among the most spectacular. No difficult hiking is involved, but those wishing to see wildlife should be prepared for some steep walks.

ITINERARY:

DAY 1 and 2: Leave U.S. Arrive Beijing. Transfer to hotel.

DAY 3 and 4: Sightseeing including the Great Wall at Badaling, dating

from the Ming Dynasty, with a stop at a beautifully carved stone gate built in the Mongol period; afternoon drive through the 15th century Avenue of Animals, with its huge stone sculptures, to visit the Ming Tombs, built during the emperor's lifetimes to be their underground palaces in the afterworld; tour the Forbidden City, once the Imperial Palace, a vast treasure-house begun in the Yuan Dynasty and enlarged over the centuries.

DAY 5: Fly to Chengdu.

DAY 6: Local sightseeing with time to explore the narrow streets of old Chengdu—a rich experience for photographers and handicraft enthusiasts. Chengdu has been called the "Storehouse of Heaven" as a center for hand-crafted treasures—embroidery, brocades, laquerware, cutlery, baskets and pottery.

DAY 7: Drive to Wolon Panda Research Station (6,435'), about a 4½ hour drive through rich agricultural plains and small villages. Common birds along the river: River Chats, Plumbeous Redstarts, Wall Creepers and Brown Dippers. Overnight at Wolon Guest House.

DAY 8: By special permit, we visit the Wolon Panda Research Station. There are some pandas living in nearby enclosures which we may be able to visit. Afternoon walks in the wilds of the Ying Chang Valley, ten minutes drive up the road. Springs and waterfalls gush from this nearly vertical mountain landscape that resembles the mystical Chinese scroll paintings. The trail is chiseled through four tunnels: Celestial, Silent, Listening to Spring and Waterfall. Ponchos and flashlights are required.

In the late afternoon, by special permit, visit the Wolon Natural History Museum, a UNESCO Project housing some fine exhibits of

A

B

C

local birds, insects, mammals and a large relief map of the area.

DAY 9: All-day drive over Palung Pass (14,500') down to Zulun (10,500') with fine views of the Sigunian Range.

DAY 10: Begin six-day trek into the Sigunian Range. Leisurely five-hour walk to a fine meadow about half way to base camp (11,500') entering deep conifer forests hung with Spanish moss. Birdlife is prolific and includes Raptors, Griffon Vultures, Lammergeiers, Chinese Goshawks and Redstarts. Horses will carry our gear.

DAY 11: Camp at about 12,500 feet in a meadow below the impressive northern face of Mt. Sigunian (21,600'). Precipitous slopes rise from the valley floor where bharal (blue sheep) and musk deer make their home. We've seen up to 22 sheep in one sighting.

DAY 12 to 14: Day hikes in the area, or optional backpacking to a spectacular side canyon that leads up around the southwest flanks of Celestial Peak, a shapely granite pyramid around 18,500 feet.

DAY 15: Return to Zulun.

DAY 16: In Zulun, with a chance to experience a day's life in a remote agricultural commune, with its population of 800. The director of the commune and chief physician will host us for special visits.

DAY 17: Drive to Wolon.

DAY 18: Drive to Chengdu, with a picnic stop at Two Kings Temple (Erwangsi) built during the Qing Dynasty (221–206 B.C.). The complex contains some of China's most beautiful traditional-style architecture.

DAY 19: Fly to Beijing.

DAY 20: Depart Beijing and connect with homeward-bound flights.

IT4PA1SFMT1

SICHUAN: SIGUNIAN EXPLORATORY TREK

DATES: Sep 15–Oct 9 (25 days)
LEADER: Jerry Coe
GRADE: C-3
LAND COST: $3600 (13–15 members) $4100 (8–12)

This is a fifteen-day exploratory trek around Mt. Sigunian (21,600'), "Four Sisters Peak," one of the most impressive granite spires in the world, situated near the world-famous Wolon Panda Reserve.

Making a circle around Mt. Sigunian, we cross three passes of about 15,000 feet in a very remote region which is excellent habitat for wildlife including bharal sheep, wild yaks and possibly snow leopard. Horses and/or porters will carry our gear.

Visits to Wolon Panda Research Station (see trip description for "Sichuan: Pandas of the Siguniang Valley"), Chengdu and Beijing are also included.

ITINERARY:

DAY 1 and 2: Leave U.S. Arrive Beijing. Transfer to hotel.

DAY 3 and 4: Sightseeing including the Great Wall at Badaling, dating from the Ming Dynasty, with a stop at a beautifully carved stone gate built in the Mongol period; afternoon drive through the 15th century Avenue of Animals, with its huge stone sculptures, to visit the Ming Tombs, built during the emperors' lifetimes to be their underground palaces in the afterworld; tour the Forbidden City, once the Imperial Palace, a vast treasure-house begun in the Yuan Dynasty and enlarged over the centuries.

DAY 5: Fly to Chengdu. Transfer to hotel.

DAY 6: Local sightseeing around Chengdu, a center for many handcrafted treasures.

> **Making a circle around Mt. Sigunian, we cross three passes of about 15,000 feet in a very remote region which is excellent habitat for wildlife.**

DAY 7: Drive to Wolong Panda Research Station (6,435') along rich agricultural plains and small villages. Visit Wolon Panda Research Station. Overnight at Wolon Guest House.

DAY 8: Bus to Zelun, hire horses at local commune and begin trek.

DAY 9 and 10: Trek into the valley and camp beneath the fantastic granite peak of Sigunian.

DAY 11 and 12: Continue north, then travel east and up towards the first high pass northeast of Sigunian.

DAY 13 to 15: Descend the eastern escarpment of the Sigunian Range into valleys seldom, if ever, visited by foreigners.

DAY 16 to 18: Continue southwards, and climb over another 15,000-foot pass, due east of the big peaks.

DAY 19 to 22: Cross a third 15,000-foot pass leading into the Hai Chi Valley and return to our starting point at the Zelun Commune.

DAY 23: Drive to Chengdu.

DAY 24: Fly to Beijing.

DAY 25: Depart Beijing and connect with homeward-bound flights.

IT4PA1SFMT1

YANGTSE VALLEY BICYCLE TOUR

DATES: Aug 26–Sep 18 (24 days)
LEADER: Joe Brennan
GRADE: B-1
LAND COST: $2145 (6–15 members)

What better way is there to travel through China than the way many Chinese do—on bicycles! On this cycling tour, we'll cross the Yangtse Valley (China's rice bowl) and the chain of cities that first brought silk, porcelain and jade to the world beyond China. One of the many advantages of touring by bicycle is that we will be able to travel on our own, admiring the beauty of rural China, stopping to explore little villages, pausing to share a cup of tea at a commune along the way, according to our own individual preferences.

The tour visits the very scenic and ancient towns of Nanjing, Zhenjiang, Yangzhou, Changzhou, Yixing, Wuxi (with a boat ride on the fantastic "Grand Canal", Suzhou, and the cities of Shanghai and Beijing.

On the cycle portion of the trip, all luggage will be transported by bus. Meals and accommodations will be in hotels. The bike touring is moderate and none of the biking days are exceptionally long.

ITINERARY:

DAY 1 to 3: Leave U.S. arrive Beijing. Transfer to hotel.

DAY 4 to 7: Touring Beijing and environs by bicycle. Excursions to the Great Wall, Ming Tombs, Forbidden City (home of the Imperial Family during the Ming and Qing Dynasties), Summer Palace and zoo.

DAY 8: Fly to Nanjing on the banks of the Yangtse River at the base of the Purple and Gold Mountains.

DAY 9 and 10: Bike tour of the city of Nanjing and out to the countryside for swimming and other sports, plus a visit to an agricultural commune.

DAY 11: Bike to Yangzhou, a charming town lying at the juncture of the Yangtse and Hua Rivers.

DAY 12 and 13: Bike around Yangzhou, known for its temples, gardens and artistic products; afternoon cross the Yangtse River by ferry to Zhenjiang.

DAY 14: Bike to Beigushan, with its hillside pagodas and pavillions.

DAY 15: Train to Changzhou; afternoon bike tour including stops at the Red Plum Pavillion and Tianning Temple.

DAY 16 and 17: Bike to Yixing, a lovely town known for its stoneware pottery. Cycling tour of Yixing, including the Temple of Confucius and Reverence Zhang Grotto, a group of 72 caves linked by hand-carved steps.

DAY 18: Bike through the countryside to Wuxi, a 2,000-year old city which produces some of the most beautiful silk in China.

> **. . . stopping to explore little villages, pausing to share a cup of tea at a commune along the way.**

DAY 19: Morning boat trip on the Grand Canal, world's longest man-made waterway, sections of which were built in the 6th Century. Afternoon cruise on Lake Tai, one of China's largest lakes.

DAY 20: Continue biking to Suzhou, "Venice of the East," through a fertile rural area adjacent to the Grand Canal.

DAY 21: Bicycle tour of Suzhou, one of China's oldest and most beautiful cities; short afternoon train ride to Shanghai.

DAY 22 and 23: Tour Shanghai, a commercially active and prosperous city.

DAY 24: Depart Shanghai and connect with homeward-bound flights.

IT4PA1SFMT1

TIBET: THE MT. EVEREST TREK

DATES: Apr 15–May 10 (26 days)
LEADER: Nigel Dabby
GRADE: A-3/C-3
LAND COST: $5700 (13–15 members)
$6100 (8–12)

"Tibet, forbidden and forbidding, the land of vast sweeping plateaus and giant ranges crowned with eternal snows, the land of a strange and colorful people. From the time of Marco Polo, it has drawn men of the Western Hemisphere to probe its mysteries . . ." R. Burdsall, *Men Against The Clouds.*

Of all the places we visit in China, only one can claim the magic and mystery of Tibet. The aim of our Tibetan travels will be a visit to the northern foot of Mt. Everest, known to Tibetans as Chomolungma, Goddess Mother of The Earth.

During our visit to Lhasa, we will visit the legendary Potala Palace, the very symbol of Tibet, a thousand-room hilltop citadel which was the traditional seat of the Dalai Lama, God-King of Tibet. We will also visit Drepung (the world's largest monastery), and Jokhang, the holiest shrine in Tibet and equivalent of Mecca for Tibetan Buddhists.

Leaving Lhasa, we drive down the Yarlung Zangbo river valley through Shigatse (Xigase) and Shegar (Xegar) (14,500'), site of an historic walled village, then drive further by truck over rough tracks to the Rongbuk Valley ("Valley of Precipices"), at the head of which stands Mt. Everest.

At the site of the old Rongbuk Monastery (16,500'), we will set up our tents and have five days to explore the area and feast our eyes on the mountain views. Those who are in good shape and well acclimatized can hike up the Rongbuk Glacier to Camp I of the historic Everest expeditions of the 1920's.

ITINERARY:

DAY 1 and 2: Leave U.S. Arrive Beijing. Transfer to hotel.

DAY 3 and 4: Sightseeing including the Great Wall at Badaling, dating from the Ming Dynasty, with a stop at a beautifully carved stone gate built in the Mongol period; afternoon drive through the 15th century Avenue of Animals, with its huge stone sculptures, to visit the Ming Tombs, built during the emperors' lifetimes to be their underground palaces in the afterworld; tour the Forbidden City, once the Imperial Palace, a vast treasure-house begun in the Yuan Dynasty and enlarged over the centuries.

We will visit the legendary Potala Palace, the very symbol of Tibet, a thousand-room hilltop citadel which was the traditional seat of the Dalai Lama, God-King of Tibet.

DAY 5: Fly to Chengdu.

DAY 6: Fly to Lhasa on one of the most spectacular mountain flights in the world. Drive 80 miles to Lhasa with a stop to visit a large stone-carved Sakyamuni Buddha.

DAY 7 to 9: Three full days in Lhasa, with visits to the Potala, the Norbulingka, and the three great monasteries of Lhasa (Ganden, Sera, and Drepung). There will also be time to stroll in the bazaar.

DAY 10: All-day bus ride to Shigatse (12,500'), with a ferry ride across the Tsangpo River. In Shigatse, second largest city in Tibet, we will visit Tashilumpo Monastery, the former seat of the Panchen Lama and one of the most important religious centers in central Tibet.

DAY 11: All-day bus ride to the town of Shegar ("White Crystal") at 14,500 feet, crossing the high passes of Tso La (14,800') and Gyatso La (17,300'), the incongruously named "Ocean Pass" which has yielded many marine fossils to casual collectors. Shegar is the site of a soaring, but sadly ruined dzong (fortress/monastery).

DAY 12: By truck to Rongbuk (16,500'), winding through numerous remote Tibetan villages. Driving over the Pang La (17,300'), there are spectacular views of the north side of the Himalaya from Makalu to Cho Oyu, including Mt. Everest.

DAY 13 to 17: Five full days at the Rongbuk area. Time for local walks and exploration. Those who are very fit can hike to the British Camp I (17,800') on the East Rongbuk Glacier.

DAY 18: Drive to Shegar by truck.

DAY 19: Bus to Gyantse, visiting Younghusband's fort and Kumbum Stupa (largest in Tibet), "the pagoda of 100,000 Buddhas."

DAY 20: Bus to Lhasa.

DAY 21: Day free in Lhasa.

DAY 22: Fly to Chengdu.

DAY 23: In Chengdu.

DAY 24: Fly to Beijing.

DAY 25: In Beijing.

DAY 26: Depart Beijing and connect with homeward-bound flights.

IT4PA1SFMT1

TIBET: THE MT. EVEREST/ EAST FACE TREK

DATES: Sep 20–Oct 23 (34 days)
LEADER: Arlene Blum
GRADE: C-3
LAND COST: $6400 (13–15 members)
$6900 (8–12)

This is a 12-day trekking adventure exploring remote and unvisited portions of the Tibetan highlands, including the deep valleys which descend from the eastern flanks of Mt. Everest (29,028') and Makalu (27,825').

After a three-day visit to Lhasa, capital of Tibet, we drive to Shigatse (12,500') and Shegar (14,500'), then over the Pang La into the Rongbuk Valley and east to Kharta.

From here, we will trek for twelve days towards the great east face of Everest, crossing several high passes and exploring the magnificent Kharta and Kama valleys, which so delighted the British mountaineers during expeditions in the 1920's. We will attempt to reach the site of the American East Face Expedition on the Kangshun Glacier at approximately 14,000 feet for a close look at the world's highest peak. Other giants of the Himalaya are also in full view from this unique vantage point, including Makalu.

Most of the hiking on this trek takes place at 12,000 feet or higher. Daily trekking distances have been calculated at about 10 miles a day, but are approximate. A lot of the daily mileage depends on the yaks and yak drivers, in combination with weather conditions. The passes are neither glaciated nor technically difficult, although glacier travel itself can present problems.

ITINERARY:

DAY 1 and 2: Leave U.S. Arrive Beijing. Transfer to Hotel.

DAY 3 and 4: Sightseeing including the Great Wall at Badaling, dating from the Ming Dynasty, with a stop at a beautifully carved stone gate built in the Mongol period; afternoon drive through the 15th century Avenue of Animals, with its huge stone sculptures, to visit the Ming Tombs, built during the emperors' lifetimes to be their underground palaces in the afterworld; tour the Forbidden City, once the Imperial Palace, a vast treasure-house begun in the Yuan Dynasty and enlarged over the centuries.

DAY 5: Fly to Chengdu.

DAY 6: Fly to Lhasa (11,700'), drive 80 miles to Lhasa via the Yarlung Tsangpo River, stopping to visit a large stone-carved Buddha Sakyamuni.

DAY 7 to 9: Visit the major temples and shrines of Lhasa, including the Jokhang, Drepung and Ganden monasteries, the Potala Palace, and Norbulinka (summer palace of the Dalai Lama).

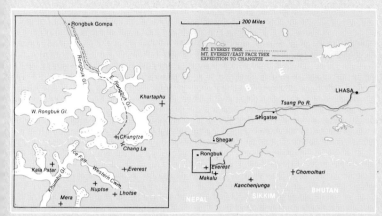

DAY 10: All-day drive to Shigatse (12,500'), second largest town in Tibet, with a ferry ride across the Tsangpo River. Visit Tashilumpo Monastery, one of the largest and most important religious centers of central Tibet.

We will trek for twelve days towards the great east face of Everest, crossing several high passes and exploring the magnificent Kharta and Kama valleys, which so delighted the British mountaineers during expeditions in the 1920's.

DAY 11: Bus to Shegar (14,500'), an all-day drive crossing several high passes, including the Tso La (14,800') and Jatso La (17,300').
DAY 12: Truck to Kharta, a small hamlet on the Arun River, with views of Makalu and Everest. Meet with our yak drivers and yaks for the trek.
DAY 13 to 24: Begin 12-day trek at Kharta, heading west up the Kharta Valley. Cross a pass and descend into the subtropical and heavily wooded Kama Valley. Slowly ascending towards the glaciers,

we reach an altitude of 14,000 feet and the site of the American Everest East Face Expedition base camp. Retrace our steps back to the Kharta Valley and town of Kharta, where we will be met by trucks for the return drive to Lhasa.
DAY 25: Drive over the Pang La (17,300') to Shegar.
DAY 26: Drive to Shigatse.
DAY 27: Drive to Gyantse. Visit Kumbum, the largest stupa in Tibet, and the beautiful Palkhor Monastery.
DAY 28: Drive to Lhasa. Visit Sakya Monastery on route (pending permission).
DAY 29: Day free in Lhasa.
DAY 30: Fly to Chengdu.
DAY 31: In Chengdu.
DAY 32: Fly to Beijing
DAY 33: In Beijing.
DAY 34: Depart Beijing and connect with homeward-bound flights.

IT4PA1SFMT1

TIBET: EXPEDITION TO CHANGTZE

DATES: Sep 25–Nov 5 (42 days)
LEADER: Lanny Johnson
GRADE: E-2
LAND COST: $7900 (8-12 members)

Mt. Everest (29,028') has three satellite peaks: Lhotse ("East Peak," 27,923'), Nuptse ("South Peak," 25,850'), and Changtze ("North Peak," 24,868').

We have planned an expedition to climb Changtze, the northern satellite peak of Mt. Everest, climbed 45 years ago by Eric Shipton's Everest expedition, and climbed once again in 1982 by a German team.

After visiting Lhasa, we drive to the Rongbuk Monastery at 16,500 feet and, with yaks carrying loads, establish camps on the East Rongbuk Glacier, ascending the peak via North Col of Everest or a new route along the northeast ridge. Solid mountaineering skills are required, with at least three years experience on snow and ice.

ITINERARY:
DAY 1 and 2: Leave U.S. Arrive Beijing.
DAY 3 and 4: Sightseeing including the Great Wall at Badaling, dating from the Ming Dynasty, with a stop at a beautifully carved stone gate built in the Mongol period; afternoon drive through the 15th century Avenue of Animals, with its huge stone sculptures, to visit the Ming Tombs, built during the emperors' lifetimes to be their underground palaces in the afterworld; tour the Forbidden City, once the Imperial Palace, a vast

treasure-house begun in the Yuan Dynasty and enlarged over the centuries.
DAY 5: Fly to Chengdu.
DAY 6: Fly to Lhasa (11,700') on one of the most spectacular mountain flights in the world.
DAY 7 to 9: In Lhasa, visiting the Jokhang, Drepung and Ganden monasteries, Potala Palace and Norbulingka.
DAY 10: Drive to Shigatse (12,500') Tibet's second largest city. Visit Tashilumpo Monastery.

Solid mountaineering skills are required, with at least three years experience on snow and ice.

DAY 11: Drive to Shegar (14,500'), crossing the Tso La and Gyatso La (17,300').
DAY 12: Drive to Rongbuk Monastery (16,500'), crossing the Pang La (17,300') with its spectacular views.
DAY 13: Move to camp at foot of Rongbuk Glacier.
DAY 14 to 17: Establish camps I, II, III on the East Rongbuk Glacier, with yaks for transport up the glacier.
DAY 18 to 33: Two weeks to make the ascent.
DAY 34 to 36: Break camp and return to base camp.
DAY 37 to 39: Return drive to Lhasa.
DAY 40: Fly to Chengdu.
DAY 41: Fly to Beijing.
DAY 42: Depart Beijing and connect with homeward-bound flights.

A St. Basil's Cathedral, Moscow/Nigel Dabby
B Mountain Columbine/Nigel Dabby
C Kazakh grandmother inside yurt/Nigel Dabby
D Traveling by camel/Nigel Dabby

ITIAF155RY

TREKKING IN MONGOLIA

DATES: Jun 25–Jul 15 (21 days)
LEADER: Dick Irvin
GRADE: B-2
LAND COST: $3950 (6–15 members)

In 1982, Mountain Travel operated the first-ever treks in Mongolia, land of Genghis Khan, whose fierce nomadic warriors once ranged from the Black Sea to the Pacific.

This year we will again return to the mountains of Mongolia, where the peaks of the High Altai rise from the great Central Asian steppes, topped by 15,266-foot Mt. Tayn Bogd Uul. This part of Mongolia borders on Sinkiang Province, China's westernmost extension.

Access to Mongolia is by way of Russia, and the trips begin with a visit to Moscow.

A long flight from Moscow over Siberia and the Central Asian heartland leads to Ulan Bator, Mongolia's capital, set in a green grassland at 5,000 feet. Here we'll visit Gandan Monastery, where there are several resident lamas and some of the most impressive Buddhist art and artifacts in Asia. The dates coincide with Ulan Bator's festive "independence day" celebrations.

From central Mongolia, we fly to Kobdt, across the vast sands of the Gobi Desert and up over cool, lake-strewn northern forests. Reaching the foot of the High

---

Reaching the foot of the High Altai, we will trek and explore, staying in tents amidst the yurt dwellings of Mongolia's shepherds.

Altai, we will trek and explore, staying in tents amidst the yurt dwellings of Mongolia's shepherds. With luck, we may catch a glimpse of some of Mongolia's rare species of wildlife including snow leopard, Argali sheep, and ibex.

After the trek, we visit the ruins of Karakorum, Genghis Khan's ancient capital, abandoned in 1260 A.D. when his son, Kublai Khan, moved the Mongol capital to Beijing.

ITINERARY:

DAY 1 and 2: Leave U.S. Arrive Moscow. Transfer to hotel.

DAY 3: All day sightseeing.

DAY 4: Morning sightseeing. Late afternoon fight to Ulan Bator, Mongolia.

DAY 5: Arrive Ulan Bator. Transfer to hotel.

DAY 6: Morning visit to Gandan Monastery, the only functioning Buddhist monastery in Mongolia. Afternoon visit to the Bogda Khan's winter palace, with its fantastic Buddhist murals dating to the 16th century

DAY 7: Spectacular four-hour flight across Mongolia to Kobdt, then five-hour drive to the trek starting point.

DAY 8: Trek up to a beautiful campsite by Khukh Serkh Nuur ("Blue Ibex Lake").

DAY 9: Optional day hike to Urt Sallah Ehk (13,500'), crossing meadows covered with wildflowers. With luck we might spot some ibex.

DAY 10: Follow the Khukh Serkh River to a Kazakh village and eventually reach a campsite beneath six pine trees.

DAY 11: Continuing south, we trek steeply uphill with views of Kobdt far in the distance.

DAY 12: Up steeply and then more gradually to camp at Burught Belchir. Optional afternoon horseback ride.

DAY 13: Trek downhill along a river, seeing many columbines and butterflies.

DAY 14: East down the valley to Tsagaan Tokhoi at the confluence of two rivers. Possible visit with a Kazakh family in their yurt.

DAY 15: End trek and drive to Kobdt along the Dund Valley. Stop at Har Us Nuur ("Black Lake") to view water birds, including the herring gull.

DAY 16: Return drive to Kobdt and fly to Ulan Bator.

DAY 17: We will have a chance to watch the colorful Independence Day celebrations, including the two traditional sports of wrestling and archery.

DAY 18: Morning flight to Khujert and overnight in yurt camp. Visit Karakorum, the ancient Mongolian capital built by Genghis Khan's successors and destroyed by the Chinese in 1368. Erdene Dzu Monastery was built on the same spot and with many of the same stones in 1586.

DAY 19: Fly to Ulan Bator.

DAY 20: Fly to Moscow. Transfer to hotel.

DAY 21: Depart Moscow and connect with homeward-bound flights.

SOVIET CENTRAL ASIA

We offer two very special trips in Soviet Central Asia (for fuller description, see our 1984 Europe Catalog):

THE ALTAI MOUNTAINS

Hiking and climbing in the remote Central Asia mountain range shared by the U.S.S.R. and Mongolia.
DATES: Jul 21–Aug 14 (25 days)
LEADER: to be announced
GRADE: B-2/D-2
LAND COST: $2875

THE PAMIRS

Expedition to climb Peak Lenin (23,406').
DATES: Jul 12–Aug 10 (30 days)
LEADER: Bruce Klepinger
GRADE: E-2
LAND COST: $2790

A River crossing/Dick McGowan
B Porters on the upper Baltoro Glacier/Dick McGowan
C Balti porters, the "Sherpas" of Pakistan/Dick McGowan
D Trekker below K2/Dick McGowan

PAKISTAN • 13

T2BA1YO46

THE BALTORO/K2 TREK

DATES: Jun 5–Jul 12 (38 days)
LEADER: Jan Zabinski
GRADE: C-3
LAND COST: $3950 (10–15 members)
*Note decrease from 1984 Trip Schedule.

The traditional expedition route up the Baltoro Glacier leads to K2 (28,741'), second highest mountain on earth, and to the great 8,000-meter peaks of the Karakorum. Eight of the thirty highest peaks in the world are located along or near this route.

The goal of our 30-day Baltoro trek is the junction of the Godwin-Austen and Baltoro glaciers, a spectacular setting called Concordia. Here, within a radius of about twelve miles, rise six peaks over 26,000 feet.

Setting out with our 100 expedition porters, we walk through the villages of Chakpo, Chango and then Askole, the last village we will see for three weeks. After Askole, human habitation ends, and we enter an incredible wilderness of ice, rock and sky. Author and mountaineer Fosco Maraini called this place "the world's greatest museum of shape and form."

Reaching Paiju Camp at the foot of the Baltoro Glacier we begin to feel the pulse of creation: the ice melts, the rocks roll, the glacier creaks and groans, rearranging its icy rivers. We walk along the rough surface of the glacier, a thin rocky moraine that covers a frozen river which is slowly flowing downstream.

At Concordia, views include K2, Marble Peak (20,460'), Broad Peak (26,400'), Gasherbrum IV (26,180'), Golden Throne (23,990'), Chogolisa (25,020') and razor-edged Mitre Peak (19,718'). We'll have five days here to explore the majestic upper Baltoro Glacier and K2 Base Camp.

Although on most of this trek we are in utter wilderness, we will take a part of the Karakorum culture with us: our 100 expedition porters, the lively Baltis and "Hunzakuts" who carry all our group trekking gear. There will be many memorable evenings spent at camp, listening to their songs and watching (and sometimes joining) their dances.

This "trek of a lifetime" is ample proof that the most difficult journeys are also the most rewarding. The rewards are too numerous to mention; the difficulties will include rough glacier travel, wild river crossings, and possible delays in the mountain flights in and out of Skardu.

ITINERARY:
DAY 1 to 3: Leave U.S. Arrive Rawalpindi. Transfer to hotel.
DAY 4: Free day in Rawalpindi. Trek preparation and briefing.
DAY 5: Fly to Skardu (weather permitting). Overnight in guest house.
DAY 6: Day to explore Skardu, a

PAKISTAN
ABOUT TREKKING IN THE KARAKORUM

A

To make your Pakistan trek as comfortable as possible, all camping gear is carried by porters hired from local villages. Pack animals are not normally available in these regions. You will only need to carry a light day-pack for your jacket, camera, and water bottle.

In addition to a Mountain Travel leader, there will be a small local camp staff including a cook. It isn't always possible to purchase local food supplies, so our meals will be a combination of local food and high-quality freeze-dried camping food (Mountain House brand) brought from the U.S. Breakfast and dinner are hot meals served in camp. A cold lunch (with hot tea) is served picnic-style each day. All water used for cooking or drinking is boiled and filtered.

The staff does all camp chores (although it will be appreciated if you help in setting up your own tent).

Our treks take place in the Karakorum Range of extreme northern Pakistan, a sparsely populated and arid mountain region. Even at moderately high altitudes (6,000 to 9,000 feet) the weather can be extremely hot. Campsites are chosen for their proximity to available water sources.

small village located on the banks of the Indus River.
DAY 7: Jeep to Basha in the Shigar Valley. Short hike to Dasso.
DAY 8: Dasso to Chakpo, a long, hot day.
DAY 9: Chakpo to Chu-mik. Rugged trekking and a thousand-foot ridge. Hot springs en route.
DAY 10: Chu-mik to Askole, passing the last cultivation we see for about three weeks.
DAY 11: Askole to Biafo Glacier

camp, farther up the Braldu Valley and across the Biafo Glacier's mouth.
DAY 12: Biafo Camp to Bardumal, past the 19,060-foot Bakhor Das monolith and across the Dumordo River.
DAY 13: Bardumal to Paiju, a moderate day's walk with first views of the Baltoro Glacier.
DAY 14: Layover day at Paiju, a rest day for the porters and ourselves.
DAY 15: Paiju to Liliwah, onto the Baltoro Glacier itself. Views of Paiju Peak and the Trango Towers.
DAY 16: Liliwah to Urdukas, a day of glacier walking with several river crossings.
DAY 17: Urdukas to Biango. Ascend the north bank of the glacier with superb views of Masherbrum and Mustagh Tower.
DAY 18: Biango to Goro, a shorter day as we approach Concordia.
DAY 19: Goro to Concordia, one of the world's most spectacular mountain locations.
DAY 20 to 24: Side trips from Concordia.
DAY 25 to 28: Return down the Baltoro Glacier.
DAY 29: Possible rest day at Paiju Camp.
DAY 30 to 35: Paiju to Dasso, retracing our route down the Braldu Valley.
DAY 36: Meet jeeps and drive to Skardu. Overnight at guest house.
DAY 37: Fy to Rawalpindi, weather permitting.
DAY 38: Leave Rawalpindi and connect with homeward-bound flights.

B

C

A

IT2BA1YO48

HUNZA & NANGA PARBAT TREK

DATES: Sep 4–Oct 1 (28 days)
LEADER: Dick Irvin
GRADE: C-3
LAND COST: $2475 (11-15 members)
$2675 (7-10)

Hunza is one of the most impressive mountain-ringed valleys in the world. The peak of Nanga Parbat which rises 23,000 feet above the arid Indus River gorge, has been called an entire mountain range in itself.

Both the Shimshal and Rupal valleys that we'll trek into on this trip have been recently derestricted. We will be among the first outsiders to visit these fascinating areas.

From Gilgit, we'll jeep south to the Astor Valley and trek for a week beneath the sheer south face of Nanga Parbat (26,660'), 9th highest mountain in the world. At midpoint on this trek, we will ascend the Mazeno Glacier towards the historic Mazeno Pass (17,000').

After returning to Gilgit, the magnificent Hunza Valley beckons. Our approach is by the paved Karakorum Highway, not the dangerous trails of yore. Fanny Bullock Workman, an early Karakorum pioneer remarked upon reaching Baltit, Hunza, in 1910: "A short distance beyond Chalt, the peerless massif Rakaposhi, called Domani by the Hunza people, first comes into view. Not a dozen miles away, it bursts upon the eye, filling a long gap between lesser mountains, a glorious 18,000 feet of steep, broken snow slopes culminating in pointed icy summits. From here to Hispar, the whole region is wild and savage to the last degree." In contrast to the forbidding mountains, however, Hunza's villages are delightful irrigated green oases of apricot orchards, wheat fields and poplar trees.

Our Hunza adventure is a nine-day trek to Shimshal, the most remote village in the valley. The precarious trail leading to Shimshal takes us along clifftops, across ledges and talus slopes, and over hanging bridges beneath the great granite walls of the Karakorum.

ITINERARY:

DAY 1 to 3: Leave U.S. Arrive Rawalpindi. Transfer to hotel.

DAY 4: In Rawalpindi.

DAY 5: Fly to Gilgit, weather permitting. Transfer to inn.

DAY 6: Long drive by jeep to Rampur via the town of Astor. Camp near the roadhead.

DAY 7: Short day up the Rupal River to camp at Tarshing. All day the immense massif of Nanga Parbat becomes nearer as we approach.

DAY 8: Cross the Chhungphar Glacier to Rupal village. Continue and cross the Bazhin Glacier to an area of lovely meadows with the south face of Nanga Parbat (26,660') rising directly above.

DAY 9: Proceed along the right bank of the Toshain Glacier on a good moraine trail.

DAY 10 and 11: Day hikes in the Mazeno Glacier area from our camp.

DAY 12 to 14: Return down-valley to Rampur.

DAY 15: Drive to Gilgit. Overnight at hotel.

DAY 16: Drive to Karimabad, capital of Hunza, along the newly-built Karakorum Highway. Overnight in Karimabad.

DAY 17: Continue along the Karakorum Highway among Hunza's magnificent mountain scenery. Meet porters at Pasu village and begin trek to Shimshal.

DAY 18: The valley begins to open out as we ascend, often crossing immense scree slopes. High peaks are visible up narrow side valleys.

B

DAY 19: After boulder-hopping along a wide plain, we pass a shrine to a Moslem saint. Camp in a river plain.

> The great explorer Eric Shipton wrote of Hunza as "the ultimate manisfestation of mountain grandeur."

DAY 20: Cross the tangled moraine of the Mulungutti Glacier with views of Disteghil Sar (25,868'), Hunza's highest peak. Reach Shimshal.

DAY 21 and 22: In Shimshal. A chance to explore the area. Shimshal is actually three villages each irrigated by a different stream.

DAY 23 to 25: Return trek to Pasu along the often-narrow path.

DAY 26: Drive from Pasu down the Hunza Valley on the Karakorum Highway to Gilgit.

DAY 27: Fly to Rawalpindi, weather permitting.

DAY 28: Depart Rawalpindi and connect with homeward-bound flights.

C

IT2BA1YO47

HUNZA & BALTISTAN

DATES: Aug 7–Aug 31 (25 days)
LEADER: Jan Zabinski
GRADE: B-3
LAND COST: $2175 (11-15 members)
$2375 (7-10)

The great explorer Eric Shipton wrote of Hunza as "the ultimate manifestation of mountain grandeur" and many present-day visitors agree with him. Located in northernmost Pakistan where the borders of Russian Turkestan, China and the tip of Afghanistan's Wakhan Corridor meet, this former princely state is a 150-mile long valley surrounded by precipitous Karakorum peaks. Hunza's most famous peak, 25,550-foot Rakaposhi, rises majestically above the valley's many apricot orchards.

We skirt directly beneath Rakaposhi while driving into Hunza from Gilgit on the Karakorum Highway, a marvel of mountain road engineering. From Hunza's old capital of Baltit, with its direct views of Rakaposhi, to the northerly town of Pasu (as close to China as foreigners are presently permitted to drive on the Karakorum Highway), we will explore the valley. We'll meet the hardy Hunzakuts, taste some of the 22 varieties of apricots, visit old garnet mines, step onto the 30-mile-long Batura

A Crossing the Shyok River by raft/Pam Shandrick
B The Hushe Valley below Masherbrum/Pam Shandrick
C Resting at Masherbrum Base Camp/Pam Shandrick

PAKISTAN • 15

A

B

Glacier and admire the awesome scenery.

From Hunza we retrace our route to Gilgit and head along the newly opened Indus Valley road to Baltistan in the midst of the Karakorum Range. Baltistan has as many 20,000-foot peaks as the Alps have 10,000-footers, but at first we won't see them as we travel up the narrow "district of defiles" by road.

Reaching Skardu, a small town on a bluff above the Indus River, we'll see the Dogra fort perched on thousand-foot high Skardu Rock. We can explore the fort and look for the ancient rock carving of Buddha.

West of Skardu we will undertake an eight-day trek up the Hushe Valley into the midst of the Karakorum Range. Starting from the large, well-irrigated town of Khapalu on the Shyok River, we hire Balti porters and walk to Masherbrum Base Camp at 13,000 feet, amost directly below the southern face of Masherbrum (25,660'). We will have a layover day at the base camp to explore the Masherbrum Glacier and experience the unmatched wilds of the Karakorum.

ITINERARY:

DAY 1 to 3: Leave U.S. Arrive Rawalpindi. Transfer to hotel.

DAY 4: In Rawalpindi.

DAY 5: Fly to Gilgit, weather permitting. Overnight at inn.

DAY 6: In Gilgit.

DAY 7: Very scenic drive to upper Hunza along the Karakorum Highway. First views of Rakaposhi (25,550'). Short hike for views of the Batura Glacier near Pasu. Overnight in guest house at Gulmit.

DAY 8: From Gulmit, hike to Borit Lake (a stop for migratory birds coming from China) and visit site

of old ruby mines. Visit Mir's palace in Baltit. Overnight in Baltit.

DAY 9: Morning walk around area near Karimabad. Afternoon return drive to Gilgit, stopping along the way for photos and garnet hunting.

DAY 10: In Gilgit.

DAY 11: All day drive to Skardu, Baltistan, on a rough road carved into the narrow Indus gorge. Overnight in rest house on a bluff overlooking the Indus.

DAY 12: In Skardu. Optional walk up to the Skardu fort.

DAY 13: Five-hour jeep ride to Khapalu, a large town at 8,550 feet on the Shyok River. Excellent views of the steep granite peaks at the entrance to the Hushe Valley across the river. Camp near government rest house. This afternoon the trip leader will be busy hiring porters for the trek.

DAY 14: Cross the Shyok River (either by jeep or by small goatskin rafts—an adventure in itself!) to the Hushe Valley and begin trek. Camp at the village of Machulu.

DAY 15: Trek directly toward Masherbrum (25,660') through many beautiful orchards, fields and villages.

DAY 16: Reach Hushe village (10,000'), with its spectacular views of Masherbrum.

DAY 17: A strenuous day's walk to Masherbrum Base Camp (13,000').

DAY 18: Optional hikes in the Masherbrum area.

DAY 19 to 21: Return trek to Khaphalu, again crossing the Shyok River.

DAY 22: Drive to Skardu.

DAY 23: In Skardu.

DAY 24: Fly to Rawalpindi, weather permitting.

DAY 25: Depart Rawalpindi and connect with homeward-bound flights.

IT2BA1YO49

VALLEYS OF THE HINDU KUSH

DATES: Aug 7–Aug 31 (25 days)
LEADER: to be announced
GRADE: C-3
LAND COST: $2175 (11-15 members)
$2375 (7-10)

The high, jagged peaks of the Hindu Kush have long been the cultural watershed between the lands of eastern Central Asia and the different valley kingdoms of the north Indian subcontinent. Alexander the Great crossed the range in 328 B.C. with his Greek soldiers and in 747 A.D. Chinese General Kao Hsien crossed the Darkot Pass into the Hindu Kush's Yasin Valley with 3,000 troops.

The terrain of these valleys is best described as mountainous desert, and it is inhabited by hardy clans, some of which are said to be descendents of Alexander's Greek army.

This 15-day trek explores some of the least visited areas of the eastern Hindu Kush: the Yasin Valley of the Gilgit region, and the Yarkhun and Turikho valleys of northern Chitral.

Starting in Gilgit, we travel 90 miles by jeep up the Gilgit River Valley to the large village of Yasin. Walking north toward the Darkot Pass, we then turn west into a series of narrow canyons dotted with small villages and summer shepherd camps. Beyond the shepherd camp of Shotali, we will ascend the Aghost Bar Glacier located between 20,000-foot peaks. At the 14,760-foot Thui An Pass there are splendid views of major peaks in the Hindu Raj Range, many of which are still unclimbed.

As we descend the Gazin Glacier into the Yarkhun Valley of Chitral District, we enter a region with strong cultural ties to Central Asia. Horsemen can be seen along the rolling valley floor, children carry the double-string bow called the tambuk, falconry is still practised, and men hunt ducks along the river with ancient muzzle-loading guns. Everyone wears the homespun pakol, a Tudor-style hat.

Traveling north along the Yarkhun River, we walk at first directly toward the wildly striated peaks of the Hindu Kush, then turn west to cross the Shah Janali Pass (14,000'). Now in the Turikho Valley, the path slowly descends to villages as we pass numerous canyons where unseen ibex graze high above. Several days along we reach the roadhead, having sampled many varieties of apricots along the way. Near the end of the long jeep ride to Chitral Bazaar, we will finally see 25,264-foot Tirich Mir, highest peak in the Hindu Kush.

Trekking in this wildly beautiful country will be exhilarating, but sometimes strenuous, since we have many days hiking on scree, boulders and glaciers.

ITINERARY:

DAY 1 to 3: Leave U.S. Arrive Rawalpindi. Transfer to hotel.

DAY 4: In Rawalpindi.

DAY 5: Fly to Gilgit, weather permitting. Overnight at inn.

DAY 6: Jeep to Yasin and camp near village.

DAY 7: Free day in Yasin's green oasis.

DAY 8: Jeep to the village of Harph and begin trek.

DAY 9: Walk to Shotali below the Aghost Bar Glacier.

DAY 10: Up to glacier camp.

DAY 11: Rest day at glacier camp. Optional climb of a 15,000 foot peak.

DAY 12: Cross Thui An Pass (14,760') and descend into Chitral District.

DAY 13: Down to Gazin village.

DAY 14 to 16: Ascend narrow Yarkhun Valley to Yashkist village near Lasht, the valley's northernmost town.

DAY 17: 3,000-foot climb up to the summer settlement of Ishperu Dok.

DAY 18: Layover day and chance to rest or climb high.

> The terrain of these valleys is best described as mountainous desert, and it is inhabited by hardy clans, some of which are said to be descendents of Alexander's Greek army.

DAY 19: Over the Shah Janali Pass (14,000'). Beautiful views of the Hindu Kush from the summit, then a long descent to a shepherds' camp.

DAY 20: Rough day from meadows to scree slopes to flat river country.

DAY 21: Down Turikho Valley from Phurgram to Uzhnu past many narrow gorges.

DAY 22: To the roadhead town of Warkup, passing fertile oases with apricot trees.

DAY 23: Jeep the long and bumpy ride to Chitral Bazaar. Overnight at rest house.

DAY 24: Fly to Rawalpindi, weather permitting.

DAY 25: Depart Rawalpindi and connect with homeward-bound flights.

C

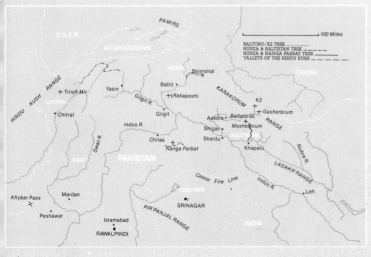

100 Miles

BALTORO/K2 TREK
HUNZA & BALTISTAN TREK
HUNZA & NANGA PARBAT TREK
VALLEYS OF THE HINDU KUSH

PAMIRS

U.S.S.R.

AFGHANISTAN

CHINA

HINDU KUSH RANGE

CHITRAL

Shimshal

Tirich Mir

Yasin

Baltit

Chitral

Rakaposhi

Gilgit R.

Gilgit

KARAKORUM RANGE

K2

Gasherbrum

Askole

Baltoro Gl.

Indus R.

Shigar

Masherbrum

Swat R.

Chilas

Skardu

Nanga Parbat

Khapalu

Nubra R.

SWAT

PAKISTAN

LADAKH RANGE

Cease Fire Line

Indus R.

Khyber Pass

Leh

Mardan

KASHMIR

Peshawar

PIR PANJAL RANGE

SRINAGAR

Islamabad

RAWALPINDI

INDIA

IT4PAlSFMT2

TREKKING IN KASHMIR & LADAKH

DATES: #1 Jul 7–Jul 27 (21 days)
　　　　#2 Aug 11–Aug 31 (21 days)
LEADER: #1 John Mueller
　　　　#2 Hugh Swift
GRADE: B-2
LAND COST: $1490 (12–15 members)
　　　　$1650 (9–11)

The Kashmir Valley is cool, green and lush in summer, its gentle mountains and hillsides dense with evergreen forests, birch groves and wildflowers. It was long the favorite mountain retreat of the Moghul Emperors and the British Raj, who came here to escape the searing summer heat of the Indian plains. Culturally, the Kashmir Valley is almost entirely Moslem, although thousands of Hindu pilgrims make annual visits to its sacred lakes and holy caves.

After a pleasant stay on houseboats in Srinagar, Kashmir's capital, we'll begin a seven-day hike. An ideal first trek in the Himalaya because of its relatively moderate elevation and terrain, we begin at Pahalgam and meander through remote forested valleys inhabited by a few colorful Gujar nomads. Views include a close look at precipitous Kolahoi Peak (17,800') and the distant giant Nanga Parbat (26,660'). Highest altitude reached on this trek is 13,500 feet, the crossing of the Yemnher Pass into the Sind Valley.

Leaving Kashmir, we drive across the Himalayan crest, passing the Himalayan rain shadow, and find ourselves in the extremely arid mountain landscape of Ladakh. At Leh and in the Indus Valley, we'll visit some of the most beautiful Tibetan Buddhist monasteries in existence, then make a four-day trek on the flanks of the Indus Valley towards the peak of Stok Kangri (21,000') for grand panoramas of the Indus Valley and mountains of Ladakh from a pass at 16,000 feet.

ITINERARY:

DAY 1 to 3: Leave U.S. Arrive Delhi. Transfer to hotel.

DAY 4: Fly to Srinagar (5,200') and transfer to houseboat on Dal Lake. Afternoon sightseeing.

DAY 5: Drive to Pahalgam (7,800') and begin trek. Hike through a forest over a deserted road to Aru (7,850'); continue uphill to a large open valley above the Lidder River, passing Gujar shepherd huts. Camp at Lidderwat (8,870').

DAY 6: Trek along the north bank of the Lidder River, heading towards Kolahoi Peak, a beautiful spire of rock, snow and ice. Cross forests of Kashmiri maple, pine and fir to Satlanjan (10,050'), a summer settlement for Gujar shepherds.

DAY 7: Rest day or optional hike up the valley to the snout of the Kolahoi Glacier.

DAY 8: Back through Lidderwat

INDIA
ABOUT TREKKING IN KASHMIR & LADAKH

A

Most of our India treks take place in portions of the Great Himalayan Range such as Ladakh and Zanskar, sparsely populated and arid regions, usually at 10,000 feet or higher. Campsites are chosen for their proximity to available sources of water and fodder for the pack animals.

All camping gear is carried by pack animals (porters are not a tradition in this region of the Himalaya). You will only need to carry a light day-pack with a jacket, camera, and water bottle.

There will be a camp manager and a small local camp staff including a cook. Breakfast and dinner are hot meals served in a dining tent; you will carry a light pack lunch each day, which you can stop and eat at any point during the day's walk.

All water used for drinking and cooking is filtered and boiled. The staff does most camp chores (although it will be appreciated if you help in setting up your own tent).

B

and begin a climb toward Sekiwas (11,150').

DAY 9: Across the Yemnher Pass (13,500') and descend into the Sind Valley. Spectacular mountain views. Continue to a lovely high camp.

DAY 10: Continue descending the whole day, sometimes steeply, ending at a meadow near Zaivan (9,300').

DAY 11: Walk to Kulan, near Sonamarg and meet with jeep. Drive to Kargil (9,000'). Overnight at hotel.

DAY 12: Continue the dusty but spectacular drive over the mountains to Leh (11,000'). Transfer to hotel.

DAY: 13: Visit the Tiksey and Hemis monasteries in the Indus Valley.

It was long the favorite mountain retreat of the Moghul Emperors and the British Raj, who came here to escape the searing summer heat of the Indian plains.

DAY 14: Begin four-day trek with a hike up through the village of Stok (11,500') and into a long, winding canyon that passes below a spectacularly situated cliffside fort.

DAY 15: Trek towards the peak of

Stok Kangri, climbing steadily all day to a camp at about 14,000 feet just below the Matho La Pass. A long day through dramatic terrain of multicolored rock formation.

DAY 16: A short but steep climb up to the Matho La Pass (16,000'), from which there are fine views of snowy 20,000-foot Ladakh ranges. Descend below a yak herders' settlement to a camp at about 14,000 feet with good views of surrounding glaciers.

DAY 17: Descend through a beautiful canyon and end the trek near the village of Matho near the Matho Gompa (monastery). Drive to Leh. Overnight at hotel.

DAY 18: Fly to Srinagar (weather permitting) and transfer to houseboats on Dal Lake.

DAY 19: Free day in Srinagar.

DAY 20: Fly to Delhi and transfer to hotel.

DAY 21: Transfer to airport and connect with homeward-bound flights.

C

IT4PAlSFMT2

THE TRANS HIMALAYA TREK

DATES: #1 Jul 28–Aug 26 (30 days)
　　　　#2 Sep 1–Sep 30 (30 days)
LEADER: #1 John Mueller
　　　　#2 Hugh Swift
GRADE: C-3
LAND COST: $1890 (12–15 members)
　　　　$2050 (9–11)

There are few places on earth where it is possible to experience the diversity of landscape seen on this 19-day foot journey, which travels from the densely forested Kashmir Valley to the desert of Ladakh. Moreover, this trek provides an ethnic odyssey, from the Moslem herders' hamlets of Kashmir to the medieval Buddhist villages of Ladakh, known as "Little Tibet".

Trekking through the deep forests for which Kashmir is famous, we hike over the Pir Panjal Range at Shilshar Pass (11,760'), passing shepherds' meadows of the Warwan Valley, a place of Moslem culture and Gujar nomad camps.

Reaching the head of the Warwan Valley, we cross the Great Himalayan Range at Lonvilad Gali Pass (14,530') into the watershed of the Indus River and enter the Suru Valley, a semi-arid canyon populated by Baltis (who are ethnically Tibetan but long ago converted to Islam). The Suru Valley is cradled between the snowy flanks of the Himalaya and the parched rock of the Zanskar Range to the north.

Continuing up the Suru Valley with views of massive Nun Kun (23,410'), we enter a landscape of dry and windswept mountains and reach our first lamaistic temple, Rangdum Gompa, on the outskirts of Zanskar. We are now in the land of the Ladakhi Buddhists.

Crossing the Zanskar Range by the Kanji La Pass (17,240'), we descend past the medieval village of Kanji, a cliff-side settlement whose inhabitants dress in thick red robes, goatskin shawls and winged stovepipe hats. Our last days take us past the multicolored cliffs of Kang Nalla and to ancient Lamayuru Monastery, from where we drive to Leh, capital of Ladakh. We spend three days visiting monasteries of the Indus Valley before flying to Srinagar and homeward.

ITINERARY:

DAY 1 to 3: Leave U.S. Arrive Delhi. Transfer to hotel.

DAY 4: Fly to Srinagar. Transfer to houseboats on Dal Lake.

DAY 5: Sightseeing in Srinagar (5,200'), capital of Kashmir.

DAY 6: Drive to Lihenwan and camp.

DAY 7: Hike across Shilshar Pass (11,760'), through forests and meadows.

DAY 8: Steep descent to Inshan (8,000') on the Warwan River, hiking through stretches of forest.

D

A   Upper Kashmir Valley/John Thune
B   Women from Zanskar/Arlene Blum
C   Mune Gompa, Zanskar/Pam Shandrick
D   Zanskari grandmother and children/Arlene Blum

INDIA • 17

Camp on the banks of the Warwan.

DAY 9: Trek past a number of villages, to Sokhniz (9,100'), the highest village in the Warwan Valley.

DAY 10: Walk alongside the river and camp at about 9,900 feet.

DAY 11: Through lovely countryside today reaching a confluence and following the eastern tributary to Humpet, leaving behind the forests and walking through rocky meadows.

DAY 12: Walk to Kaintal (11,500') at the snout of a glacier.

DAY 13: A long day over the Lonvilad Gali Pass (14,530') along the terminal moraine and glacier.

DAY 14: Rest day.

DAY 15: Descent to the Suru River. The countryside, now in the Himalayan rain shadow, is noticeably drier and more barren. First views of Nun Kun and the Zanskar Range. We are now out of Kashmir and entering Zanskar.

This trek provides an ethnic odyssey, from the Moslem herders' hamlets of Kashmir to the medieval Buddhist villages of Ladakh, known as "Little Tibet".

DAY 16: Continue over the Pukartse La (12,500'), with its spectacular view of Nun Kun as well as the crevassed Ganri Glacier, and descend to Parkachick, a fascinating adobe village at the foot of the Zanskar Range.

DAY 17: An easy walk along a road to camp at Golmatung Meadow (12,650').

DAY 18: Rest day.

DAY 19: Trek to beautifully situated Rangdum Gompa, a Tibetan Buddhist monastery.

DAY 20: Visit Rangdum Gompa then walk to the Kanji La South Base Camp (13,900').

DAY 21: A long but not steep hike up to the Kanji La where there are breathtaking views of the peaks of the Karakorum. A sharp descent brings us into Ladakh proper.

DAY 22: An easy walk down a dramatic maze of canyons to camp near the medieval village of Kanji, a classic Ladakhi town at about 12,000 feet.

DAY 23: Rest day.

DAY 24: Emerge at Hiniskut from between high, steep ridges and pass into a wide valley with an old caravan trail and modernday road high above.

DAY 25: End trek and proceed to Leh by jeep. En route, visit Lamayuru Monastery (11,300'), perched dramatically on an erosionsculpted cliff above the river.

DAY 26 and 27: Visit Hemis, Tiksey, and other major sites around Leh.

DAY 28: Fly to Srinagar (weather permitting). Transfer to houseboats on Dal Lake.

DAY 29: Fly to Delhi. Transfer to hotel.

DAY 30: Depart Delhi and connect with homeward-bound flights.

THE OLD CODGERS' EXPEDITION TO THE EASTERN KARAKORUM

DATES: Jun 30–Aug 11 (43 days)
LEADER: Leo Le Bon
GRADE: D-3
LAND COST: Special celebration price of $3100

This is an expedition for mountaineers 50 years or older (and only by special dispensation for those younger) in celebration of the 50th birthday of Leo Le Bon, Mountain Travel's president and founder.

The expedition will attempt a first ascent of a 24,000-foot peak at the head of the Siachen Glacier in the eastern Karakorum. The approach will be via the Nubra Valley, and there will be plenty of skiing on the Siachen Glacier, longest in the Karakorum.

NOTE: This expedition is subject to granting of permits and the official opening of the restricted Nubra Valley.

ITINERARY:

DAY 1 to 3: Leave U.S. Arrive Delhi. Transfer to hotel.

DAY 4: Day free in Delhi.

DAY 5: Morning flight to Srinagar. Transfer to houseboats on Dal Lake.

DAY 6: Fly to Leh (weather permitting). Transfer to hotel.

DAY 7: Visit several monasteries of the Indus Valley.

DAY 8 and 9: By truck convoy over the Kardung La, highest road pass in the world, and descend into the Nubra Valley. Continue to the roadhead at Panamik.

DAY 10 to 12: Organize gear and start expedition. About 40 kilometers of glacier travel along the huge Siachen Glacier will be required to get to a base camp at the foot of an unclimbed and moderately easy 24,000-foot peak in the eastern Karakorum. We expect to ski up the glacier and enjoy some great runs on this vast expanse of snow. Porters will carry expedition gear to base camp.

DAY 13 to 35: We are allowing about 22 days for the ascent and descent of our unclimbed (and probably unnamed) peak. It might take less time than this, but with old codgers, one never knows. We just want to be sure we get up there!

DAY 36 to 38: Pack up base camp and descend glacier to Panamik.

DAY 39 and 40: Drive back to Leh.

DAY 41: A day in Leh, drinking beer at the Officers Mess (unlimited quantities will be available).

DAY 42: Fly to Delhi (weather permitting).

DAY 43: Depart Delhi and connect with homeward bound flights.

A Tiksey Monastery, Ladakh
B Lama/Leo Le Bon
C Phuktal Gompa, Zanskar/Arlene Blum
D Himalayan ski mountaineering/Fred Harper

A

IT4PA1SFMT2

HIMALAYAN PASSAGES

DATES: #1 Jul 7–Aug 7 (32 days)
#2 Aug 4–Sep 4 (32 days)
LEADER: #1 Nigel Dabby
#2 Jeff Campbell
GRADE: C-3
LAND COST: $2190 (12–15 members)
$2350 (9–11)

This rugged 21-day trek in the Great Himalayan Range traverses the parched canyons of the ancient "kingdom" of Zanskar, once part of western Tibet, then crosses over the Kishtwar Himalaya, one of the mountain ranges that forms the backdrop to the green and fertile plains of Punjab.

After visiting Srinagar, capital of Kashmir, we'll drive to Leh (11,000') and begin the trek near Lamayuru, an ancient monastery perched atop a high, eroded shelf. Entering Zanskar, we'll walk through a dramatic high landscape of narrow river gorges with spectacular views of Zanskar's rugged peaks.

Zanskar is a fascinating Tibetan Buddhist enclave which has had little contact with the outside world—indeed, even the famous Himalayan caravan routes didn't pass this way, since snows keep Zanskar's high passes inaccessible most of the year. Two ceremonial monarchs still reside here, one in Padum and one in the tiny hamlet of Zangla. There are several ancient monasteries in Zanskar, including the large and spectacularly-situated complex at Karsha.

Descending momentarily from the high country, we'll follow the Zanskar River to Padum (11,800') the area's largest town. Turning westerly, our route takes us over the 17,300-foot Umasi La and down into flower-filled meadows containing the rare blue poppy.

As we continue downward into the Kishtwar Himalaya through the deep Chenab Valley, we enter an area of Hindu culture with small villages and intriguing temples, both Hindu and animistic. Finally, we trek to the roadhead east of Kishtwar in the steep Chenab gorge. After returning to Srinagar, we fly back to Delhi.

ITINERARY:
DAY 1 to 3: Leave U.S. Arrive Delhi. Transfer to hotel.
DAY 4: Morning flight to Srinagar (5,200'). Transfer to houseboat on Dal Lake. Afternoon sightseeing.
DAY 5: Drive from the green Kashmir Valley over the Zoji La (11,580') into a different world—the western periphery of Ladakh. Arrive at Kargil (9,000').
DAY 6: Reach Leh after crossing two high passes and descending into the Indus Valley.
DAY 7: Visit the monasteries of Hemis and Tiksey, the latter on a hilltop overlooking the Indus.
DAY 8: Drive to Lamayuru Monastery (11,300') and begin trek, crossing the Prinkiti La and descending through barren "badlands."
DAY 9: Proceed past Shila with its

small monastery, old castle and apricot orchards into a canyon with numerous river crossings.
DAY 10: Ascend the Snigoutse La (16,120') amongst the brown folds of the Zanskar Range and walk into a moonscape of orange and amber-colored rocks criss-crossed with brilliant serpentine.
DAY 11: Cross the Sirsir La (15,200') and wind down into a valley across from Photoskar village, set among fields of wheat and potatoes.

Zanskar is a fascinating Tibetan Buddhist enclave which has had little contact with the outside world —indeed, even the famous Himalayan caravan routes didn't pass this way.

DAY 12: Continue through brilliantly colored, twisted layers of rock and cross the 14,000-foot Kuba La; then, after a short descent, cross the Netushi La.
DAY 13 and 14: Over the Hanuma La (16,000') and Parfi La, then plunge down into the Zanskar River Valley, walking up and down along steep trails in the river gorge.
DAY 15 and 16: Trek along a flat, dusty trail marked with long rows of Buddhist *chortens*. We'll pass small villages and have fine panoramas of the Great Himalayan Range. Reach Karsha, Zanskar's largest and most important monastery.
DAY 17: Trek across the wide, flat river plain to Padum, Zanskar's "capital," a village of some 400 inhabitants.
DAY 18 and 19: Hike west past the village of Ating (12,000') into the Bardar Chu Valley. Ascend to a high camp next to the Zanskar Glacier.

DAY 20: Climb the steep north side of the Zanskar Glacier onto the Umasi La (17,300'). Spectacular last views into Zanskar.
DAY 21: Steeply down alongside the Umasi Glacier. We'll camp in a small meadow at about 12,500 feet.
DAY 22: Rest day. Bid goodbye to our porters and meet the horsemen from Kishtwar.
DAY 23 and 24: Descend the Zanskar Nalla into a valley with idyllic meadows. Pass several Buddhist villages.
DAY 25 and 26: After we reach the Bhut Nalla, the villages become Hindu and the weather warms up. Reach Gulab Garh in the Chenab River gorge.
DAY 27 and 28: Trek up and down through dense forests in the Chenab canyon, passing caravans of Gujar and Gaddi, sheepherding nomads.
DAY 29: Drive to Kishtwar (5,200') after reaching the roadhead.
DAY 30: Drive to Srinagar.
DAY 31: Fly to Delhi.
DAY 32: Depart Delhi and connect with homeward-bound flights.

IT3TG1MTO2

KEDARNATH SKI EXPEDITION

DATES: Sep 2–Oct 4 (33 days)
LEADER: to be announced
GRADE: E-1
LAND COST: $3190 (10–12 members)
$3390 (8–9)

Kedarnath Peak in the Garhwal Himalaya consists of five peaks: Kedarnath Dome (22,410'), Kedarnath Peak (22,770'), Bharte Khunta (21,580'), Shivaling (21,470')—sometimes called the Indian Matterhorn), and Mt. Meru (21,850').

This expedition's goal is an ascent and descent on skis of Kedarnath Dome and Kedarnath Peak. Both peaks are accessible from a high camp at about 18,000 feet, and the long high altitude slopes of these mountains offer unexcelled skiing possibilities in a magnificent setting.

The approach to the peaks is through the Garhwal Himalaya, a spectacular alpine region containing the headwaters of the holy Ganges River. The Garhwal's peaks are considered the traditional abode of Shiva and many other dieties, and the region has always been a major pilgrimage center for Hindus. From the village of Rishikesh on the banks of the Ganges, we head north and trek to base camp along the Bhagirithi River. Further up along the Gangotri Glacier, we establish a base camp at about 14,300 feet and spend about 19 days on the climbs.

This expedition is for advanced skiers with at least three years of climbing experience.

D

ITINERARY:
DAY 1 to 3: Leave U.S. Arrive Delhi. Transfer to hotel.
DAY 4: In Delhi.
DAY 5 to 7: Drive via Rishikesh and Uttarkashi to Harsil.
DAY 8 to 10: Trek to Gangotri and Gaumukh (13,000').
DAY 11 to 27: Establish base camp, higher camps and make summit attempts.
DAY 28 to 31: Return to Delhi.
DAY 32: Depart Delhi on homeward-bound flights.
DAY 33: Arrive home.

C

A "Sutee" handprints, Bikaner Fort, Rajasthan/Marsha Parker
B Children of Rajasthan/Marsha Parker
C Thar Desert campsite/Marsha Parker
D Ready for the day's ride/Marsha Parker

INDIA • 19

IT3TGIMTO1

RAJASTHAN CAMEL SAFARI

DATES: #1 Jan 21–Feb 10 (21 days)
   *#2 Nov 10–Nov 30 (21 days)
   1985: Feb 10–Mar 2 (21 days)
LEADER: Raj Singh
GRADE: *B-2
LAND COST: $1975 (12–15 members)
   $2140 (9–11)
*Note change from 1984 Trip Schedule.

Rajasthan—land of the maharajas —is one of India's most historic and picturesque regions, a semi-desert graced with the legacy of the Moghul Empire.

In the Moghul cities of Jodphur, Jaisalmer and Jaipur, which we visit, there are massive princely forts and exquisite marble palaces (one of which we tour on elephant back). In Jodphur, Jaipur, Gajner and Bikaner, our accommodations will be in maharajas' palaces. Outside the cities is a little-known stretch of land called the Great Indian (or Thar) Desert, through which we'll travel by camel.

Unlike the Sahara, the Thar is a younger desert and supports a flora and fauna which is fascinating and diverse. This desert is habitat for nilgai, black buck antelope, Indian gazelle and desert fox. It is also home to some of the rarest birds in the world, including the great Indian bustard, and a wide range of birds of prey, such as griffin vultures, eagles and falcons.

An ancient civilization once flourished in the Thar Desert, as is apparent from desert archaeological finds such as Kaligangan, and it is currently inhabited by nomadic and pastoral tribes who retain unique customs of the traditional desert way of life, tending livestock and riding camels with colorful tasseled saddles.

Our seven-day camel safari is designed to explore a small section of this historic desert traveling from one village to another by camel (or on foot if one chooses).

NOTE: The dates of Trip #2 allow for a visit to the famous annual Puskhar Camel Fair. Contact us for details.

Rajasthan—land of the maharajas—is one of India's most historic and picturesque regions, a semi-desert graced with the legacy of the Moghul Empire.

ITINERARY:

DAY 1 to 3: Leave U.S. Arrive Delhi. Transfer to hotel.

DAY 4: Sightseeing in Old and New Delhi.

DAY 5: Fly to Jaipur. Sightseeing at Amber, a complex of forts and palaces (including the carved white marble "Diwan-i-Am" or Hall of Public Audience) and other temples and museums.

A

B

DAY 6: Drive to Dunlod Castle, home of Rajvir Singh. Overnight accommodations at the castle with traditional village banquet, which may include music and local dancers from the village of Dunlod.

DAY 7:Leave Mr. Singh's castle and drive to Bikaner Palace. Stroll around palace grounds and museum. Overnight in palace guestrooms.

DAY 8: Visit Bikaner Fort and the city. After lunch, short drive to Gajner Palace. Overnight at Gajner Wildlife Sanctuary, where the forests shelter black buck, nilgai, wild boar and a variety of birds.

DAY 9: Morning visit to wildlife sanctuary. After lunch, visit camel breeding farm. Drive to Bithnok and camp.

DAY 10 to 15: On camel safari through the remote villages of

Granthi, Pabuser, Burana, Chinnu, Nachna, and Ghantiali. We can either ride the camels or walk, according to individual preference. The Thar Desert is dotted with small nomadic encampments and is habitat for nilgai, black buck antelope, Indian gazelle and desert fox, plus a wide range

RAJASTHAN CAMEL SAFARI ....
|— 200 Miles

of birds of prey.

DAY 16: End camel safari and drive to Jaisalmer. Afternoon sightseeing of fort and city. Overnight at Narayan Niwas Palace.

DAY 17: Morning sightseeing in this 12th century desert stronghold, "a mirage of golden yellow stone" rising from the Thar Desert. Overnight train to Jodphur.

DAY 18: Arrive in Jodphur in the morning. Sightseeing in Jodphur, gateway to the desert and home of the Rathore rulers of Marwar who settled here after the Moslems conquered Delhi and Kanauj. The city has seven gates and colorful bazaars. Overnight at Umaidbhavan Palace.

DAY 19: Fly to Delhi. Transfer to hotel. Rest of day free.

DAY 20: In Delhi for shopping and sightseeing.

DAY 21: Transfer to airport and connect with homeward-bound flights.

C

D

IT4PA1SFMT2

INDIAN WILDLIFE SAFARI

DATES: #1 Feb 11–Feb 27 (17 days)
*#2 Dec 6–Dec 22 (17 days)
LEADER: Raj Singh
GRADE: A-1
LAND COST: $1765 (12–15 members)
$1890 (9–11)
*Note change from 1984 Trip Schedule.

The Indian Subcontinent houses an impressive array of wildlife, including Royal Bengal tiger, leopard, one-horned rhino, Indian bison, wild elephant, many varieties of deer and 2,000 species of birds.

With Indian naturalist Raj Singh, we visit Kanha National Park, situated in the heart of the sal forests of central India. This rolling parkland is one of the finest places in all India to see tiger, and on our pre-dawn elephant rides, we may also see blackbuck, chital, hyena and jungle fowl.

At the well-known Bharatpur Bird Sanctuary, once a private princely shooting reserve, we will see vast numbers of waterfowl, including the rare Siberian crane.

In the forests of Dudhwa National Park near the Nepal border, we'll visit Tiger Haven and meet conservation pioneer and "big cat" expert, Arjan Singh, to learn about his efforts to reintroduce zoo-reared tigers and leopards into the wilds.

Accommodations in the wildlife parks will be in bungalows and lodges. We will also tour the cities of Bombay and Delhi and the Taj Mahal in Agra.

ITINERARY:

DAY 1 and 2: Leave U.S. Arrive Bombay and transfer to hotel.

DAY 3: Half-day city tour of Bombay. Afternoon free.

DAY 4: Fly to Nagpur, drive to Kanha National Park. Overnight at forest lodge.

DAY 5 and 6: Game viewing by elephant and landrover in Kanha National Park, where large open meadows give us an excellent chance of seeing beautiful blackbuck, five species of deer, wild pigs, and chausingha (four-horned antelope). In the forests, we're likely to find langur monkeys, the magnificent gaur (Indian

A

bison) and perhaps a tiger. There is also an abundance of birdlife, including pied hornbill, black ibis and racket-tailed drongos.

DAY 7: Drive to Nagpur and fly to Delhi.

DAY 8: All day sightseeing tour of Old and New Delhi.

DAY 9: Four hour drive to Bharatpur. Transfer to forest lodge.

DAY 10: Bird watching by boat in the marshes of Keoladeo Ghana Bird Sanctuary and nature walks on foot. This sanctuary, a large shallow lake, is a breeding ground for waterbirds, including painted storks, spoon-bills, ibis and jacanas. Migratory birds include the Siberian crane.

DAY 11: Morning of birding, then drive to Delhi via Agra to visit the Taj Mahal.

> **We'll visit Tiger Haven and meet conservation pioneer and "big cat" expert, Arjan Singh, to learn about his efforts to reintroduce zoo-reared tigers and leopards into the wilds.**

DAY: 12 to 14: Fly to Lucknow, and drive to "Tiger Haven," the ranch of Indian conservationist, Billy Arjan Singh. Singh has been instrumental in establishing sanctuaries for Indian wildlife. His book, *Tiger Haven*, recounts his experiences in raising two leopards named Harriet and Juliet, who were the subject of a Survival Anglia wildlife film on leopards called "Prince of Cats." Morning and evening game drives through 20-foot tall "elephant grass" in Dudhwa National Park.

DAY 15: Drive to Lucknow and fly to Delhi.

DAY 16: Free day in Delhi. Late evening transfer to airport and depart on homeward-bound flights.

DAY 17: Arrive home.

INDIA WILDLIFE SAFARI
VARANASI/KATHMANDU
DARJEELING OVERLAND — — —

Srinagar

TIBET

Bharatpur
Bird Sanctuary · Corbett N.P.
KATHMANDU
DELHI · Dudhwa
N.P. · Lumbini · Darjeeling
Jaipur · Agra
Varanasi
Kanha N.P. · Calcutta
Bombay
Periyar

400 Miles

IT3TG1MTO3

TREKKING IN SIKKIM

DATES: Oct 20–Nov 11 (23 days)
LEADER: Daku Tenzing Norgay
GRADE: B-2
LAND COST: $1795 (12–15 members)
$1975 (9–11)

The summit crest of Mt. Kanchenjunga (28,208'), third highest mountain in the world, forms the border between Sikkim and Nepal. Its satellite peaks—Jannu (25,294'), Tent Peak (24,089'), Siniolchu (22,610') and Kangbachan (25,925')—are called "The Five Treasures of the Great Snows." At the present time, the only access to this peak is on a picturesque trail through the foothills on the Sikkimese side, a route we'll travel on our 14-day trek towards Kanchenjunga.

We start our trip in highland India at Darjeeling (8,000'), queen of the British colonial hill stations. We'll walk its steep, narrow streets, sip tea at one of Darjeeling's lovely tea estates, and, from Tiger Hill, view the magnificent sunrise reflected on Kanchenjunga.

Driving into the Sikkimese hills on winding roads through terraced fields of rice, we visit Gangtok, the capital, the Rumtek Monastery and Sikkim's Institute of Tibetology, then begin the trek near the great monastery at Pemayangtse.

The walk begins at 6,000 feet in moss-laden forests of pine, magnolia and rhododendron, venturing gradually up into high alpine country. At about mid-point in the trek, we'll have a layover day at a 13,000-foot campsite for an optional side trip up to the Goecha La (16,400') for classic views of Kanchenjunga.

ITINERARY:

DAY 1 to 3: Leave U.S. Arrive Delhi. Continue by air to Bagdogra. Drive to Darjeeling along the route of the "Toy Train," the old steam engine line. Overnight at hotel.

DAY 4: Morning sightseeing in Darjeeling, afternoon drive to Gangtok (5,000').

DAY 5: Visit Rumtek Monastery, the largest in Sikkim, and Institute of Tibetology.

DAY 6: All day drive to Yoksum (6,000'). Overnight at Dak Bungalow.

DAY 7: Begin trek, leaving a cultivated area for a wilderness region. Trek through rich wooded hills to Bakhim forest bungalow at 9,000 feet.

DAY 8: A moderately demanding climb through yak and sheep grazing areas to Choka, a resettlement camp for Tibetans and the last village encountered on the trek. Camp at Pittang (12,000').

> **The walk begins at 6,000 feet in moss-laden forests of pine, magnolia and rhododendron, venturing gradually up into high alpine country.**

DAY 9: Continue through rhododendron forest to Dzongri (13,221'), with its awe-inspiring views of the Sikkimese Himalaya.

DAY 10: Leisurely walk through meadows and gorges to Thangsing (12,467'), magnificent campsite in a giant valley surrounded by high peaks.

DAY 11: Walk toward Kanchenjunga through the great Onglathang Valley, past splendid glacial lakes and numerous glaciers. Camp at Chemathang (15,748') below Pamdim (21,952'), a beautiful peak only recently climbed by the Indian Army.

DAY 12: Optional four-hour hike up through lichen-covered moraine and steep boulder fields to the top

B

C

A Footbridge below Pandim/Ken Scott
B Trekkers, porters, guides/Ken Scott
C Mt. Chomolhari/Leo Le Bon
D Monks at Tashichho Dzong/Leo Le Bon

INDIA • 21

A

C

IT3TG1MTO4

BHUTAN: THE CHOMOLHARI TREK

DATES: #1 May 17–Jun 3 (18 days)
#2 Sep 13–Sep 30 (18 days)
LEADER: #1 to be announced
#2 Jan Zabinski
GRADE: C-2
LAND COST: $2190 (10–15 members)
$2390 (6–9)

of the Goecha La, with its classic views of Kanchenjunga and the Talung Glacier.

DAY 13: Descend the valley to Dzongri (13,221') via the same route.

DAY 14: North toward the base camp of the Himalayan Mountaineering School beneath a peak called Kabur (15,781'). Cross a 14,000-foot pass en route.

DAY 15: Rest day or exploratory hikes up to the Himalayan Mountaineering School or Ratong Glacier (16,000'). There are unexplored 6000-meter peaks all around and the views are spectacular (Forked Peak, 20,039', Kabru Dome, 21,653', and Kabru 23,228').

DAY 16: Trek along Ratong Chu to Zamlin Gang Camp, perched on a hillside in dense forest.

DAY 17: Continue trekking to Bakhim Dak Bungalow (9,000').

DAY 18: Trek to Yoksum ("the meeting place of the three saints"). It was here in 1641 that the first Chogyal was consecrated as the ruler and religious leader of the Sikkimese people. Optional hike to a very old monastery atop a nearby hill. Continue trekking to a campsite perched on the rim of a valley with magnificent terraced rice fields as far as the eye can see.

DAY 19: Trek to Tashiding Monastery atop a hill overlooking the town of Tashiding, the "holiest" of the 60 or so monasteries in Sikkim. Very few groups of tourists are allowed to stay at Tashiding.

DAY 20: Hike down to Legship, meet with vehicles and drive to Pemayangtse. Overnight at lodge.

DAY 21: Morning sightseeing at Pemayangtse Monastery, Sikkim's most important monastery, then drive to Darjeeling.

DAY 22: Sightseeing, including a visit to Tiger Hill (if weather didn't permit on DAY 4). Afternoon drive to Bagdogra and fly to Delhi. Transfer to hotel.

DAY 23: Depart Delhi and connect with homeward-bound flights.

Bhutan, or Druk Yul ("Land of the Peaceful Dragon") is a secluded kingdom whose quiet, ancient ways and Tibetan Buddhist culture are virtually untouched by the "modern" world. In enormous medieval fortress-monasteries, red-robed lamas continue age-old traditions of manuscript illustration and scroll painting.

The Bhutanese are a self-sufficient and highly religious people whose art and architecture are strikingly beautiful. Their national sport is archery and dance and song are a way of life.

Our Bhutan visit begins in the Shangri La setting of the Paro Valley, where we'll ride by pony up to Taksang Monastery, the "Tiger's Nest" overlooking the Paro Valley.

From here we undertake a seven-day trek between Paro and Thimphu (the two major "cities" of Bhutan), hiking through pine forests and yak herders' settlements and enjoying views of Chomolhari (23,977'), the "divine mountain" of Bhutan. The highest altitude reached on the trek is the Yalila Pass (15,800').

ITINERARY:

DAY 1 to 3: Leave U.S. Arrive Delhi. Continue by air to Bagdogra. Drive through subtropical hillsides to Phuntsoling, Bhutan. Overnight at hotel.

DAY 4: Morning visit to Kharbandi Monastery, then begin a long drive on a twisting mountain highway to Paro (7,000') in the beautiful Paro Valley. Overnight at hotel.

DAY 5 and 6: Two days of sightseeing in Paro Valley, including visits to Paro Dzong, the ancient

Drugyel Dzong (a ruined fortress where the Bhutanese defeated the Tibetans), and Kyichu, built in the 7th century and dating back to the time of the Tibetan King Songtsen Gampo. All-day excursion on ponies up to the fantastically situated Taksang Monastery, clinging to a spot on a cliffside where the "precious teacher" Guru Rimpoche is said to have landed, traveling from Tibet on the back of a flying tiger.

DAY 7: Drive to Drugyel Dzong and begin trekking along the Paro River.

DAY 8: Continue walking along the Paro River through pine and juniper forests.

DAY 9 to 11: Trek to Tengethang, visiting a yak herder's home, cross Nyela Pass (13,940') and Yalila Pass (15,800'). Excellent views of Mt. Chomolhari en route.

DAY 12 and 13: Trek through rhododendron forests past the ruins of Barshong Dzong and visit Chenri, the first monastery built by Shabdrung Ngawang Namgyal. End trek in the afternoon. Drive to Thimphu, Bhutan's capital, and

transfer to hotel.

DAY 14: Sightseeing in Thimphu, set at 7,600 feet in the Wang Chu Valley. Visit the great Tashichho Dzong and the government handicraft center.

> **In enormous medieval fortress-monasteries, red-robed lamas continue age-old traditions of manuscript illustration and scroll painting.**

DAY 15: All day excursion by road to Punakha and the Wangdi Valley. visit the spectacular Punakha Dzong. Picnic lunch and return drive to Thimphu.

DAY 16: Morning performance of traditional mask and folk dances by Bhutanese dance troupe. Afternoon drive down to the lowlands at Phuntsoling.

DAY 17: Drive to Bagdogra and fly to Delhi.

DAY 18: Depart Delhi and connect with homeward-bound flights.

B

D

IT4PAISFMT2

VARANASI/ KATHMANDU/ DARJEELING OVERLAND

DATES: #1 Feb 18–Mar 4 (16 days)
#2 Mar 2–Mar 17 (16 days)
#3 Nov 20–Dec 5 (16 days)
#4 Dec 3–Dec 18 (16 days)
LEADER: Local guides
GRADE: A-1
LAND COST: $1490 (12-15 members)
$1590 (6-11)

Touring northern India and Nepal by mini-bus, we'll travel from the broad plains of the Ganges Basin to the delightful Himalayan foothills of Nepal and highland India.

In India, we begin at Varanasi (also called Benares), one of India's most mysterious and ancient holy cities. Here the Ganges River, the "mother of India," flows wide and placid, its banks lined with ancient temples, burning *ghats* and an exotic crowd of Hindu pilgrims, holy men and assorted mystics.

Crossing the border into Nepal, we make a pilgrimage to Lumbini, birthplace of Lord Buddha. Driving ever closer to the Himalaya, we visit Pokhara, a town famous for its mountain views. In Kathmandu, we'll tour many temples, the famous bazaar and the historic towns of the Kathmandu Valley.

Driving east across the plains back into India, we end our trip with a visit to Darjeeling (8,000'), a mountain town with a British colonial flavor, home to a colorful blend of Tibetans, Sikkimese and Nepalis.

NOTE: Trips #1 and #3 begin in Varanasi; Trips #2 and #4 begin in Darjeeling.

ITINERARY:
DAY 1 to 3: Leave U.S. Arrive Delhi and continue by air to Varanasi. Transfer to hotel.

DAY 4: Varanasi is a religious center for Buddhists as well as Hindus, since Buddha gave his first sermon at nearby Sarnath. Morning boat cruise on the Ganges River to watch sunrise. Afternoon tour of many ancient shrines and temples.

DAY 5: Cross into Nepal and visit Lumbini, Buddha's birthplace.

DAY 6: Sightseeing around Lumbini, and drive to Pokhara.

DAY 7: A day in Pokhara to enjoy superb mountain views and perhaps take a day hike or pony trek in the Pokhara Valley.

DAY 8: We'll drive to Kathmandu via Gorkha, a historic town where the ruling dynasty of Nepal had its origins in the late 18th century.

DAY 9 to 11: Three days of sightseeing in Kathmandu and around the Kathmandu Valley, including Swayambhunath, Boudhanath, Patan, Bhaktapur, Pashupatinath and an excursion to the Tibetan border. Optional sightseeing flight to view Mt. Everest.

NEPAL
ABOUT TREKKING IN THE HIMALAYA

Each trekking expedition is accompanied by Sherpa guides, kitchen staff and porters, all under the direction of a sirdar, or Sherpa leader.

All camp gear and your own duffle bag of personal gear will be carried by hired porters or yaks; you carry only a small daypack for your water bottle, camera, extra sweater, etc.

The daily schedule is usually as follows: up at 6 a.m., pack up your duffle and have a light breakfast of oatmeal and tea. The Sherpas break camp and the porters head up the trail with their assigned loads. Trekkers and Sherpas start on the trail around 7 a.m.

Despite the fact that there may be about a dozen trekkers in the group, it is always possible to walk alone if one chooses, since everyone is encouraged to walk at his/her own pace.

Lunch stop is about 11 a.m., and consists of a hearty "brunch": eggs, home fries, sausage, beans, etc. The afternoon walk begins around 1 p.m. and continues until 4:30, when camp is reached. While camp is being set up, light snacks and tea are served. Dinner is served around 6:30 in a dining tent with a dinner table and small rattan stools.

After dinner one can linger in the dinner tent to talk about events of the day, or retire to read or write by flashlight. We provide large, comfortable, specially designed trekking tents which comfortably accommodate two people and all their gear.

Food on the trek will be plentiful. Fresh vegetables, eggs, chickens and other food stuffs are purchased as available. Meals are supplemented with tinned foods, such as peanut butter, fruit, coffee and fish. The Sherpa cook and his staff are trained professionals.

Mountain Travel of Albany, California, does not employ the services of Mountain Travel, Pvt., Ltd., Kathmandu, a Nepalese trek outfitter.

A WORD ABOUT COSTS
The Land Cost listed for Nepal treks is for groups of 6 to 15 members (and some 6-12 members). If group size falls below 6, there will be a surcharge of $200 per person.

MALLA HOTEL
The Hotel Malla is one of Nepal's finest luxury hotels. Located near the Royal Palace, the Malla boasts neo-traditional Nepalese architecture, private gardens, beautifully appointed rooms and suites, and a gourmet restaurant. To top it all off, the hospitality is Nepalese, and that's hard to beat anywhere in the world.

For reservations, contact Mountain Travel, Inc., Albany, Ca. 94706

DAY 12: Drive to Janakpur, crossing the border into India.

DAY 13: Drive from the Indian plains into the cool hill country and arrive at Darjeeling.

DAY 14: Darjeeling is a charming old "hill station" built as a mountain resort in the days of the British Raj. It has a cross-section of ethnic groups including Nepalis, Gurungs, Tibetans, Lepchas, Bhotias and Drukpas. Visit a tea plantation, Tibetan Handicraft Center and Himalayan Mountaineering Institute.

DAY 15: Early morning drive to Tiger Hill, where (weather permitting) there are beautiful views of sunrise on Kanchenjunga (28,208'), third highest mountain in the world.

DAY 16: Drive to Bagdogra and connect with homeward-bound flights.

DISCOVER NEPAL & THAILAND

TOUR COST: (including round trip air fare to Kathmandu on Thai Airways):
$2390 from Seattle.
$2590 from Dallas/Ft. Worth.
$2520 from San Francisco/ Los Angeles
DATES: 17-day tours depart weekly every Monday and return Wednesdays. 1984/1985 dates: weekly from October 1, 1984 to May 30, 1985.
LEADER: Local guides
GRADE: B-1

Tour Price (including airfare) is based on prices in effect at time of printing (May 1983) and is subject to change.

This 17-day adventure offered in conjunction with THAI Airways, is a travel bargain and a fine introduction to two ancient kingdoms: Nepal and Thailand.

The small country of Nepal contains one of the greatest environmental transitions in the world: its northern border is a Himalayan barrier containing eight of the ten highest mountains on earth. Its southern border, just 100 miles away, is deep terai jungle, haunt of tigers and rhinos.

Cultural transitions abound in Nepal, too, from the Hindu culture of subtropical Kathmandu Valley to the Tibetan Buddhist enclaves of the high country. To really discover Nepal (where there are few roads) one must "trek"—that is, walk the network of serpentine trails which connect one village to the next. This tour features a delightful, non-strenuous five-day hill walk with magnificent Himalayan views.

In addition to a five-day visit to Kathmandu, Nepal's capital, we will also tour Bangkok, capital of Thailand. We'll visit Bangkok's world-famous temples, canals and "floating markets," with plenty of free time for shopping sightseeing and individual pursuits.

B

A Royal Bengal tiger cubs
B Temple detail, Kathmandu/Alla Schmitz
C Fields of mustard, Modi Khola Valley/Lanny Johnson
D Springtime rhododendron/Alla Schmitz
E Children of Nepal/Susan Thiele
F Machapuchare from Pokhara Valley/Alla Schmitz

A

ITINERARY:

DAY 1: Depart Seattle, San Francisco, Los Angeles or Dallas/Ft. Worth on THAI's Royal Orchid Service to Bangkok.

To really discover Nepal (where there are few roads) one must "trek"— that is, walk the network of serpentine trails which connect one village to the next.

DAY 2: Arrive Bangkok in the evening; transfer to hotel.

DAY 3: Fly to Kathmandu on THAI. Transfer to hotel. Trek briefing.

DAY 4: Excursion to Nagarkot at 7,000 feet to watch sunrise over the Himalayas, or to Dhulikhel, a small town at 5,000 feet with panoramic Himalayan views. Visit the ancient town of Bhaktapur.

DAY 5: Morning tour of Chovar

Gorge and Kirtipur, the oldest village in the Kathmandu Valley.

DAY 6: Morning tour of Pashupatinath (a riverside temple dedicated to Shiva), Boudhanath (a large Buddhist stupa), and Swayambhunath, a Hindu shrine on a hill overlooking Kathmandu Valley.

DAY 7: Fly (or drive if flights unavailable) to Pokhara. Meet with Sherpa crew and begin five-day trek. Short walk to Henja (3,500').

DAY 8: Continue up the Yangdi Khola river valley to Dhampus (5,900') overlooking the Pokhara Valley.

DAY 9: Hike a scenic ridge path to Khare (5,600'), sharing the trails with pony caravans.

B

DAY 10: Descend to Sarangkot (4,800') with excellent views of Annapurna and Dhaulagiri.

DAY 11: End trek, descend into the Pokhara Valley and drive to Pokhara. Overnight at Fishtail Lodge on Phewa Lake.

DAY 12: Fly (or drive if flights not available) to Kathmandu and transfer to hotel.

DAY 13: Depart on THAI to Bangkok. Transfer to hotel.

DAY 14: Temple tour or "floating market" tour.

DAY 15 and 16: Optional sightseeing in Bangkok

DAY 17: Transfer to airport and fly via THAI to Seattle, San Francisco, Los Angeles or Dallas/Ft. Worth.

C

D   E

PRIVATE TREKS IN NEPAL

DATES: September through May (8 to 36 days)
LEADER: Sherpa sirdars
GRADE: B-1 to C-3
LAND COST: depends on number in party and services requested

In addition to our scheduled Nepal treks, we can arrange treks for private groups and individuals. Ideally, a group of four or more persons is the best number from a cost standpoint, but we can make arrangements for fewer than that.

Since there are so many wonderful trekking routes in Nepal, selecting a trek itinerary can be bewildering! We suggest that you read the descriptions of the treks listed here and pick the one that sounds best for you, according to your time schedule. We can then adapt the itinerary to suit your specific needs.

Let us know your trek route, travel dates, and number in party (preferably at least three months before the planned departure) and we will plan an exact itinerary and quote a cost.

CLIMBING:
For mountaineers, we can arrange expeditions on peaks which are authorized by the Nepalese Government for climbing expeditions.

F

IT3TGIMTO5

THE NEPAL ADVENTURE

DATES: #1 Jan 19–Feb 4 (17 days)
#2 Feb 4–Feb 20 (17 days)
#3 Dec 1–Dec 17 (17 days)
LEADER: #1 Bruce Klepinger
#2 & #3 to be announced
GRADE: B-1
LAND COST: $1595 (6–15 members)

This 17-day adventure samples Nepal's three worlds: its mountains, rivers and jungles.

For a taste of mountain trekking, we will walk a scenic six-day route in the Annapurna foothills near Pokhara and circle up through cool forests and lovely Gurung villages such as Ghandrung (6,400'), with views of Annapurna and Dhaulagiri.

Returning from the mountains, we board rafts and set off on a leisurely float trip down the Seti Khola ("White River"), which flows into the jungles of Chitwan National Park.

Arriving at rustic Gaida Wildlife Camp, we'll spend several days searching for game by elephant-back, by dugout canoe, and on foot. The deep *terai* jungle is the haunt of one-horned rhinos, leopards, elusive Bengal tigers, and numerous species of exotic tropical birds.

ITINERARY:

DAY 1 to 3: Leave U.S. Arrive Kathmandu. Transfer to hotel.

DAY 4: Sightseeing in Kathmandu. Briefing on trek arrangements.

DAY 5: Fly along the Himalayan skyline to the little town of Pokhara. Meet with Sherpas and porters and begin trekking in the Pokhara Valley to a campsite on the outskirts near the Tibetan Camp at Henja (3,500').

DAY 6: Across rice fields to the small village of Suikhet, climb a steep crest to 6,500 feet then descend to Landrung (5,280').

DAY 7: Down to the Modi Khola river, then up 2,300 feet to a grazing pasture above Ghandrung (6,400'). Spectacular views of Annapurna and Machapuchare (the "Matterhorn" of Nepal).

DAY 8: Back down to the Modi Khola, walking along its right bank to Birethanti (4,300').

DAY 9: Cross the Modi Khola and ascend to the hamlet of Chandrakot, then further up to Lumle (5,000'), over a small pass at Khare (5,600'), and finally down to Naudana (4,800').

Arriving at rustic Gaida Wildlife Camp, we'll spend several days searching for game by elephant-back, by dugout canoe, and on foot.

DAY 10: End trek in the afternoon, arrive in Pokhara and check into Fishtail Lodge on Phewa Lake.

DAY 11: Drive to Damauli, the put-in point for our raft trip on the Seti Khola.

DAY 12: On the river.

DAY 13: Arrive by raft near Gaida Wildlife Camp. Transfer to jeep for a short drive to Gaida. Check into camp and take an afternoon jungle walk.

DAY 14: Game viewing on the river by dugout canoe. Optional nature walk and late afternoon game viewing ride by elephant.

DAY 15: Morning visit to game viewing blind, then depart for five-hour drive to Kathmandu.

DAY 16: Depart Kathmandu on homeward-bound flights.

DAY 17: Arrive home.

A

IT2TGIMTO6

AROUND ANNAPURNA

DATES: #1 Apr 16–May 15 (30 days)
#2 Jul 30–Aug 28 (30 days)
#3 Oct 11–Nov 9 (30 days)
#4 Oct 25–Nov 23 (30 days)
LEADER: #1 Hugh Swift
#2 Jeff Campbell
#3 Dick Irvin
#4 John Mueller
GRADE: C-3
LAND COST: #1, #3 & #4 $1990
(6–15 members)
#2 $1845 (6–15)

One of our favorite treks and a classic walk in Nepal is the 22-day circuit around Annapurna, crossing north of the Annapurna massif via the Thorong La (17,771').

The walk begins in the lush valley of the Marsyandi River, which cuts steeply between the Annapurnas to the west and the Manaslu/Himalchuli peaks to the east.

Turning west into the Manang Valley, a longitudinal gorge which makes a deep furrow behind the Annapurnas, we'll find ourselves in an increasingly Tibetan landscape and culture.

The Manang Valley is inhabited by gypsy traders of Tibetan origin whose villages are striking clusters of medieval stone dwellings often nestled into eroded sandstone cliffs. The main villages are Chame, Pisang, Braga (where there is a magnificent monastery) and Manang (11,450'). Above Pisang, there is a sudden environmental transition as the dense forests of the lower valley give way to rocky and arid Tibetan scenery and high yak pastures.

The Manang Valley is walled on the south by Annapurnas II and IV, Annapurna III (24,767'), Gangapurna (24,457') and Glacier Dome (23,191'); to the north, and barring the way to Tibet, is a long ridge of 20,000 to 22,000-foot peaks.

At the head of the valley we cross north of the Annapurnas at the Thorong La and descend by way of the Hindu and Buddhist shrines at Muktinath. Now in the deep gorge of the Kali Gandaki, we descend gradually into green, terraced hillsides and the rhododendron groves of Lete. There are continuous and beautiful views of Dhaulagiri (26,810'), Tukche and the Annapurnas all the way back to Pokhara.

ITINERARY:

DAY 1 to 3: Leave U.S. Arrive Kathmandu. Transfer to hotel.

DAY 4: Sightseeing in Kathmandu. Briefing on trek arrangements.

DAY 5 to 8: Begin trek, hiking gently upward through lush subtropical vegetation and the cultivated fields along the Marsyandi River. Excellent views of Manaslu, Peak 29, Himalchuli, Annapurnas II and IV, Lamjung and Machapuchare. Ascend past canyons coming off rocky ramparts of Peak 29 and Namun Bhanjyang, climbing high above the river to about 7,000 feet among Tibetan settlements.

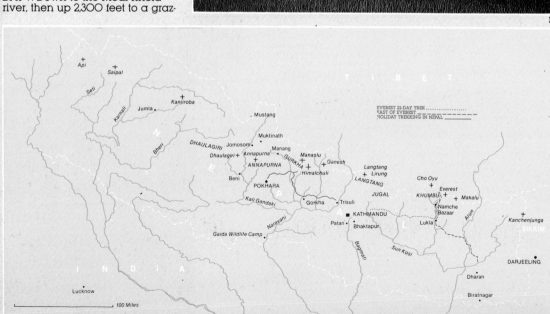

B

EVEREST 22-DAY TREK ....
EAST OF EVEREST ....
HOLIDAY TREKKING IN NEPAL _____

100 Miles

A   Tibetan traders of Manang/Alla Schmitz
B   Crossing Thorong La/Gordon Wiltsie
C   Braga village in Manang Valley/Gordon Wiltsie

A

DAY 9 and 10: Enter the heavily wooded lower Manang Valley and pass the villages of Chame (8,800') and Pisang (10,450').

DAY 11 and 12: A beautiful walk on easy terrain through forests to the upper Manang Valley. Rest day at the village of Braga (11,250'). A half-hour's walk above camp leads to a splendid view of the Annapurnas and Manaslu.

DAY 13: Past Manang village and continue up past yak huts to Chakar Dhunga (13,500').

DAY 14: Continue through alpine country past Leder (14,200') to a high camp at Phedi (14,500'), just at the foot of the climb to the Thorong La.

DAY 15: Long day, ascending steeply on a yak and pony trail. Cross Thorong La and descend steeply to Muktinath (12,500').

DAY 16: Rest day at Muktinath. Visit Hindu and Buddhist shrines and enjoy views of Dhaulagiri.

DAY 17: Descend about 3,000 feet down the Jhong Khola canyon. Camp at the medieval village of Kagbeni (9,000').

DAY 18: Down along a level but rocky trail through juniper thickets to Jomosom and then Marpha (8,760'), a large Thakali village with an important monastery.

DAY 19 and 20: Continue down the Kali Gandaki flood plain to Larjung (8,400'). Rest day or optional hike to the Dhaulagiri icefall at 12,000 feet.

DAY 21: Through pine woods to Ghasa (6,400'). The Kali Gandaki gorge begins to narrow here and there are marvelous views of Dhaulagiri, Annapurna-I and Tukche.

DAY 22 and 23: Descend lower into the Kali Gandaki canyon, through Tatopani, known for its hot springs, on to Ghorapani (9,300') and over Deorali Pass (10,000'), with its great views of Dhaulagiri and Annapurna South.

B

DAY 24 and 25: Descend through rhododendron forests to Ghandrung (6,400'), a large Gurung village, and down a wide set of stone stairs (the best example of this type of trail in the country) to the Modi Khola. Ascend to Landrung, another Gurung village, and descend to Dhampus (5,900'), a meadow with one of the most spectacular views in Nepal, seen to its best advantage in the morning.

DAY 26: Descend to the Yangri Valley, then walk along flat fields to Pokhara (2,800'). Overnight at Fishtail Lodge on Phewa Lake.

DAY 27: Fly or drive to Kathmandu. Transfer to hotel.

DAY 28: Day free in Kathmandu.

DAY 29: Depart Kathmandu on homeward-bound flights.

DAY 30: Arrive home.

C

The Manang Valley is inhabited by gypsy traders of Tibetan origin whose villages are striking clusters of medieval stone dwellings often nestled into eroded standstone cliffs.

IT2TGIMTO9

THE ANNAPURNA SANCTUARY TREK

DATES: #1 Apr 23–May 15 (23 days)
#2 Nov 5–Nov 27 (23 days)
LEADER: #1 Charles Gay
#2 Scot Macbeth
GRADE: B-3
LAND COST: $1650 (6–15 members)

The Annapurna Sanctuary is a glacier-covered amphitheatre at 13,300 feet formed by a circle of the principal peaks of the western Annapurna Himal—including Annapurna South (23,814'), Fang (25,089'), Annapurna I (26,545'), Gangapurna (24,457'), Annapurna III (24,787'), and the spire of Machapuchare (23,942').

This spectacular mountain-ringed basin can be reached on a relatively short trek (15 days) that goes right to the base of some of the most famous peaks in the Himalaya.

We trek up the Modi Khola through forests of bamboo, rhododendron and oak, and villages of the Gurung and Tamang people. We'll reach the Sanctuary on about the 7th day and spend two days within its spectacular confines with a possible visit visit to Annapurna South Base Camp.

Return to Pokhara is via the Gurung settlements of Landrung and Ghandrung, with a final grand mountain panorama from our last campsite.

ITINERARY:

DAY 1 to 3: Leave U.S. Arrive Kathmandu. Briefing on trek arrangements.

DAY 4: Sightseeing in Kathmandu. Briefing on trek arrangements.

DAY 5: Drive to Pokhara, about 100 miles west of Kathmandu, meet with Sherpa crew and begin trek, reaching Henja (3,500'), on the outskirts of the Pokhara Valley.

DAY 6 to 8: Cross the Yangdi Khola and wind through rice fields, climb up a steep hill to Naudanda and continue on to Khare (5,600'). Drop down to the Modi Khola and climb very steeply uphill through forests to Ghorapani Pass, from where there are good mountain views. Camp at Ghorapani (9,300').

The Annapurna Sanctuary is a glacier-covered amphitheatre at 13,300 feet formed by a circle of the principal peaks of the western Annapurna Himal.

DAY 9: Early morning visit to Poon Hill for a spectacular view of Dhaulagiri. Trek eastward along the ridge to forest camp at 9,500 feet.

DAY 10 and 11: Cross the pass leading to Ghandrung and then steeply down to a bridge at about 6,000 feet, then back up high above the Modi Khola, through forests of rhododendron, oak, and hemlock

to British sheep breeding project at Kuldi Ghar (7,000').

DAY 12: Climb steeply high above the river in a bamboo forest to the tiny campsite at Hinko (9,900').

DAY 13 and 14: A short walk to the Sanctuary (13,300') and spend these days exploring, photographing and enjoying the mountain scenery.

DAY 15 to 18: Retrace our steps back down through Kuldi Ghar, then continue to the large Gurung village of Ghandrung. Descend on wide stone stairs to the Modi Khola and make a steep climb through Landrung to the pass at Dhampus and camp on the ridge at Tolka.

DAY 19: Down the Yangri Khola valley to Pokhara. Overnight at Fishtail Lodge.

DAY 20: Fly or drive to Kathmandu. Transfer to hotel.

DAY 21: In Kathmandu

DAY 22: Depart Kathmandu on homeward-bound flights.

DAY 23: Arrive home.

Map labels: Kagbeni, Muktinath, TIBET, French Col, Jomosom, Thorong La, Tukche, Chulu, Tilicho Lake, Chulu East, Dhaulagiri I, Nilgiri, Manang, Pisang Peak, Lete, Annapurna I, Glacier Dome, Gangapurna, Pisang, NEPAL, Fang, Annapurna Sanctuary, Annapurna III, Chame, Thonje, Manaslu, Tatopani, Annapurna S., ANNAPURNA, HIMAL, Annapurna IV, Annapurna II, Peak 29, Hiuchuli, Machapuchare, Lamjung Himal, Sikha, Himalchuli, Ghorapani, Ghandrung, Landrung, Beni, Modi, Naudanda, Henja, Bara Pokhari Lake, Kali Gandaki, Marsyandi, Seti, Mardi, POKHARA, Lamjung, Phewa Tal, Phalesangu, Gorkha, Dumre

AROUND ANNAPURNA ....
DHAULAGIRI & ANNAPURNA _____
ANNAPURNA SANCTUARY TREK ....

IT2TGIMTO8

DHAULAGIRI & ANNAPURNA

DATES: #1 Feb 20–Mar 12 (22 days)
#2 Apr 5–May 1 (27 days)
#3 Nov 22–Dec 13 (22 days)
1985: Feb 22–Mar 15 (22 days)
LEADER: #1 Bruce Klepinger
#2 to be announced
#3 Charles Gay
GRADE: B-2
LAND COST: #1 & #3 $1590
(6–15 members)
#2 $1790 (6–15)

The Kali Gandaki River has carved a tremendous gorge which splits the Himalaya sharply between the massifs of Dhaulagiri (26,810') and Annapurna (26,545'), creating the deepest canyon in the world. A trek through this great gorge, which for centuries has been a major trade route between Tibet and India, has impressive changes in landscape, population and culture, great views of Dhaulagiri and Annapurna, and doesn't involve crossing any high mountain passes.

Starting at Pokhara and winding through Gurung villages, rhododendron forests and green woodlands, we cross Deorali Pass (10,000'). At Tatopani with its welcome hot springs, we join the Kali Gandaki and walk on ancient pathways as far as the Thakali village of Marpha (8,760').

Treks #1 and #3 (14 days) turn around here, and Trek #2 (19 days) continues as far as the shrines and temples at Muktinath (12,500').

This is very much a people-watching trek and we'll see a whole range of fascinating Himalayan groups— the village Chettris and Gurungs (from which the British Army has long recruited its famed "Gurkha" regiments), the Thakalis (renowned traders of central Nepal), and wild-looking Tibetans who frequent this trail with their yak and donkey caravans.

ITINERARY: 14-DAY TREK

DAY 1 to 3: Leave U.S. Arrive Kathmandu. Transfer to hotel.

DAY 4: Sightseeing in Kathmandu. Briefing on trek arrangements.

DAY 5: Fly or drive to Pokhara, meet with Sherpa crew and begin trek with a short walk to Henja (3,500').

DAY 6 and 7: Cross rice fields to Suikhet, climb up to Dhampus (5,900'), descend to the Modi Khola river before a steep climb to a grazing pasture below Ghandrung (6,400'). Spectacular

A Machapuchare/Stan Armington
B Tibetan pony caravans/Alla Schmitz
C Dzarkot village/Alla Schmitz
D Gorge of the upper Kali Gandaki/
   Alla Schmitz

views of the Annapurna Himal and Machapuchare (the "Matter-horn" of Nepal).

DAY 8: Pass through thick rhodo-dendron forests with a few clear-ings and climb up through lush growth to a clearing at Deorali Pass (10,000') where there is a spectacular view of Dhaulagiri. Further along, Machapuchare and Annapurna can be seen.

DAY 9: The trail sweeps down the Ghatte Khola canyon during an easy but long descent dominated by the Dhaulagiri ice peaks. Tatopani (3,900') is a town of lemon trees and a hot spring just north of the bridge over the Kali Gandaki.

DAY 10 and 11: We travel up the gorge of the Kali Gandaki taking a trail literally carved out of the walls high above the gorge. Tran-sition from the tropical zone into the alpine and climb to Lete village. Annapurna-I appears east of the gorge as we trek toward the village of Larjung (8,400').

DAY 12: The pine woods of Lete give way here to the juniper thickets of Tukche. We reach the government fruit and vegetable farm at the large village of Marpha (8,760').

DAY 13 to 15: Retrace trails back to Tatopani and Ghorapani.

DAY 16 to 17: Descend the valley of the Bhurungdi Khola toward the Modi Khola, over a pass at Khare (5,600') and gradually descend to Naudanda (4,800').

DAY 18: Trek down to Pokhara and check into Fishtail Lodge on the shores of Phewa Lake.

DAY 19: Fly or drive to Kathmandu. Transfer to hotel.

DAY 20: In Kathmandu.

DAY 21: Depart Kathmandu on homewardbound flights.

DAY 22: Arrive home.

ITINERARY: 19-DAY TREK
SAME UNTIL DAY 12, then:
DAY 13: Continue through the juniper thickets of Tukche to Jomosom (8,900'), where the scenery is Tibetan: arid and rocky but grand, with occasional splashes of green cultivation.

DAY 14 and 15: Walk up to the holy shrine of Muktinath, sheltered from the winds of the upper Kali Gan-daki, and decorated with small temples and shrines with magnifi-

cent Dhaulagiri as a backdrop. Layover day at Muktinath.

DAY 16 and 17: Return through the Kali Gandaki and down to the Ghatte Khola.

DAY 18 to 20: Down to the village of Kalopani with time for a side trip to visit the Dhaulagiri icefall, on through Tatopani to Ghorapani.

> **The Kali Gandaki River has carved a tremendous gorge which splits the Himalayas sharply between the massifs of Dhaulagiri (26,810') and Annapurna (26,545'), creating the deepest canyon in the world.**

DAY 21 and 22: The trail descends the Bhurungdi Khola Valley across the Modi Khola river and over a pass at Khare (5,600').

DAY 23: Trek to Pokhara and check into Fishtail Lodge on Phewa Lake.

DAY 24: Fly or drive to Kathman-du. Transfer to hotel.

DAY 25: In Kathmandu.

DAY 26: Depart Kathmandu on homeward-bound flights.

DAY 27: Arrive home.

Chomolungma, "Mother Goddess of the Earth." It is a mountain to describe in superlatives—the most photographed and most written about mountain on earth.

The classic view of Mt. Everest (29,028') and the Khumbu Icefall from the vantage point of Kala Patar (18,192'), a three-hour hike from camp at Gorak Shep at 17,000 feet/Hugh Swift

A Sherpanis of the Khumbu/Bruce Klepinger
B Thyangboche Monastery portrayed by Sherpa artist Kappa Khalden/Gordon Wiltsie
C Rice terraces at Kirantichap/Lanny Johnson
D Campsite in Gokyo Valley/Hugh Swift

A

IT2TGIMT17

22-DAY EVEREST BASE CAMP TREK

DATES: #1 Mar 17–Apr 16 (31 days)
      #2 Oct 8–Nov 7 (31 days)
LEADER: #1 Bruce Klepinger
       #2 Scot Macbeth
GRADE: C-3
LAND COST: #1 $1690
          (6–15 members)
       #2 $2090 (6–15)

Mt. Everest (29,028'), the world's highest mountain, is known to Tibetans as Chomolungma, "Mother Goddess of the Earth." It is a mountain to describe in superlatives—the most photographed and most written about mountain on earth.

The region below Mt. Everest is now designated as Sagarmatha National Park. It is Nepal's most popular trekking destination. Although the walk from the 4,000-foot lowlands near the Kathmandu Valley to Everest Base Camp at 18,000 feet is long and demanding, the experience of gazing on the majesty of Everest is an indescribable thrill and the realization of a dream for many.

The 22-day Everest Base Camp trek is the classic walk to Everest, following the traditional long base camp march used by most Everest expeditions. The trail from Kirantichap to Everest heads generally eastwards at first. Since the deep valleys which drain the Himalaya lie north to south, we'll be cutting "across the grain," for the first week, hiking up and down over many ridges. This is Nepal's "banana belt", lush subtropical scenery of bamboo thickets and rhododendron forests. The villages of this region are inhabited by a variety of Hindu hill tribes.

After about nine days of lowland walking (great for altitude acclimatization), we enter the Tibetan Buddhist culture of the Khumbu region, the Sherpa homeland, and spend the rest of our trek in a wonderland of Himalayan grandeur. The trek culminates in a hike to Kala Patar (18,192') for classic Everest views near the site of Everest Base Camp.

The trek ends with a walk down to Lukla for a flight to Kathmandu.

ITINERARY:

DAY 1 to 3: Leave U.S. Arrive Kathmandu. Transfer to hotel.

DAY 4: Sightseeing in Kathmandu. Briefing on trek arrangements.

DAY 5 to 7: Meet with Sherpa crew and begin trek. Drive to Kirantichap (4,200'). Trek through a pine forest to the Bhote Kosi River, then over to Yarsa (6,400'), across Chisopani Pass (8,200'), descend to Sikri Khola, and cross a low pass to Those (5,700').

B

DAY 8 to 10: Along the river to Shivalaya; over Chyangma Pass (8,900') to Bhandar (6,700'). Optional visit to a small dairy and cheese factory at Thodung. Down to the Likhu River and the market town of Kenja. Over Lamjura Pass (11,600')) to Junbesi (8,800'), with beautiful mountain views including Numbur.

DAY 11 to 14: Enter the Sherpa-inhabited Solu Valley for a first glimpse of Mt. Everest in the distance. Over Takshindu Pass to Takshindu Monastery (10,000'), a long, steep descent to the Dudh Kosi canyon then up and down along the Dudh Kosi gorge to Phakding (8,700').

DAY 15 and 16: Entering the Khumbu region, we ascend to the busy market town of Namche Bazaar (11,300') and on to Khumjung (12,500'), one of Khumbu's prettiest villages, known for its views of Kangtega (22,340'), Thamserku (22,208') and Ama Dablam (22,494')

DAY 17: To Thyangboche Monastery (12,700'), spiritual center of the Khumbu.

DAY 18: To Pheriche (14,000'), site of the Himalayan Rescue Association's Trekkers Aid Post.

DAY 19: To the yak grazing pastures at Lobouje (16,200').

DAY 20: A long day to Gorak Shep (17,000'), walking on boulder fields and glacial debris to the edge of the Khumbu Glacier. Nuptse (25,850') and Pumori (23,442') loom above camp.

DAY 21: Hike to the summit of Kala Patar (18,192') for classic views of Mt. Everest, or hike to base camp itself. Return to Lobouje.

DAY 22 to 25: Back down the Khumbu Valley on a scenic high trail to Dingboche (14,500'), down through Pangboche and around a steep mountainside to Phortse, then through Khumjung, past Namche Bazaar and down to Lukla (9,300'), the mountain airstrip where we will fly out to Kathmandu.

DAY 26 to 29: The next few days will be spent either in Kathmandu or Lukla, depending on flying weather and other factors which often delay the mountain flights. Upon arrival in Kathmandu, transfer to hotel.

DAY 30: Depart Kathmandu on homeward-bound flights.

DAY 31: Arrive home.

C

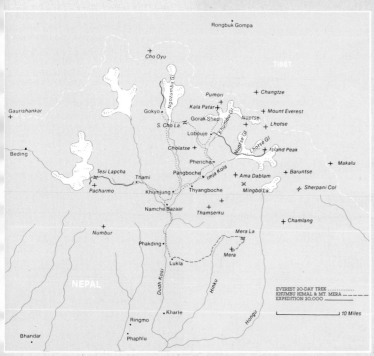
D

EVEREST 20-DAY TREK ....
KHUMBU HIMAL & MT. MERA ____ ____
EXPEDITION 20,000

|———————————| 10 Miles

IT2TGIMTI7

20-DAY EVEREST BASE CAMP TREK

DATES: #1 Mar 26–Apr 23 (29 days)
     #2 Oct 25–Nov 22 (29 days)
     #3 Nov 22–Dec 20 (29 days)
LEADER: #1 Hugh Swift
       #2 to be announced
       #3 John Mueller
GRADE: C-3
LAND COST: $1990 (6–15 members)

The 20-day trek to Everest Base Camp begins with a flight to Lukla airstrip at 9,300 feet, bypassing the lowland scenery. Most of the trek is spent well above 11,000 feet in the Khumbu region, at the head of which stand Mt. Everest (and many other of the most magnificent peaks in all the Himalayas). Khumbu is decorated everywhere with prayer flags and carved *mani* stones, and is the homeland of the Sherpa people, Tibetan Buddhist mountain dwellers who have gained fame as high altitude porters on mountaineering expeditions. Besides their traditional occupations as traders and yak herders, many Sherpas also work as trekking guides throughout Nepal's mountain regions.

> **Khumbu is decorated everywhere with prayer flags and carved mani stones, and is the homeland of the Sherpa people, Tibetan Buddhist mountain dwellers who have gained fame as high altitude porters on mountaineering expeditions.**

The 20-day Everest treks include a trip up the Gokyo Valley for a chance to hike up Gokyo Ri (18,000'), a "hill" with stupendous views of the summits of Everest, Makalu and many other peaks. From the Gokyo Valley, a hike across the snow-covered South Cho La Pass (17,800') is an adventurous way to approach the upper Khumbu Valley en route to Everest Base Camp. (If the South Cho La crossing is not possible due to snow conditions or other factors, we will approach Everest Base Camp via the usual route up the Khumbu Valley). These treks end with a flight out of Lukla to Kathmandu.

ITINERARY:

DAY 1 to 3: Leave U.S. Arrive Kathmandu. Transfer to hotel.

DAY 4: Sightseeing in Kathmandu. Briefing on trek arrangements.

DAY 5 to 7: Fly to Lukla, weather permitting. Meet with Sherpa crew and trek along the Dudh Kosi to Phakding, then steeply up to Namche Bazaar (11,300'), the Sherpa "capital". Spare day at Namche.

DAY 8 and 9: Ascend the Bhote Kosi Valley and trek to Thame (12,500'). Visit Thame Monastery, known for its frescoes, and trek to Khumjung (12,500'), a beautifully situated village with views of Kangtega (22,340'), Thamserku (22,208') and Ama Dablam (22,494').

DAY 10: Trek to Phortse bridge (11,500').

DAY 11 to 13: Trek gradually up Gokyo Valley, through birch-woods with fine views of Kangtega and on to the yak pasture of Machherma (14,500'). Continue up a rocky gulch beside the Ngozumba Glacier to beautiful Gokyo Lake (15,800'). Rest day and optional hike up Gokyo Ri, for magnificent views including Everest (29,028'), Makalu (27,825'), Cho Oyu (26,750'), and a vast expanse of other peaks.

DAY 14: Cross the Ngozumba Glacier and camp at 16,500 feet.

DAY 15: Ascend the 17,300-foot South Cho La pass on boulder fields and a steep, but short, snow slope. Descend the glacier to the beautiful glen of Dzonglha (15,900').

DAY 16: Contour the steep, grassy hillsides above Tshola Lake, enter the upper Khumbu Valley and walk to Lobouje (16,200').

DAY 17: To Gorak Shep (17,000'), up and down by the Khumbu Glacier passing over a tangle of moraine.

DAY 18: Morning hike to the summit of Kala Pater (18,192') for classic views of Mt. Everest. Afternoon walk all the way back down to Lobouje.

DAY 19 to 21: Down past the Trekkers' Aid Post at Pheriche to the Imja Khola, on to Pangboche (12,800'), then continue down the Imja Khola for a short climb to Thyangboche Monastery (12,700'). Spare day at Thyangboche.

DAY 22 and 23: Down to Namche Bazaar and continue along the gorge of the Dudh Kosi to Lukla.

DAY 24 to 27: The next few days will be spent either in Kathmandu or Lukla, depending on flying weather and other factors which often delay the mountain flights. Upon arrival in Kathmandu, transfer to hotel.

DAY 28: Depart Kathmandu on homeward-bound flights.

DAY 29: Arrive home.

IT2TG1MT17

SHERPA VILLAGES & MT. EVEREST

DATES: Dec 8–Dec 30 (23 days)
LEADER: Charles Gay
GRADE: B-2
LAND COST: $1790 (6–15 members)

The 14-day Everest trek circles up through the Khumbu region at a leisurely pace, enjoying the unbeatable mountain scenery and Sherpa culture. We'll visit all the major Sherpa villages including Namche Bazaar, Thame, Khumjung, and of course the famed Thyangboche Monastery (12,700'), where there are views of Everest. Although the trek doesn't walk the extra few days up the Khumbu Valley to Everest Base Camp, it is nevertheless a fantastic trekking experience with close-up views of some of the most beautiful peaks in the Himalaya. There will be much interaction with the Sherpa people and their Tibetan Buddhist culture. The trek begins and ends at the mountain airstrip at Lukla.

ITINERARY:

DAY 1 to 3: Leave U.S. Arrive Kathmandu. Transfer to hotel.

DAY 4: Sightseeing in Kathmandu. Briefing on trek arrangements.

DAY 5: Begin trek. Fly to Lukla (9,300'), weather permitting. Meet with Sherpa crew and trek for a few hours along the Dudh Kosi to the village of Phakding (8,700').

DAY 6 and 7: Follow the Dudh Kosi, crossing it at intervals, then hike up the steep Namche hill to Namche Bazaar (11,300'), main trading center for the Khumbu area. Rest day to explore Namche and environs.

DAY 8: Trek to the village of Thame (12,500').

DAY 9 and 10: Visit Thame Monastery and then trek to Khumjung (12,500'). Rest day at Khumjung, with time to visit the Khumjung Monastery, Everest View Hotel, and Khunde Hospital.

DAY 11 and 12: Descend into the deep gorge of the Dudh Kosi and up the other side to reach Thyangboche Monastery, the best-known monastery in Nepal.

DAY 13: Up the Khumbu Valley to Pangboche (12,800') and, time permitting, further on to Orso (13,600').

DAY 14 and 15: Return to Thyang-

A

boche, with a stop at the Pangboche Gompa en route, then continue down to Khunde (12,500') via the steep Dudh Kosi gorge.

DAY 16 and 17: Down past Namche Bazaar to Lukla.

DAY 18 to 21: The next few days will be spent either in Kathmandu or Lukla, depending on flying weather and other factors which often delay mountain flights. Upon arrival in Kathmandu, transfer to Malla Hotel.

DAY 22: Transfer to airport. Leave Kathmandu on homeward-bound flights.

DAY 23: Arrive home.

IT2TG1MT02

FAMILY TREK IN NEPAL

DATES: Apr 5–Apr 27 (23 days)
LEADER: Charles Gay & Pam Ross
GRADE: B-2
LAND COST: $1790 (6–15 members)
Children:
    ages 7–14: $835
       2–6: $745
      under 2: $345

This special trek, visiting the Sherpa villages of the Mt. Everest region, is a wonderful opportunity for parents and children to share the fun of a Nepal trek. On a very relaxed trekking schedule, the 14-day trek begins at Lukla (9,300') and circles up into the Khumbu region at a moderate pace (see itinerary for "Sherpa Villages & Mt. Everest"). Certain extra amenities will be added to help make things run as smoothly as possible (i.e., extra Sherpa staff and porters to carry the very young children and the older kids when necessary). Much of the emphasis will be on interaction with the Sherpa population. Sherpa families are close-knit and they love being with children. They and their own children are always fascinated to meet "foreign" youngsters, a relative rarity in the Khumbu.

ITINERARY:
(see "Sherpa Villages & Mt. Everest")

B

D

C

IT2TGIMT17

MOUNTAIN MEDICINE SEMINAR & TREK

DATES: Mar 15–Apr 12 (29 days)
LEADER: Peter Hackett, M.D.
GRADE: C-3
LAND COST: $2550 (6–15 members)

The 20-day Mountain Medicine Seminar & Trek is designed for persons with a keen interest in high alitutde physiology and mountain medicine.

En route to Everest Base Camp, there will be lectures on various topics including medical preparation for trekking and climbing, survey of diseases indigenous to the Himalaya, overview of acute mountain sickness, high altitude pulmonary and cerebral edema, hypothermia, frostbite, expedition medicine and mountain rescue. Visits will be made to the Himalayan Rescue Association's Trekkers Aid Post at Pheriche and to the Hillary Hospital at Khunde.

C.M.E. credit has been applied for. A portion of the Land Cost is a donation to the Himalayan Rescue Association.

The seminar will be taught by Peter Hackett, M.D., Director of Medical Research for the Himalayan Rescue Association of Kathmandu and Director of High Altitude Research in the Department of High Latitude Studies of the University of Alaska, Anchorage. He was chief medical officer of the 1981 American Medical Research Expedition to Everest, on which he became the fourth person (and first American) to climb to the summit of Everest alone.

ITINERARY:

DAY 1 to 3: Leave U.S. Arrive Kathmandu. Transfer to hotel.

DAY 4: Sightseeing in Kathmandu. Briefing on trek arrangements, afternoon and evening lectures.

DAY 5 to 7: Fly to Lukla (9,300'), weather permitting. Meet with Sherpa crew and trek along the Dudh Kosi to Phakding (8,700'), then steeply up to Namche Bazaar (11,300'), the Sherpa "capital". Spare day at Namche.

DAY 8 and 9: Ascend the Bhote Kosi valley to Thame (12,500'). Visit Thame Monastery on a hill above town and trek to Khunde (12,500'). Here a visit will be made to the Hillary Hospital.

DAY 10: Cross the valley to Thyangboche Monastery (12,700') beneath Ama Dablam (22,494').

DAY 11 to 13: Trek to Pheriche (14,000') for acclimatization and studies on adaptation to elevation. Visit the Trekkers' Aid Post operated by the Himalayan Rescue Association.

DAY 14: Up past the mouth of the Khumbu Glacier to Lobouje at 16,200 feet.

DAY 15: Ascend and cross the Changri Glacier to camp at Gorak Shep (17,000') near an ice-covered tarn.

DAY 16: Morning hike to the summit of Kala Patar (18,192') for classic views of Mt. Everest. Afternoon walk down to Lobouje.

DAY 17: Walk to Chukung (15,515') in the Imja valley south of the massive Lhotse-Nuptse wall.

There will be lectures on various topics including medical preparation for trekking and climbing, survey of diseases indigenous to the Himalaya, overview of acute mountain sickness, high altitude pulmonary and cerebral edema, hypothermia, frostbite, expedition medicine and mountain rescue.

DAY 18: Day hike for a close-up view of Lhotse's spectacular south face.

DAY 19 to 21: Down past Dingboche along the Imja Valley to Pangboche (12,800'). Continue through an enchanting moss-draped forest to Thyangboche Monastery. Rest day at Thyangboche.

DAY 22 and 23: Down to Namche Bazaar and continue along the Dudh Kosi gorge to Lukla.

DAY 24 to DAY 27: The next few days will be spent either in Kathmandu or Lukla, depending on flying weather and other factors which often delay the mountain flights. Upon arrival in Kathmandu, transfer to hotel.

DAY 28: Depart Kathmandu on homeward-bound flights.

DAY 29: Arrive home.

IT2TGIMTO5

EXPEDITION 20,000

DATES: Nov 5–Dec 13 (39 days)
LEADER: Dick Irvin
GRADE: D-2
LAND COST: $2690 (6–12 members)

A 30-day climbing adventure, "Expedition 20,000" will attempt ascents of Island Peak (20,238'), Pokhalde (19,044'), and Parcharmo (21,097').

Island Peak is a moderately technical snow climb in an unbelievably magnificent setting. It stands isolated at the foot of the huge Lhotse Wall surrounded by the giants ringing the Lhotse Glacier—Lhotse Shar (27,644'), Nuptse (25,850'), Ama Dablam (22,494'), Baruntse (23,826') and Cho Polu (22,222').

Pokhalde stands to the southwest of the Lhotse Wall, east of the Khumbu Glacier. Views from its summit include Makalu, Pumori and Cholatse.

B

A Monks at Mani Rimdu festival/Bruce Klepinger
B Summit ridge of Baruntse/Bruce Klepinger
C Yak/Dick McGowan

NEPAL • 33

> **The peaks are very challenging but not technically demanding. The trekking itinerary includes a visit to Everest Base Camp and the crossing of two rarely-used passes, the Changri La and Kongma La.**

Parcharmo is situated above the Tesi Lapcha Pass on the edge of the Rolwaling Valley. Summit views extend into the heart of the Rolwaling, dominated by the peaks of Melungtse and Gauri Shankar (23,452') (with the Drolambao Glacier below) and countless peaks stretching into Tibet.

The peaks are very challenging but not technically demanding. The trekking itinerary includes a visit to Everest Base Camp and the crossing of two rarely-used passes, the Changri La and Kongma La.

ITINERARY:

DAY 1 to 3: Leave U.S. Arrive Kathmandu. Transfer to hotel.

DAY 4: Sightseeing in Kathmandu. Briefing on trek arrangements.

DAY 5: Fly to Lukla (weather permitting). Trek to Phakding (8,700').

DAY 6: Trek to Namche Bazaar (11,300').

DAY 7: Short trek to Khumjung (12,500'). Views stretching from Kwangde (20,293') to Thamserku (21,723') and Kangtega (22,334'), plus Everest (29,028') and Lhotse (27,916').

DAY 8 to 11: Trek up the valley of the Dudh Kosi through Phortse and Machhermo to Gokyo Lake (15,800'). Day free at lake.

DAY 12 to 14: Cross the Ngozumba Glacier and Changri La Pass to Changri Nup Glacier. If conditions are bad on this pass, cross the South Cho La Pass (17,800') into the Khumbu.

DAY 15 and 16: Trek to Gorak Shep (17,000') and hike up Kala Patar (18,192') for views of Everest. Return to Lobouje.

DAY 17: Cross the lower portion

of the Khumbu Glacier and camp at 17,200 feet en route to the Kongma La.

DAY 18: Ascend Pokhalde (19,044'), with its fine views of Makalu, Nuptse, Lhotse, Ama Dablam, Pumori, and Cholatse. Return to camp in the Kongma La.

DAY 19 to 21: Hike to Chukung and farther up the Imja Khola to Pareshaya Gyab, camping by a small lake with fine views up the Lhotse Glacier and Lhotse-Nuptse wall.

DAY 22: and 23: Establish a high camp on Island Peak, and, conditions permitting, attempt the summit the following day. The approach is relatively easy but the final pitches are considerably more difficult, perhaps impossible in foul weather.

DAY 24 to 27: Trek back down past Pheriche, Thyangboche Monastery and Namche Bazaar to Thame, situated below the Tesi Lapcha Pass.

DAY 28 to 32: Tengbo (14,300') to Glacier Camp at about 17,000 feet, then up to a high camp at 19,000 feet for the ascent of Parcharmo (21,097').

DAY 33 and 34: Trek from Thame to Lukla (9,300').

DAY 35 to 37: The next few days will be spent either in Kathmandu or Lukla, depending on flying weather and other factors which often delay the mountain flights. Upon arrival in Kathmandu, transfer to hotel.

DAY 38: Leave Kathmandu on homeward-bound flights.

DAY 39: Arrive home.

A

IT2TGIMT17

EAST OF EVEREST

DATES: #1 Mar 10–Apr 12 (34 days)
      #2 Dec 6, 1984–Jan 8, 1985 (34 days)
LEADER: #1 to be announced
       #2 Bruce Klepinger
GRADE: C-3
LAND COST: $2290 (6-15 members)

Nepal is most verdant in its lush eastern reaches, where more rain falls than any other part of the country. On this 25-day trek, we will pass from these green tropics to the high Khumbu area and reach Kala Patar with its world-renowned views of Mt. Everest.

This approach to Everest's base is different from the 22-day trek in its remoteness, its distance from well-trodden paths and in the abundance of vegetation we see along the way.

The trails we follow are those walked by the lowland porters who supply Namche Bazaar with its food grains. These were also the trails walked by the first Mt. Everest reconnaissance expedition from the south in 1951, led by Eric Shipton.

Our trek begins from a roadhead between the towns of Dharan and Dhankuta and soon heads up the steamy Arun Valley toward Makalu (27,825'). After crossing the Arun (most likely by dugout), we head northwest along the Irkhua River valley, over narrow bamboo bridges and among millet and rice fields.

We cross three passes before reaching Khumbu. The first is the 11,400-foot Salpa Bhanjang, crowned by a twelve-foot-high stupa. Descending into the deep Hongu Valley, we pass the first Sherpa village en route, then trek for several days across two steep gorges before arriving in the Dudh Kosi Valley south of Mt. Everest. Here, perhaps for the first time on our trek, we begin to see other trekkers as we join the well-traveled path north of the Lukla airfield.

The last twelve days of the trek follow the regular hiking route into the Khumbu region and up to Kala Patar (18,192') for superb views of Everest. (See "22-day Everest Trek" for more details on the last half of the trek.)

ITINERARY:

DAY 1 to 3: Leave U.S. Arrive Kathmandu. Transfer to hotel.

DAY 4: Sightseeing in Kathmandu. Briefing on trek arrangements.

DAY 5: Fly to Biratnagar and drive to Dharan (1,200') at the edge of the low Siwalik hills.

DAY 6: Drive to the roadhead near Dhankuta (3,900') and meet Sherpa crew and porters. Begin trek in afternoon.

DAY 7: Ascend to the village of Hile (6,100') on a ridgetop with its Bhotia community and new monastery. Begin walk down ridge, passing a British-run agricultural station.

DAY 8: Magnificent distant views

of Makalu as we descend to the hot Arun Valley floor at about 850 feet.

DAY 9: Up the Arun's left bank past Tumlingtar airstrip on a long, low plateau.

DAY 10: Cross the Arun River in a dugout "ferry" and begin walking away from the Arun through low hills.

DAY 11: Passing lush fields, we ascend the Irkhua Valley populated by people of the Brahmin, Chettri and Rai clans. Reach Phedi (6,500').

DAY 12: Now in oak and rhododendron forest, we cross the Salpa Bhanjang (11,400') and descend to Sanam village.

DAY 13: Down into the Hongu gorge with views of snow peaks up-valley, we pass the town of Gudel and reach the village of Bung.

DAY 14: Ascend past a small monastery completely surrounded by evergreens and a wall of prayer stones. Cross the Sipkie Pass (10,120').

DAY 15: We are now in the Inukhu (also called Hinku) Valley. Climb to the Pangum La (10,400') with superb views of peaks both ahead and behind us.

DAY 16: Here in the Dudh Kosi Valley, south of Khumbu, we begin walking north.

> **This approach to Everest's base is different from the 22-day trek in its remoteness, its distance from well-trodden paths and in the abundance of vegetation we see along the way.**

DAY 17: Cross a high ridge and join the busy trail beyond Lukla airfield. White peaks appear on both sides of the valley.

DAY 18 to 20: Trek to Namche Bazaar, Khumjung and Thyangboche (12,700').

DAY 21 to 23: Trek to Pheriche (14,000'), Lobouje (16,200') and Gorak Shep (17,000').

DAY 24: Hike to top of Kala Patar (18,192') for classic Everest views.

DAY 29 to 32: The next few days will be spent either in Kathmandu or Lukla, depending on flying weather and other factors which often delay the mountain flights. Upon arrival in Kathmandu, transfer to hotel.

DAY 33: Depart Kathmandu on homeward-bound flighs.

DAY 34: Arrive home.

C

IT2TGIMTO3

KHUMBU HIMAL & MT. MERA

DATES: Oct 25–Dec 2 (39 days)
LEADER: Bruce Klepinger
GRADE: C-3/D-2
LAND COST: $2690 (6–15 members)

Always one of our most popular alpine trips, this trek and climb combines a visit to Everest Base Camp and an ascent of Mt. Mera (21,247'), from the summit of which one can see four of the five highest mountains in the world: Everest (29,028'), Kanchenjunga (28,208'), Lhotse (27,923') and Makalu (27,825').

The first half of our trek, which begins with a flight to Lukla, takes us to Everest Base Camp (see "20-Day Everest Treks").

The second half takes us back down to Lukla then east into the high Hinku valley, a wild and uninhabited area. The entire trip from Lukla to Mt. Mera and back is one of high adventure amidst superb mountain wilderness. We'll establish high camp on the Mera La, an 18,000-foot pass from which qualified climbers can attempt Mera's summit. The climb is not technicaly difficult but the altitude makes it physically demanding.

ITINERARY:

DAY 1 to 3: Leave U.S. Arrive Kathmandu. Transfer to hotel.

DAY 4: Sightseeing in Kathmandu. Briefing on trek arrangements.

DAY 5: Begin trek. Fly to Lukla (9,300') (weather permitting) and trek to Phakding.

DAY 6 and 7: Trek to Namche Bazaar and Khumjung (12,500').

DAY 8 to 10: Trek up the Gokyo Valley to Gokyo Lake at 15,800 feet. Optional hike to Gokyo Ri (18,000').

DAY 11: Cross the Ngozumba Glacier and camp at 16,500 feet.

DAY 12: Weather and other factors permitting, cross the snow-covered South Cho La Pass (17,800'), a flat glacier plateau with magnificent views to the east and west. Descend to Dzonghla.

DAY 13: Trek to the yak pastures of Lobouje (16,200').

DAY 14: To Gorak Shep (17,000') along the edge of the Khumbu Glacier.

DAY 15: Hike to summit of Kala Patar (18,182') or Everest Base Camp itself. Return to Lobouje.

DAY 16: Past the Trekkers' Aid Post and along the Imja Khola to Thyangboche Monastery (12,700').

DAY 17: Trek back to Namche Bazaar.

DAY 18: Trek back to Lukla, where we prepare for the second stage of the trek.

DAY 19: Climb through pine and rhododendron forests then yak pastures to Chutenga (11,300').

DAY 20: Climb over a series of three passes at about 14,900 feet. Descend to Chetara (13,700').

DAY 21: Climb up over a rocky spur and descend into the Hinku Valley. Camp near a cave at Kote (11,500').

DAY 22: Through forests and summer pastures to Duhphu, a tiny stone gompa said to be several hundred years old. Camp at Tangnag (13,750').

DAY 23: Climb over moraines and up a ridge to Khare, a yak pasture at 15,800 feet.

DAY 24 to 26: Ascend to the Mera La (18,000') and prepare for the climb. Extra days here to allow for acclimatization and inclement weather.

. . . an ascent of Mt. Mera (21,247'), from the summit of which one can see four of the five highest mountains in the world.

DAY 27: Establish high camp at approximately 19,500 feet.

DAY 28: Summit attempt today.

DAY 29 to 33: Trek back out to Lukla.

DAY 34 to 37: The next days will be spent either in Kathmandu or Lukla, depending on flying weather and other factors which often delay the mountain flights. Upon arrival in Kathmandu, transfer to hotel.

DAY 38: Depart Kathmandu on homeward-bound flights.

DAY 39: Arrive home.

IT3TGIMTO7

THE MANASLU TREK

DATES: Oct 11–Nov 12 (33 days)
LEADER: Hugh Swift
GRADE: B-3
LAND COST: $1990 (6–15 members)

This 25-day trek in central Nepal explores remote, uninhabited valleys and scenic ridges south of the magnificent "Gurkha Himal": Manaslu (26,760'), Himalchuli (25,895') and Peak 29 (25,705').

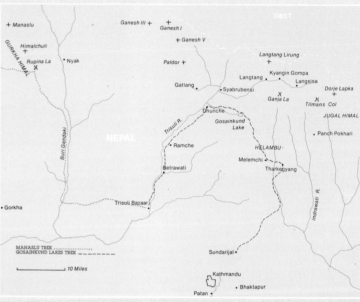

A

This region is newly opened for trekking and few Westerners have ever traveled here.

Walking from Trisuli to Pokhara, we first pass south of Ganesh (24,298'), the peak most easily visible from Kathmandu. Soon our path heads north of the usual trading routes into rarely traveled gorges beneath Bauda (21,890'), a high outlier of Manaslu.

'As we leave the terraced fields and villages of the lower hills, our route will take us along narrow

A

paths leading to upper grazing pastures and dense forests. We reach our highest point on the ascent of the Rupina La (15,400'), an unfrequented pass that lies just east of Bauda Peak. (We won't actually cross the pass, which requires technical skills, and will descend the same side.) Afterwards, we may be able to visit the secluded upper lake of Dudh Pokhari on a ridge south of Bauda with commanding views.

Our return to civilization first takes us down through thick rhododendron forests with gnarled trunks and moss-covered vines. By the time we descend to chartreuse-hued rice fields, we'll have seen nearly the full range of vegetation that Nepal has to offer. Most areas on this trek are far from the main hiking routes and the welcome accorded us by Gurung, Tamang and Brahmin-Chettri villagers will be delightfully spontaneous.

This region is newly opened for trekking and few Westerners have ever traveled here.

ITINERARY:
DAY 1 to 3: Leave U.S. Arrive Kathmandu. Transfer to hotel.
DAY 4: Sightseeing in Kathmandu. Briefing on trek arrangements.
DAY 5: Drive from Kathmandu to Trisuli (1,600'). Here we'll meet the Sherpa staff and porters and begin the trek.
DAY 6 to 8: Walk westerly on old paths now nearly deserted, passing ancient *chautaras* (resting places shaded by pipal and banyan trees). At Arughat, we'll see a temple with both Buddhist and Hindu images.
DAY 9 to 11: Walk up the Buri Gandaki Valley which narrows into a gorge as we continue northward. We are now entering a region rarely visited by foreigners.
DAY 12: Climbing, we turn into a narrow side-valley and arrive at the town of Laprok.
DAY 13 and 14: Leave human habitation and cross a wooded ridge into the upper Darondi Valley. Reach high camp.
DAY 15: Rest day at high camp with a chance to explore this remote area.
DAY 16: Climb high to the Rupina La, below which lies all of central Nepal. Return to high camp.
DAY 17 to 19: Possible walk to Dudh Pokhari, an isolated lake south of Bauda Peak. Descend southward along a ridge west of the Darondi Valley. Here we'll see Gurung herders in the upper pastures with their flocks of sheep and goats.
DAY 20 to 22: Continue descent to the upper Chepe Valley, cross the river and proceed over a forested spur to the village of Simi.
DAY 23 and 24: Down the Dordi Valley and into lower country,

reaching the town of Phalesangu by the Marsyandi River.
DAY 25: Today we follow the busy Marsyandi Valley trade route to the large bazaar of Khudi.
DAY 26: Ascending the Khudi Valley, we reach the ridgetop town of Ghanpokhara with its excellent perspective of Lamjung Himal (22,740')
DAY 27 and 28: Now we walk across low ridges into Nepal's middle hills where we'll have superb views of Lamjung, Annapurna II and IV and the fishtail peak, Machapuchare (22,942').
DAY 29: Descending into the broad Pokhara Valley, we will overnight at the Fishtail Lodge on Phewa Lake.
DAY 30: Fly or drive to Kathmandu. Transfer to hotel.
DAY 31: Day free in Kathmandu.
DAY 32: Depart Kathmandu on homeward-bound flights.
DAY 33: Arrive home.

B

IT2TG1MT18
THE GOSAINKUND LAKES TREK

DATES: #1 April 16–May 7 (22 days)
#2 Oct 4–Oct 25 (22 days)
LEADER: #1 Bruce Klepinger
#2 John Mueller
GRADE: B-2
LAND COST: $1575 (6–15 members)

This 15-day route is an excellent first trek in Nepal, offering a good overall impression of the contrasting Hindu-Buddhist hill cultures of Nepal. It circles through a Sherpa enclave on a picturesque trail which is regularly traveled by Hindu pilgrims on their way to worship at the "holy lake" of Gosainkund (14,200'), site of an ancient shrine to Shiva. As we climb up to the lake, we'll have excellent views of high peaks nearby at Kyirong, a former Tibetan trading town. Above the lakes, as we cross Lauribina Pass (15,100'), we'll have sweeping views of Himalchuli (25,895'), Manaslu (26,750'), and the Ganesh Himal.

We start the trek in the Trisuli Valley, just northeast of Kathmandu, skirting along green ridges with small Tamang villages and some of the most enchanting forests imaginable.

After visiting the holy lakes, we descend to Tharepati, a ridgetop summer settlement which has a wide view along the Himalayan range, then to Tarke Gyang, a compact Sherpa settlement which looks like a Swiss mountain village. Our last few days take us through the Helambu Sherpa district back to Kathmandu.

ITINERARY:
DAY 1 to 3: Leave U.S. Arrive Kathmandu. Transfer to hotel.
DAY 4: Sightseeing in Kathmandu. Briefing on trek arrangements.

DAY 5: Drive from Kathmandu to the roadhead at Trisuli Bazaar, meet with porters and Sherpa crew and trek along the Trisuli River to Betrawati (2,000').
DAY 6 and 7: Follow the course of the Trisuli Gorge, climbing high above the bank of the river to about 6,000 feet. This is a beautifully forested canyon with a mixture of subtropical and temperate/ deciduous trees. The Trisuli drains the peaks of the Gosainkund Range.
DAY 8: Down steeply and across the Trisuli, then steeply up the other side to Syabru (8,000').
DAY 9 and 10: Up through fir and rhododendron forests to Sing Gompa, a seldom used Buddhist monastery, and a small cheese factory at Chandan Bari (11,200'). Rest day in area.
DAY 11: Climbing steeply in the morning, we will have spectacular views of the peaks of Himalchuli, Manaslu, and the Ganesh Himal. We descend to the shore of the third high lake we pass, which is Gosainkund. A white rock at Gosainkund Lake is reputed to be the remains of an ancient shrine to Shiva and hence the lake has been visited by Hindu pilgrims for centuries.
DAY 12: Wonderful views of the Annapurna, Himalchuli, and Ganesh ranges make a pleasant walk out of our climb past three more lakes to the Lauribina Pass (15,100'). Descend steeply to camp near a cave at Gopte (11,700').
DAY 13: Continue hiking up and down through forests to a ridge crest named Tharepati with a magnificent view across the central Nepal Himalaya. Camp in a pasture at 9,500 with fine views.
DAY 14: Passing the Sherpa village of Malemchi (8,300'), we descend to the Malemchi Khola, then make a long climb up to Tarke Gyang (8,400'), where there is a recently renovated monastery. We are now amidst the Sherpa people of Helambu, who differ from the Khumbu Sherpas in many ways (including dress and language).
DAY 15: Rest day at Tarke Gyang. Optional day hikes and visits to Sherpa houses.
DAY 16: A day of great cultural change as we descend from the Sherpa mountain villages to the Tamang villages of the valley. Camp at Gheltum (3,200').
DAY 17 and 18: Cross the river at Taramarang and follow the south bank, then climb steeply to the village of Thakani (6,500'). Good mountain views from the crest of the ridge at Borlang Bhanjang (8,200').
DAY 19: A long and steep descent brings us to the edge of the Kathmandu Valley. Drive to Kathmandu and transfer to hotel.
DAY 20: In Kathmandu.
DAY 21: Depart Kathmandu on homeward-bound flights.
DAY 22: Arrive home.

C

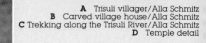

A   Trisuli villager/Alla Schmitz
B   Carved village house/Alla Schmitz
C Trekking along the Trisuli River/Alla Schmitz
D   Temple detail

IT2TG1MT11

HOLIDAY TREKKING IN NEPAL

DATES: Dec 6–Jan 1 (27 days)
LEADER: Bill Henderson
GRADE: B-2
LAND COST: $1590 (6–15 members)

Timed to coincide with mid-winter school holidays, this 19-day walk traverses middle hills of central Nepal south of three great ranges: Ganesh, Manaslu and Annapurna.

Most of the year these trails would be too hot for trekking, but in December there will be pleasant weather and clear skies. We will have plenty of opportunities to meet the hospitable hill people— Brahmins, Chettris and Gurungs— as we pass by their fields and villages.

The high point of the trip is a hike of several days onto Bara Pokhari Lekh, a high, forested ridge at 12,500 feet extending directly out from 25,895-foot Himalchuli.

We begin in Trisuli and head west along paths that were once the primary route between Kathmandu and Pokhara before a road was built. En route, we'll visit the historic, fortress-topped town of Gorkha, where Prithvinarayan Shah began his conquests that founded the kingdom of Nepal. At this point, we'll be south of quadruple-peaked Ganesh Himal (24,298').

By the time we begin our hike up Bara Pokhari Lekh, our path will lead us straight toward Himalchuli's glacier-cloaked southern slopes. Views of Manaslu (26,760'), Peak 29 (25,705') and Bauda (21,890') will be spectacular.

As we approach our destination of Pokhara, we'll see north of us the 22,910-foot peak of Lamjung and ahead of us the symmetrical spire of Machapuchare.

NOTE: Academic credit is available for this trek. Write for details.

ITINERARY:
DAY 1 to 3: Leave U.S. Arrive Kathmandu. Transfer to hotel.

DAY 4: Sightseeing in Kathmandu. Briefing on trek arrangements.

DAY 5: Drive from Kathmandu to Trisuli Bazaar (1,600') where we'll meet with porters and Sherpa crew. Begin trek west along the Samri Valley

DAY 6: Cross the low Samri Ridge (4,200'). We'll be passing Bhotia people from the restricted area north of Manaslu as they head south for winter trading.

DAY 7: Past Kitunge Bazaar to a ridgetop with sweeping views of Ganesh and Himalchuli. Camp along Ankhu River.

DAY 8: Cross the low, flat plain of Sallentar to a suspension bridge over the Buri Gandaki at Arughat Bazaar.

DAY 9: Ascend a long ridge toward Gorkha, all the while enjoying views of Ganesh, Himalchuli and Manaslu.

DAY 10: We'll see the birthplace of modern Nepal at Gorkha's fortress (6,000') and may observe the Kanpat yogis as they perform their sacred rituals.

DAY 11: After crossing the Darondi River, we'll walk over the Luitel Bhanjang, at 2,300 feet the lowest "pass" on the trek.

DAY 12: Beyond a flat plain, we reach the Marsyandi River near Tarkughat and begin a level hike up-valley.

DAY 13: Today, at Phalesangu, we begin the ascent of Bara Pokhari Lekh and leave the low valley behind.

DAY 14: We continue up the forested ridge beyond the last village, entering rhododendron groves and camp at about 10,200 feet.

> **En route, we'll visit the historic, fortress-topped town of Gorkha, where Prithvinarayan Shah began his conquests that founded the kingdom of Nepal.**

DAY 15: Walking right toward Himalchuli, we ascend to a higher camp at 12,500 feet.

DAY 16: Rest day for admiring the spectacular view and exploring the upper ridge.

C

B

DAY 17: Descend all day, following a different trail in the lower sections.

DAY 18: Reach the Marsyandi River and turn south along a deep, green gorge.

DAY 19: Passing Khudi town, we head upstream at the junction of the Marsyandi and Khudi rivers.

DAY 20: At the large Gurung town of Ghanpokhara, we'll admire the views of Lamjung and descend to the Midam Khola.

DAY 21 and 22: Walk down the Midam Valley and cross onto Arghuan Ridge at the edge of Pokhara Valley.

DAY 23: End trek at the roadhead and transfer to Fishtail Lodge on Phewa Tal Lake.

DAY 24: Fly or drive to Kathmandu.

DAY 25: Free day in Kathmandu.

DAY 26: Depart Kathmandu on homeward-bound flights.

DAY 27: Arrive home.

RESTRICTED REGIONS OF NEPAL

We have tentatively scheduled treks to both Kanchenjunga and Dhaulagiri, pending the official opening of these restricted regions by the Nepalese Government. As soon as we have official confirmation and permits, we will publish a bulletin with trek details.

IT2TG1MT10

THE DHAULAGIRI TREK

DATES: Oct 1–Oct 31 (31 days)
LEADER: to be announced
GRADE: C-3
LAND COST: $1975 (6–15 members)

23-day trek up the Kali Gandaki gorge, over French Col (17,000') and into Dhaulagiri Base Camp. Although it was one of the first 8,000-meter peaks attempted, Dhaulagiri (26,810') was one of the last to be successfully climbed (by the Swiss in 1960). In Tibetan, the name Dhaulagiri means "the rock that stands alone," and it is indeed an impressive mountain.

IT2TG1MT16

THE KANCHENJUNGA TREK

DATES: Oct 11–Nov 12 (33 days)
LEADER: to be announced
GRADE: B-3
LAND COST: $2190 (6–15 members)

The Eastern Himalaya is crowned by Kanchenjunga (28,208'), third highest mountain in the world, whose icy crest forms the frontier between eastern Nepal and Sikkim.

For this 25-day trek, we fly to Biratnagar in east Nepal, drive to Dharan, and walk through the dense forests of east Nepal— rhododendron, bamboo, cedar, hemlock and spruce, visiting settlements of Bhotias, Rais, Limbus, Gurungs. Our approach to the Kanchenjunga massif will be via the Yalung Glacier.

D

Karen tribe/Ken Scott
Yao tribe/Ken Scott
Temple at Pagan, Burma/Ken Scott
Ramayana mural, Wat Phra Keo/Ken Scott
Akha hill tribe village/Ken Scott
Akha headdress/Ken Scott
Koh Samui/Ken Scott

T2TG1MT15

HILL TRIBES OF THAILAND

DATES: #1 Feb 4–Feb 21 (18 days)
#2 Dec 1–Dec 18 (18 days)
1985: Feb 3–Feb 20 (18 days)

LEADER: #1 Bruce Klepinger
#2 to be announced

GRADE: B-2

LAND COST: $1575 (10–15 members)
$1750 (6–9)
1985: $1690

Thailand's hill tribes live in relative isolation in northern mountain enclaves along the Burmese and Laotian borders, the infamous opium-growing region known as "the Golden Triangle." This is a sparsely populated mountainous jungle at about 6,000 feet, largely hardwood forest where elephants are still employed to exploit the lucrative hardwood logging industry.

About twenty different tribes live here. Tibeto-Burmese in origin, they are semi-nomadic and vary from well-known groups such as the Meos to tiny elusive clans such as the Phi Thong Luang ("Spirits of the Yellow Leaves"), who were just recently encountered. Each tribe has its own language and distinctive embroidered clothing, complete with beautifully beaded turbans and massive silver jewelry.

Our journey here will be a leisurely seven-day walk in a seldom-visited region west of Chiang Mai, ancient capital of Thailand and center for fine hill tribe crafts. We'll hike from village to village and meet members of various tribes, including Akha, Yao, Lisu, Karen and Shan. En route, we stay in village huts. Daily hiking time is four to six hours a day.

After the trek, we'll fly south to Koh Samui, a remote island in the Gulf of Thailand to relax and enjoy swimming, snorkeling and fresh seafood in an undiscovered island paradise.

ITINERARY:

DAY 1 and 2: Leave U.S. Arrive Bangkok. Transfer to hotel.

DAY 3: All day sightseeing in Bangkok, including Wat Phra Keo, the Royal Chapel of the Grand Palace which contains one of Thailand's most venerated religious images, the Emerald Buddha. Afternoon boat tour of the "klongs," quiet waterways removed from the bustle of modern Bang-

kok. "Welcome to Thailand" dinner at one of Bangkok's best seafood restaurants.

DAY 4: Fly to Chiang Mai. Afternoon tours of silk, wood, silver and lacquerware handicraft centers. Traditional "Kantoke" dinner and dancing by northern hill tribes and/or classical Thai groups. Overnight at hotel.

DAY 5: Drive to Mae Hong Son via Chomthong Obluang Gorge. Lunch en route. Dinner and overnight at Ban Salaklo.

DAY 6: to 12: On trek, walking from village to village. Meals and accommodations in village huts.

DAY 13: Drive to Chiang Mai via Khun Youam. In the evening, Thai dinner and visit to the colorful night market.

DAY 14: Fly to Bangkok and transfer to hotel. Evening free to sample Bangkok's internationally famous nightlife.

DAY 15: Fly to Surat Thani. Transfer to Ban Don for the three-hour ferry trip to Koh Samui. Overnight at rustic but comfortable beach cottages.

DAY 16: Boat tour to National Marine Park where we can hike to a high volcanic lake. Fishing en route, local style. Lunch on the island and return to Koh Samui for a special seafood barbecue dinner.

DAY 17: By boat to Ban Don and transfer to Surat Thani for flight to Bangkok. Farewell dinner and traditional Thai dance performance.

DAY 18: Depart Bangkok and connect with homeward-bound flights.

BURMA: OPTIONAL SIX-DAY TOUR

TOUR PRICE: $780 per person (including meals, English-speaking guide, round trip air fare Bangkok/Rangoon and within Burma)
Available only in conjunction with a Mountain Travel trip.

Burma is a secluded country of pagodas, rice paddies and Tibeto-Burman, Mon-Khmer and Thai-Chinese hill tribes. Foreigners are only allowed to visit certain regions, and 7-day stays are the lengthiest permitted.

This optional tour fits in nicely before or after a Nepal trek, or for trip members who are traveling via Bangkok.

We visit Pagan, one of the most amazing places in southeast Asia, where in the beautiful rural setting of the Irawaddy River Valley there are hundreds of ruined pagodas of all sizes—huge and glorious temples like the Ananda and many small, graceful ones standing alone in the fields. Most of these temples were abandoned in 1287 A.D. when the area was overrun by Kublai Khan's Tartars.

In the Shan State, we visit picturesque Inle Lake with its floating villages, and in Mandalay, we visit important Buddhist monasteries and watch water buffalos hauling teak logs on the banks of the Irrawaddy.

The tour begins and ends in Rangoon, the capital, and site of the 300-foot-high, golden-domed Shwe Dagon Pagoda, the very essence of Burma.

This optional tour fits in nicely before or after a Nepal trek, or for trip members who are traveling via Bangkok.

ITINERARY: (from Bangkok)

DAY 1: Fly Bangkok/Rangoon.

DAY 2: Fly to Pagan. Full day touring.

DAY 3: Morning tour in Pagan. After lunch fly to Mandalay. Afternoon tour.

DAY 4: Morning tour in Mandalay. After lunch, fly to Heho and visit Inle Lake

DAY 5: Morning tour. After lunch fly to Rangoon. Afternoon tour.

DAY 6: Morning tour. After lunch, fly to Bangkok.

A Village near Takayama/Ken Scott
B Mt. Yari, Japanese Alps/Jerry Coe
C Sunrise on Fuji/Ken Scott
D Temple detail, Kyoto/Ken Scott

IT4PA1SFMT3

THE NORTH ALPS OF JAPAN

DATES: Sep 15–Oct 5 (21 days)
LEADER: Muneo Nukita
GRADE: B-3
LAND COST: $1790 (10–15 members)

Japan is one of the most mountainous countries on earth, with more than 80% of its total terrain too steep for habitation. This trip features a nine-day walk across Japan's most beautiful and precipitous mountain range, the North Alps. At present we are the only foreign group to trek across the entire North Alps.

This trip is for people who want to experience Japan exactly as the Japanese do. In the places we go, there is almost no English spoken or written. There are no Western-style accommodations, no Western-style food (and virtually no Westerners!

Although less than 10,500 feet high, the North Alps rise over a vertical mile above their immediate bases. Their cliff-hung sides are draped with dense forests which give cover to wild bear, deer, mountain goat, racoon, badger and monkey. At the time of our visit the slopes will be covered with wild splashes of red and yellow autumn coloring.

In general, the trails are steep, rocky, narrow and exposed. Japanese literature lists these walks as "climbing" but all of it can actually be done on what we call a trail in the U.S. Hiking time will be about 6 or 7 hours a day. We prefer to have strong, experienced hikers but we have taken brave novices.

In addition to our time in the mountains, we will have some days to enjoy the temples, gardens, palaces, gourmet dining and great shopping of Kyoto, Nara and Tokyo.

NOTE: We can arrange an optional climb of Mt. Fuji before or after the trip.

ITINERARY: .
DAY 1 and 2: Leave U.S. Arrive Tokyo. Transfer to hotel.

DAY 3 and 4: Days free for sightseeing or optional two-day climb of Mt. Fuji.

DAY 5: By train through the mountains to Ariake. Continue by bus or taxi up a steep dirt road to the trailhead. Overnight at hut.

DAY 6 Begin 9-day trek, walking on a very steep forest path to a high ridge at timberline. Overnight at Enzanso.

DAY 7 and 8: Along a ridge to Nishidake Hut and continue (partly climbing ladders on steep narrow ridges) to "Spear Mountain". Overnight at Yarigatake Hut.

DAY 9: Optional climb and/or walk down the canyon of the Karasawa. Optional climb of Mt. Yari. Long descent through a canyon with Hawaiian-like scenery. Overnight at Yokoo Sanso.

DAY 10: Walk up canyon under

A

B

Japan's "Yosemite," Mt. Byobu, to a famous ski resort. Optional climb. Cool forest walk to Karasawa Hut.

DAY 11: Walk to the bases of the highest peaks of the North Alps. Good views of Mt. Fuji. Overnight at Karasawa Hut.

DAY 12 and 13: Walk along forested ridges to Nishiitoya Hut. Extra day in the area for optional walks.

DAY 14: Walk to Nakao Pass and descend to Nakao Onsen. Overnight at Okuhida Hut.

In the places we go, there is almost no English spoken or written. There are no Western-style accommodations, no Western-style food (and virtually no Westerners!).

DAY 15: Spectacular bus ride over the mountains to Takayama, a famous mountain village. Afternoon exploring the village, overnight at a Japanese-style hotel.

DAY 16: By train to Kyoto via Nagoya. Overnight at hotel.

DAY 17 to 19: Sightseeing in Kyoto.

DAY 20: By "bullet" train to Tokyo. Overnight at hotel.

DAY 21: Depart Tokyo and connect with homeward-bound flights.

IT4PA1SFMT4

TREKKING IN NEW ZEALAND

DATES: #1 Mar 7–Mar 27 (21 days)
#2 Nov 23–Dec 13 (21 days)
LEADER: Mike Perry
GRADE: B-2
LAND COST: $2190 (9–12 members)
Domestic flights: $445

The spectacular, snow-capped Southern Alps of New Zealand are the setting for this in-depth trekking tour.

We'll make a three-day trek on the famous Milford Track in Fjordland National Park, walking in densely wooded valleys and alpine grasslands with grand views of glacier-flanked peaks. We cross MacKinnon Pass and take a side trip to Sutherland Falls ending at the serene mountain-ringed fjord called Milford Sound.

In Mt. Aspiring National Park, we hike for three days on the Routeburn Walk, 25 miles of untouched beech forests, a luxuriant growth of ferns, magnificent waterfalls, river valleys and mountain ridges.

In the heart of Mt. Cook National Park, we'll find ourselves in the most spectacular part of the Southern Alps, where 17 snow-covered peaks rise to 10,000 feet or higher, including precipitous Mt. Cook (12,349'). Our choices here include a ski-plane flight to the ice cap of the Tasman Glacier

C

D

The Southern Alps/Dick McGowan
Mt. Cook, New Zealand/Dick McGowan
Antarctic excursion/W. Kahler
Wildlife viewing/W. Kahler

ANTARCTICA • 39

A

Mt. Cook
Mt. Aspiring
Milford Sd.
Te Anau
Auckland
Queenstown
Wellington
Fjordland N.P.
Queenstown
Christchurch

TREKKING IN NEW ZEALAND ....

200 Miles

ollowed by a two-day trek back
o Mt. Cook Lodge, or a hike up
Mt. Olivier, a day's walk on the
Tasman Glacier, and a scenic
overflight of the park.

Our accommodations on trek will
be in New Zealand's well-stocked
and convenient wilderness huts.

ITINERARY:

DAY 1 to 3: Leave U.S. Arrive
Auckland, New Zealand. Transfer
o hotel.

DAY 4: Fly to Te Anau, a long
light stopping at Rotorua, Christchurch, Mt. Cook and Queens-
own. Transfer to hotel.

DAY 5: Morning free. Afternoon
ide by motor launch to the head
of Lake Te Anau. Begin hike on
he Milford Track with a short
walk to the Glade House.

DAY 6: Today's walk gives us time
o get acquainted with Fjordland's
birdlife and enjoy views of Mac-
Kinnon Pass way in the distance.
Overnight at Pompolona Hut.

**In the heart of Mt. Cook
National Park, we'll find
ourselves in the most
spectacular part of the
Southern Alps, where 17
snow-covered peaks rise
to 10,000 feet or higher,
including precipitous
Mt. Cook (12,349')**

DAY 7: Steadily uphill today to
bushline and cross MacKinnon
Pass, descending to Quintin, with
a side trip to Sutherland Falls.
Overnight at Quintin Hut.

DAY 8: Long day of downhill
hiking, our last day on the Milford
Track. A break at Boatshed,
Mackay Falls, Lake Ada, Giant's
Gate Falls, en route to the Milford
Sound hotel.

DAY 9: Launch cruise on Milford
Sound, following the walls of this
beautiful fjord where we might
see seals perched on ledges
along the cliffs. Short afternoon
flight around the coast to Martin's
Bay. Afternoon for strolling on the
beach.

DAY 10: A choice of jet-boating on
the Hollyford River and Lake
McKerrow, local bush walks, or a
day of beachcombing.

DAY 11: Short flight up the valley
and continue by mini-coach ride
to start the Routeburn Walk. Walk
to Lake MacKenzie Lodge for
overnight.

DAY 12: Hike across the Harris
Saddle, highest point on the trail,
to the Routeburn Falls Hut.

DAY 13: Free day at Routeburn
Falls for day hikes or relaxation.

DAY 14: Morning hike out to the
trailhead and drive to Queenstown. Arrive late afternoon and
transfer to inn.

DAY 15: Drive to Mt. Cook National
Park. Overnight in chalets

DAY 16 to 19: At Mt. Cook National
Park. Strong mountain walkers
can take a ski plane flights onto
the Tasman Glacier, spend two
nights in mountain huts, climb
Hochstetter Dome (a glacial snow
peak on which ice axe and
crampons are required), and
make a two-day trek back down
the Tasman Glacier to the lodge.
Those who want an easier schedule can spend one night in a
mountain hut, climb Mt. Olivier,
walk on the Tasman Glacier to
Hochstetter Icefall, and take a
scenic overflight of the area.

DAY 20: Morning tour of a high
country sheep station, then fly to
Auckland. Arrive early evening
and transfer to hotel.

DAY 21: Depart Auckland and connect with homeward-bound flights.

B

IT3EA1MT21

ANTARCTIC CIRCUM-NAVIGATION

DATES: Jan 15–Feb 18 (35 days)
LEADER: Leo Le Bon
GRADE: A-1
LAND COST: From $8000, not
including airfare.

In the comfort afforded by the
expedition ship *World Discoverer*,
we will circumnavigate the Antarctic continent for 30 days,
beginning at Punta Arenas, Chile,
skirting along the Antarctic Peninsula and the coast of the Ross Sea,
ending the journey in New
Zealand.

Except on days of exploration into
the pack ice, we will use the
ship's fleet of Zodiac inflatable
rafts to land on remote beaches,
photograph and observe penguins and other wildlife we encounter. We plan to visit several
scientific stations en route.

The *World Discoverer* has all the
conveniences of a conventional
cruise ship, including lecture
room, movie theatre, two lounge/
bars and observation lounge,
gym, sauna, outdoor pool and
sundecks. Meals are prepared by
European chefs. The ship holds a
maximum of 130 passengers.

As with all Antarctic expeditions,
weather and ice conditions will
dictate our schedule, although we
will make every effort to adhere
to the itinerary below.

ITINERARY:

DAY 1 and 2: Fly from Miami to
Punta Arenas, Chile.

DAY 3: Excursion to Fitzroy Channel, where we hope to see many
unusual species of birds.

DAY 4: Board the *World Discoverer*
and cruise the Strait of Magellan
and Beagle Channel.

DAY 5: Into Drake Passage, past
Cape Horn, hoping for the rare
ideal weather which would allow
us to land.

DAY 6: Sail the Drake Passage.

DAY 7 to 11: During these days, we
visit many Antarctic highlights,
such as King George, Anvers,
Nelson and Deception Islands,
Paradise Bay and Port Lockroy.
Along the route, study wildlife colonies, observing seals, penguins
and other bird species.

DAY 12 to 20: Cruise the Amundsen and Bellinghausen seas and
enter into the Ross Sea, an expeditionary route very few have
taken. We see hundreds of
beautiful icebergs and tabular ice
floes carrying seals or penguins.
We may spot some whales or
elusive emperor penguins as well.

DAY 21: Lost to International
Dateline!

DAY 22: Ice conditions permitting,
cruise along the Ross Ice Shelf.

DAY 23: Enter McMurdo Sound
and land at America's McMurdo
Station and New Zealand's Scott
Base.

DAY 24: At Cape Evans and Cape
Royds, visit the huts of fabled Ant-
arctic explorers Scott and
Shackleton.

DAY 25: At sea.

DAY 26: Ice conditions permitting,
land at Cape Adere and Cape
Hallett.

DAY 27: Wind conditions permitting, cruise between the Balleny
Islands.

DAY 28 and 29: At sea.

DAY 30: Visit the Australian scientific station at MacQuarie Island.
Photograph huge sea elephants
and thousands of king, royal and
rockhopper penguins.

DAY 31: At sea.

DAY 32: At the Auckland Islands,
see royal albatross and yellow-
eyed penguins.

DAY 33: Cruise in our Zodiac landing craft along the Snares Islands,
where we have a good chance
to see Snares penguins.

DAY 34 and 35: Arrive at Port Bluff
New Zealand. Morning sightseeing at Invercargill and depart for
Auckland and homeward-bound
flights.

C

D

Tibetan traders crossing the floodplain of the Kali Gandaki, Nepal/Susan Thiele

AFRICA
& THE MIDDLE EAST

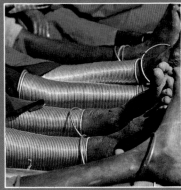

For centuries, Africa has lured the world's greatest adventurers, all determined to solve its geographical mysteries and encounter its lost tribes.

Today's Africa remains a continent of mystery, encompassing enormous tracts of still untamed country which beckons the modern-day adventurer.

Mountain Travel fields camping safaris—from deluxe to rugged—in every major wildlife reserve south of the Sahara. From the well-known Serengeti to the remote Etosha Pan, we are there with our naturalist guides and expedition expertise.

In the south of Africa, we boat the flooded forests of Zimbabwe's Matusadona National Park, tour Kruger National Park (Africa's oldest park), and go birding in Botswana's Makgadikgadi Pans.

In east Africa, we climb to the snows of Kilimanjaro, explore Kenya's Tsavo National Park on foot, ride horses along the edge of the Masai Mara, and search for walia ibex in Ethiopia's Semyen Mountains.

In central Africa, we trek in Zaire's mist-shrouded Mountains of the Moon and look for mountain gorilla families on Rwanda's Virunga Volcanoes.

In north Africa, we travel the Sahara by camel with blue-robed Touareg nomad guides, wander among the archaeological relics of Egypt's Nile Valley, hike the rugged High Atlas of Morocco, and jeep along the southern fringe of the Sahara to legendary Timbuktu.

Our group size is kept very small and each trip is led by a top professional guide who will enrich your discoveries with a storehouse of knowledge.

1984 CALENDAR INDEX

Most of our 1984 trips will be repeated in 1985 on approximately the same dates.

LEADERSHIP

Whether the journey's emphasis is wildlife, natural history or cultural exploration, our African trip leaders bring a special dimension to African travel with their extensive experience.

IAIN ALLAN, 34, has lived in East Africa most of his life. A journalist by profession and one of Kenya's leading mountaineers, he is author of the definitive *Guide Book to Mt. Kenya and Kilimanjaro*. He has pioneered new climbing routes on both mountains and is also an experienced safari leader.

ALLEN BECHKY, 36, is an expert naturalist and avid ornithologist with a decade of experience as a professional safari guide in Africa, the Indian Subcontinent and Latin America.

JEAN-LOUIS & ODETTE BERNEZAT, ages 44 and 38, are professional Sahara adventurers who have spent more than a dozen years exploring the expanses of this great desert, which they love with a passion. Odette is author of a book on Touareg nomads.

Panthera leo

African flora/Alla Schmitz

Front cover left to right:

Serengeti lion/Skip Horner
Porter on Mt. Kilimanjaro/Allen Bechky
Touareg camel/Alla Schmitz
Masai leg jewelry/Dick McGowan
Seychelles Islands/Allen Bechky
Exotic pod/Alla Schmitz
Canoeing the Zambesi/Dick McGowan
Pt. Lenana, Mt. Kenya/Ian Allan
Mountain gorilla and park ranger/Allen Bechky
Mt. Kilimanjaro from Amboseli/Alla Schmitz
Temple at Abu Simbel, Egypt/Allen Bechky
Coptic ceremonies at Lalibela/Allen Bechky
Hippo in the Zambesi/Skip Horner
Samburu tribesmen/Alla Schmitz
Game viewing in Masai Mara/Tony Church
Sunset in the Serengeti/Allen Bechky

Iain Allan

Loxodonta africana

ROB FLOWERS, 25, has guided Kenyan mountain and gameland trips for three years. Born in Kenya, Rob speaks fluent Swahili and is an authority on wildlife conservation, Kenyan tribal culture and East African game.

CHRIS MACINTYRE, 26, is a New Zealander by birth but raised and educated in southern Africa. He was a game ranger for two years in the Zambesi Valley as well as a mineral prospector in the Kalahari and Namib deserts. He is an excellent all-around naturalist and has been a professional safari leader in southern Africa for the last four years.

PETER OURUSOFF, 43, is a professional naturalist, formerly with the Massachusetts Audubon Society. He holds an M.A. in Teaching Natural Sciences from Harvard University.

WILLIE POTGEITER, 25, has lived in East Africa all his life and is an authority on African bushcraft and tracking wild game. Willie is familiar with the remotest areas of Kenya, speaks fluent Swahili and guides wildlife treks.

NED ST. JOHN, 30, is an American who has lived in Africa for more than ten years. A professional safari guide, he speaks Swahili and other African dialects and has traveled throughout the continent.

TONY CHURCH, 45, was raised in Kenya and has spent most of his life operating safaris in East Africa, particularly horseback safaris, which are his specialty.

Allen Bechky

Jean Louis Bernezat

Tony Church

Rob Flowers

Chris MacIntyre

Willie Potgeiter

Diceros bicornis

AFRICA
CAMPING SAFARIS

IT3BA1YO17

DISCOVER KENYA

DATES: #1 Feb 18–Mar 8 (20 days)
#2 Jun 16–Jul 5 (20 days)
#3 Jul 14–Aug 2 (20 days)
#4 Aug 11–Aug 30 (20 days)
#5 Sep 22–Oct 11 (20 days)
#6 Dec 15, 1984–Jan 3, 1985
(20 days)
LEADER: Iain Allan
GRADE: B-2/C-2
LAND COST: $1850 (10–16 members)

Discover the diversity of Kenya the Mountain Travel way. On trek, we experience the grandeur of Mt. Kenya's forests and peaks; on foot and by landrover, we safari to the game-filled savannahs of the national parks, then taste the tropical exuberance of the historic Kenya coast. This is an African safari for the adventurer.

On a five-day hiking traverse of Mt. Kenya, we'll explore its varied environments: the forest (home of the leopard, buffalo and elephant); the moorlands, and the peak-studded alpine zone. The trail scales glaciers and scree to Point Lenana (16,355'), then descends into the beautiful Teliki Valley on the southwest side of the peak.

Our best game viewing adventure is in Amboseli National Park, where permanent water attracts a wide variety of wildlife: elephant, giraffe, antelope, lion and rhino are commonly seen. The park is also well known for its views of Mt. Kilimanjaro.

On the edge of the Taru Desert in Tsavo National Park (a game reserve the size of Massachusetts), we make a three-day "foot safari" along the banks of the Tsavo River and experience intimately the sight, sound and feel of the African bush. Game seen on this non-strenuous trek will include hippo, crocodile and elephant.

On Kenya's coast, we camp and relax on white sand beaches near Mombasa, with time for swimming, snorkeling, shopping, and touring this historic Arab town. We return to Nairobi by an overnight train ride on the turn-of-the-century "Lunatic Express."

MASAI MARA OPTION: For those who want more wildlife viewing after the trip, we can arrange an optional three-day "fly-in" safari to a deluxe tented camp (Governor's Camp) in the fabulous Masai Mara Reserve. Cost: approximately $285.

ITINERARY:
DAY 1 to 3: Leave U.S. Arrive Nairobi. Transfer to Norfolk Hotel.

DAY 4: Drive 120 miles to the western slopes of Mt. Kenya, and camp in the forest at Sirimon Camp (8,000').

DAY 5: Hike for five miles across open moorland, descending in the afternoon to the Liki North Valley. Camp by a stream at 13,000 feet.

DAY 6: We spend the day trekking up the Mackinder Valley to its head.

DAY 7: Making a pre-dawn start, we ascend Point Lenana from the north, reaching the summit at

about 9 a.m. Point Lenana (16,355') is the highest point accessible to walkers. Descend into the Teliki Valley on the south side of the mountain. (We grade this trip a "B-2/C-2" because members who don't want to make the Point Lenana hike can traverse around the mountain by an easier route, catching up with the group at Teliki Camp.)

DAY 8: Descend the Teliki Valley to camp at a forest clearing at 10,000 feet. Monkeys, bushbuck and buffalo are often seen here.

DAY 9: Drive to Nairobi.

DAY 10: Drive south into plains country to Amboseli Game Reserve, where the full panoply of African plains animals can be observed and photographed with magnificent Mt. Kilimanjaro as a backdrop.

Africa is an exciting place to camp—the whoop of hyenas and distant roar of lions is often heard around the evening campfire! While animals do come around the camp, they are not dangerous to people who observe the rules of the bush; our expert safari guides will be there to instruct us.

Generally, we prefer to camp in remote sites where we have the isolation of the bush all to ourselves. In some national parks, official regulations restrict us to designated campgrounds.

In bush campsites, we bring drinking water, which we boil and filter, but washing water is from a local source, usually a river.

Our camp staff prepares good meals from fresh local supplies. We maintain a very high standard of camp hygiene. Travel is usually by four-wheel-drive vehicle with four or five persons plus a driver.

> On Kenya's coast, we camp and relax on white sand beaches near Mombasa, with time for swimming, snorkeling, shopping, and touring this historic Arab town.

DAY 11: Full day to explore Amboesli.

DAY 12: Drive through Masailand, gradually entering the dry country of the vast wilderness of Tsavo National Park.

DAY 13 to 15: Three days for trekking along the Tsavo River, a warm-water river running along the edge of the Taru Desert. This is a totally different wildlife experience, tiptoeing quietly through the rugged bush country and meeting wildlife on its own terms. An armed park ranger will be with us at all times for our protection. In our three nights here, we'll have two or three different campsites, each very scenic and on the banks of the river.

DAY 16: A complete change of environment from the semi-desert to the inviting tropical coast. Stay at Nomad Tented Camp, a permanent camp on the beach which has walk-in tents with twin beds and private showers.

DAY 17: Day free to relax on the beach, arrange for snorkeling or visit Mombasa.

DAY 18: Free day in Mombasa, then catch the train to Nairobi, a memorable overnight ride on a historic railway line.

DAY 19: Breakfast on the train, as the Lunatic Express chugs through the bush country of Tsavo National Park, and arrive in Nairobi about 8 a.m. Late evening depart Nairobi on homeward-bound flights.

DAY 20: Arrive home.

Masai women/Dick McGowan
Cape buffalo/Alla Schmitz
Hippos in the Tsavo River/Iain Allan

A

T3BA1YO16

WILDLIFE TREKKING SAFARI

DATES: #1 Jan 14–Feb 2 (20 days)
#2 Jun 23–Jul 12 (20 days)
#3 Jul 24–Aug 12 (20 days)
#4 Nov 24–Dec 13 (20 days)

LEADER: #1, #3 & #4 Rob Flowers
#2 Willie Potgeiter

GRADE: B-2

LAND COST: $1775 (9–16 members)

Tracking game on foot allows for extraordinary wildlife encounters, an intimate appreciation of the African countryside, and a chance to experience Africa as did the early explorers.

Hiking in the forested Loita Hills, we search for cape buffalo, elephant, and plains game such as impala, wildebeest and giraffe. We also meet the Masai, traditional herders of the plains, visiting a manyatta for a glimpse of life in a typical Masai village.

At the world famous Masai Mara Game Reserve, we do our game viewing by landrover, allowing us to range widely through the verdant plains of this fantastic park to search for lion, cheetah, and leopard and to photograph elephant, rhino and an astounding variety of wildlife.

Entering the vast thornbush wilderness of Tsavo National Park, we'll make a three-day "foot safari" along the Tsavo River through the heart of Kenya's largest reserve, accompanied by an armed "askari" (park ranger).

Our last two days are spent relaxing on the tropical beaches of the Indian Ocean at Mombasa, with a return to Nairobi by overnight train, the historic "Lunatic Express."

Tracking game on foot allows for extraordinary wildlife encounters, an intimate appreciation of the African countryside, and a chance to experience Africa as did the early explorers.

ITINERARY:

DAY 1 to 3: Leave U.S. Arrive Nairobi. Transfer to Norfolk Hotel.

DAY 4 to 6: Drive through the Great Rift Valley to the green Loita Hills and camp. Two days of game walks in the hills and forests.

DAY 7 to 9: Drive to the incomparable Masai Mara Game Reserve, Kenya's finest game country, and camp by the Mara River on the boundary of the reserve. In this famous park, we see an abundance of wildlife including elephant, cape buffalo, lion, cheetah, leopard, hippo, zebra and many species of antelope found in great herds.

DAY 10: Return to Nairobi.

DAY 11: Drive to the desert country of Tsavo National Park, one of the largest in Africa. Camp by the Tsavo River.

DAY 12 to 15: The next four days will be spent trekking along the palm-fringed banks of the Tsavo River, a warm-water river running along the edge of the Taru Desert. The river is home to many hippos and Nile crocodiles, and wildlife to be seen along the banks might include elephant, cape buffalo

and plains game. Although on this section of the trip we won't see game in the vast numbers one sees in the Mara, we will have the unique experience of tiptoeing quietly through the bush and meeting the wildlife on its own terms—with the excitement of sudden chance encounters. An armed park ranger will be with us at all times for our protection. Tsavo National Park was the setting for some historic confrontations between the British and Germans during World War I, and on our hikes we'll see remnants of some of their fortifications and bridges.

DAY 16: Drive to Mombasa. Camp by the beach at a permanent tent accommodation with walk-in tents and private showers.

DAY 17: Day for relaxing, arranging snorkeling trips and enjoying the beach.

DAY 18: Day in town or at the beach, and evening departure on the "Lunatic Express," an overnight train ride to Nairobi.

DAY 19: Arrive in Nairobi in the morning. Evening depart Nairobi on homeward-bound flights.

DAY 20: Arrive home.

B

C

IT3BA1YO19

GREAT PARKS OF EAST AFRICA

DATES: #1 Mar 12–Apr 1 (21 days)
#2 Jul 2–Jul 22 (21 days)
#3 Aug 13–Sep 2 (21 days)
#4 Sep 10–Sep 30 (21 days)
LEADER: #1 Allen Bechky
#2 Rob Flowers
#3 Peter Ourusoff
#4 to be announced
GRADE: A-1
LAND COST: $2850 (10–16 members)

This is the "grand safari," visiting the best wildlife areas in both Kenya and Tanzania. We do our game viewing by landrover, and stay in our own private camps or permanent bush camps, enjoying the flavor and excitement of the African wilderness.

In Samburu Game Reserve we watch elephants come to bathe near our river camp, and we search the surrounding scrub for Grevy's zebra, reticulated giraffe, oryx and gerenuk, all special to Kenya's desert.

In the lush mountain forests of Aberdares National Park, with Mt. Kenya distantly visible, we see concentrations of rhino, buffalo and elephant, plus unusual species such as giant forest hog, duiker and bongo.

On the celebrated plains of the Masai Mara, we find many wonders including hippo-filled rivers, vast herds of topi, buffalo and zebra and numerous predators.

In Tanzania, we adjust our itinerary to the seasonal rhythms of animal migration. Our March trip features the Serengeti, when the vast herds of wildebeest cover the plain. Our August/September trips take advantage of the dry season concentrations of game in Tarangire National Park. All three trips feature the unforgettable experience of camping on the floor of the Ngorongoro Crater, where the variety of wildlife, from prowling lions to throngs of flamingos, never ceases to amaze.

ITINERARY:

DAY 1 to 3: Leave U.S. Arrive Nairobi. Transfer to Norfolk Hotel.

DAY 4: Drive into the bush country of Samburu Game Reserve. In dry thorn thickets we search for the graceful gerenuk; on grassy plains we find the pin-striped Grevy's as well as the common zebra, often feeding along with groups of magnificent Beisa oryx, while reticulated giraffes gaze at us over the crowns of flat-topped acacia trees.

DAY 5: A full day to explore Samburu, where along the Samburu River we see crocodile, waterbuck, baboon, impala and groups of elephants. Lion and cheetah are also found in the park.

DAY 6: Drive to the coolness of Kenya's highlands and the Aberdares National Park.

DAY 7: A full day to explore the Aberdares, a beautiful forest environment of tall cedars, African olive, podocarpus, lush bamboo

A

zone and alpine moorlands, where trout streams tumble in thousand-foot waterfalls. Rhino and leopard are frequently seen here.

DAY 8: Drive into the Great Rift Valley and visit Lake Naivasha, a large freshwater lake with good birdwatching.

DAY 9: Drive to the Masai Mara Reserve. Camp on the Mara River, where we'll have Masai herdsmen for neighbors. Wildlife abounds here, and we'll hear the roar of lions and the whooping call of hyena while we sit around our campfire.

DAY 10 and 11: Two days to explore the Masai Mara Game Reserve, Kenya's premier park in its abundance and variety of wildlife.

DAY 12: Drive to Nairobi.

DAY 13: Fly to Kilimanjaro Airport, Tanzania.

Sometimes it seems that we are passing through a sea of wildebeest, zebra and gazelle, dotted with little islands where a predator (perhaps a lion or cheetah) rests on the plain.

DAY 14: Drive into the cool forests of the crater highlands to Ngorongoro Crater, truly one of the great natural wonders of the world. Its 100-square-mile floor is framed by steep green crater walls and presents a spectacular setting for wildlife. There is a large year-round population of grazing animals, including wildebeest, zebra, eland, buffalo and elephant, as well as many predators —lion, hyena and jackels. Our camp will be on the crater floor.

DAY 15: We'll watch the sun rising over Lake Magagidi, see the rhinos coming out of the Lerai forest, and spend the whole day observing wildlife on a circuit of the crater.

For March departure:

DAY 16 to 18: Enter the world of the Serengeti Plains, the last place on earth where vast herds are free to follow their traditional patterns of migration. Sometimes it seems that we are passing through a sea of wildebeest, zebra and gazelle, dotted with little islands where a predator (perhaps a lion or cheetah) rests on the plain. We will spend our nights at Ndutu Camp and follow the herds.

DAY 19: Visit the historic archaeological site at Olduvai Gorge, where the Leakey family has made some of their most important discoveries in the search for early man. Back to the crater highlands and overnight on a charming coffee plantation.

DAY 20: Visit Lake Manyara National Park, set at the foot of a spectacular Rift escarpment. The birdlife here makes this an orithologist's paradise. Continue to Arusha and depart for the airport in the evening.

DAY 21: Arrive London and connect with homeward-bound flights.

B

For August and September departures:

In the summer months, our itinerar is different because the migratior has gone too far north to be accessible and Trip #2 will probably see it in Kenya's Masai Mara.

DAY 16: Morning game viewing ir Ngorongoro Crater, then overnigh at a coffee plantation.

DAY 17: Visit Lake Manyara National Park then drive through the Rift to Tarangire National Park. Stay at a permanent tented camp

DAY 18 and 19: Two days to explore Tarangire, where the river attracts game from all over the Masai steppe in the dry season. In the parklike baobob woodlands, we find zebra, gnu and lion, then search the drier parts of the park fo fringe-eared oryx and lesser kudu

DAY 20: Drive to Arusha transfer to the airport and depart Tanzania.

DAY 21: Arrive London and connect with homeward-bound flights

C

D   E

A

B

C

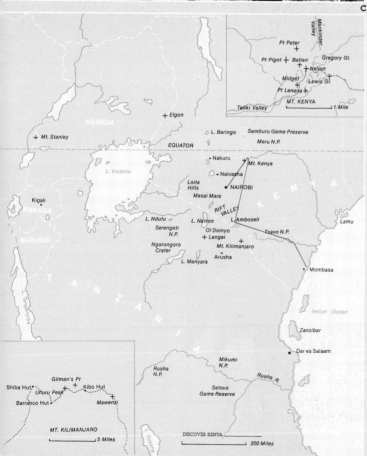

IT3BA1YO15

MT. KENYA & KILIMANJARO

DATES: #1 Feb 6–Feb 26 (21 days)
#2 Jun 25–Jul 15 (21 days)
#3 Sep 10–Sep 30 (21 days)
LEADER: in Kenya: Rob Flowers
in Tanzania:
to be announced
GRADE: C-3
LAND COST: $2490 (10–15 members)

The two highest peaks in Africa are Mt. Kenya (17,058') in Kenya, and Mt. Kilimanjaro (19,340'), in Tanzania. Both mountains rise in regal isolation from surrounding plateaus and plains. Hiking these equatorial giants takes one through three worlds of fascinating beauty: tropical forest, mist-shrouded moorlands, and high altitude alpine zone.

Our Mt. Kenya hike is a five-day traverse beginning in the forests of the little-known Sirimon Route. We ascend to the heights of Point Lenana and descend the other side through the splendid "tropical alpine" flora of the Teliki Valley. Point Lenana (16,355') is the highest point that can be reached without technical cimbing, and has an astounding view of Mt. Kenya's two jagged summits, Batian and Nelion, surrounded by lesser needles and some fifteen glaciers.

Before leaving Kenya, we'll enjoy excellent game viewing in the forests of Aberdares National Park and the magnificent Samburu Game Reserve.

In Tanzania, our six-day Kilimanjaro trek takes us along the Machame Route, a remote trail skirting the southern glaciers of the mountain. Beginning in rain forest at 6,400 feet, we hike in isolation, enjoying fabulous alpine scenery as we make an altitude gain of nearly 13,000 feet on the way to the "snows of Kilimanjaro" —Uhuru Peak at 19,340 feet.

After the trip, we can arrange an optional seven-day safari in Tanzania's fantastic national parks.

ITINERARY:

DAY 1 to 3: Leave U.S. Arrive Nairobi. Transfer to Norfolk Hotel.

DAY 4: Drive 120 miles to the western slopes of Mt. Kenya and camp in the forest at Sirimon Camp (8,000').

DAY 5: Hike for five miles across open moorland, descending to camp in Liki North Valley (13,000').

DAY 6: Trek up the deep Mackinder's Valley and camp at 14,500 feet.

DAY 7: Making a pre-dawn start, we hike steeply up to Point Lenana from the north, reaching it at about 9 a.m. Descend to the south side of the mountain and camp at 13,600 feet beneath the south face.

DAY 8 and 9: Descend the Teliki Valley and its infamous "vertical bog" to the forest clearing at 10,000 feet. Drive to the Ark Lodge in the highlands of Aberdares National Park. This famous lodge features nighttime viewing and the possibility of seeing such rare forest creatures as giant forest hog, bongo and rhino.

DAY 10 and 11: Drive north to the Samburu Game Reserve in the arid Northern Frontier District. By landrover, we'll find the animals of northern Kenya such as Beisa oryx, Grevy's zebra, reticulated giraffe and Somali ostrich. We'll also see large herds of elephant and cape buffalo, and with a bit of luck, lion and cheetah.

DAY 12: Drive to Nairobi.

DAY 13: Fly to Arusha, Tanzania. Transfer to Kibo Hotel at the base of Kilimanjaro.

DAY 14: Drive to Machame Route and begin hiking at about 6,400 feet. Follow trails up through rain forest and heather to Uniport Hut (10,000').

> **Hiking these equatorial giants takes one through three worlds of fascinating beauty: tropical forest, mist-shrouded moorlands, and high altitude alpine zone.**

DAY 15: Climb up to and cross the Shira Plateau to Shira Hut (12,600'). The plateau is often roamed by herds of eland and offers spectacular views of the glaciers of Kilimanjaro.

DAY 16: Trek to Barranco Hut (13,500').

DAY 17: Trek beneath the wild south face of Kilimanjaro to the Barafu Hut (15,000'), situated high on a ridge with views of Mawenzi Peak, Mt. Meru and Moshi on the plains below.

DAY 18: A long, memorable and very strenuous day: up at 1 a.m. and hike about five to nine hours (depending on your speed) to the crater rim, then an hour along the rim to Uhuru Peak (19,340'), and return via crater rim to Gilman's Point (about one hour). Descend to Kibo Hut (15,000') and down to Horambu Hut (12,200'), hopefully reaching it by about 5 to 7 p.m.

DAY 19: Pleasant descent on a good trail through the forest down to the Kibo Hotel.

DAY 20: Day free. Evening depart Tanzania on homeward-bound flights.

DAY 21: Arrive home.

D

Map labels:

Mackinder Valley · Pt Peter · Pt Pigot · Batian · Nelion · Gregory Gl. · Midget · Lewis Gl. · Pt Lenana · Teliki Valley · MT. KENYA · 1 Mile

UGANDA · Mt. Stanley · Elgon · L. Baringo · Samburu Game Preserve · Meru N.P. · EQUATOR · L. Victoria · Nakuru · Mt. Kenya · Naivasha · Loita Hills · NAIROBI · Masai Mara · KENYA · Kigali · RWANDA · BURUNDI · L. Ndutu · L. Natron · RIFT VALLEY · L. Amboseli · Lamu · Serengeti N.P. · Ol Doinyo Lengai · Tsavo N.P. · Ngorongoro Crater · Mt. Kilimanjaro · Arusha · Mombasa · L. Manyara · TANZANIA · Indian Ocean · Zanzibar · Ruaha N.P. · Mikumi N.P. · Dar es Salaam · Ruaha R. · Selous Game Reserve · Tanganyika · Gilman's Pt · Kibo Hut · Shiba Hut · Uhuru Peak · Mawenzi · Barranco Hut · MT. KILIMANJARO · 5 Miles · Nyanza · DISCOVER KENYA · 200 Miles

A

IT3KL1342AZZ

TREKKING IN MASAILAND

DATES: #1 Aug 10–Aug 28 (19 days)
#2 Dec 21, 1984–Jan 8, 1985
(19 days)
LEADER: Allen Bechky
GRADE: B-2
LAND COST: $1990 (9–12 members)

Vast tracks of northern Tanzania's bush country outside the boundaries of the famous game parks remains beautiful wild country teeming with game.

Visiting such areas allows one to enter an Africa unknown to tourism and unfettered by the rules of park administrations. One can walk and wander in total freedom.

On the trip, we explore a remote part of unspoiled Masailand. The Rift Valley scenery is picture-book dramatic. One vista of green, acacia-dotted plains unfolds endlessly into another of forest-covered hilltops, and above it all looms the expansive African sky.

Here we can track animals on foot. With expert guides, we learn to read the signs of the bush, to see what the gazelle nibbled and where the lion passed. We quietly enjoy such unique experiences as waiting at waterholes for kudu to appear, avoiding cape buffalo on forest game trails, relishing the downwind stalk of an unsuspecting elephant group, and chancing a glimpse of a lioness before she vanishes into the long grass.

We spend one week sharpening our bushcraft skills in Masailand. We use our landrovers to reach base camps, then do our explorations on foot.

We shall also enjoy superb traditional game viewing on a seven-day landrover safari into the Serengeti, Ngorongoro and Lake Manyara parks.

ITINERARY:
DAY 1 to 3: Leave U.S. Arrive Kilimanjaro Airport, Tanzania. Overnight at Ngare Sero Lodge.

DAY 4: Begin camping safari with a visit to Lake Manyara National Park.

DAY 5 to 8: Explore the superlative Serengeti National Park. Wildlife viewing among the great herds and attendant predators is fabulous!

DAY 9 and 10: We visit the archaeological site at Olduvai Gorge, then descend to the floor of the Ngorongoro Crater. We camp for two nights in this modern Garden of Eden, surely one of the world's most beautiful game parks.

> **Visiting such areas allows one to enter an Africa unknown to tourism and unfettered by the rules of park administrations. One can walk and wander in total freedom.**

DAY 11 to 16: We move into Masailand and begin our explorations. Here we are alone to discover for ourselves the quiet delights of undisturbed wilderness. We use landrovers to establish our base camps, then explore the bush on foot, a real outdoor learning experience.
DAY 17: Drive to a lodge outside Arusha.
DAY 18: Morning depart Tanzania on homeward-bound flights.

DAY 19: Arrive home.

IT3BA1YO18

KENYA HORSEBACK SAFARI

DATES: #1 Jun 30–Jul 17 (18 days)
#2 Dec 1–Dec 18 (18 days)
LEADER: Tony Church
GRADE: B-1
LAND COST: $1990 (7–12 members)
$2190 (5–6)

Kenya is a great riding country: its beautiful unfenced landscapes and pleasant climate are a delight for the horseman, and its wildlife is wondrous. Game viewing on horseback is particularly interesting, as most animals allow a rider a fairly close approach. This safari will put us in close touch with the land, as we spend our days in the saddle and our nights under canvas in wilderness camps.

Our horseback safari takes place in the beautiful Loita Hills and along the edge of the Masai Mara, Kenya's finest game country.

Time is set aside for wildlife viewing by landrover into the Mara gamelands and the rugged moorlands of the Aberdares, as well as some fine birding at lakes Naivasha and Bogoria.

All riding gear is supplied, including English saddles that are modified for the kind of riding one will experience in Kenya. The horses are accustomed to riding through the savannahs in close contact with game animals. Our camping equipment will be transported by vehicles from one campsite to the next. Previous riding experience is required.

ITINERARY:
DAY 1 to 3: Leave U.S. Arrive Nairobi and transfer to Norfolk Hotel.
DAY 4: Drive west into Masailand and the lovely unspoiled Loita Hills at about 7,000 feet. Our horses and camp equipment will

have been trucked in the day before.
DAY 5: A full day out on horseback exploring the wooded Loita Hills immediately above the impressive Nguruman Escarpment. In the forest glades we shall see eland, kongoni, impala, bushbuck, and waterbuck. We picnic on a high ridge looking towards Ol Doinyo Lengai and Ngorongoro Crater in Tanzania.
DAY 6: We rise early, strike camp, feed our ponies and ride out over the Loita Hills in a northerly direction, finally dropping down into the Morijo Valley.
DAY 7: Today we ride across the rolling highlands up to Subugo (8,000'), the highest point on the Loita Hills, before descending to Narosura Springs, a favorite haunt for baboons and vervet monkeys.
DAY 8: Saddle up and cross open plains interspersed with acacia to Maji Moto (Hot Springs), where there are a number of Masai villages.
DAY 9: A long day in the saddle riding across the vast Loita Plain, home of thousands of wildebeest and gazelles, arriving in the acacia-forested Lemek Valley.
DAY 10: A shorter ride today reaching Aitong, on the edge of the Mara plains where the enormous concentration of game migrating from the Serengeti gathers before moving south again in late September.
DAY 11: Ride across the grassy Mara Plain literally surrounded by large herds of plains game. (Our horses are quite accustomed to this).
DAY 12: The horses have a rest day and we go by landcruiser into the Masai Mara Game Reserve to photograph wildlife including lion, hyena, elephant and rhino at close quarters from the safety of a vehicle.
DAY 13: We ride across the river and up onto the Soit Ololol escarpment, with its superb views into the Mara Game Reserve, perhaps the most densely populated game sanctuary in Africa.
DAY 14: Leave the horses and drive back into the Great Rift Valley via Lake Nakuru to Lake Baringo. By launch over to our charming island camp.
DAY 15: Early morning launch cruise to photograph a multitude of birds, such as the African fish eagle, the African jacana, kingfishers, egrets and herons. Then by landcruiser to Lake Bogoria to see the huge assembly of flamingoes.
DAY 16: Drive to the Aberdares for an overnight at the Ark Lodge, with its nighttime game viewing.
DAY 17: Drive to Nairobi. Evening depart Nairobi on homeward-bound flights.
DAY 18: Arrive home.

B

A Masais meet child on "family safari"/Dick McGowan
B Kenya's coast
C Camel trek in Tsavo East/Iain Allan

EAST AFRICA • 9

IT2BAIYO44

FAMILY SAFARI IN KENYA

DATES: #1 Jul 14–Jul 27 (14 days)
#2 Jul 31–Aug 13 (14 days)
LEADER: Willie Potgeiter
GRADE: A-1
LAND COST: $1390 (adults)
$590 (ages 8–12)
$295 (ages 2–7)

A wildlife safari opens doors of learning for both parents and children. Most children love animals. To see large numbers and varieties in the wild is a great opportunity for a child to expand his perception of the wonder of life on our planet. Nowhere but Africa is such a spectacle possible. Combine the learning experience with the fun of an outdoor camping adventure in one of the most beautiful countries on earth, and you have a fantastic experience to share with your children.

This special safari, designed with children in mind, visits the major game reserves in Kenya: Meru National Park, Samburu Game Reserve, Lake Nakuru and the fantastic Masai Mara.

Travel is by four-wheel-drive vehicle and mini-bus.

ITINERARY:
DAY 1 to 3: Leave U.S. Arrive Nairobi. Transfer to Norfolk Hotel.
DAY 4: Drive north, skirting the western flanks of Mt. Kenya to beautiful Meru National Park
DAY 5: A full day of landrover exploration in this lovely park, a typically beautiful Kenyan landscape of golden plains and woodlands, once home to Elsa, the famed lioness of *Born Free*. Elsa is gone, but elephant, buffalo and many antelope species such as oryx and dikdik are found here. The Tana River shelters hippos and crocodile.
DAY 6: Drive north to the Samburu Game Reserve, on the fringes of the great desert of northern Kenya, in an area which features good concentrations of wildlife including waterbuck, elephant, and baboon. The surrounding thornbush desert is the habitat of celebrated desert animals such as reticulated giraffe, Grevy's zebra, oryx and gerenuk. We will also be able to see the very traditional Samburu people, who roam nomadically with their cattle. We may visit one of their villages.
DAY 7: In addition to the unique desert wildlife of Samburu, we have a good chance to find the cats here: lion, cheetah and leopard. Overnight at camp.
DAY 8: Drive into Africa's Great Rift Valley via Thompson's Falls to Lake Naivasha.
DAY 9: Drive into the Masai Mara Game Reserve, one of the finest wildlife areas in all Africa and home of the well known Masai people, who retain their traditional pastoral way of life.
DAY 10 and 11: Two full days to explore the Mara by landrover. This is the classic African landscape:

acacia-studded plains with roving herds of wildebeest, zebra, giraffe and an astounding variety of antelopes. Elephant and the now-endangered black rhino can be found here, and it is the best bush country in Kenya for finding the big predators such as lion, cheetah, hyena, and the always-elusive leopard.
DAY 12: Drive to Nairobi.
DAY 13: Day free in Nairobi. Late evening depart Nairobi on homeward-bound flights.
DAY 14: Arrive home.

A

IT2BAIYO43

KENYA: CAMEL TREK & COASTAL SAIL

DATES: #1 Feb 3–Feb 22 (20 days)
#2 Oct 6–Oct 25 (20 days)
LEADER: Willie Potgeiter
GRADE: B-2
LAND COST: $2290 (9–12 members)

This trip has a very exotic itinerary with unique attractions. As far as we know, no similar itinerary is offered in Kenya today. We trek by camel through the wild bushlands of Tsavo East, sail by Arab "dhow" among the luxuriant tropical islands of the Lamu Archipelago, and make traditional landrover safaris in the little-visited Shimba Hills and magnificent Amboseli National Park.

We begin with game drives in Amboseli, a park dominated by the peak of Mt. Kilimanjaro, then move on to Tsavo East National Park for a four-day camel trek, stalking wildlife on foot and riding camels through a rugged semidesert landscape.

From the pleasant beach town of Malindi, we fly to Lamu, an island off the northern Kenya coast. The

Lamu Archipelago has a blend of Arab and African influences from which the Swahili culture was born. Lamu Island has retained a charming centuries-old flavor, born of its narrow, white-washed streets, Arab architecture and a timeless tranquility enhanced by the absence of motor vehicles on the islands. From Lamu, we board small sailboats (traditional Arab dhows) and sail the archipelago for two days, camping at night.

The trip ends with game drives in Shimba Hills National Reserve, a wildlife park located only 20 miles inland from the Indian Ocean.

ITINERARY:
DAY 1 to 3: Leave U.S. Arrive in Nairobi. Transfer to Norfolk Hotel.
DAY 4: Drive south towards Africa's highest mountain, Kilimanjaro and enter Amboseli Game Reserve. Camp in the shade of flat-topped acacia trees with good views of Kilimanjaro.
DAY 5: Game viewing by land-rover in Amboseli, known for its wealth of predators—lion and cheetah. Elephant and rhino can also be seen.
DAY 6: Drive to Tsavo East National Park and reach the Galana area, starting point for our camel trek.
DAY 7 to 10: Days spent wandering through the remote Lali Hills, where we may see herds of elephant and the elusive greater kudu in these hills. All camping equipment and personal baggage will be transported on camels and several passenger-carrying camels will be available.
DAY 11: Drive to the coastal town of Malindi. Overnight in hotel.
DAY 12: Short flight to the delightful Arab island of Lamu, where our accommodations will be in a large Arab house. Lamu is much like an Arab port in the Middle Ages—a scene of dhows full of mangrove headed for Arabia, shipwrights building wooden sailing ships, with a backdrop of dozens of ancient mosques.
DAY 13 and 14: During these days, we sail an Arab "dhow" around the Lamu Archipelago, camping at night, visiting Manda Island, Matondoni, Takwa National Monument and a dhow-building village.
DAY 15: Sail back to Lamu Island and spend the day exploring town. Overnight in Arab house.
DAY 16: Fly to Malindi and drive down the coast to Mombasa, then continue southwards to Shimba Hills National Reserve. Camp.
DAY 17: A day spent driving in these green rolling hills, East African home of the rare roan and sable antelope, and also an environment where elephant and bushbuck can be seen. Camp.
DAY 18: Drive to Nairobi and check into the Norfolk Hotel.
DAY 19: Day free in Nairobi. Evening depart on homeward-bound flights.
DAY 20: Arrive home.

B

C

IT3KL1342AZZ

TANZANIA WILDLIFE SAFARI

DATES: #1 Jan 13–Jan 31 (19 days)
      #2 Feb 17–Mar 6 (19 days)
      #3 Jun 29–Jul 17 (19 days)
      #5 Nov 30–Dec 18 (19 days)
LEADER: #1, #2 & #5 Allen Bechky
       #3 Peter Ourusoff
GRADE: B-2
LAND COST: $2490 (8–15 members)

This is the Africa buff's "connoisseur" safari. By four-wheel-drive vehicle and on foot, we travel through some of the best landscapes the continent has to offer and visit the best gamelands on earth at the very best time of year. This area, celebrated in Peter Matthiessen's *The Tree Where Man Was Born*, is truly "Old Africa" as we all have imagined it.

In Arusha National Park, we hike in the company of armed rangers, following game trails through Mt. Meru's lush cloud forest, and peering into Ngordoto Crater, where humans are forbidden to tread.

Leaving the cool highlands, we descend into the Great Rift Valley, land of wild animals and Masai herds, of baobab and whistling thorn.

We then enter the Serengeti ecosystem to witness the greatest wildlife spectacle on earth. Here vast herds of wildebeest, zebra and gazelle stretch to every horizon. It will be calving season and we may well witness the miracle of birth and the drama of predation and death. Our schedule is flexible, allowing us to follow the migration.

We also visit another natural wonder, the 100-square-mile expanse of Ngorongoro Crater, for a mind-boggling wildlife experience within the confines of the earth's largest relic caldera.

At Lake Manyara National Park, we enjoy unbelievably close-up observations of elephant family groups, marvel at massed flocks of waterbirds, and (with luck), find the celebrated tree-climbing lions.

This is a deluxe African camping safari. We travel four or five per-

sons to a landrover, which gives us tremendous flexibility in catering to the personal interests and energies of trip members. We are supported by a full staff of experienced camp assistants. There are Tanzania safaris which are lower in cost, but if you compare, you'll find that Mountain Travel's safaris offer more time in the bush and fuller service, leading to a better wildlife experience.

OPTIONAL TRIPS: After the safari, we offer a seven-day Kilimanjaro hike or a visit to the Selous. See "Africa Options."

ITINERARY:
DAY 1 to 3: Leave U.S. Arrive Kilimanjaro Airport, Tanzania. Drive to Momella Lodge in Arusha National Park.

DAY 4: With park rangers as escorts, we hike through the forests of Mt. Meru (14,990') to its beautiful crater.

DAY 5: Drive into Rift Valley wilderness country.

DAY 6: Hike into a gorge that emerges from the steep Rift Valley escarpment. We may see baboon and klipspringer, and can swim near a wild date palm oasis. Camp in the shadow of the active volcano Ol Doinyo Lengai, the Masai "Mountain of God," and hike to the shores of Lake Natron to enjoy the hospitality of nearby Masai manyattas. These traditional people will enliven our camp with memorable cultural exchanges!

DAY 7: Drive out of the Rift Valley toward the Gol Mountains, and camp along a dry river overlooking a short grass plain.

We then enter the Serengeti ecosystem to witness the greatest wildlife spectacle on earth. Here vast herds of wildebeest, zebra and gazelle stretch to every horizon.

A Ol Doinyo Lengai, Tanzania/Allen Bechky
B Elephant/Allen Bechky
C Rhino in Masai Mara/Allen Bechky
D Warthog in the Aberdares/Allen Bechky
E Somali ostrich/Allen Bechky
F The Seychelles/Allen Bechky
G Giraffa camelopardalis

EAST AFRICA • 11

DAY 8: Hike into a spectacular gorge to view a large colony of griffon vultures, then drive across the short grass plains of the western Serengeti, encountering large herds of wildebeest, zebra and gazelle en route to Lake Ndutu.

DAY 9 to 12: In the Serengeti, our itinerary is flexible so we can stay in proximity to the migrating animals. Generally, from December to May, the great herds (mostly wildebeest, zebra and gazelle) are on the short grass plain of the southeast. Our June departure will catch migration moving through the western corridor and may even be lucky enough to witness the mass exodus from the plains. In addition to the spectacle of migration, Serengeti is "a kingdom of predators," and we shall see lion, cheetah, hyena, jackal, the elusive leopard and wide-ranging wild hunting dogs.

DAY 13: Visit the famed archaeological site at Olduvai Gorge and drive to the Crater Highland massif. Descend and camp on the floor of Ngorongoro Crater.

DAY 14: We have the Crater entirely to ourselves for our dawn game drive, on which we will see an incredible variety of wildlife in great abundance. Elephant, eland and kongoni live here as well as the larger herds of wildebeest and zebra. Lion and hyena are very numerous.

DAY 15: After a morning game run, drive through fertile farmlands to Gibb's Farm to sample Tanzanian coffee, and continue to Lake Manyara National Park.

DAY 16: Lake Manyara is famed for wonderful concentrations of waterbirds and its numerous elephant herds. Our camp is situated in a lovely groundwater forest, alive with the calls of blue monkeys and silvery-cheeked hornbills.

DAY 17: Drive to Arusha, stopping en route at an African country market.

DAY 18: Morning depart Tanzania on homeward-bound flights.

DAY 19: Arrive home.

AFRICA OPTIONS

The following programs are excellent travel options for people visiting Africa on our trips or independently. Contact Mountain Travel for rates and further details.

KENYA'S COAST

Kenya's luxuriant tropical coast, with its inviting Indian Ocean beaches, is a perfect place to relax after a safari. You can swim, snorkel and taste gourmet seafood at a beach resort in Mombasa, fly to the romantic Arab island of Lamu, or visit the marine national parks at Malindi and Shimoni. We can arrange a coast experience to suit your taste. Time: Two days or longer. Season: All year.

SEYCHELLES ISLANDS

The Seychelles, set in the mid-Indian Ocean, present the true "island paradise" that one dreams of being marooned on. Crowned with tropical vegetation and graced by the most scenic beaches imaginable, the Seychelles are remote enough that they are still unspoiled. The sea life on the outlying coral reefs is remarkable, an endless delight for the snorkeler, and the islands' bird life is well known by the world's ornithologists. The people of the Seychelles —of French, African and Asian extraction—give the islands a distinctive culture. Time: Four days or longer. Season: All year. (Travel to the Seychelles increases air fare by approximately $600.)

KILIMANJARO HIKING

Mt. Kilimanjaro, the "mountain of springs," is a challenge to strong hikers but those who have trekked to its summit know that the effort is well rewarded—to stand on its glaciers and look down over the hot African plains is an unforgettable thrill. We offer a six-day hike starting from the forests at 7,000 feet and pushing upward to Uhuru Peak (19,340'). Accommodations are in alpine huts and porters carry the gear. This is a great addition to our Tanzania Wildlife Safari and many other East Africa trips. Time: Seven days. Season: Most of the year (avoid April/May and October/November).

SELOUS GAME RESERVE

The Selous of southern Tanzania is Africa's largest and wildest game reserve. (See "Selous Safari" for description.) Access is by air charter from Dar es Salaam and we stay at the permanent Mbuyu Camp on the banks of the wide Rufigi River, exploring by land-rover, on foot and by launch on the river. Party size: four or more. Time: Four or more days.

ZAMBIA: THE LUANGWA VALLEY FOOT SAFARI

Zambia's Luangwa Valley is one of Africa's premier national parks. Massive concentrations of wildlife inhabit its vast wooded plains. More than 60,000 elephants live here, and the park's 2000 rhinos are the last truly viable population of that endangered species. With an armed ranger and naturalist guide, one can take a marvelous five-day "foot safari" in the game-filled bushlands. This option works well with our Botswana and Namibia safaris. Time: Six days or longer. Season: June through November.

PRIVATE TRIPS

In addition to our regular programs, we can make arrangements for private groups or individuals in Kenya, Tanzania, Rwanda, Zambia, Botswana, Namibia and Egypt.

Ideally, a group of four or more persons is the best number from a cost standpoint, be we will make arrangements for individuals and couples.

Let us know your travel dates, number in party, and lodging preferences about three months (or more) in advance of your proposed trip so we can plan an exact itinerary for you and quote a cost.

A

B

C

E

F

G

A

IT3KL1342BZZ

THE SELOUS SAFARI

DATES: *Sep 1–Sep 18 (18 days)
LEADER: Allen Bechky
GRADE: A-2
LAND COST: $2950 (8–12 members)
*Note change from 1984 Trip Schedule.

The game reserves of southern Tanzania are among the most spectacular of the entire continent, but because of their remoteness, they are almost totally unvisited by tourists. On this trip, we discover a still-pristine piece of wild Africa, a superb wildlife habitat encompassing the flood plains of mighty rivers and vast tracks of deciduous "miombo" woodlands. To explore these wild areas before they are inevitably discovered by tourism is a unique opportunity.

We initiate ourselves to safari life in the picturesque wooded hills of Mikumi National Park, then continue to superb Ruaha Park. Ruaha is unfrequented by tourists, but well-known to afficionados as one of Africa's foremost wildlife paradises. We camp for four days here, observing elephant and kudu along forested river tracks, scouring the miombo for the magnificent sable and roan antelope, and checking rocky outcrops for leopard.

We then move to the renowned Selous Game Reserve, setting of Peter Mathiessen's *Sand Rivers*. The Selous, at 21,000 square miles, is the largest and wildest reserve in Tanzania. For the drama and variety of its landscapes, the Selous is superlative. Waterbuck and impala graze its grassy flats, watchful for lion and wild dog. Rhino still frequent forest glades, and the game-harboring miombo stretches endlessly to the distant south. It is a land of rivers, greatest of which is the Rufigi, whose waters teem with hippos and crocodile, while huge bull elephants (the largest tuskers in Africa) patrol the stately palm forests of its flood plain.

Walking trips are permitted in the Selous, and during our stay here, foot safaris will give us a particularly intimate feel for the wild, while excursions by landrover allow us the best photographic opportunities and the flexibility to explore different sections of this vast park. We do our wildlife viewing on the Rufigi River by boat.

ITINERARY:
DAY 1 to 3: Leave U.S. Arrive Dar Es Salaam. Transfer to hotel.

DAY 4 and 5: Camp in Mikumi National Park, a small but delightful reserve with abundant wildlife.

DAY 6: Drive to Ruaha National Park, establishing camp on the beautiful Ruaha River.

DAY 7 to 9: Three days to explore remote Ruaha by landrover. On the Mdonya woodlands circuit, we hope to find sable and roan and the unusual Lichenstein's Hartebeest.

DAY 10 and 11: Move to the cool highlands of the fertile Morogoro district, then enter the Selous, exploring the woodlands around precipitous Steigler's Gorge on the Rufigi River.

This is the setting of Peter Mathiessen's *Sand Rivers*. The Selous, at 21,000-square-miles, is the largest and wildest reserve in Tanzania.

DAY 12 and 13: By landrover and on foot, we investigate the complete mosaic of Selous landscapes: oxbow lakes crowded with storks and waterfowl; lush green swards of seasonally-flooded *mbugas* (swamps) which attract impala, yellow baboon and elephant; acacia woodlands, haunts of blue gnu, kudu and rhino. We camp in splendid isolation and enjoy a natural bath at Behobeho hot springs. We also visit the grave of explorer Frederick Courtenay Selous, after whom this great reserve was named.

DAY 14 and 15: We base ourselves at Mbuyu Camp, overlooking the Rufigi River. On boats we cruise the river, while foot safaris allow us to stalk the game and birds of the flood plain.

DAY 16 and 17: We return to Dar and have time to relax at a beach hotel on the tropical Indian Ocean.

DAY 18: Depart Dar and connect with homeward-bound flights.

IT3SN1476

RWANDA GORILLA SAFARI

DATES: #1 Jan 5–Jan 23 (19 days)
        #2 Jun 28–Jul 16 (19 days)
    1985: Jan 10–Jan 28 (19 days)
LEADER: #1 to be announced
        #2 Allen Bechky
GRADE: B-2
LAND COST: $2750 (11–15 members)
        $3125 (6–10)

Straddling the border of Rwanda and Zaire, the Virunga Volcanoes offer a most unusual wildlife experience: observation of one of the rarest animals on earth, the mountain gorilla.

These great anthropoid apes live a very secluded life, avoiding all contact with their one enemy: man. But in Virunga Volcanoes National Park several family groups of wild-living gorillas have become habituated to the presence of observers and can be approached quite closely in their natural habitat. In very small groups, we'll be able to sit down right in the midst of these gentle apes, observing them in their daily activities. It is quite fair to say that no other wild animal has shown as much tolerance for quiet human observance. This is really a one-of-a-kind wildlife experience. We spend three days at Virunga, hiking the lush slopes of these steep, emerald-green mountains.

We combine the gorilla experience with a camping/landrover safari in some of Kenya's premier parks, including Masai Mara, Samburu and the Aberdares.

ITINERARY:
DAY 1 and 2: Leave U.S. Arrive Kigali. Meet with trip leader and drive to Akagera National Park.

DAY 3 and 4: Akagera Park is a unique piece of wild Africa. It is known for its vast papyrus swamps, where the birdlife is always stunning in its diversity. We explore the papyrus by boat. On land, we hope to see lion and leopard as well as waterbuck, warthog, and a variety of other game.

DAY 5: Drive through northern Rwanda, "the land of a thousand hills," and arrive at Ruhengi with its views of the Virunga Volcanoes.

DAY 6: Drive to Virunga Volcanoes Park, and divide into small groups to search for gorillas. We shall attempt to track and observe two different family groups. "Group 11" lives on the slopes of Visoke Volcano where its steep flanks are covered with thick forest. "Group 13" inhabits Sabinyo Volcano and can often be found in the extensive bamboo zone. Sometimes finding the gorillas is easy, as they may have remained close to the area where they had been feeding the previous day. Sometimes, they require constant tracking which can be arduous. The reward is an extraordinary opportunity to observe the gorillas at close range. The gorillas are not tame, but they have been scientifically habituated to accept the presence of quiet and unthreatening observers. (We may also encounter groups of unhabituated gorillas during our stalks, but they will run from us). We can expect to observe the animals for an hour to an hour-and-a-half after we have first found them.

DAY 7: We climb Visoke Volcano (12,139') through the montane forest and an upper forest zone characterized by magnificent moss-

B

C

D

> **In very small groups, we'll be able to sit down right in the midst of these gentle apes, observing them in their daily activities.**

strewn hagenia trees and giant St. John's worts (hypercium). Still higher, we reach the zone of Africa's bizarre alpine vegetation: giant groundsels (senecios) and lobelias growing amidst a profusion of everlasting flowers. Nowhere in East Africa is this alpine zone vegetation as lush and mysteriously beautiful as on the misty heads of the Virunga

A

Volcanoes. Descend through a valley filled with untouched hagenia-hypercium woodland, prime gorilla habitat. We may also see bushbuck, duicker, forest buffalo, golden monkeys and possibly elephant.

DAY 8: Another morning to search for gorillas. Short afternoon drive, enjoying magnificent views of jagged Mikeno Volcano and the still-active Nyorangonga (in Zaire). Overnight at Gisenye, on the shores of beautiful Lake Kivu, nestled between the rugged hills of Rwanda and Zaire.

DAY 9: Drive to Kigali and fly to Nairobi, Kenya. Transfer to hotel.

DAY 10 and 11: Drive to Samburu/Shaba Game Reserve. Explore dramatic semi-desert country looking for endemic species—Grevy's pin-striped zebra, reticulated giraffe, beisa oryx and diminutive dikdik. Watch elephant herds bathe in the palm-fringed Uaso Nyiro River.

DAY 12: We visit the forests of the Aberdares, where we stay at the Ark Lodge. We enjoy extended nighttime viewing of animals, often including such rarities as rhino and bongo.

DAY 13: Drive over the top of the Aberdares Mountains and descend to the Rift Valley. Overnight at Lake Naivasha.

DAY 14 to 16: Fabulous game viewing in Kenya's premier park, the Masai Mara Game Reserve. Here we find and photograph a huge variety of animals of the plains savannah. Herds of topi, gazelle, zebra, buffalo, large prides of lion, cheetah, hyena and rhino can all be found.

DAY 17: Return drive to Nairobi.

DAY 18: Day free in Nairobi. Late evening depart Nairobi on homeward-bound flights.

DAY 19: Arrive home.

B

IT3BA1YO13

RUWENZORIS: THE "MOUNTAINS OF THE MOON"

DATES: Jul 1–Jul 19 (19 days)
LEADER: to be announced
GRADE: B-3/C-3
LAND COST: $2290 (8–12 members)

Since ancient times, legends of the mist-shrouded Ruwenzori Mountains nestled in the heart of the African continent have stimulated the imaginations of armchair geographers and intrepid adventurers alike.

Ptolemy named them the "Mountains of the Moon" and thought that they contained the long-sought source of the Nile. Generations of Greek, Roman and Arab explorers told fantastic stories of snow-covered equatorial mountains inhabited by hairy giants. The geographic questions were finally solved by Stanley, one of Africa's greatest explorers, who applied a native name to the range: Ruwenzori, "The Rainmaker."

Impenetrable jungle (home of chimpanzees) surrounds the range. Hot air rising from tropical forests enshrouds the mountains in perpetual swirling mists. Vegetation which is normally quite small in temperate climates has grown riotously luxuriant on the mist-soaked Ruwenzori ridges. Tree-sized groundsels, lobelia and other bizarre flora, all heavily moss-laden, abound in vertical bogs.

There are six Ruwenzori peaks rising to over 15,000 feet and carrying permanent snow and glaciers. The highest is Mt. Stanley (16,673'), first climbed by the Italian Duke of Abruzzi in 1906.

We begin our expedition by exploring the scenic area around Goma in eastern Zaire, enjoying the beauty of Lake Kivu. We hike up Nyiragongo Volcano, still quite active and named for a fiery local god. Camping on the crater rim, we may be treated to a pyrotechnic display in the volcano's bubbling lava lake. We then enjoy superb wildlife viewing by vehicle along the shores of Lake Albert in Virunga National Park.

Commencing our rugged seven-day trekking expedition in the Ruwenzoris, we approach through the wet forests of the western slopes where resident wildlife includes elephant and leopard. Porters will carry our gear, and our accommodations will be in mountain huts or tents. We will attempt to trek up onto the glacial moraine of Mt. Stanley. Conditions permitting, members experienced in glacier travel can attempt to climb to Point Margharita, the highest of Mt. Stanley's nine separate summits.

These peaks are very seldom frequented by climbers or trekkers due to their remoteness and the difficulties of terrain and climate. This is an expedition for the true African explorer.

ITINERARY:

DAY 1 to 3: Leave U.S. Arrive Goma, Zaire. Transfer to hotel.

DAY 4: Hike to summit of Nyiragongo Volcano and camp on the crater rim.

DAY 5: Explore the lava flows of Nyirongongo. Return to Goma for overnight.

DAY 6 to 8: Wildlife viewing in Zaire's Virunga National Park, a lake environment which supports elephant, buffalo, topi, lion and hippos.

DAY 9: Drive to Mutsora, starting point for the Ruwenzori trek.

DAY 10 to 15: Trekking in the "Mountains of the Moon."

DAY 16: Return to Goma for some well-deserved relaxation

> **Generations of Greek, Roman and Arab explorers told fantastic stories of snow-covered equatorial mountains inhabited by hairy giants.**

DAY 17: Fly to Kinshasha, modern capital of Zaire.

DAY 18: Depart Kinshasha and connect with homeward-bound flights.

DAY 19: Arrive home.

C

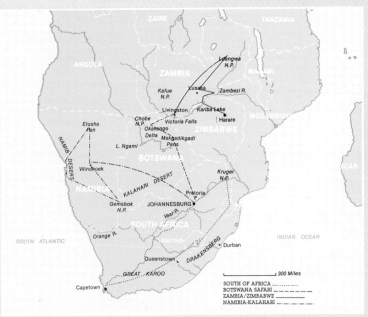

IT3BA1YO14

ZAMBIA/ ZIMBABWE EXPEDITION

DATES: *#1 May 29–Jun 18 (21 days)
   *#2 Aug 7–Aug 27 (21 days)
LEADER: Ned St. John
GRADE: B-1
LAND COST: $2350 (8-12 members)
*Note date change from 1984 Trip Schedule

This special new safari offers unique gameviewing possibilities from houseboats, canoes and on foot in a spectacular region of Africa.

A scenic charter flight takes us to Matusadona National Park. Backed by the steep foothills of the Matusadona Range and facing man-made Lake Kariba, the park is known for its uniquely beautiful tree silhouettes in the flooded forests along its shores. This area is a photographer's and birdwatcher's paradise. Staying in houseboats on a river tributary of the lake, we'll take game viewing excursions, boat along the shoreline, and walk into the mopane scrub forest of the national park. Game likely to be seen includes impala, kudu, rhino, lion, eland and sable.

A five-day canoe safari on the Zambesi River gives a thrilling perspective on African bush game as we glide past hippo pools and sunning crocodiles, watching elephant and cape buffalo grazing along the banks. This historic river figured prominently in the epic explorations of Livingston and Stanley. We'll paddle down it in stable, easy-to-maneuver two-man canoes and camp under the stars at night.

In Zambia's Luangwa Valley National Park, we'll undertake an exciting five-day foot safari, hiking to remote bush camps through a national park which is home to 60,000 elephant, 2,000 black rhino, and vast herds of buffalo. Hippos and crocodiles abound in the Luangwa River, and there are more than 400 species of birds in the park.

Our last stop is famous Victoria Falls, with the option of a one-day Zambesi whitewater adventure.

ITINERARY:
DAY 1 to 3: Leave U.S. Arrive Harare, Zimbabwe. Transfer to hotel.

DAY 4: Morning flight to Kariba. Connect with charter flight to Matusadona National Park. Transfer to houseboat accommodations on Lake Kariba.

DAY 5 and 6: Game viewing excursions by boat and on foot from Matusadona House Boat Camp.

DAY 7: Morning charter flight back to Kariba. Begin five-day canoe trip on the Zambesi River. Canoe from the Kariba Gorge to Nyamuomba Island.

DAY 8: Full day on the Zambesi, reaching Chirundu in the late afternoon.

DAY 9: A more relaxed day with

time to spend on extended "drifts" and refreshing stops under shady trees. Camp at Kakomakamorara Hill.

> **A five-day canoe safari on the Zambesi River gives a thrilling perspective on African bush game as we glide past hippo pools and sunning crocodiles, watching elephant and cape buffalo grazing along the banks.**

DAY 10: Continue the canoe safari as the Zambesi flows into a wilder area and more wildlife is encountered. Reach Rukomeche River in the late afternoon and camp.

DAY 11: End river journey in the afternoon at Nyamepi Camp in Mana Pools National Park. Transfer to Chikwenya Camp. Late afternoon game drives by landrover.

DAY 12: Game drives and walks from Chikwenya Camp in Mana Pools National Park.

DAY 13: Drive to Lusaka for charter flight to Zambia's Luangwa Valley. Overnight at Chibembi Camp.

DAY 14 to 17: Foot safari in Luangwa Valley.

DAY 18: Fly by charter to Lusaka, continue by air to Livingston, and transfer to Victoria Falls Hotel.

DAY 19: Optional excursions at the falls. Overnight at Victoria Falls Hotel.

DAY 20 Fly to Harare. Late evening depart for London and connect with homeward-bound flights.

DAY 21: Arrive home.

A

B

IT4PA1SFMT14

NAMIBIA-KALAHARI EXPLORATION

DATES: *#1 Apr 28–May 18 (21 days)
   #2 Sep 8–Sep 28 (21 days)
LEADER: Chris MacIntyre
GRADE: B-1
LAND COST: $2190 (12-13 members)
   $2390 (6-11)
*Note change from 1984 Trip Schedule.

Namibia (South West Africa) is one of the least known parts of the African continent. A former German colony on the southern tip of the Atlantic coast, it contains some amazing environments: the Namib Desert, with its towering dunes in vivid colors, the vast thornland of the Kalahari Desert, the Fish River Canyon ("Grand Canyon" of Africa), and the eerie Skeleton Coast, so called for the treachery of its fog-bound shores, where countless ships have wrecked while rounding the Cape. This southwestern tip of the continent is home to hardy wildlife like the noble gemsbok and mountain zebra, which cling miraculously to sparse desert niches.

A major safari highlight is Etosha National Park, recently celebrated in a *National Geographic* television special. The vast salt pan of Etosha is a wildlife paradise where herds of delicate springbok dot the land and elephants emerge from the shimmering haze of the salt pan like distant ships approaching land. Both prey and predator thrive near each water hole. Giraffe, kudu, cheetah, lion and plenty of small game are found here.

We also explore Namib Desert Park, where ocean-born fog is the only moisture to reach its unique plants and wildlife, and Fish River Canyon, little known outside Africa but as spectacular in its savage rock-hewn grandeur as our own Grand Canyon.

At Kalahari-Gemsbok National Park, named for the graceful oryx of the southern deserts, we should encounter cheetah, bat-eared foxes, secretary birds, kori bustard, large herds of springbok and the Kalahari lion.

ITINERARY:
DAY 1 and 2: Leave U.S. Arrive Johannesburg. Transfer to airport hotel.

DAY 3: Continue by air to Windhoek, capital of Namibia, a small, very modern city with its blend of Namibian peoples: Afrikaners, Germans, English, Namas (Hottentots), Hereros and Ovambos.

DAY 4: Drive northward through bush country to Etosha National Park.

DAY 5 to 7: Three full days at Etosha National Park. We'll wait near the waterholes to watch the parade of animals come to drink. Lion, jackals, hyena and cheetah may be seen as well as black rhino and the very rare blackfaced impala. The birdlife at

A

Etosha is always very impressive.

DAY 8: Drive south through dry bush country, explore a forest of petrified wood and look for Bushman rock engravings.

DAY 9: Drive through increasingly desolate country to the Skeleton Coast, whose shores were much feared by sailing men. To be shipwrecked here meant certain death because the land behind the beach holds no fresh water.

> **The vast salt pan of Etosha is a wildlife paradise where herds of delicate springbok dot the land and elephants emerge from the shimmering haze of the salt pan like distant ships approaching land.**

DAY 10: A full day exploring the Skeleton Coast. We may be able to find shipwrecks locked in the sands.

DAY 11: Drive southward along the Skeleton Coast, with a possible visit to the great colonies of southern fur seals found at Cape Cross. Arrive at Swakopmund, a town that maintains much of its German colonial character.

DAY 12 and 13: Enter the Namib Desert, one of the driest deserts in the world. We may be lucky enough to encounter gemsbok and the rare Hartman's mountain zebra. Explore the moonscape of the eroded bed of the Swakop River.

DAY 14: Drive to Sossusvlei, scenic bed of a seasonal lake which is surrounded by the highest sand dunes in the world (up to 1000 feet). Hike to the dunes for spectacular views of the desert landscape.

DAY 15: Drive to Fish River Canyon National Park, camping on the rim of the canyon.

DAY 16: Hike down to the floor of the canyon and spend the day exploring and possibly swimming in Fish River.

DAY 17: Drive to Kalahari Gemsbok National Park.

DAY 18: A full day to explore Kalahari Gemsbok National Park, with its bare dunes interspersed with thornbush.

DAY 19: Drive back to Windhoek.

DAY 20: Fly to Johannesburg. Afternoon free. Evening depart Johannesburg on homeward-bound flights.

DAY 21: Arrive home.

IT4PA1SFMT13

THE BOTSWANA SAFARI

DATES: #1 May 18-Jun 4 (18 days)
#2 Jul 27-Aug 13 (18 days)
#3 Oct 5-Oct 22 (18 days)
LEADER: #1 & #3 Chris MacIntyre
#2 Allen Bechky
GRADE: B-1
LAND COST: $2190 (5-13 members)

A safari into northern Botswana is a true expedition, a journey into a very wild and remote land. We'll travel by four-wheel drive vehicle, carrying our own mobile camps, and visit all of Botswana's great wildlife areas.

We begin with a camp in the Makgadikgadi Pans, where we meet the wildlife of the open plains: gemsbok, zebra and gnu. Here we sharpen our senses to the pleasures of the "veld"—the rush of zebra through high grass, and pink mirage that materializes into a throng of flamingos, the unfamiliar night sounds around our campfire. Game sometimes congregate here in such great numbers that Makgadikgadi is called a "southern Serengeti."

In the celebrated Okavango Delta, we travel by boat to enjoy the environs of this great swamp, a gentle, timeless wilderness where lechwe stamp through the grassy shallows, sitatunga take shelter in the reeds, and hippo and crocs reside in the clear black waters. The birdlife is spectacular.

We also visit Moremi Wildlife Reserve and the famed Savuti Channel, whose waters attract fantastic concentrations of game.

We end with a safari in the "big game" woodlands of Chobe National Park (elephant country at its finest) and a visit to Mosi-oa-Tunya ("The Smoke That Thunders"), better known as Victoria Falls.

ITINERARY:

DAY 1 and 2: Leave U.S. Arrive Johannesburg, South Africa. Transfer to hotel.

DAY 3 and 4: Charter flight to Botswana and proceed into the game reserves of Makgadikgadi Pans or Nxai Pans. (Our exact destination will depend on the seasonal migration of game.) In this area, we shall see animals of the open grass plains like wildebeest and zebra, as well as gemsbok, the beautiful oryx of the deserts of southern Africa. When the pans hold water, they are a paradise for birds, often hosting great masses of flamingos.

DAY 5: Dawn explorations around camp then drive through the plains of north central Botswana to Maun, for a charter flight into Xaxaba Camp in the Okavango Delta. Here in crystal clear waters, the magnificent fish eagle is a common sight, as are a wide variety of storks, herons, ibises and other water birds including pygmy geese and malachite kingfishers. Larger wildlife includes lechwe and sitatunga, hippo and crocodile are common.

DAY 6 and 7: We board makoros, the traditional dugout canoes of the Delta natives, and paddle into the waterways of the Delta, for fishing, swimming and wildlife viewing. We explore the larger Delta islands on foot.

DAY 8: Paddle our makoros back to Xaxaba for an afternoon charter flight back to Maun. We may have time to explore Maun, meet people of the Tswana and Herero tribes, and the colorful bush characters who frequent Botswana's safari capital.

DAY 9 to 11: Drive to Moremi Game Reserve, one of the most interesting and beautiful reserves of southern Africa. Antelope such as sassaby, kudu, roan and impala can be found here, as well as buffalo, elephant and the ever elusive predators: lion, cheetah, leopard, and wild dog. We spend three days in the reserve, for game drives, explorations on foot and swimming.

DAY 12 and 13: Drive northward into the drier bush country of the Mababe Depression, a section of Chobe National Park. We camp

B

along the Savuti Channel, an impermanent waterway which holds the floodwater spill of the Chobe River. The numbers of hippo and elephants in this area can be very impressive. In the bushier areas, we have good chances to encounter the magnificent sable antelope, as well as kudu and roan. Camping along the Savuti Channel is always an experience, as hippo, buffalo and elephant frequently graze through the camp and the roaring of lions is a common night sound.

DAY 14 and 15: Move to the Chobe River, elephant country par excellence. We may see congregations numbering in the hundreds. We hope to see the beautifully marked Chobe bushbuck here, and perhaps find colonies of Carmine bee-eaters.

DAY 16: Drive across the Zimbabwe border to Victoria Falls. Check into the elegant Victoria Falls Hotel and visit this spectacular waterfall which has a flow of more than 200 million gallons per minute in flood!

DAY 17: Optional excursions around Victoria Falls. Evening depart Johannesburg on homeward-bound flights.

DAY 18: Arrive home.

> **A safari into northern Botswana is a true expedition, a journey into a very wild and remote land.**

IT4PA1SFMT15

THE SOUTH OF AFRICA

DATES: #1 Mar 7–Mar 27 (21 days)
    *#2 Aug 8–Aug 28 (21 days)
    #3 Nov 7–Nov 27 (21 days)
LEADER: Chris MacIntyre
GRADE: A-2
LAND COST: $2390 (8–15 members)
+ "Blue Train" fare $299–$561
*Note change from 1984 Trip Schedule

By pony, by landrover and on foot, this is a journey of discovery in the South of Africa, a region with a spectacular landscape and a justly-famed variety of African wildlife, protected in the oldest game reserves on the continent.

Much of the fascination of this part of Africa, chronicled in James Michener's recent best-seller, *The Covenant*, lies in observing the rich diversity of cultures that have shaped the history of the continent. Zulu, Basutho, Swazi, Cape Dutch, English and Indian have all left their mark on the land.

We begin in Kruger National Park (Africa's oldest, established in 1898), celebrated for its variety of animals. We visit nearby Londolozi, which shares Kruger's magnificent fauna and has the advantage of being privately owned, allowing us the freedom to seek game on foot as well as by landrover.

We visit Swaziland, an independent African kingdom, and browse the Swazi markets for crafts, then continue to Umfolozi Game Reserve, situated in the heart of Zululand.

A

With a local Zulu-speaking guide, we will move from one Zulu village to another, meeting the people and perhaps observing a "coming of age" ceremony, a wedding or other local festivity.

Moving southwest to the Drakensburg Range, highest mountains of southern Africa, we visit the independent country of Lesotho to make a four-day pony trek through its mountainous highlands. En route, we ride across grassy plains, stop to swim in sparkling rivers, and enjoy the unique opportunity of meeting local villagers.

With three days in Capetown ("the Fairest Cape of them all"), we can hike to the top of Table Mountain, drive to the Cape of Good Hope, and visit wine country, where we'll stay in a traditional Cape Dutch homestead.

Return travel to Johannesburg is by the famed "Blue Train," one of the most prestigious and luxurious rail journeys in the world.

B

ITINERARY:

DAY 1 and 2: Leave U.S. Arrive Johannesburg. Overnight in airport hotel.

DAY 3 and 4: Fly to Nelspruit in the Transvaal *lowveld*, meet with trip leader and drive to Londolozi Game Reserve. Game drives and wildlife hikes.

DAY 5: Game viewing by vehicle in Kruger National Park.

DAY 6 and 7: Visit Swaziland, an independent kingdom, and Mlilwane National Park.

DAY 8 and 9: Visit Umfolozi Game reserve and Zululand.

DAY 10: Travel to Nk Walini and drive by bush vehicle into the more remote areas of Zululand, moving from village to village with a Zulu-speaking guide.

DAY 11: Drive to the Drankensburg Mountains. Overnight at lodge.

DAY 12: Travel to Maseru, capital of Lesotho, a mountainous land inhabited by the Basotho tribe.

DAY 13 to 16: Pony trekking in the mountains of Lesotho.

DAY 17 to 19: In Capetown area, with many optional side trips.

DAY 20: Board the "Blue Train" in the morning for the journey to Johannesburg.

DAY 21: Arrive Johannesburg in the morning. Afternoon visit to a gold mine. Evening depart Johannesburg on homeward-bound flights.

Moving southwest to the Drakensburg Range, highest mountains of southern Africa, we visit the independent country of Lesotho to make a four-day pony trek through its mountainous highlands.

C

D

A Ethiopian park ranger/Allen Bechky
B Camp in the Semyen Mountains, Ethiopia/Allen Bechky
C Rock-hewn church at Lalibela/Allen Bechky

IT3ETIMT4

THE ETHIOPIAN HIGHLANDS

DATES: #1 1 Mar 15–Apr 2 (19 days)
#2 Oct 4–Oct 22 (19 days)
LEADER: #1 Angela Gardner
#2 to be announced
GRADE: B-2
LAND COST: $2190 (10-15 members)
$2390 (7-9)

Ethiopia, the land that slept for 1,000 years as an early Christian enclave surrounded by a sea of Islam, possesses a vast store of Coptic Christian antiquities. There are also many natural wonders, such as the amba-studded mountain country of the Semyen, with its Grand Canyon-like scenery, and the Tississat Falls of the Blue Nile.

We first visit the much-storied Blue Nile at the place where it enters Lake Tana (6,000'). Here we'll hike to Tississat Falls (2nd in height only to Victoria Falls in southern Africa), and visit several ancient Coptic monasteries on Laka Tana.

On a five-day trek in the Semyen Mountains, we'll see Ethiopia's rare endemic wildlife: walia ibex, klipspringer, the Semyen fox, and lion-maned gelada baboons who live on the sheer walls of the Semyen cliffs. Pack animals will carry our camping gear.

After the trek, we visit Lalibela, with its amazing complex of 11th century churches, hewn underground out of solid rock. A living medieval site, the shrines at Lalibela still ring with the ceremonies of Coptic worship.

We finish our trip in lowland Ethiopia, with its largely Moslem population, visiting the market towns of Harrar and Dera Dawa.

NOTE: For those with additional time, we can offer an optional one-week extension to trek the remote Bale Mountains.

ITINERARY:

DAY 1 to 3: Leave U.S. Arrive Addis Ababa. Transfer to hotel.

DAY 4: Fly to Barhdar on the shores of Lake Tana and take a short hike to the base of the thundering Tississat Falls on the Blue Nile.

DAY 5: Boat cruise on Lake Tana (6,000'), highest lake in Ethiopia, to visit several beautifully decorated Coptic monasteries, which still practice a form of Christian worship founded in the 4th century A.D.

DAY 6: Fly to Gondar, seat of the 16th century empire of the Fasillide kings. We explore the castles of the royal enclosure and the church of Debre Berhan Selassie, with its beautiful 17th century frescoes depicting Biblical and Ethiopian scenes.

DAY 7: Drive to Debarek, and begin trek into the Semyen Mountains. Horses will be available for those who prefer to ride. Camp in Semyen National Park at Senkabar (9,500').

DAY 8: Trek through forests of giant heath, past Amharic villages finally emerging into the alpine country. Camp at 11,500 feet.

A living medieval site, the shrines at Lalibela still ring with the ceremonies of Coptic worship.

DAY 9: Day hike in the sub-alpine highlands, with views over the Semyen escarpment. Gelada baboons live on the edge of this abyss and the skies are alive with Augur buzzards, an unbelievable variety of corvid birds (white-naped ravens, pied crows, thick-billed ravens, choughs) and the spectacular Lammergeier vulture.

DAY 10: Trek back to Senkabar and watch for ibex on the giant heather along the escarpment.

DAY 11: Return to Debarek and drive back to Gondar, with a possible visit to a village of Falashas, a sect of Black Jews who trace their origins back to the time of King Solomon.

DAY 12: Fly to Lalibela, a highland village featuring an 11th century underground church complex. The Christian churches were chiseled down into the limestone bedrock of the ground in order to hide them from the view of marauding Muslim aries. Con-

nected by underground tunnels, they are among the holiest sites in Ethiopia, greatly animated by the current-day activities of priests, monks and pilgrims.

DAY 13: Hike several hours through rugged hill country to the rock-hewn Church of Ganeta Mariam, another of King Lalibela's creations.

DAY 14: Fly back to Addis, and visit the National Museum, which features the remains of "Lucy," the earliest discovered remains of the genus homo (man).

DAY 15: Fly to Dire Dawa and drive to Harrar, a city of Islamic tribespeople founded in the 7th century. Its charm, which induced the French poet Rimbaud to settle there for a time, is not diminished today. We'll pass through the ancient city gates into a bazaar of narrow streets thronged with colorfully attired shoppers.

DAY 16: Afternoon drive to Kulubi to visit St. Gabriel's Church. Continue to Dire Dawa.

DAY 17: By train to Addis.

DAY 18: Depart Addis on homeward-bound flights.

DAY 19: Arrive home.

IT1AF155RZ

TIMBUKTU AND BEYOND

DATES: *Jan 6–Jan 28 (23 days)
LEADER: to be announced
GRADE: A-1
LAND COST: $3090 (8–15 members)
*Note change from 1984 Trip Schedule.

It was only a matter of time before Mountain Travel went to Timbuktu, that sandy city of legend made famous by the French Foreign Legion and by its very remoteness.

Timbuktu was once an important watering stop for the camel cara- vans traveling from Arabia to the Atlantic, but nowadays nobody stops in Timbuktu anymore, except maybe thirsty drivers on the famous Paris-to-Dakar road rally which roars past once a year.

Although the name Timbuktu may entice, the real attractions of this trip will be meeting the diverse tribes of western Africa, and ob- serving life along the Niger River, which forms a geographical and cultural frontier between the sands of the southern Sahara and west Africa's savannah—the *sahel* zone.

Driving out on the lonely Gossi Track from Niamey (capital of Niger), we'll cross a parched land where Touareg nomads on camels may appear out of nowhere to visit our nightly camps. Reaching Sangha, the landscape is more fertile and farmers of the Dogon tribe grow maize, millet and fra- grant onions.

At the town of Mopti, with its harbor on the wide Niger River, we'll see all the different tribal people of Mali come to sell goods in a busy market place.

Djenne, also on the Niger River, is a fascinating town dominated by the most beautiful mosque in western Africa. Most of the people around Djenne are of the semi- nomadic Peul tribe, and during the annual floods of the Niger Delta, their town becomes an island.

Our tour reaches Bamako, capital of Mali, then circles back to Niamey via Timbuktu.

Niger and Mali are countries which are slowly emerging into the modern world; while the countryside is beautiful and the people are very friendly, please be prepared for very primitive conditions, as well as long days on the road.

ITINERARY:
DAY 1 and 2: Leave U.S. Arrive Paris and fly to Niamey.
DAY 3: Arrive Niamey, Niger. Transfer to hotel.
DAY 4: Begin our overland adven- ture with a drive to Ayorou, a small village in the Niger Valley populated by the Sonhai tribe and known for its lively market where thousands of zebus (Indian ox), sheep and goat are sold each week.
DAY 5: Drive to Gao, crossing the border into Mali, following along the Niger River. As we approach

Gao, the surrounding brush begins to get paler in color and then gives way to the golden sands of the Sahara. The intense green waters of the Niger River present a striking contrast to the sands of the Sahara. We'll see the Laptot tribe, sailors of the Niger, poling their long pirogues (dugout canoes) along the water. Camp overnight.

DAY 6 to 9: For the next four days, our landrovers will take us across a wide stretch called the "Gossi Track," a road which is merely tire tracks in the hardened sand. We'll camp en route. This region is seemingly uninhabited, but our nightly camps may be visited by small groups of nomadic Touar- egs, blue-robed desert dwellers pushing their herds along in their continuous search for water. This road is tough going even for land- rovers and we may all have to pitch in and help with pushing the vehicle should it get stuck in soft sections of the track.

DAY 10 and 11: Arrive at Mopti, a market town where the Niger and Bani rivers meet. We'll visit the harbor and see a fantastic variety of tribal peoples at the market, then explore the village of Sangha, where clusters of old houses are perched along a high cliff overlooking the valley.

DAY 12: Reach the town of Djenne, which is built on high land in the Niger River (and during the an- nual Niger floods, stands as an island). It is dominated by a beau- tiful mosque and we'll have time to stroll along the cool, narrow streets of this history-filled town.

A

EXPLORATOR
NORTH AFRICA & THE MIDDLE EAST

Mountain Travel is North American repre- sentative for EXPLORATOR, the major French adventure firm. Owned and managed by Jean Picon, EXPLORATOR'S odysseys range throughout the world and extensively in North Africa & the Middle East. These trips are not as "trekking" oriented as ours and instead often feature jeep travel and over- landing. Many of their leaders are English- speaking. We think EXPLORATOR's journeys capture the spirit of adventure and will be of interest to Mountain Travel enthusiasts. If you would like to join one of their trips, write to us for a copy of the current EXPLORATOR catalog (text in French) and we'll arrange the rest.

DAY 13 to 17: On these five days, we'll circle south to Segou, cross the Niger River and continue along its northern banks finally reaching remote Timbuktu, where we'll spend two days.

DAY 18 and 19: Push west back to Gao, completing our long over- land circle. Camp en route.

DAY 20 and 21: Continue driving back to Niamey. Overnight in hotel.

DAY 22: Day free. Late evening depart Niamey on homeward- bound flight.

DAY 23: Arrive home.

> Driving out on the lonely Gossi Track from Niamey (capital of Niger), we'll cross a parched land where Touareg nomads on camels may appear out of nowhere to visit our nightly camps.

IT2BA1Y033

SUDAN: THE NILE & THE NUBIAN DESERT

DATES: Nov 13–Dec 1 (19 days)
LEADER: to be announced
GRADE: A-2
LAND COST: $1990 (8–15 members)

We invite you to discover Sudan, a country visited often by archae- ologists and ethnologists, and seldom (if ever) by tourists.

The beauty of this country lies no just in the wild Nubian Desert with its volcanic summits, long pla- teaus and the ever-changing pat- terns of its ochre and yellow dunes, but in its civilizations, past and present.

As we journey for eleven days by landrover along the Nile and across the desert, we'll see the im pressive remains of royal cities, pyramids and temples dating back 5,000 years, the vestiges of such kingdoms as Meroe and Kush.

At Naga, we'll see surprising ruins which combine the art of Rome, Greece and Egypt. At the royal city of Meroe, we'll walk amidst Roman baths and hundreds of pyramids and try to imagine how verdant and populous this land once was.

Crossing the Nile, we'll admire temples to the God Amun. Furthe along in Argo, we'll see wonderfu Nubian clay houses and find the oldest ruin in Sudan: Kerma, built around 4,000 B.C. and still an enigma to archaeologists.

We'll also have a look at present- day civilization in Sudan, as we wander through the villages of the Nile, seeing the rich riverside gardens and orchards and enjoy ing the celebrated hospitality of the Nubian people.

ITINERARY:
DAY 1 and 2: Leave U.S. Arrive

B

C

A Pyramid ruin at Meroe/Jean Ribat
B Sudanese children/Jean Ribat
C Overland in the Sahara/Jean Ribat

ALGERIA • 19

A

IT4PA1SFMT5

THE SAHARA OVERLAND

DATES: Nov 28–Dec 15 (18 days)
LEADER: to be announced
GRADE: B-1
LAND COST: $2450 (8–15 members)

A desert odyssey by jeep, this trip covers the full range of spectacular Saharan landscapes, including the wind-sculpted dunes of the Killian Erg and the sharp volcanic peaks of the Hoggar Mountains.

From the oasis town of Tamanrasset, we jeep past Touareg nomad encampments in sight of the huge, black and impressive basalt peaks of the Hoggar Mountains, then visit the high refuge of Father de Foucauld, situated at 10,000 feet on the Assekrem Plateau, overlooking the Hoggar Range.

After a visit to the town of Djanet, we drive along wild ravines and sandy washes where gazelles graze as we head for the well of In Afaleleh, an important stopping point for Touareg nomad caravans on their way to Niger. In the Tenere Desert, we'll discover Mt. Gauthiers, a fairy-tale peak on the "shore" of the vast sandy sea of the Tenere. Our final lap takes us through the dramatic dune country of the Killian Erg.

ITINERARY:
DAY 1 and 2: Leave U.S. Arrive Paris and fly to Algiers. Transfer to hotel.
DAY 3: Fly to Tamanrasset. Transfer to hotel.
DAY 4: Jeep northwards toward the Hoggar Range. Hike to the refuge of Father Charles de Foucauld.

DAY 5 and 6: Leaving the Assekrem Plateau, we head northeast through a hilly landscape to a small oasis.
DAY 7 and 8: Reach the Fadnouin Plateau and explore the rock paintings at Tintehert. Continue on a winding track to the rock towers of Tin Teradjeli, then on through sand and rose-laurels to Oued Essendilene, along the eastern edge of the Admer Erg, arriving at the town of Djanet in the afternoon. Overnight at grass hut accommodations.

A desert odyssey by jeep, this trip covers the full range of spectacular Saharan landscapes, including the wind-sculpted dunes of the Killian Erg and the sharp volcanic peaks of the Hoggar Mountains.

DAY 9: Visit a site of neolithic engravings in Terarart and camp near the well at In Afaleleh.
DAY 10: Arrive at Mt. Gauthiers in the Tenere Desert by mid-day and camp nearby.
DAY 11: A day of hiking around the spectacular rock massif of Mt. Gauthiers.
DAY 12 and 13: Head south across the great dunes of the Killian Erg, farthest extension of the Tenere Desert. Arrive at the stone citadels of Tahaggart.
DAY 14: Morning hike in Tahaggart, then drive across the dunes of the Tin Tarabin Erg to the Tassili Tin Meskor. Camp in the Tagrera grottos.
DAY 15: Hiking in the Tagrera region.
DAY 16: A long and final day's jeeping to reach Tamanrasset.
DAY 17: Fly to Algiers and on to Paris. Overnight at hotel.
DAY 18: Depart Paris on homeward-bound flights.

C

...aris. Overnight at hotel.
DAY 3: Fly to Khartoum, Sudan. Transfer to hotel.
DAY 4: Visit the wonderful museum of Khartoum, then travel by land-rover to the 6th cataract on the Nile.
DAY 5: Jeep to Naga, where there are surprising archaeological remains. A Roman kiosk and Egyptian-inspired temple here give a good impression of the once-great kingdom of Meroe. We also visit Musawarat, with its temples and ruined castles.
DAY 6: Explore ruins of the royal city of Meroe. It's difficult to envision how this land once supported a large civilization, since it is now a windswept desert.
DAY 7: Cross the Nile to the Bayuda Desert.
DAY 8: Visit ruins, among which is the high pyramid of Taharka, Nubian pharaoh of Egypt.
DAY 9: We spend a day exploring the villages along the banks of the Nile, which have orchards of grapefruit, oranges, limes, and fields of vegetables. Cross the Nile to visit pyramid sites and a temple to the god Amun.
DAY 10: Leave the Nile Valley and head through the desert to the city of Argo.

DAY 11: Visit the oldest ruin in Sudan, Kerma, whose origin is unknown.

The beauty of this country lies not just in the wild Nubian Desert with its volcanic summits, long plateaus and the ever-changing patterns of its ochre and yellow dunes, but in its civilizations, past and present.

DAY 12: Onward to the Third Cataract, with its Egyptian temple sites.
DAY 13 and 14: Cross the Nile once more and reach Dongola, the main city of northern Sudan, which until the 14th-15th century formed a stronghold against the Muslim attempts to conquer East Africa.
DAY 15 and 16: Drive back to Khartoum through the desert. Overnight in hotel.
DAY 17: Free day in Khartoum for sightseeing and shopping.
DAY 18: Fly Khartoum/Paris and connect with homeward-bound flights.
DAY 19: Arrive home.

B

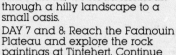

A Neolithic rock painting/Alla Schmitz
B Lunch stop in the Sahara/Alla Schmitz
C Across the Hoggar/Alla Schmitz

IT4PA1SFMT5

SAHARA CAMEL EXPEDITION

DATES: #1 Jan 28–Feb 14 (18 days)
#2 Oct 30–Nov 16 (18 days)
LEADER: Jean Louis Bernezat
GRADE: B-2
LAND COST: $2100 (8–15 members)

The Sahara, the largest desert in the world, is not an unending sea of sand, as fiction and film would have us believe. It has an infinite variety of landscapes: rock-ribbed plateaus, sandstone canyons, the volcanic Hoggar Mountains, beach-like golden washes filled with oleander, tamarisk, acacia-thorn trees, date palms, and many wildflowers.

We will travel a mountainous region of the Sahara—the Hoggar Mountains—by camel and on foot, enjoying the mystique of the Sahara and experiencing the way of life of our nomadic Tou-areg guides, the blue-robed "nobles of the desert."

Our circular trek from Tamanras-set will last two weeks, traveling around the central Atakor pillar, a geological remnant dating back to the Pre-Cambrian era. There are rock carvings, paintings, archae-ological remains, unclimbed domes, basalt gorges, awesome volcanic spires, shifting sands and erosion-carved river beds.

We will also hike up to the famous hermitage of Father Charles de Foucauld, 10,000 feet high on the summit of the Assekrem Plateau. Experienced climbers may climb one or more of the famous Hog-gar peaks, such as the Tezouiaig.

We will sleep under the stars, as there is no need for tents. NOTE: no previous camel riding experi-ence is required!

B

ITINERARY:

DAY 1 and 2: Leave U.S. Arrive Paris. Transfer to flight to Algiers, Algeria. Transfer to hotel.

DAY 3: Fly to the oasis town of Tamanrasset. Overnight at hotel.

DAY 4: Early morning rendezvous with our Touareg guides and
C

There are rock carvings, paintings, archaeological remains, unclimbed domes, basalt gorges, awesome volcanic spires, shifting sands and erosion-carved river beds.

camels, and set off into the desert, traversing the plain of Tam. Camp near the Daouda, a magnificent rock spire.

DAY 5: Follow the Oued ("dry river bed") Takecherouat through a setting of enormous and beautiful granite boulders. Cross a series of small passes and plains, and camp at the base of the rocky hills of Aleheg, where there are neolithic engravings of cattle and hunters as well as grafitti in Tifinar (the written language of the Touaregs).

DAY 6: Today we can either go north around the massif of Aleheg with our camel caravan, or send the camels by another route while we hike across Aleheg Mountain on foot for some beautiful views. Camp in Oued In Dalag ("Place of the Palm Trees").

DAY 7: Cross a plateau to large dry riverbeds bordered by green tamarisks.

DAY 8: Along Oued Isigen toward the beautiful peak of Aguelzam. Afternoon at leisure, or for those who wish, an easy climb up Aguelzam for panoramic views.

DAY 9: Heading east, we'll see a multitude of sharp peaks, each more needle-like than the next. We'll spend the day walking around the base of the peaks and into the gorge of Terara with its fine neolithic drawings of giraffes.

DAY 10: Across a narrow pass where an epic battle among the Touaregs took place around 1880. We'll see many old gravesites. The path ascends to the Assekrem Plateau. Side hike to see some engravings.

DAY 11: Today we arrive at the foot of the Tezouiag (9,000'), among the most beautiful summits of Atakor. We leave the camels to go around the south side and hike up a pass with magnificent views. Descend the west slope and join the route which comes from Tam.

DAY 12: If possible, we will visit a small Touareg encampment en route. Optional hike up Saouinane, a beautiful volcano. Two-hour hike to Assekrem Plateau to visit the rock hermitage of Father Charles de Foucauld. In the afternoon, rejoin our camels at the foot of the Assekrem Pass.

DAY 13: Cross Aril Pass with majestic views of the summit of Ilaman, and descend past the old site of a battle between the Touaregs and the French Foreign Legion.

DAY 14: Up onto a plateau and descend the Oued Terhenanet.

DAY 15: Over a series of plateaus and plains bordered by smooth-faced mountains. Afternoon visit to the village of Tagmart, where we'll have a tea with some local Touaregs.

DAY 16: Arrive in the afternoon in Tamanrasset. Overnight at hotel.

DAY 17: Morning flight to Algiers. Overnight in hotel.

DAY 18: Fly Algiers/Paris and connect with homeward-bound flights.

IT4PA1SFMT6

TREKKING IN MOROCCO

DATES: May 18–Jun 2 (16 days)
LEADER: to be announced
GRADE: B-2
LAND COST: $1190 (10–15 members)
$1390 (6–9)

The great red city of Marrakech is a medley of thousand-year-old mud ramparts, olive groves, palm trees, ornate mosques and bazaars full of medieval delights. Above and behind this scene, some 60 miles distant, is the unbelievable sight of a wall of snowy mountains. This is the High Atlas, a range which runs for a thousand miles across Morocco, Algeria, and Tunisia.

The focus of the trip is a ten-day trek in the High Atlas, crossing a landscape of great escarpments, dry plateaus, and small villages of Berber farmers and shepherds.

In addition to enjoying Morocco's special mountain-and-desert scenery, we'll have much cultural interaction with our friendly Berber mountain guides and learn something of their way of life. Nights will be spent sleeping under the stars or in remote Berber villages, where we may be invited to share a meal of cous-cous and mint tea.

The hiking on the trip, though non-technical, will occasionally be strenuous (between altitudes of 6,000 and 10,000 feet).

ITINERARY:

DAY 1 and 2: Leave U.S. Arrive Marrakech. Overnight at hotel.

DAY 3: Free day in Marrakech.

DAY 4: By bus and truck to Iskattafem, across Tighist Pass (8,600'). Meet our Berber guides and their families and spend the night in a Berber home.

DAY 5: Mules are loaded with our gear and we begin trekking in a

beautiful valley, seeing many villagers working their fields and gardens. As the valley narrows we continue along terraced fields with views of the Mgoun Massif in the distance. Camp near a river at 7,200 feet.

> **The great red city of Marrakech is a medley of thousand-year-old mud ramparts, olive groves, palm trees, ornate mosques and bazaars full of medieval delights.**

DAY 6: Gently upwards to a pass crossing the summit of the Ighil N'Ikkis. From here we follow a ridge which leads us to another summit, Jbel Tarkeddit at 10,330 feet. Camp at 9,000 feet near the source of the Tessaout River.

A

DAY 7: Hike up and over N'Oumsoud Pass (11,800') and descend towards the sheep-grazing areas of Tagoulzit (8,500'), a green oasis-like pasture.

DAY 8: Walking through the gorges of the Tessaout River, with cliffs rising as much as 2,000 feet on either side, we ford the river from time to time. While the mules take a detour to avoid the waterfalls at the end of the gorges, we will continue to the village of Tasgaiwalt. Camp at 7,000 feet.

DAY 9: Continue along the Tessaout Valley through willows and poplars, crossing the river several times, and arrive at the beautiful village of Ichbakene, where houses are perched high above the river on a rocky promontory. Camp at Megdaz (6,000').

DAY 10: Cross a pass at 7,800 feet to the Taghout Valley, hiking through gorges and delightful terraced fields of grapevines, fig trees, and nut trees—a sharp contrast from the high arid pass which we have just crossed.

DAY 11: Continue along the river to the village of Tissili. Camp between Jbel Tignost and Aguenso N'Iss at 7,800 feet.

DAY 12: Cross a 10,000-foot pass and camp in a valley at Imi N'Isk (6,200').

DAY 13: Head up along red hillsides dotted with chestnut trees. Spectacular views of the Tarkeddit Range, the valleys of Ghougoult and the pass we crossed yesterday.

DAY 14: Our last day of trekking, we head down a valley to the Ait Bougemez River. Tonight we spend the evening at Iskattafem, celebrating and bidding farewell to our Berber friends.

DAY 15: By truck and bus back to Marrakech. Overnight at hotel.

DAY 16: Depart Marrakech and connect with homeward-bound flights.

B

IT4W14046

ANCIENT EGYPT

DATES: #1 Feb 12–Feb 27 (16 days)
#2 Oct 14–Oct 29 (16 days)
#3 Nov 4–Nov 19 (16 days)
LEADER: to be announced
GRADE: A-2
LAND COST: $1590 (11–16 members)
$1690 (8–10)

Herodutus wrote of Egypt in the 5th century A.D. "there is no other country which possesses such wonders." And that is still true today.

In Cairo, we visit the Great Pyramids, the Sphinx, and the Egyptian Museum of Antiquities (filled with King Tut's treasures). From Aswan, we visit Abu Simbel, site of the Nile-side temples of Ramses II. We then begin a special part of our Egypt tour, a leisurely four-day *felucca* sail on the Nile from Aswan to Luxor.

Our vessels for the sail will be feluccas, the traditional native open sailboats. Living on these little boats involves "roughing it" by Western standards. Toilet facilities are primitive, privacy is limited, and since there are no berths on the boat, we will sleep on the beaches at night. What the boats lack in comfort, they make up for in flexibility. We think they provide a far better Nile experience than the sterile cruise ships which are floating hotels. Egyptian sailors handle the boat and do all the cooking. We'll have a relaxed pace on the river, visiting the major temples on route, and meeting white-robed Nubians as they conduct the commerce of the Nile from their felucca boats.

Arriving at Luxor, where the legacy of the pharaohs is at its most astonishing, we'll discover the world of ancient Thebes, visiting the Valley of the Kings, Tutankhamen's tomb and other wonders.

All trips are escorted by a professional Egyptologist. Travel between Cairo and Aswan is by sleeper train.

NOTE: We can arrange a one-week trekking option in the Sinai or Judean Desert after the trip.

ITINERARY:

DAY 1 and 2: Leave U.S. Arrive Cairo and transfer to hotel.

DAY 3 and 4: Two full days sightseeing, including Egyptian Museum, Great Pyramids, and an excursion to Memphis, ancient capital of Lower Egypt and its necropolis, Sakarra. Evening of Day 4, board the night train to Aswan.

DAY 5: Arrive in Aswan about noon. Visit Kitchener Island, Elephantine Island and the Mausoleum of the Aga Khan.

DAY 6: Short morning flight to Abu Simbel. Visit the dramatic temples of Ramses II and his wife, Queen Nefertari. These Nile-side temples were dismantled by an international engineering project and reassembled several hundred feet above their original site to save them from the rising waters of Lake Nassar. Fly back to Aswan

and take a short sail to Philae, site of a lovely temple to Isis.

DAY 7 to 10: Board the felucca boats, our floating homes for the next four nights, and enjoy the quiet pleasures of the Nile, a beautiful river whose waters are edged by green palm thickets and flanked by golden desert escarpments. We'll stop each day to visit the major temples en route and have close contact with the friendly Nubian people living along the banks of the Nile, getting a glimpse into the lives of Egyptian shepherds and farmers. This experience is totally different than a Nile cruise in a big luxury liner.

> **Our vessels for the sail will be feluccas, the traditional native open sailboats. Living on these little boats involves "roughing it" by Western standards.**

DAY 11: Arrive in Luxor, bid our felucca crew goodbye, and transfer to a hotel for showers and cleanup.

DAY 12 and 13: Visit the "Thebes Necropolis," Valley of the Kings, Queens and Nobles, funerary temples of Queen Hatshepsut and Ramses III, the tombs of Ramses IV and Tutankhamen, and the extensive temple sites of Karnak and Luxor.

DAY 14: Morning visit to a small village; afternoon depart on the overnight train to Cairo.

DAY 15: Arrive in Cairo and transfer to hotel. Day free.

DAY 16: Depart Cairo and connect with homeward-bound fights.

Camel trekking in the Sinai/Allen Bechky
Bedouin guides/Allen Bechky
Petroglyphs in the Sinai/Allen Bechky

EGYPT • 23

4TW14047

EGYPTIAN SINAI CAMEL TREK

DATES: Dec 1–Dec 19 (19 days)
LEADER: to be announced
GRADE: B-2
LAND COST: *$1725 (13–15 members)
$1860 (9–12)
*Note increase from 1984 Trip Schedule.

This trip combines the delights of desert travel—austere landscapes, Bedouin campfires, oasis pools and star-studded nights—with the mystery of exploring the Mediterranean's last great wilderness, the Sinai.

Flying from Cairo to the coast of the Sinai Peninsula, we'll make a five-day trek with a camel cara-

van, then stop for a visit to St. Catherine's Monastery (with its Byzantine treasures) and a hike up Mt. Sinai. We then continue our desert trek for four more days, hiking through steep canyons and Bedouin encampments.

Our desert trek takes us through a multicolored sandstone region where flat valleys are strewn with huge, fantastically-shaped sandstone blocks. Traversing narrow canyons, swimming in clear, cool pools, visiting nomadic settlements and sleeping under the starry desert sky, we'll appreciate the mysterious power which the desert has always had over the human soul.

Bedouin mountain guides will ac-

company us; camels will carry our gear and be available for riding on some stretches.

After the trek, we tour some of the many wonders of ancient Egypt, including the Pyramids at Giza, Memphis and Sakara.

ITINERARY:
DAY 1 and 2: Leave U.S. Arrive Cairo and transfer to hotel.

DAY 3: Fly to Sharm al-Sheikh. Drive north along the coast, stopping to swim and snorkel at colorful coral reefs. Camp on the beach at the beautiful oasis of Dahab.

DAY 4: Visit the oasis of Bir Ugda and return to beach camp.

DAY 5: Meet with camel caravan and begin Sinai camel trek. Ride and hike through a canyon to the lovely oasis of Moyet Malha. Continue to the geologically interesting valley of Freia and camp.

DAY 6: Hike through the fantastically shaped and colorful sandstone canyons of the Laglug abu Arta ("Canyon of Colors"), ride and hike to the oases of Bir Biriya, Bir Sawra and Moyet Sawana.

DAY 7: Ride and hike over Ras al Galb Pass to the large oasis of Ein umm Ahmad, shared by the Tarabin and M'zeina tribes. Time for swimming in pools and visiting the Nawamis, a necropolis of well-preserved burial structures from the early Bronze Age (c. 3200 B.C.)

DAY 8: Day hike up the huge dome of Jabel Burga (3,800'), the highest peak in the area.

DAY 9: Hike out to the oasis of Ein Khodra, leave our Bedouin guides and camels, and proceed to St. Catherine's Monastery.

DAY 10: Day to visit the monastery and hike up Mt. Sinai.

> **Traversing narrow canyons, swimming in clear, cool pools, visiting nomadic settlements and sleeping under the starry desert sky, we'll appreciate the mysterious power which the desert has always had over the human soul.**

DAY 11: Begin another trek, this one starting with a hike up Jabal Abbass Basha for breathtaking views of the entire area. Descend the canyon of Wadi Shag and swim in its pools. Hike on through another canyon and camp in the gardens of the Tweita canyon.

DAY 12: Descend into a gorge and spend the day swimming in pools. Hike along a stream to our night's camp near the Bedouin encampment of Farsh Rumana.

DAY 13: Hike up Jabel Bab Peak for a magnificent westward view. Camp near a Bedouin garden in Wadi Jbal.

DAY 14: Walk through cultivated and steep canyons, hike up Jabel Ahmar and descend to the village of Milga.

DAY 15: Transfer to the Mt. Sinai airport and fly to Cairo. Overnight at hotel.

DAY 16 and 17: Two full days of sightseeing in Cairo and environs.

DAY 18: Depart Cairo and connect with homeward-bound flights.

DAY 19: Arrive home.

B

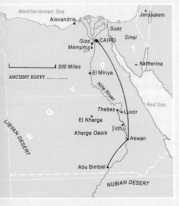

C

D

Traveling with a Touareg caravan in the Sahara/Alla Schmitz

EUROPE
& CENTRAL ASIA

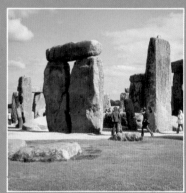

We see the continent of Europe as an ideal place for an outdoor adventure because of its easy access from America, and its still-pristine wilderness regions side by side with the creature comforts for which Europe is known.

Mountain Travel's journeys take in the full panoply of European adventure travel, from hikes and ski tours in Norway to mountain trekking in Turkey, a surprising country full of fabulous antiquities and beautiful mountains.

Our walking tours in Britain have been hailed for many years as a fine combination of hiking and sightseeing. We have successfully applied this walking/touring concept to many other regions of Europe, including Ireland, France, Spain, Germany and Switzerland.

In the Italian Alps, we have a comprehensive program of treks, from an easy walk in pastoral Piemonte foothills, to a rugged trek beneath the limestone spires of the Dolomites.

Most of our European trips don't involve backpacking but for those who want that challenge, we offer several backpacking expeditions and guided climbs in the French and Swiss Alps, the alpine wonderland where the sport of mountaineering was born 100 years ago.

In the U.S.S.R.'s Caucasus and in the Pamirs of Soviet Central Asia, we offer hiking and climbing camps which are unique and very reasonably priced.

With us, you'll see a Europe that you didn't think still existed, in many places where travelers may be a rarity. Our group sizes are very small—usually not more than 10, and our European leaders are superb and experienced guides.

1984 CALENDAR INDEX

Most of our 1984 trips will be repeated in 1985 on approximately the same dates.

LEADERSHIP

Our exceptionally talented staff of European trip leaders have skills, enthusiasm and an understanding of the local culture which adds immeasurably to the success of each trip.

MIKE BANKS, 57, is one of Britain's leading polar explorers and mountaineers. He was awarded the Polar Medal by Queen Elizabeth for his epic 800-mile crossing of the Greenland icecap and received the M.B.E. (Member of th Brifish Empire) for climbing Rakaposhi (25,550') without oxygen. He is the author of six books on the polar regions and mountaineering.
ROD BUNTZ, 63, is a retired colonel in the French Marine Corps and a world traveler who with his wife, Maryvonne leads the "Other France" walking tour

Mike Bank

Frozen wildflowers/Beppe Tenti

The Grandes Jorasses, Italian Alps

Wolfgang Koch

PIERRE JAMET, 50, of France, leads mountain treks and ski tours in France, Switzerland, Italy and Austria. A mathematics professor turned trekking guide, he has been a member of several climbing expeditions in Nepal and India.

BRUCE KLEPINGER, 42, has led more than 50 Mountain Travel treks in Asia and South America. His mountaineering background includes over 1,000 climbs, and he has led expeditions on Aconcagua (highest peak in the Western Hemisphere), Huascaran (highest peak in Peru), and several peaks in Nepal and India. Bruce also has ten years experience as a boatman on the Grand Canyon of the Colorado River and on several South American rivers.

WOLFGANG KOCH, 31, of Stuttgart, a chemist by profession, has been hiking, skiing and climbing in Europe for many years. He knows the German and Tyrolean Alps well and leads our Bavarian hiking tours.

MAKI IDOSIDIS, 36, is a Greek mountaineer who divides his time between living in Greece and the U.S. He knows Greece well, is a fine Greek dancer and leads our Greek sailing and hiking journeys.

JOHN NOBLE, 39, has taught mountaineering both in his native Britain and at Colorado Outward Bound. A Fellow of the Royal Geographic Society, he was Field Leader of the British Antarctic Survey and has led treks and ski-mountaineering expeditions in the Himalaya and the Alps.

PADDY O'LEARY, 47, director of Ireland's National Association for Adventure Sports, has 25 years of mountaineering experience in Britain and the Alps and has led expeditions in the Karakorum, Himalayas and Andes.

DAVE PARKER, 37, spent three years as a ski instructor in Norway, speaks fluent Norwegian and is a professional nordic guide as well as a member of the Mountain Travel reservations staff.

ALLEN STECK, 55, one of the founding partners of Mountain Travel, is a veteran mountaineer and one of America's pioneer rock climbers with first ascents throughout the world. He is co-author of *Fifty Classic Climbs*, a climbing guide for North America. Allen is also a noted Greek dancer and specializes in leading our "vagabond" trips in Greece.

MARTIN ZABALETA, 33, is a Basque mountaineer who in 1981 became the first Spaniard to climb to the summit of Mt. Everest. He has worked professionally as both a safari leader and climbing guide and has a passion for nature photography and Basque cuisine.

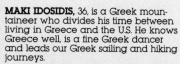

Rodolphe and Marie Buntz

Dave Parker

Maki Idosidis

Allen Steck

Martin Zabaleta

"Scrambles In The Alps"

A

IT4PA1SFMT7

THE OTHER BRITAIN

DATES: *#1 May 10–May 27 (18 days)
#2 Aug 16–Sep 2 (18 days)
LEADER: Mike Banks
GRADE: A-1
LAND COST: $1990 (10–12 members)
$2190 (8–9)
*Note change from 1984 Trip Schedule.

This is an exclusive opportunity to experience a totally different Britain from that seen by the crowds who trudge around the usual tourist attractions. Mike Banks, the well-known British author, mountaineer and explorer, will take us on some of his favorite walks among the British hills and along cliff paths. The basic aim is to strike a balance between sightseeing and hiking.

Visits have been arranged to beautiful and unusual places: the gaunt, prehistoric standing stones on Dartmoor; centuries-old Cotswold villages of timeless tranquillity; mountains and castles in Wales, a land where English is still the people's second language; and the walled medieval city of York with its magnificent thousand-year-old Minster.

One night we stay in a lovely manor house, Langton Hall, as guests of the owner, Robert Spencer, a relative of Princess Diana, future queen of England.

Travel between centers of interest will be by two luxury minibuses, allowing us to range from Cornwall to Yorkshire. Lodging will be in small country inns and guesthouses of character.

ITINERARY:
DAY 1 and 2: Leave U.S. Arrive London, meet with trip leaders. Drive to Westcountry with a stop at Stonehenge. Overnight at hotel in the county of Wilshire.

DAY 3: Continue west to Devon and explore Plymouth's historic Barbican, down whose cobbled streets the Pilgrim Fathers strode to begin their epic journey, as did Raleigh, Drake and Captain Cook. Afternoon hike in the stern wilderness of Dartmoor to view prehistoric remains and glimpse wild ponies.

DAY 4 to 6: In "Cornwall near England," legend-laden land of King Arthur, we hike on the Celtic Peninsula, then drive up-country to visit Bath, the elegant Georgian spa built over an ancient Roman city.

DAY 7: Heading north, we visit England's charming Cotswolds villages, whose honey-colored stone cottages and flower-filled gardens blend with perfection into the soft green landscape. Explore Burford, a timeless village of 14th century wool merchant's houses and cottages set beside the River Windrush.

DAY 8: to 10: In North Wales, we hike part of the way along the great defense earthwork of Offa's Dyke, a boundary dug between England and Wales about A.D.

785, and now one of Britain's favorite walks. We'll explore the mountains of Snowdonia, training area for the first successful Everest team, and visit one of the massive castles of the early Welsh princes. One evening we'll be entertained by harp and song at a banquet in ancient Ruthin Castle.

DAY 11 and 12: In the Lake District, we climb its fells and follow its becks down to the famous waters that inspired Beatrix Potter to weave her fairytale world, and by which still stands Dove Cottage, where Wordsworth lived and wrote.

> **Mike Banks, the well-known British author, mountaineer and explorer, will take us on some of his favorite walks among the British hills and along cliff paths.**

DAY 13 to 15: Driving east to Yorkshire, we stay within the walled city of York, one of Britain's historical treasures, still entered by its medieval gates. We explore its narrow cobbled streets, museums and colorful taverns, and marvel at the soaring splendor of the superb Minster, the largest Gothic church in England, whose magnificent windows contain nearly half of Britain's medieval stained glass. We drive over the Yorkshire dales and moors, where green stone-walled valleys stretch like ribs from the mountain spine of the Pennine Chain, known as the "backbone of England."

DAY 16: Drive south to Leichestershire and stay in Langton Hall, a manor house which dates back to 1550 and is set in beautiful countryside.

DAY 17: Drive to London with afternoon at leisure.

DAY 18: Depart London and connect with homeward-bound flights.

IT4PA1SFMT7

ELEGANT ENGLAND

DATES: #1 Jun 16–Jun 29 (14 days)
#2 Jul 7–Jul 20 (14 days)
LEADER: Mike Banks
GRADE: A-1
LAND COST: $2690 (8–10 members)
$2950 (4–7)

In this rapidly changing world, England is one of the few countries left where, in its historic country castles, the traditional way of life and the hospitality of a bygone age can still be found and enjoyed.

This special trip is really two tours in one: by day, we have a delightful walking tour of rural England at its loveliest; by night, we delight in the grandeur of four of England's "great houses," where we'll stay as private guests of the owners.

Our days will be taken up exploring medieval villages and mysterious prehistoric sites, and hiking the unspoiled English countryside and coastline from Cornwall to Yorkshire.

Our evenings will be spent in elegant castles surrounded by beautiful gardens and estates, enjoying gourmet food and wine with our hosts. Activities such as tennis, riding, golf and croquet will be made available at the various castles.

ITINERARY:
DAY 1 and 2: Leave U.S. Arrive London. Meet with trip leader and drive to the charming Georgian city of Bath. Overnight in hotel.

DAY 3 to 5: Drive further west to Cornwall and stay with Lord Eliot at his house, Port Eliot, in the village of St. Germans. Port Eliot is one of the most historic houses in Cornwall and was acquired by the Eliot family from King Henry VIII in 1564. Time to explore the wild and beautiful country of Cornwall which has inspired many of England's greatest painters and writers.

DAY 6 to 8: Leaving Port Eliot, we visit the port of Plymouth then continue to Dorset and Forde Abbey, home of the Roper family. Forde Abby was founded in 1141 by the Normans as a Cistercian monastery. Our hosts will show us around their ancient and magnificent home with its famous Mortlake tapestries, great baronial hall, extensive gardens, arboretum and ornamental lakes. While here, we will enjoy the unspoiled beauty of the Dorset countryside and view some of the greatest prehistoric earthworks and hillside carvings in Britain.

> **By day, we have a delightful walking tour of rural England at its loveliest; by night, we delight in the grandeur of four of England's "great houses," where we'll stay as private guests of the owners.**

DAY 9 and 10: Drive to Croxton Park, the home of David Smollett, set amid its own 3,000 acres of park and farmland. David is a direct descendant of Tobias Smollett, the influencial 18th century novelist. From Croxton, we explore the venerable environs of Cambridge University.

DAY 11 and 12: We drive northwest to Locko Park, one of the finest of the "great houses" in the district. Our host will be Captain Patrick Drury-Lowe, whose family has lived in Locko Park for over 200 years. His gracious home contains a notable collection of artwork. There is also an impressive private chapel which is older than the house.

DAY 13: Drive to London and check into hotel. Afternoon free.

DAY 14: Depart London and connect with homeward-bound flights.

THE OTHER BRITAIN

B

2BAIYO36

IRELAND & BRITAIN

DATES: Jul 22–Aug 11 (21 days)
LEADER: Mike Banks &
Paddy O'Leary
GRADE: A-1
LAND COST: $1890 (10–12 members)
$2350 (7–9)

This tour combines walks in Ireland, Wales, England and Scotland all in one trip, with an itinerary that does not overlap any ground covered by our other Ireland and Britain journeys.

A week-long Irish ramble will take us through the lake-dotted territory of "the Ferocious O'Flaherty's", and the Atlantic-washed haunts of the great pirate queen, Grace O'Malley. We'll visit the fabled "Mountains of Mourne" overlooking the Irish Sea, and walk in a lovely green landscape filled with Ireland's storied past, including 4000-year-old dolmens, early Christian settlements and Norman castles.

Crossing the Irish Sea to Wales, land of music and song (with a language older than English) we hike the spectacular Pembroke Coast and visit the fishing village said to have inspired Dylan Thomas' "Under Milk Wood."

Journeying to England, we tour the Wye Valley, beloved of composer Elgar and poet Housman. Driving northwards, we visit Chester, a 2000-year-old city with medieval city walls, then north again to hike the Pennine Way along the mountainous backbone of England.

Lastly, we cross into Scotland to hike its glens and explore "Robert Burns" country before ending our tour in ancient Rowallan Castle as guests of its owner.

ITINERARY:
DAY 1 and 2: Leave U.S. Arrive Shannon, Ireland. Meet with trip leader and drive through County Clare to our hotel. Afternoon walk along the 700-foot Cliffs of Moher.

DAY 3: Hike in the Burren, with its many reminders of Ireland's past from megalithic tombs to Norman castles. Drive around Galway Bay, a Gaelic-speaking area. Free time in Galway, the "city of tribes".

DAY 4: Drive north to Westport, County Mayo, and hike on Achill Island, past whitewashed cottages and onto a beach with views of Clare Island, once the stronghold of pirate queen, Grace O'Malley.

DAY 5: Travel through County Mayo and Sligo, visiting the hilltop grave of the great Queen Maeve and the haunts of poet W.B. Yeats, then continue through lake country to Enniskillen in Northern Ireland.

DAY 6: Visit the cathedral city of Armagh and hike the famous Mountains of Mourne along the Brandy Pad, an old smugglers' trail.

DAY 7: Drive down the coast to Dublin. Visit the favorite pubs of playwrights Behan and O'Casey, and enjoy traditional Irish music in the Abbey Tavern.

DAY 8: Visit the hills of County Wicklow, walk in the historic valley of Glendalough, and continue to Wexford.

DAY 9 and 10: Depart Ireland on a three-hour ferry ride from Rosslare to Fishguard, Wales, where our British leaders, Pat and Mike Banks, will meet us. Hike the Pembroke hills, legendary land of Merlin the magician and the Druids. Walk the spectacular St. David's Peninsula with its soaring granite cliffs.

DAY 11: Head east past the varied landscape of South Wales and stop at Laugharne, home of poet Dylan Thomas. At the ancient border town of Monmouth, we spend the night in a 300-year-old inn.

DAY 12 to 14: In Gloucestorshire, one of the most unspoiled counties of England, we explore tranquil villages and hike gentle green uplands on trails used long before the Romans came to Britain.

DAY 15 and 16: Drive north and visit the historic walled city of Chester, founded by the Romans 2000 years ago.

DAY 17 and 18: Continuing north, we visit Martin Mere Wildfowl Reserve in Lancashire and have tea in a great historic mansion, Brownsholme Hall, built in 1507 by the Parker family who still live there. The next day we hike in the Pennine Mountains and venture into the largest limestone cavern in Britain.

> **A week-long Irish ramble will take us through the lake-dotted territory of "the Ferocious O'Flaherty's," and the Atlantic-washed haunts of the great pirate queen, Grace O'Malley.**

DAY 19 and 20: North again to the Scottish border, a region immortalized by poet Robert Burns, whose house we visit. We'll hike the border hills and spend a night at Rowallan Castle.

DAY 21: Depart Glasgow and connect with homeward-bound flights.

IT4EI15O27

THE IRISH COUNTRYSIDE

DATES: #1 May 12–May 29 (18 days)
#2 Sep 8–Sep 25 (18 days)
LEADER: Paddy O'Leary
GRADE: A-1
LAND COST: $1695 (10–12 members)
$1895 (7–9)

This walking tour is a relaxed and low-key look at little-known areas and aspects of Ireland, conducted by an Irish mountaineer, Paddy O'Leary. It's an unusual chance to see "an Irishman's Ireland," with its quiet county towns, wild moors, and lonely coastal cliffs.

We begin with a visit to Clare, "Land of Castles," and the peculiar landscape of the Burren country, where mild weather and the proximity of the sea has led to exquisite flora.

We take a ferry to the Aran Islands, then return to Galway and visit the lake-dotted wilds of Connemara, one of Ireland's most beautiful regions.

Driving south, we tackle the rough mountain and coastal country of South West Kerry, staying in a secluded cove on the Ring of Kerry.

Heading through a region steeped in the lore of the Norman Conquest, we tour Kinsale with its sheltered harbor then walk in St. Mullins, an unspoiled river village and burial place of the Kings of Leinster.

Our last lap takes us through the prosperous farms of County Wexford and the Wicklow Hills, where we'll walk in wooded and historic valleys and glens, including Glendalough, with its 6th century monastery founded by St. Kevin.

Travel will be by minibus; accommodations are in small hotels.

ITINERARY:
DAY 1 and 2: Leave U.S. Arrive Shannon, Ireland. Meet with trip leader and drive to a hotel in the Burren. Afternoon stroll on the Cliffs of Moher.

DAY 3: Walk in Burren country and enjoy a session of Irish traditional music in a pub at Doolin.

DAY 4: By ferry to Inisheer and on to the Aran Islands, where islanders proudly foster the Gaelic language and traditions. In the evening, attend a banquet and pageant at Knappogue Castle, 15th century home of the McNamara clan.

DAY 5: Drive around Galway Bay to Galway, called "City of the Tribes", in reference to the fourteen Anglo-Norman families which once dominated the town. Continue through the lake-dotted wilds of Connemara, and on to Kylemore Abbey and Gaeltacht.

DAY 6: Drive through Limerick to Adare, with its thatched cottages, and ruins dating from the 13th to 15th century, and on to Tralee, county town of Kerry.

DAY 7: Walk in the vicinity of Carrauntoohil (3,414'), Ireland's highest mountain, and drive around the glorious Ring of Kerry. Overnight in the seaside village of Waterville.

DAY 8: By fishing boat to Skellig Michael, a dramatic rock pinnacle with an old church clinging to its 700-foot-high summit. Skelligs is a bird sanctuary with thousands of puffins, guillemots, kittiwakes and gannets.

DAY 9: Walk along flower-hung country lanes and skirt the lovely shoreline of Lamb's Head. Afternoon visit to the home of Daniel O'Connor, the Liberator.

DAY 10: Drive to Kinsale, stopping at Staigue Fort, a well-preserved circular stone fort, the origin of which was lost somewhere in the misty past some 30 centuries ago.

> **An unusual chance to see "an Irishman's Ireland", with its quiet county towns, wild moors, and lonely coastal cliffs.**

DAY 11: Day in Kinsale, with its sheltered harbor and history-filled streets. This was once an important Norman stronghold, later a prosperous seaport and site of one of the great sieges and battles of Irish history.

DAY 12: Drive through Cork to Waterford, with its famous glass factory. Continue to a secluded guest house on the banks of the peaceful River Barrow.

DAY 13: Stroll through the little hamlet of St. Mullins, with its village green and fine example of early Norman fortification. Walk along a tow path beside River Barrow.

DAY 14: Drive to Kilkenny.

DAY 15 and 16: Drive through the farm country of County Wexford to the Wicklow Hills.

DAY 17: Drive to Dublin. Evening at the Abbey Tavern in the nearby fishing village of Howth to enjoy traditional music and dancing.

DAY 18: Depart Dublin and connect with homeward-bound flights.

IT4PA1SFM8

THE OTHER FRANCE

DATES: #1 Jun 2–Jun 19 (18 days)
#2 Sep 4–Sep 21 (18 days)
LEADER: Rod & Maryvonne Buntz
GRADE: A-1
LAND COST: $2350 (10–12 members)
$2575 (7–9)

In the style of our popular "Other Britain" walking tours, we will tour rural western France, immersing ourselves in French country life as we visit the Basque hills, the Pyrenees, the coastal plains of Aquitaine, the vineyards of Bordeaux, and the Loire countryside with its famed chateaux.

We begin with a swift train ride from Paris south to the French Pyrenees. Here we tour Basque villages and hike in the beautiful high altitude mountain pastures of the Ossau Valley.

Driving north through the largest conifer forest in Europe, we discover the medieval city of St. Emilion, known for its wines. We hike its vineyards, sample some wine, then stop in Cognac and visit the Hennessy cellars.

At La Rochelle, we stroll the streets along this 17th century city's fortified harbor and enjoy delicious fresh seafood.

Heading for the Loire Valley and the heart of France, we visit some famous chateaux and take walks in the countryside of Sologne and forests of Fontaineblue.

Travel will be by comfortable minibus, with accommodations in hotels and inns.

ITINERARY:

DAY 1 and 2: Leave U.S. Arrive Paris. Continue by train to Dax in the south of France. Overnight in hotel.

DAY 3: Morning visit to a spa known for its healing mudbaths. Afternoon boat ride on the "courant d'Huchet" through an almost tropical underwood. On the return trip, we'll hike in a lofty pine forest, visit immense sand beaches on the Atlantic Coast and drive back to Dax.

> **We will tour rural western France, immersing ourselves in French country life as we visit the Basque hills, the Pyrenees, the coastal plains of Aquitaine, the vineyards of Bordeaux, and the Loire countryside with its famed chateaux.**

DAY 4: Morning drive to Pomarez to visit a typical poultry market of this region. Drive to Orthez and hike along the river Adour, ending at the trip leaders' 17th century country house, where we'll have dinner. Overnight at hotel in Dax.

DAY 5: Drive to Bayonne, Biarritz and St. Jean de Luz, with short visits to these typical old towns.

Picnic in a private summer house with time to enjoy the wonderful scenery of the bay at St. Jean de Luz. Afternoon drive through the Basque hills and visits to Basque villages. Overnight at St. Jean-pied-de-port, a very attractive old fortified town.

DAY 6: An entire day's hike in the beautiful "Foret des Arbailles," then drive to Louvie-Juzon.

DAY 7: Early morning drive to one of the wildest valleys in the Pyrenees, the Ossau Valley. Here we can choose either a full day's hike or two shorter walks before and after lunch.

DAY 8: Drive to St. Emilion, the world-famous wine city, through the Landes forest. Afternoon walk in the forest. Overnight at St. Emilion.

DAY 9: Morning walk in the vineyards, Visit the wine cellar at Chateau Lignac, owned by friends of the trip leaders.

DAY 10: Driving north, we visit a monolithic 6th century cathedral and a 17th century papermill where hand-made paper is still produced. Lunch in a country bistro, then drive to La Rochelle through the Cognac vineyards. Visit the old town of Saintes, where there are important Roman ruins.

DAY 11: Day at leisure in La Rochelle, strolling along the harbor.

DAY 12: Drive to Montreuil Bellay, a little town surrounded by the Anjou vineyards. We shall tour a "fairy-tale castle," visit a mushroom farm, and sample excellent Saumur wine. Overnight at Chinon, Joan of Arc's town.

DAY 13: Drive to Candes, where St. Martin died in the year 397. Morning walk on the hills above the Loire and Vienne rivers. Back to Chinon in time to enjoy a stroll down its narrow, medieval streets.

DAY 14: Visit the Loire Valley, "valley of the kings," and the chateaux of Usse-Villandry and Chenonceaux.

DAY 15: Full day's wildlife walk along the Sologne ponds.

DAY 16: Drive to the Fontainebleu forest for a walk and picnic, arrive in Paris in the evening and transfer to hotel.

DAY 17: Free day in Paris.

DAY 18: Depart Paris and connect with homeward-bound flights.

IT4PA1SFMT8

SOUTH ALPS OF FRANCE

DATES: Jun 16–Jul 1 (16 days)
LEADER: Pierre Jamet
GRADE: B-3
LAND COST: $990 (9–12 members)
$1150 (6–8)

Beginning at Menton on the Cote d'Azur, we will hike from the shores of the Mediterranean into the pastoral foothills of the South Alps, following the French side of the French/Italian border, mostly along the "sentier de grande randonnee."

The South Alps do not have sharp high peaks but in their favor they have a sunny climate and are relatively untraveled.

As we walk through the South Alps' larch forests and pastures, we'll find reminders of earlier civilizations, including the mysterious prehistoric stone engravings in the Vallee des Merveilles. Abandoned villages and little-used foot trails have taken on new life with the growing interest in hiking, and a portion of this route is now protected as Parc National du Mercantour. The walking—all under 9,200 feet—will not be difficult, but even in June, crossing the highest passes on the trek involves some walking over snow. Daily hiking time is four to six hours.

ITINERARY:

DAY 1 and 2: Leave U.S. Arrive Paris. Continue by air to Nice. Overnight at hotel.

DAY 3: By train to Menton along the coast. Hike over Col du Razet (3,369') to Sospel (1,140'), a village with an 11th century bridge and church. Overnight in hotel.

DAY 4: Up a stone-paved trail and along a long ridge all day, meeting shepherds with their flocks. Overnight in hotel at Col de Turin (5,272').

DAY 5: Follow a high ridge over the Pas du Diable (7,992') to the Refuge du Merveilles (6,925'). This area is well known for its prehistoric engravings.

DAY 6: Morning spent looking at the prehistoric engravings, then hike over two passes of about 8,000 feet and descend to the Refuge de Nice (7,322').

DAY 7: Up and over several small passes through larch forests to the Refuge de Cougourde.

IT4PA1SFMT8

NORTH ALPS OF FRANCE

DATES: Sep 5–Sep 20 (16 days)
LEADER: Pierre Jamet
GRADE: B-2
LAND COST: $990 (9–12 members)
$1150 (6–8)

Beginning in the border town of Mondane, on the French side of a tunnel which connects France and northern Italy, this trek leads north all the way to Mont Blanc, highest peak in the Alps, which we'll see in the distance on the first days of our hike and many more times as we trek toward our destination, the Chamonix Valley.

En route we cross two separate ranges of mountains; the Vanoise and the Beaufortain. The Beaufortain, not as high as the Vanoise, has kept its traditional pastoral flavor. Here in flower-filled meadows, shepherds still prepare cheese in their alpine huts (one of France's best cheeses, Beaufort, is made here).

Much of the alpine Vanoise region is now a national park. It contains some of the largest glaciers in France and has spectacular views not only of Mont Blanc, but of the Matterhorn and Monte Rosa. Our North Alps hike ends near the foot of Mont Blanc.

Although the hiking days are not long, there are some steep climbs and the hiking takes place mostly above 6,500 feet. Our accommodations will be mountain refuges and occasional hotels. Some of the huts do not provide food, and on part of the trip we carry our own food supplies and cook our own meals.

ITINERARY:
DAY 1 and 2: Leave U.S. Arrive Geneva. Transfer to hotel.
DAY 3: By train to Mondane, and hike up to the Refuge de l'Orgere (6,348') on a wooded trail.
DAY 4: Continue above timberline to the Col de Chaviere (9,100') and down to the Refuge de Peclet-Polset (8,310').
DAY 5: Climb to the Col du Soufre (9,320'), descend the Gebroulaz Glacier, then up again over Col de Chanrouge (8,303') to Refuge des Lacs Merlet (7,844') near two little lakes.
DAY 6: Down to about 6,100 feet, then climb steeply up to the Breche de la Porteta (8,694'), a narrow gap between vertical towers and pinnacles of rock. From here, descend steeply to the ski resort of Pralognan (4,652'). Beautiful views of the Grande Casse (12,647'), highest summit in the Vanoise, and the Domes de la Vanoise, which are covered by a glacier more than 10 kms. long. Overnight in hotel.
DAY 7: Short hike up to the Col de la Vanoise (8,257'), a beautiful pass. Overnight at mountain refuge.
DAY 8: Over Col de le Leisse (9,048'), steep descent, then up

again to Col du Palet (8,700'). Overnight at mountain refuge.
DAY 9: Short detour for a beautiful view of the steep northern face of the Grande Casse, then down the valley of the Pontuirn to Landry (2,559'). Overnight in hotel.
DAY 10: Cross the valley of the Isere River and hike to the hamlet of Forand. Overnight at Refuge de la Balme (6,591').
DAY 11: Rest day or hikes in the area. Weather permitting, climb the Point de Combe Neuve (9,714'), an easy non-technical climb with a beautiful view of all the summits in the North Alps, including the Matterhorn and Monte Rosa.
DAY 12: Upwards to the Lac de Presset (8,202') and Col du Grand Fond (8,694'), down the valley of

Combe Neuve, straight towards Mont Blanc, then traverse the wide-open pass of the Cormet de Roselend to the Refuge du Plan de la Laie (6,069').
DAY 13: Up green pastures to Col de la Sauce (7,217'), and traverse down to the village of Les Contamines (3,805'), a ski resort. Overnight in hotel.

> **Beginning in the border town of Mondane, on the French side of a tunnel which connects France and northern Italy, this trek leads north all the way to Mont Blanc, highest peak in the Alps.**

DAY 14: Up to the Col de Voza (5,423'), below which lies the Chamonix Valley, on the north side of Mont Blanc. Descend to Les Houches (3,248') and proceed to Chamonix. Overnight in hotel.
DAY 15: Morning free in Chamonix. Afternoon train to Geneva. Overnight in hotel.
DAY 16: Depart Geneva and connect with homeward-bound flights.

DAY 8: Down along the Boreon valley, up through green pastures to Refuge des Adous (7,100'). Optional climb of Mont Archas (8,287').
DAY 9: Through forest to Molieres, summer home for shepherds, and further to the abandoned hamlet of Tiecs (2,952'), whose only inhabitants are a young couple who sell goat cheese. Overnight at Refuge de Longon (6,177') in open meadows.
DAY 10: Over the Portes de Longon (7,400') and steeply down to the hamlet of Vignols, then along the east ridge of Mont Mouneir (9,500'). Descend to Roya. Overnight in abandoned school house.

> **Abandoned villages and little-used foot trails have taken on new life with the growing interest in hiking, and a portion of this route is now protected as Parc National du Mercantour.**

DAY 11: Up to the Cime du Pal (9,242'), then down along several lakes to Saint Dalmas le Selvage. Overnight in hotel.
DAY 12: Over the Col de la Colombire (7,339'), Col des Fourches (7,417') and Pas de la Cavale (8,759') to Larche, a village on the highway which leads to Italy. Overnight in hotel.
DAY 13: Cross several 9,000-foot passes to the Refuge de Chameryon with a spectacular view of the tower-like summit of the Brec de Chambeyron.
DAY 14: On our last day of hiking, we walk in the gorge of the Ubaye River, over Col de Serenne (8,772') and down to the town of Guillestre. Overnight at hotel.
DAY 15: Morning visit to the fortified village of Montdauphin and return to Paris by train. Overnight in hotel.
DAY 16: Depart Paris and connect with homeward-bound flights from Paris.

A   Trekking in the Pyrenees/Dick McGowan
B   Church at St. Nectaire/Pierre Jamet
C   Alpine meadow, Pyrenees/Dick McGowan

IT4PA1SFMT8

FRANCE: TREKKING THE MASSIF CENTRAL

DATES: Apr 20–May 5 (16 days)
LEADER: Pierre Jamet
GRADE: B-2
LAND COST: $1190 (9–12 members)
$1350 (6–8)

This hiking odyssey in central France consists of two separate sections: the first is a six-day hike in the "Chaine des Domes," a range of volcanoes about 10,000 years old. We'll hike its high ridges to crater lakes, tiny hamlets and visit the ruins of medieval strongholds and Romanesque churches.

The second hike starts in the unspoiled Cevennes, a lovely region of moors, chestnut forests and apple orchards. This route was traveled in and written about by Robert Louis Stevenson in 1878, and much of the region remains little changed in the last 100 years. We then continue across the flat plateaus and deep gorges of the Causse Mejean, a setting of sheer cliffs, natural arches and rock towers of fantastic shapes.

Most nights will be spent in small hotels, with one night in a barn and one in a mountain refuge.

ITINERARY:
DAY 1 and 2: Leave U.S. Arrive Paris. Transfer to hotel.

DAY 3: By train to Riom. Overnight at hotel in Tournoel.

DAY 4: Drive to the Col de la Nugere and begin hike along the Chaine des Domes, the highest of which is dome-shaped Puy de Dome (4,806'). Hike up Puy de Pariou (3,966'), visit its crater, then hike the Puy de Dome for views of the whole volcanic range. Visit the ruins of a Roman temple dedicated to the god Mercury and hike down the old Roman road to Col de la Moreno (3,484'). Overnight in an old house now converted into a hotel.

DAY 5: Continue southwards along the Chaine des Domes, hiking up the twin volcanoes of Lassolas (3,920') and La Vache (3,828'), remarkable for their large reddish craters. Reach the village of Saulzet-le-Froid (3,346').

DAY 6: Hike into another range of mountains called "Monts Dore" which are remnants of larger and much older volcanoes than the Chaine des Domes. Walk to a little lake in an ancient crater, then climb up the Puy de Combe Perret (4,527') and the Puy de l'Auire (4,937'), which overlook two spectacular rock peaks. Continue to Le Mont Dore (3,444'), a health resort since the time of the Romans, who appreciated its hot mineral springs; nowadays it is a ski resort.

DAY 7: Up to the Col de la Croix Saint Robert (4,747') passing a waterfall called "La Grande Cascade," then along to the spectacular ruins of the medieval castle of Murol. Overnight in hotel below the castle.

DAY 8: Short walk to Saint-Nectaire. Drive to Issoire.

DAY 9: Visit the Romanesque church at Issoire. Afternoon train to Villefort. Overnight in hotel.

DAY 10: Start the Cevennes hike. From Villefort (1,984'), hike along the long ridge of Mont Lozere. Overnight at Mas de la Barque.

DAY 11: Continue along the ridge and hike over Roc Malpertus (5,511'), continuing to the hamlets of Salarial and l'Hopital. Follow the "draille," a shepherd trail to the hamlet of L'Aubaret. Overnight in a hotel at the Col De la Croix de Berthel (3,569').

DAY 12: Follow the ridge of Montagne du Bouges (4,662') to the town of Florac (1,788'). Fine views of the various Cevennes ridges.

> **This route was traveled in and written about by Robert Louis Stevenson in 1878, and much of the region remains little changed in the last 100 years.**

DAY 13: Climb steeply to the rim of the Causse Mejean (3,280') and walk across a dry chalky plateau to La Parade where there is a rustic hotel. The villages in this area are inhabited by shepherds.

DAY 14: Short walk to Aven Armand, a beautiful cave. Walk to the little hamlet of La Viale. Dinner at a farm and overnight in its barn.

DAY 15: Reach the south rim of the Causse Mejean, hike down to Le Rozier (1,279') by a spectacular trail amidst rocks with bizarre shapes. At Le Rozier, drive to Millau and take an overnight train to Paris.

DAY 16: Arrive Paris. Depart Paris and connect with homeward-bound flights.

IT4PA1SFMT8

TREKKING IN THE PYRENEES

DATES: #1 Jul 8–Jul 22 (15 days)
#2 Sep 2–Sep 16 (15 days)
LEADER: #1 Pierre Jamet
#2 Sophie Ginnier-Gillet
GRADE: B-3
LAND COST: $1190 (6–10 members)

This 11-day trek offers challenging hiking in the beautiful Vallee d'Aspe of the western Pyrenees, part of the French national park system.

One of the great attractions of the Pyrenees, besides the peaks themselves (50 over 10,000 feet), is the large alpine area between timberline and the summits. Timberline is about 6,800 feet and snowline is about 9,000 feet. For those who love to wander through alpine high country at its finest, this is one of the most appealing regions in Europe. The climate favors a wide-ranging and lovely flora, including daffodils and alpine roses.

We'll hike about eight to ten hours a day carrying rucksacks. Accommodations and meals will be in mountain huts maintained by the French Alpine Club.

The route is almost all on the French side of the frontier, except for two brief crossings into Spain. No technical climbing skills are necessary, but crampons and ice axes will be necessary to cross some snowfields on the passes. For those interested, there are several non-technical peaks to climb en route.

ITINERARY:
DAY 1 and 2: Leave U.S. Arrive Paris. Continue by train to Pau. Transfer to hotel.

DAY 3: Travel to Urdos by train and bus. Overnight at hotel.

DAY 4: Drive to the trailhead and begin trek with a long day's walk over the Col d'Ayous (7,168'). Descend to the Refuge d'Ayous.

DAY 5: Descend past the three Lacs d'Ayous into the Bious Valley (4,900') and climb to the Lac de Peyreget (6,804') and Col de

Peyreget (7,545'). Overnight at Refuge de Pombie (6,663'), situated below the south face of the Pic du Midi d'Ossau, one of the classic climbs of the Pyrenees.

DAY 6: Day for rest or optional hikes.

DAY 7: A long and strenuous day down to the Brousett Valley (4,600'), where a major highway crosses into Spain. Continue steeply into the Arrious Valley and over the Col d'Arrious (7,411') overlooking Lac d'Artouste. Overnight at a refuge with views of several lakes and snow-clad peaks.

DAY 8: Another long day to the Col du Palas (8,257'), where we cross into Spain, traverse to the Port du Lavedan (8,597'), and cross back into France. This section is without a trail. On part of it we cross rocks on small footholds and traverse steep shifting scree. Overnight at Refuge de Larribet (6,758').

DAY 9: Rest day. Optional hikes or easy climbs.

DAY 10: The route drops into the Azun Valley (5,100'), then up to the Campo Plano (7,043') followed by a climb to the Col de la Fache (8,740') on the border. Overnight at Refuge Wallon (6,118').

DAY 11: Two trail routes are possible today on our way to the Refuge des Oulettes (7,057'). The choice depends on weather, route conditions and group interest. The Oulettes Refuge lies at the base of the Vignemale (10,820') and has an inspiring view of this sheer-walled limestone peak and the glaciers at its base. This is a major climbing area in the Pyrenees.

C

DAY 12: Climb steeply over a 9,000-foot pass and descend to Refuge Bayssellance (8,401'). Optional hikes available here, including a scramble up the Petit Vignemale (9,914').

DAY 13: Rest day or optional hike.

For those who love to wander through alpine high country at its finest, this is one of the most appealing regions in Europe.

DAY 14: Hike back to Hourquette d'Ossau, descend part way to the Oulettes Refuge, and continue into the Lutour Valley which we follow to the roadhead at La Raillere (3,389'). Continue down a paved road to Cauterets. In the afternoon, take the train to Pau. Overnight at hotel.

DAY 15: Fly to Paris. Depart Paris and connect with homeward-bound flights.

IT4TW14O48

THE OTHER SPAIN

DATES: *#1 Jun 5–Jun 22 (18 days)
*#2 Nov 3–Nov 20 (18 days)
LEADER: Martin Zabaleta
GRADE: A-2
LAND COST: $1590 (6-12 members)
*Note change from 1984 Trip Schedule.

Exploring the mountains, villages and coasts of Spain, this tour is a combination of hikes in completely untouristed areas and visits to the ancient towns of Aragon, Catalonia, and Castile.

With our guide, a Basque mountaineer who climbed Everest, we begin in Cuenca, land of La Mancha, and walk in the forested mountains of La Serrania. After exploring the Moorish town of Albarracin, we bathe on the beaches of Tarragona then head up into Huesca, ancient capital of Aragon. Here in the Sierra de Guara, we hike into fantastically carved and colored "badlands" reminiscent of our own southwestern desert.

In the Pyrenees at Ordesa, we follow a canyon with 3,000-foot

escarpments towering above an alpine meadowland. Passing through San Sebastian, we dine on fresh seafood and hike along the fertile Cantabrian coast.

Lastly, we roam into the Picos de Europa, a mountain range with a mysterious labyrinth of gorges and valleys. Traveling across the golden plateaus of old Castile, we visit the walled city of Avila, then return to Madrid.

ITINERARY:
DAY 1 and 2: Leave U.S. Arrive Madrid. Drive to Chincon in the province of Cuenca. Overnight at hotel.

DAY 3: Morning hike through the Serrania of Cuenca, with wonderful gorges, alpine meadows. Afternoon tour the old quarter of Cuenca.

DAY 4: Morning walk through the Ciudad Encantada ("Enchanted City") of La Serrania to see fantastic rock formations. Lunch at Albarracin, with time to stroll its narrow, winding streets. Overnight in Teruel.

DAY 5: Easy hike up a peak in the Maestrazgo (Sierra de Gudar), picnic amidst the olive groves of Alcaniz, and overnight in a 12th-century castle of the Order of Calatrava.

DAY 6: Drive through silvery olive groves, almond orchards, and the vineyards of Catalunan to the beaches of Tarragona. Afternoon to explore the wealth of Roman treasures and medieval ruins found here.

DAY 7: Drive to Monzon, visiting several great Cistercian abbeys; afternoon hike through the fig groves, cork oak and pine-covered woodlands of the Sierra de Montsant.

DAY 8: Hike in the Sierra de Guara, the foothills of the Aragonese Pyrenees. Afternoon visit to San Juan de la Pena, a 9th century monastery with great views of the harshly beautiful landscape at the foot of the Pyrenees.

DAY 9: Day hike in Ordesa National Park, walking through a canyon ringed with vertical walls and along the alpine banks of the River Arazas, with its myriad waterfalls and wildlife such as mountain goats and chamoix. Overnight in a splendidly refurbished parador in the medieval town of Castejon de Sos.

DAY 10: Hike in Sierra de Leire, encountering vestiges of Roman civilization in the peaceful oak and pine forest. Afternoon drive into the Pays Basque ("Basque Country"). Overnight in Ulzama Valley.

DAY 11: Roam through pastoral countryside of the Baztan Valley. Lunch at a *caserio* (farm) owned by friends of the trip leader. Overnight in San Sebastian, with an unforgettable dinner at "Arzak" restaurant.

DAY 12: Sightseeing in San Sebastian, then continue along the Cantabrian coast, stopping at hidden beaches and in the fishing village of Lequeitio. Visit the caves of Santimamine with their prehistoric cave paintings. Overnight in Guernica.

DAY 13: Continue driving along the Costa Verde ("Green Coast"), a fertile setting of pasturelands and steep cliffs. Overnight in San Vicente de ia Barquera.

DAY 14 and 15: Day hikes in the Picos de Europa.

DAY 16: From Leon, drive to Avila, passing through the golden wheat fields of Castile. Overnight in the walled city of Avila.

DAY 17: Drive to Madrid. Afternoon free. Overnight at hotel.

DAY 18: Depart Madrid and connect with homeward-bound flights.

IT4SRIMO1

SCRAMBLES IN THE ALPS

DATES: Aug 3–Aug 24 (22 days)
LEADER: John Noble
GRADE: D-2
LAND COST: $2450 (5–9 members)

On this mountaineering journey, we will attempt to climb some of the most famous peaks of the Swiss and French Alps, including the Matterhorn and Mont Blanc.

Flying to Geneva, we drive directly to a camp at Arolla (6,560') and have a day for checking out our techniques and gear on some local glaciers and peaks.

We then traverse hut-to-hut for five days across peaks, passes and glaciers of the Pennine Alps—the classic route of the alpine "Golden Age," beneath such striking mountains as the Dent Blanche (14,295'), which we will attempt. We descend into Zermatt, the most well-known mountain resort in the world, nestled at the foot of the Matterhorn.

Based in the mountains above Zermatt for the next five days, we will attempt an ascent of the Matterhorn (14,962'), then drive across the border to Chamonix, France.

Little needs to be added to the wealth of material written about the Chamonix-Mont Blanc area. It is one of the world's great climbing places and the birthplace of mountaineering. Here in the Mont Blanc Range we will attempt the Aiguille Chardonnet (12,546') and Mont Blanc (15,771'), the highest point in Europe west of the Caucasus.

Note: As on all mountaineering expeditions, weather and snow conditions will determine our exact itinerary. Given a good climbing party and good luck with the weather, the program above is what we hope to accomplish.

ITINERARY:

DAY 1 and 2: Leave U.S. Arrive Geneva. Drive to Arolla (6,560'). Overnight in hotel.

DAY 3: Climbing practice above Arolla.

DAY 4: Trek to Vignettes Hut. Snow and ice climbing seminar en route. Overnight at hut.

DAY 5: 4 a.m. start for a climb of L'Eveque, a fine snow and ice peak. Overnight at hut.

DAY 6: A 3 a.m. start for ascent of Pigne D'Arolla and traverse to Mt. Blanc D'Cheilon, a fine high level route. Descend to Cabane Dix. Overnight at hut.

DAY 7: Traverse the Pas D'Chevres and descend through beautiful flower-filled alpine pastures to Arolla. Overnight at hotel.

DAY 8: Leave Arolla for Ferpecle and ascend to the Dent Blanche Hut.

DAY 9: A 3 a.m. start for ascent of Dent Blanche, one of the finest and most sought-after climbs in the Alps. Return to Dent Blanche Hut.

DAY 10: Ascend Tete Blanche and

EUROPE
ABOUT MOUNTAIN TREKKING

Most European mountain regions have an organized system of mountain "refuges," specially built for hikers and mountaineers. They are often spectacularly situated, and vary widely in the comforts they provide. Some have spacious facilities and serve hot meals. Others aren't much more than rustic hut shelters. Most are built to accommodate 50 to 100 hikers, with dorm-style rooms, bunk beds and blankets provided.

Most hut systems work on a first-come, first-serve basis. This means that, on the more popular trails, some huts may be a bit crowded on some nights. But part of the enjoyment of European-style trekking is meeting and interacting with hikers and climbers from other nations, people who share your love of the mountains.

On most of the treks graded "B-2," trip members only have to carry rucksacks. Trips which are graded "B-3" involve some sections of backpacking.

descend the Tiefmatten Glacier to the Stokje and Schonbuhl Hut.

DAY 11: Descend to Zermatt via Zmutt. Overnight at hotel.

DAY 12: In and around Zermatt. Local sightseeing and walks.

DAY 13: Walk to the Hornli Hut beneath the Matterhorn.

DAY 14: Local hikes around Schwartzsee. Overnight at hut.

DAY 15: Ascend Matterhorn (weather permitting). Descend to hut.

DAY 16: Descend to Zermatt. Continue to Chamonix. Overnight at hotel.

DAY 17: Ascend to the Grand Mulettes Hut. Overnight at hut.

DAY 18: A 1 a.m. start for the ascent of Mont Blanc (weather permitting). Traverse Aiguille and the Dome D'Gouter. Descend to the Tete Rouse Hut.

DAY 19: Descend to Chamonix. Afternoon free. Overnight at hotel.

DAY 20: Climb the Aiguille L'M and descend to Chamonix. Overnight at hotel.

> We will attempt to climb some of the most famous peaks of the Swiss and French Alps, including the Matterhorn and Mont Blanc.

DAY 21: A day of rock climbing at the Guillands and local sightseeing. Overnight at hotel.

DAY 22: Travel to Geneva. Depart Geneva and connect with homeward-bound flights.

IT4SRIMO2

MONT BLANC CIRCUIT

DATES: #1 Jun 12–Jun 26 (15 days)
　　　　#2 Jun 26–Jul 10 (15 days)
　　　　#3 Aug 28–Sep 11 (15 days)
LEADER: to be announced
GRADE: B-2
LAND COST: $1090 (6–12 members)

This is one of the world's great walks, a complete circuit around Mont Blanc, highest peak in Europe.

The classic *tour du Mont Blanc* takes about twelve days. The trail passes in and out of France, Italy and Switzerland. Views en route make it a photographer's dream, with a background of tumbling glaciers and famous peaks like the Aiguille du Midi, Les Grandes Jorasses, and Mont Dolanot.

Mont Blanc (15,771') presents an 11,000-foot flank of Himalayan scale and grandeur on the Italian side; the French flank is less steep but higher still. From this massif, seven valleys extend into France, Italy and Switzerland. Each of these alpine countries has its own unique culture, architecture and landscape. In circling Mont Blanc we pass from one to the other and take time to enjoy their individual delights amidst alpine scenery which has few equals in the world.

This is a vehicle-supported trek, so we only need to carry small daypacks. We'll camp each night, either in our own camps or at organized camping areas with shower facilities. This makes us independent of local mountain refuges, which can be crowded.

ITINERARY:

DAY 1 and 2: Leave U.S. Arrive Geneva. Transfer to hotel.

DAY 3: By train to Martigny and camp.

DAY 4: To Champex for the start of the trek, and hike around the Col Bovine to Forclas. Camp below the Trient Glacier.

> The classic *tour du Mont Blanc* takes about twelve days. The trail passes in and out of France, Italy and Switzerland.

C

Descent from Convercle Hut, Mont Blanc Range/Benjamin Ailes
European ibex

IT4SRIMO5

THE BERNESE OBERLAND

DATES: #1 Jun 25–Jul 10 (16 days)
#2 Aug 20–Sep 4 (16 days)
LEADER: to be announced
GRADE: B-3
LAND COST: $1190 (6–12 members)

The Bernese Alps, the "North Face of the Alps," contain massive glaciers and a wall of impressive peaks including the Jungfrau, the Monch and the famed Eiger.

Our backpacking tour among these peaks begins in the Swiss village of Lenk and follows a route over high passes between the Valais and the Oberland. Optional guided climbs of Grosstrubel, Blumisalphorn, the Monch or Jungfrau can be arranged during the trek at an additional cost. En route we'll stay in alpine mountain huts.

ITINERARY:

DAY 1 and 2: Leave U.S. Arrive Geneva. By train and bus to the village of Lenk (3,569').

DAY 3 to 5: Trek south to Iffigenalp beneath the peaks of Wildstrubel and Wildhorn, and continue to Engstiglenalp. Rest day at Engstiglenalp. Weather permitting, optional guided climb (cost not included) of Grosstrubel.

DAY 6 to 9: Trek via Engstiglengrat and the Gemmipass (7,680') into the Valais and Leukerbad (4,593'). Continue via the Restipass (7,742') and the Lotschenpas to Selden, then to Oeschinesee.

> **The Bernese Alps, the "North Face of the Alps," contain massive glaciers and a wall of impressive peaks including the Jungfrau, the Monch and the famed Eiger.**

DAY 10: Rest day at Oeschenesee. Weather permitting, optional guided climb (cost not included) of Blumlisalphorn (12,043').

DAY 11 to 13: Trek via the Hohturli to Griesalp, and to the unspoiled village of Murren, which lies beneath the Schilthorn (9,744'). Continue via Lauterbrunnen to Kleine Scheidegg (6,761').

DAY 14: If weather permits, by rail to Jungfraujoch to climb the Monch or Jungfrau with guide (at extra cost). Non-climbers can make some rewarding day hikes in the area.

DAY 15: Trek to Grindelwald, where the famous peaks of the Eiger, the Monch and Jungfrau dominate the views.

DAY 16: By train to Geneva. Depart Geneva and connect with homeward-bound flights.

AY 5: We cross into France via
e Col de Balme, and camp at
es Frasserands (4,537'). Afternoon
isit to Argentiere.

AY 6: Hike via Tre le Champ
,649') and Lac Chessery, visiting
cenic Lac Blanc before rejoining
e Grand Balcon route, which
oks across the Chamonix Valley
ward Mont Blanc. Descend to
e valley and camp.

AY 7: Using the cable car, we re-
in the trail and continue along
e Grand Balcon to the Col de
event (8,284'), a longish day
ith some of the finest views on
e route. Descend to Les Houches
,400') and camp.

AY 8: Climb to the Col Tricot
,955'), descend steeply to
halets de Miage, climb over

Truc and descend to Les Contamines. Camp near the chapel of Notre Dame De La Gorge.

DAY 9: We cross the Col De Vonhomme to Chapieux, or alternatively via the Tete Nord du Fours (8,500') to the Ville des Glaciers. Scenic campsite.

DAY 10: Over the Col de la Seigne into Italy. Camp in the Val Veni, east of Courmayeur.

DAY 11: Walk via the Plan Checrouit and picturesque Dolonne to Courmayeur. Continue by bus to Lavachey, our night stop at the head of the Val Ferret, beneath the Grand Jorasses.

DAY 12: Pass close by Mont Dolent, cross the Col Ferret and re-enter Switzerland. Camp at La Fouly.

DAY 13: Optional climb of Cab D'Ornay or easier route through the Swiss Val Ferret. Dinner in Champex and return to Martigny.

DAY 14: Free day to be used as necessary, or to allow for weather delays.

DAY 15: Return to Geneva. Depart Geneva on homeward-bound flights.

A

IT4SRIMTO3

THE ALPINE TRAVERSE

DATES: #1 Jul 9–Jul 24 (16 days)
#2 Aug 5–Aug 20 (16 days)
LEADER: to be announced
GRADE: B-3
LAND COST: $1190 (6–12 members)

This challenging trek visits some of the most beautiful and rarely visited parts of the Swiss Valais, traversing over high, rugged passes of true alpine character and through charming villages where the style of farming has remained unchanged for centuries. Most of the trails are relatively untrodden, giving excellent opportunity to see a variety of alpine flowers and wildlife.

From the Chamonix Valley we cross the northern part of the Mont Blanc range via the Col de Balme into Switzerland. The remainder of our trek will be in Switzerland, concluding at the famous alpine resort of Zermatt, where we spend three days on hikes with classic views of the Matterhorn, Monte Rosa and their huge surrounding glaciers.

Wherever possible, accommodations will be in mountain refuges, to maintain the high mountain ambiance.

ITINERARY:
DAY 1 and 2: Leave U.S. Arrive Geneva. Transfer to hotel.

DAY 3: By train to Chamonix and Argentiere. Overnight in mountain refuge at Les Frasserands.

DAY 4: Hike from the Chamonix Valley to the Col de Balme (7,559') and descend to Trient (4,196'). Overnight in mountain refuge.

DAY 5: From Trient there is a steep ascent to the Fenetre d'Arpett, followed by a descent into the beautiful Val d'Arpette and Champex (4,812'), a particularly charming spot in summer with its lakeside setting.

DAY 6: By bus from Champex to Le Chable, then by train up the Bagnes Valley to Verbier (4,921'), magnificently located on a plateau with impressive views. Overnight in Cabane Monte Fort (8,061').

DAY 7: Steep ascent to the Col du Gele (9,186'). On the northeast side we descend a snowfield. Though not steep, it may be icy and an ice axe would come in handy. Keeping to the left of Lac de Cleuson, follow a jeep track and overnight at the Refuge St. Laurent (8,274').

DAY 8: Ascend to Gouli de Cleuson and follow the path southeast past alpine lakes and up to a large snowfield. Cross the snowfield or descend to the valley and follow a path to Plan de Chaux to the Col de Prazfleuri (9,727'). Overnight at Cabane Prazfleuri (8,608')

DAY 9: Cross a pass to La Barma and walk to Arolla via the Col de Riedmatten (9,576'). Overnight in Arolla (6,555') or continue by bus down the valley to Evolene (4,498'). Arolla and Evolene, which lie at the heart of the Valais Alps, are very attractive villages with good restaurants and shops.

DAY 10: Bus and train to St. Luc (5,390') and walk to Cabane de Weisshorn (7,667'), a dortoir-type accommodation.

> ### Most of the trails are relatively untrodden, giving excellent opportunity to see a variety of alpine flowers and wildlife.

DAY 11: A very pleasant walk over the Meidpass (9,818') with excellent views to Gruben (5,961'). Overnight in dortoir at Gruben.

DAY 12: Ascend from Gruben to cross the Augstbordpass (9,494'). The long but delightful descent offers splendid views of Mischabel (14,911'). From Jungu we can either walk or take the cable car to St. Niklaus (3,661'). By train to Zermatt (5,265') and our hotel.

DAY 13 to 15: All around Zermatt, with its wonderful panorama of mountain peaks, there are many excellent day walks, including a hike to the Gorner Gorges and Furi, or to the Hornli Hut at the base of the Matterhorn (14,691'). Or one could take the exciting cable car ride (the highest in the Alps) to Klein Matterhorn (12,532'). For those who want to do a little climbing, we can arrange a guided climb of the Breithorn at extra cost.

DAY 16: By train to Geneva and connect with homeward-bound flights.

IT4SRIMO4

SKIING THE HAUTE ROUTE

DATES: *Apr 21–May 5
LEADER: Lanny Johnson
GRADE: B-3
LAND COST: *$1275 (8–10 members)
*Note change from 1984 Trip Schedule.

This is the most famous ski tour in the world, the "Haute Route," a high level traverse of eleven glacier passes between the greatest peaks of the Alps.

Among its many attractions are unbelievably beautiful winter views of the snowy backbone of Europe, including the Matterhorn, Monte Rosa, Mont Blanc and other great peaks of the Alps.

The classic "Haute Route" tour starts near Chamonix and ends near Saas Fee. It can be completed in about a week, but we have allowed several extra days to adjust to weather conditions and make possible ascents along the route, according to members' abilities.

Alpine skiing experience or strong parallel skiing technique on downhill skis is required. We will cover about 75 miles, most of it at an altitude of 10,000 feet.

ITINERARY:
DAY 1 and 2: Leave U.S. Arrive Geneva. Drive to Chamonix. Overnight in pension.

DAY 3: Check equipment, practice avalanche procedures and generally tone up for ski mountaineering. Overnight in pension in Chamonix.

DAY 4: By cableway to a point just below the summit of the Aiguille des Grand Montets, then descend via the Rognons Glacier to the Argentiere Glacier. Ski up to Argentiere Hut.

DAY 5: A strenuous day crossing part of another popular ski route, the Tour de Trois Cols ("Three Col Traverse") via the Plateau du Trient. Overnight at Trient Hut.

DAY 6: Ski down Trient Glacier to the Fenetre du Chamonis and the Col des Ecandies, further down into the Val d'Arpette, then Champex. On certain sections we may require the use of a rope to cross bergschrunds.

DAY 7 and 8: Via the Valsorey or Mont Fort huts, as dictated by the prevailing weather and snow conditions.

DAY 9: Climb the Pigne d'Arolla en route to the Vignettes Hut. Superb views of the Dent Blanch and surrounding peaks.

DAY 10: Spectacular Haute Route scenery as we cross Col de l'Eveque, Col du Mont Brule, Col de Valpelline, and finally the long descent beneath the Matterhorn into Zermatt. Overnight at hotel.

DAY 11: Rest day or ski ascent of the Breithorn, in part by uphill ski lifts.

DAY 12: From the Monte Rosa Hut we are among the highest conglomeration of 4,000-meter peaks in the Alps, all accessible to the ski mountaineer.

> ### Alpine skiing experience or strong parallel skiing technique on downhill skis is required. We will cover about 75 miles, most of it at an altitude of 10,000 feet.

DAY 13: To Saas Fee via the Adler Pass. Depending on conditions, we stay at Britannia Hut or Saas Fee.

DAY 14: Drive from Saas Fee to Geneva. Overnight at hotel.

DAY 15: Depart Geneva on homeward-bound flights.

B

A   Ascending the Pigne Arolla, Haute Route/Lanny Johnson
B   Bavarian villager/Wolfgang Koch
C   The Karwendel Mountains/Wolfgang Koch

GERMANY • 13

IT4PA1SFMT9

ALPINE TREKS IN BAVARIA & TYROL

DATES: #1 Jun 8–Jun 23 (16 days)
       #2 Sep 7–Sep 22 (16 days)
LEADER: Wolfgang Koch
GRADE: B-2
LAND COST: $1090 (12–14 members)
           $1395 (8–11)

This journey combines alpine trekking with visits to some of the prettiest mountain towns in Germany and Austria.

From Innsbruck, Austria's most famous alpine center, we will trek for five days through the Karwendel Mountains, a region with lovely alpine flora and fine peaks. Ending at Achensee, we drive through green alpine valleys to Berchtesgaden, famed for its landscape and romantic Bavarian architecture.

In the high mountains around Berchtesgaden, we make a four-day alpine trek which takes us over Watzmann Peak and to St. Bartholoma, a monastery on Lake Konigsee. We'll boat across the lake back to Berchtesgaden and end the trip with a visit to Salzburg.

ITINERARY:
DAY 1 and 2: Leave U.S. Arrive Munich. Drive to Innsbruck. Overnight at hotel.
DAY 3: Visit Innsbruck.
DAY 4 to 8: Alpine trek through Karwendel Mountains.
DAY 9: Drive to Berchtesgaden via Kitzbuhel.
DAY 10: Visit Berchtesgaden.

> **From Innsbruck, Austria's most famous alpine center, we will trek for five days through the Karwendel Mountains, a region with lovely alpine flora and fine peaks.**

DAY 11 to 14: Alpine trek in Berchtesgaden Mountains.
DAY 15: Visit Salzburg.
DAY 16: Depart Munich and connect with homeward-bound flights.

A

IT4PA1SFMT9

BAVARIA WALKING TOUR

DATES: #1 May 13–May 30 (18 days)
       #2 Jul 8–Jul 25 (18 days)
LEADER: Wolfgang Koch
GRADE: A-2
LAND COST: $1425 (12–14 members)
           $1620 (8–11)

This tour visits the hidden valleys and rural villages of Bavaria, where the mountain lifestyle hasn't changed in centuries.

Based in Garmisch for the first few days, we'll take day hikes into the surrounding mountains and ascend the Zugspitze (10,000'), Germany's highest peak, by cable car.

From Berchtesgaden, with its typical Bavarian architecture, we'll take some leisurely walks to high viewpoints, cross Konigsee (the most beautiful alpine lake in Germany) and visit St. Bartholoma's Monastery. In Austria, we'll visit the city of Salzburg.

Continuing into more rural and little-traveled parts of Bavaria, we'll spend several days on leisurely hikes in Bayerischer Wald National Park and Altmuhltal National Park.

Travel will be by van with accommodations in Bavarian-style pensions or castles.

ITINERARY:
DAY 1 and 2: Leave U.S. Arrive Munich. Continue to Garmisch.

DAY 3 and 4: Hikes around Garmisch area.
DAY 5: Drive to Berchtesgaden.
DAY 6 and 7: Hikes around Berchtesgaden.
DAY 8: Day trip to Salzburg.
DAY 9 and 10: Visit Passau.
DAY 11 to 13: Hiking in Bayerischer Wald National Park.
DAY 14: Visit Regensburg.
DAY 15 and 16: Hiking in Altmuhltal National Park.
DAY 17: Drive to Munich.
DAY 18: Connect with homeward-bound flights.

B

C

IT4PA1SFMT9

EASTERN ALPS CLIMBING CIRCUIT

DATES: Aug 5–Aug 26 (22 days)
LEADER: Wolfgang Koch
GRADE: B-3/D-1
LAND COST: $1490 (10–13 members)
$1755 (8–9)

This trip visits the major mountain areas of the Eastern Alps for hut-to-hut trekking and easy, non-technical ascents of the three highest points within Germany, Austria and Italy.

Traveling to the German mountain town of Garmisch, we trek for five days on a circuit through the Wetterstein Mountains. Our route takes us past Schachenhaus (an old castle at the very top of a peak) and along narrow valleys with impressive waterfalls. During the trek, we'll hike up the Zugspitze (10,000'), Germany's highest peak.

Traveling to Vent, a highland village in Austria, we trek for four days in the Otzaler Alps, with an ascent of Wildspitze (12,850'), the highest peak in Austria. Crossing the border into Italy, we'll visit the famed Dolomites for some trekking and a climb of Italy's highest peak, Ortler (13,016').

This circuit is for strong hikers or

> **Hut-to-hut trekking and easy, non-technical ascents of the three highest points within Germany, Austria and Italy.**

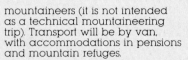

mountaineers (it is not intended as a technical mountaineering trip). Transport will be by van, with accommodations in pensions and mountain refuges.

ITINERARY:
DAY 1 and 2: Leave U.S. Arrive Munich. Continue to Garmisch.
DAY 3 to 7: Hike through the Wetterstein Mountains and climb Zugspitze.
DAY 8: Drive to Vent, Austria.
DAY 9 to 12: Hike in Otzaler Alps and climb Wildspitze.
DAY 13: Drive to Grodner Joch, Italy.
DAY 14 to 16: Hiking and scrambling in the Dolomites.
DAY 17: Drive to Trafoi, Italy.
DAY 18 to 20: Ascent of Ortler.
DAY 21: Drive to Milan via Gardasee.
· DAY 22: Transfer to airport and connect with homeward-bound flights.

IT4LH131A

LOMBARDIA TREK

DATES: *#1 Jun 29–Jul 15 (17 days)
*#2 Jul 27–Aug 12 (17 days)
*#3 Sep 7–Sep 23 (17 days)
LEADER: local guides
GRADE: B-2
LAND COST: $1295 (8–12 members)
*Note date change from 1984 Trip Schedule.

Lombardia is the region of north central Italy which extends from the fertile plains of the Po River to the snow-crowned Bernina Alps and the peaks of Bregaglia, which mark Italy's border with Switzerland.

Its alpine landscape, crowned with rock spires and snowy peaks, is seen in the background in many of Leonardo da Vinci's most beautiful paintings. In fact, da Vinci spent the most productive years of his career in Lombardia and traveled widely through the region.

We shall trek across two of the most interesting and remote valleys of Lombardia: the Val Masino and Val Malenco, both on the Swiss border. Here we find beautiful snow peaks, including Mt. Bernina (13,284') and Mt. Disgrazia (12,066'), a huge, isolated massif and one of the most picturesque in the Alps. Great glaciers flow from these mountains, among which are the Scerscen and Fellaria, which feed the large lakes of the lowlands. Also situated here is the rock massif of Mt. Badile (10,853'), well known among European climbers. The 3,000-foot high granite slabs of its northern flanks are considered by mountaineers to be one of the "six classic north faces in the Alps."

As we walk from hut to hut, the chestnut woods gradually give way to pine forests. Higher, above the 7,000-foot level, thickets of stunted rhododendrons and wildflowers compliment a typically grand apline landscape. Marmots and royal eagles are very commonly seen.

At night, we will sleep in traditional mountain "refuges," similar to the refuges in the Dolomites and many other mountain regions of Eruope.

Visits are also included to Lake Como and Milan.

Shepherd/Beppe Tenti
Mountain goat/Beppe Tenti
Village church/Beppe Tenti
Val Masino, Lombardia/Beppe Tenti

ITINERARY:

DAY 1 and 2: Leave U.S. Arrive Milan. Transfer to hotel.

DAY 3: Drive to Bagni Masino. Overnight at inn.

DAY 4: Begin 11-day trek. From Bagni Masino (3,845'), we trek through fields and pastures to the end of the Oro Valley. Overnight at Refuge Omio (6,890').

DAY 5: To Refuge Giannetti (8,310'), a long traverse along the foot of the Oro peaks.

DAY 8: To Refuge Ponti (8,395'), with spectacular views along the way of Mt. Disgrazia.

DAY 9: To Refuge Bosio (6,840'), crossing Corna Rossa Pass and entering Valle Airola, with its lovely waterfalls.

DAY 10: To Refuge Porro (6,430'), across the remote Val Torreggio with its huge granite walls, and over Ventina Pass with views of Mt. Disgrazia from the glacier.

DAY 11: To Refuge Tartaglione, through pastures and shepherds' huts, passing the peaks of Alpe de Locca and Alpe Sentieri.

DAY 12: To Refuge Longoni. Wildflowers decorate the trailsides today.

DAY 13: To Chiesa de Val Malenco (2,952'), descending to the main village of the Malenco area. Overnight at inn.

DAY 14: Visit stone quarries and a small historical museum at Chiesa de Valmelenco.

DAY 15: Sightseeing around Lake Como. Overnight at hotel.

DAY 16: Drive to Milan. Afternoon sightseeing. Overnight at hotel.

DAY 17: Depart Milan and connect with homeward-bound flights.

> **Its alpine landscape, crowned with rock spires and snowy peaks, is seen in the background in many of Leonardo da Vinci's most beautiful paintings.**

DAY 6: To Refuge Allievi (8,395'), crossing two passes: Camerozzo (8,925') and Qualido (8,760'). This is a typical alpine trail surrounded by snow-covered peaks.

DAY 7: To Cataeggio (2,580'), along the Val di Mello, a rock climbing area. Overnight at a small inn in the village of Cataeggio.

IT4LH131A

VAL D'AOSTA TREK

DATES: *#1 Jun 22–Jul 8 (17 days)
        *#2 Jul 6–Jul 22 (17 days)
        *#3 Aug 17–Sep 2 (17 days)
LEADER: local guides
GRADE: B-3
LAND COST: $1295 (8–12 members)
*Note date change from 1984 Trip Schedule.

Val d'Aosta is a spectacular valley in the heart of the highest Alps of Europe, where the mountainous borders of Italy, Switzerland and France meet.

Surrounding Val d'Aosta are some of the most magnificent and well-known peaks in the Alps: the Mont Blanc massif, whose 15,771-foot summit is the highest point in Europe west of the Caucasus, and the great peaks of the Pennine Alps, including the Matterhorn (14,692'), Monte Rosa (15,203') and Gran Combin (14,154').

The first part of our trek will take us along miles and miles of ancient paths connecting valleys, villages and alpine meadows, all with views extending from Monte Rosa to the Matterhorn to Mont Blanc. The second portion of the trek will take us through Gran Paradiso National Park, where the delicate mountain environment remains unspoiled and we may see a graceful ibex or chamois posed among the rocks. In the summer, a profusion of wildflowers add brilliant color to every vista. The climate here is generally fair and dry, since the massive flanks of Mont Blanc shelter the valley from wet weather and storms.

Rich in human history since the Neolithic Age, Val d'Aosta was conquered by the Romans in the first century B.C. In the town of Aosta (founded in 23 B.C.), a fine Roman theater and arch still remain. Val d'Aosta's medieval era is represented by many ancient forts, castles and churches.

The region is bilingual and bicultural in French and Italian. There are other ethnic communities such as the Walsers, who migrated here in the 12th century, and still speak their own German-based language.

At night we will stay in small inns, alpine villages or in mountain refuges.

ITINERARY:

DAY 1 and 2: Leave U.S. Arrive Milan. Transfer to hotel.

DAY 3: Drive to Aosta, main town of the Aosta Valley. Afternoon free to explore the city.

DAY 4: Drive to St. Jacques. Overnight at inn.

DAY 5: Begin 11-day trek. Leaving the last village in the Val d'Ayas, we cross the Col di Nana (9,100') to Chamois, a tiny village that can only be reached on foot or by cable car. Views en route include Monte Rosa, Breithorn and the Matterhorn.

DAY 6: To Cheneil (6,975'), through meadows and high pastures with wildflowers all along the trail. Views of the Matterhorn (14,492') will be spectacular today.

A

DAY 7: Descend to the village of Valtournanche (5,000'), with its ancient houses and church, then up the other side of the valley to Cignana Lake (7,086'). Overnight at a refuge close to the lake shore.

DAY 8: To Torgnon (5,577'), passing by alpine houses and open meadows. Overnight at a village inn.

DAY 9: Cross over the Col Fenetre (7,158') and reach the village of Lignan (5,357'). Overnight at inn.

DAY 10: To Oratoire de Cuney (8,700'). The trail heads uphill to a 17th century church. Overnight in a small refuge next to the church.

DAY 11: Cross over the Col Versona, with its views of Monte Rosa (and our first views of Mont Blanc and Gran Combin), and reach Valpelline. Drive to Aosta. Overnight in hotel.

DAY 12: Visit Aosta and nearby Roman ruins, stop for lunch in a local restaurant in Cogne, then hike up to the Refuge Vittorio Sella (8,477').

DAY 13: To Eaux Rousses (5,446'). Today we are in the heart of Gran Paradiso National Park. Cross the Col Lauson (10,813'), with its views of the peaks of La Grivola (13,021') and Gran Paradiso (13,641') and surrounding glaciers.

DAY 14: Up again to the Col de Sort (9,724') then descend to the village of Rhemes Notre Dame, located in the park.

> **Val d'Aosta is a spectacular valley in the heart of the highest Alps of Europe, where the mountainous borders of Italy, Switzerland and France meet.**

DAY 15: We cross from one valley into another, over the Col Fenetre (9,317') and end our trek at Valgrisenche.

DAY 16: Drive to Milan. Afternoon sightseeing. Overnight at hotel.

DAY 17: Depart Milan and connect with homeward-bound flights.

IT4LH131A

PIEMONTE TREK

DATES: *#1 Jun 8–Jun 24 (17 days)
        *#2 Jul 13–Jul 29 (17 days)
        *#3 Aug 31–Sep 16 (17 days)
LEADER: local guides
GRADE: B-2
LAND COST: $1295 (8–12 members)
*Note change from 1984 Trip Schedule.

In the western part of the Italian Alps, near the Maritime Alps, lies Piemonte (literally "foothills"), an area of green and gently rolling hills at altitudes of 5,000 to 7,000 feet.

Piemonte traces its human history back to medieval times. The oldest existing historical documents on this area date to 1200 A.D., as do many of its fine old churches.

With a geography which has left it relatively isolated from the mainstream of modern Italy, the pastoral villages of Piemonte have maintained a traditional way of life, ruled by the passing seasons. Farming and cattle raising are the summer activities, and the making of handicrafts (particularly wood carving) fills the winter.

To walk these valleys is to wander back in time, strolling on stonepaved paths, exploring ancient churches with historic wall paintings, meeting shepherds, and enjoying old-style Italian country life.

The people of Piemonte descend from an ethnic group which still speaks an ancient dialect of French called "provencal." They are proud of their heritage and celebrate it often in their dances and festivals.

The walks will be easy, with our baggage carried by pack mules. Our longest walking day will be about six hours. From the highest point on the trek (8,000'), we have a close view of the isolated pyramid of Monviso (12,600'), highest peak in the area, nearby which springs the source of Italy's longest river, the historic Po.

Our accommodations will be farmhouses or small inns.

Visits are also included to Torino, 19th century capital of Italy, and Milan.

ITINERARY:

DAY 1 and 2: Leave U.S. Arrive Milan. Transfer to hotel.

DAY 3: Drive to Rore. Overnight at inn.

DAY 4: Begin 11-day trek. Rore to Ciampanesio (4,980'), a panoramic and varied trek through woods, pastures and small villages. Overnight at farmhouse.

DAY 5: Cross the Collie de Lua Pass (8,000') to Refuge Quintano Sella, one of the oldest and most famous mountain huts in the Alps, located at the foot of Monviso Peak.

DAY 6: To Pian Melze (5,623'), a short trek descending to the Po River springs, with beautiful views of the north face of Monviso.

DAY 7: Hike to the little village of

Val D'Aosta farmer/Beppe Tenti
Spires of the Dolomites/Beppe Tenti
Autumn colors/Beppe Tenti
Wildflowers/Beppe Tenti
Ridge trail/Beppe Tenti

Crissolo then walk through the woods to Oncino (4,200').

DAY 8: Up to Testa de Garitta Nuova (7,800') and down to the village of Gilba (3,800'). Views of Monte Rosa.

DAY 9: To Becetto (4,553'), into an environment of terraced fields, stone-paved paths and small villages where farmers have worked for centuries.

To walk these valleys is to wander back in time, strolling on stone-paved paths, exploring ancient churches with historic wall paintings, meeting shepherds, and enjoying old-style Italian country life.

DAY 10: Up again to Cima de Crosa (8,300') with panoramic views. Descend through pastures to Ciampanesio (4,900').

DAY 11: Trek through one of the most extensive forests in northern Italy, and along the shores of Lake Pontechianale (5,300').

DAY 12: From Pontechianale to Blins (4,855'), over Colle della Battagliola (7,400'), with beautiful views of the south face of Monviso. The Blins Valley is inhabited by "Ousitanes," people who settled here in the Middle Ages.

DAY 13: To Elva (5,370'), through pastures and pine woods, past houses built in the old-style architecture.

DAY 14: To Colle de Macra (4,160'), across the Maira Valley, with its cobbled pathways and small chapels.

DAY 15: Drive to Milan via Torino. Overnight at hotel.

DAY 16: Sightseeing in Milan. Overnight at hotel.

DAY 17: Depart Milan and connect with homeward-bound flights.

IT4LH131A

THE DOLOMITES TREK

DATES: *#1 Jun 15–Jul 1 (17 days)
*#2 Aug 24–Sep 9 (17 days)
*#3 Sep 14–Sep 30 (17 days)
LEADER: local guides
GRADE: B-3
LAND COST: $1295 (8–12 members)
*Note date change from 1984 Trip Schedule.

Although the mountains of the Dolomites are not exceptionally high (the highest peak is 10,965-foot Mt. Marmolada), they are among the most striking mountains in Europe, steep spires of fantastic form colored in weathered hues of rose, yellow and grey.

Below the "fairytale" spires and dramatic walls lie bright green meadows alive with wildflowers all summer. In the lower valleys, there are orchards, vineyards and a checkerboard of cultivated fields.

Continuously sheer cliffs flank most of the Dolomite's peaks. The great mountaineers of the 1920's and 1930's practiced the emerging sport of rock climbing on these cliffs, forging routes which remain classics to this day.

The name Dolomites is generally considered to include all the limestone mountains of the alto Adige, Trentino and Veneto, a region favored with sunny, dry weather.

Up until World War I, this was part of the Austrian South Tyrol. The present-day people of the Dolomites speak their own special patois (Ladin) as well as Italian and German.

Our nights will be in traditional mountain "refuges," often spectacularly situated and offering rustic dorm-style accommodations.

Visits are also included to the resort town of Cortina, Verona (city of Romeo and Juliet) and Milan.

ITINERARY:
DAY 1 and 2: Leave U.S. Arrive Milan. Overnight at hotel.

DAY 3: Drive to Belluno. Overnight at hotel.

DAY 4: Begin 11-day trek. Drive to Agordo (2,700') and walk up to the new Refuge Bianchet through pine woods and alpine meadows.

DAY 5: To Refuge Pramperet (6,000'), through high pastures dotted with wildflowers.

DAY 6: To Refuge Carestiato (6,300'), through a wild and remote area where we might see wildlife such as chamois, a small goat-like antelope found in the mountains of Europe.

DAY 7: To Refuge Tissi (7,500'), a spectacularly situated refuge with exceptional views of the great buttresses and rock towers of the Civetta Range.

DAY 8: To Refuge Venezia (6,300'), through the heart of the Dolomites, passing along the base of Civetta (10,588'), (known as the "wall of walls"). Civetta's perpendicular white cliffs make it a popular climbing spot.

DAY 9: To Refuge Palmieri (6,700'). Fine views of Mt. Pelmo (10,394'), an impressive rock tower.

DAY 10: To Refuge Nuvolau (8,450'), with beautiful views of Croda de Lago and Becco de Mezzodi, peaks rising majestically from thickly wooded slopes. Walk up to the refuge at 8,450 feet.

DAY 11: To Refuge Cantore (8,350'). Views of the entire range today, including Tofana, Marmolada and the Cortina Valley. Overnight at Cantore Refuge, situated immediately below the crest of the Forcella de Fontana Negra.

DAY 12 and 13: To Refuge Lagazzuoi, at 9,000 feet in the Tofana area, then on to the Fanes Valley.

DAY 14: On the last day of our trek, we descend to the green valley of Braies, where the peak of Croda del Becco is beautifully reflected in Lake Braies. Overnight at a local hotel.

Continuously sheer cliffs flank most of the Dolomite's peaks. The great mountaineers of the 1920's and 1930's practiced the emerging sport of rock climbing on these cliffs, forging routes which remain classics to this day.

DAY 15: Sightseeing in Cortina, a winter sports center situated amid a great cirque of magnificent mountains. Two aerial tramways give easy access to superb viewpoints of the Valle d'Ampezzo, one of the most beautiful in the Dolomites.

DAY 16: Drive to Milan via historic Verona. Overnight at hotel.

DAY 17: Depart Milan and connect with homeward-bound flights.

ITIAFI55SC

THE CAUCASUS & MT. ELBRUS

DATES: Sep 1–Sep 24 (24 days)
LEADER: Bruce Klepinger
GRADE: B-2/C-3
LAND COST: $1890 (8–15 members)

This is a special trekking and climbing journey to the Caucasus Mountains of the U.S.S.R. Mountain Travel's first trip here was in 1974, when we sent the first-ever American trekking/climbing party to visit the region.

Our itinerary focuses around the Central Caucasus in the Baksan Valley. The mountain scenery here is as beautiful as any in the heart of the Swiss and French Alps. There are deep forests of poplar and beech, high thickets of stunted birch and rhododendron and alpine meadows carpeted with wildflowers. The highest peak in Europe is located here—Mt. Elbrus (18,841'). Around it are other major peaks such as Shikhra (16,529'), Katyntau (16,355'), Jangitau, (16,571'), and Ushba (15,453'), the "Matterhorn of the Caucasus."

Our base will be a hotel in the Baksan Valley below Mt. Elbrus. From this central location, we'll make a variety of excursions, including a seven-day backpacking trip across the major passes of the Caucasus into Svanetia, a Georgian mountain region with 1000 years of history dating back to the Crusades.

Returning to the Baksan Valley, climbers in the group will have a chance to ascend Mt. Elbrus, a challenging (but not technically difficult) high altitude climb. During the two-day climb, trekkers in the group can hike up to the Priutt Refuge on Mt. Elbrus for great mountain views.

ITINERARY:

DAY 1 and 2: Leave U.S. Arrive Moscow. Transfer to hotel.

DAY 3: Fly to Mineralnye Vody. Continue by bus to the Baksan Valley. Overnight at hotel.

DAY 4: By chair lift up to Cheget (11,480'), for a leisurely hike with panoramic views of the Baksan Valley and the two white peaks of Mt. Elbrus. Return to hotel.

DAY 5: Day excursion to "Refuge of Eleven" on Mt. Elbrus, up by tram to 11,480 feet, then a two-hour hike over snow to the refuge, which is located at 13,800 feet. Descend by tram and return to hotel.

DAY 6: Begin seven-day trek across the passes of the Caucasus and into Svanetia, Georgia, with a hike to a campsite below Betcho Pass (10,580'), which leads from the Baksan Valley into Georgia.

DAY 7: Cross the Betcho Pass over a steep trail and easy snow slopes. Descend into the Betcho Valley and camp.

DAY 8: Descend through meadows and forests to about 9,200 feet. Camp along the Betcho River near the roadhead.

DAY 9: Short hike through the village of Masery. Continue by bus to Mestia, a small Georgian village famous for its ancient watchtowers. This is the main town of Svanetia. Camp or overnight at hotel.

> The mountain scenery here is as beautiful as any in the heart of the Swiss and French Alps. There are deep forests of poplar and beech, high thickets of stunted birch and rhododendron and alpine meadows carpeted with wildflowers.

DAY 10: Sightseeing in Mestia, with its little stone streets and ancient town squares, many of which date back to the time of Genghis Khan. Overnight at hotel.

DAY 11: By bus to the Nacra Valley, then hike up through forests and meadows to a camp along the Nacra River (8,800').

DAY 12: Cross Dongus-Orun Pass (12,795') and descend into the valley on the other side. Traverse through meadows to the middle station of a chairlift by which we descend back into the Baksan Valley. Arrive back at our hotel.

DAY 13: Rest day, optional local walks.

DAY 14 to 16: For mountaineers, an optional climb of Mt. Elbrus; for non-climbers, hike to refuge on Elbrus.

DAY 17: Descend to the Baksan Valley. Overnight at hotel.

DAY 18: Rest day at hotel.

DAY 19 to 21: Three-day excursion by road to Georgia, including visits to Kasbegi and Tbilissi.

DAY 22: Fly to Moscow. Transfer to hotel.

DAY 23: Day free in Moscow for sightseeing.

DAY 24: Depart Moscow and connect with homeward-bound flights.

ITIAFI55SB

THE ALTAI MOUNTAINS

DATES: approx. Jul 21–Aug 14 (25 days)
LEADER: to be announced
GRADE: B-2/D-2
LAND COST: *$2875 (8–15 members
*Note change from 1984 Trip Schedule.

Few mountain regions in the world are so unknown as the Altai of the U.S.S.R., a range which rises above the deep Siberian taiga forests near the Mongolian and Chinese borders.

Britisher Samuel Turner, first Western explorer of the Altai, made a ten-week expedition here in 1904, which he chronicled in his book *Siberia: A Record of Travel, Climbing and Exploration.* He traveled in March and April (a most unlikely time of year, journeying from the railhead at Novo Nicolaevsk by troika to the Akker Valley in the heart of the Altai. During his stay he made a first ascent of Willer's Peak and evidently came within a few hundred feet of climbing Belukha (14,800'), highest in the range. Few, if any, Westerners have been here since.

Mountain Travel's explorations will begin in July 1983, when Dick and Louise McGowan travel to the Altai to establish the 1984 itinerary.

THE CAUCASUS & MT. ELBRUS ....
ALTAI MOUNTAINS — — — — — —
THE PAMIRS _____

800 Miles

C

D

A Altai explorer Samuel Turner
B Kirghiz yurt houses, Pamirs/Allen Steck
C Summit of Peak Lenin/Allen Steck
D Descending Peak Lenin/Allen Steck
E Dinner at climbing camp/Allen Steck

Our proposed 1984 Altai journey will include trekking, backpacking and optional climbs. Unlike Turner, we'll travel during optimum weather conditions and have the convenience of modern transportation to get us to our remote destination. Flying from Moscow to Barnaul, we'll be whisked to an Altai camp by helicopter, and operate from a well-stocked base camp. Besides Mt. Belukha, our research indicates that the summits of Berelsky, Delone, Pik Heroic Korea and Rerikh present interesting scrambles. We may also undertake a circular trek across several passes into the valleys of Kucherlja and Men-Su.

Few mountain regions in the world are so unknown as the Altai of the U.S.S.R., a range which rises above the deep Siberian taiga forests near the Mongolian and Chinese borders.

ITINERARY:
DAY 1 and 2: Leave U.S. Arrive Moscow. Transfer to hotel.
DAY 3: Fly to Barnaul.
DAY 4 to 22: In the Altai.
DAY 23: Return to Moscow by air.
DAY 24: In Moscow.
DAY 25: Depart Moscow and connect with homeward-bound flights.

ITIAF155SC

THE PAMIRS & PEAK LENIN

DATES: approx. *Jul 12–Aug 10 (30 days)
LEADER: Bruce Klepinger
GRADE: E-2
LAND COST: *$2790 (8–12 members)
*Note change from 1984 Trip Schedule.

Within the U.S.S.R., four peaks rise to over 7,000 meters. Three of these lie in the Pamirs, a unique cluster of mountains in the southeast corner of the Tadzhik S.S.R., where China, the Soviet Union and Afghanistan meet.

The peaks of the Pamirs are situated above a high, windswept plateau sparsely populated by nomadic Kirghiz tribesmen, and long ago traveled by the great merchant caravans of the Silk Road between China and Rome.

The goal of our expedition is an ascent of Peak Lenin (23,406'), the most frequently climbed high peak in the world. While the climb is not technically difficult, extreme altitude and potentially severe weather conditions on the mountain make it a demanding ascent.

From Moscow, we fly to Osh, capital of the Kirghiz S.S.R., and on to Daraut Kurgan, an old Silk Road fortress city built by Kothand warriors. Here we continue by truck across the 10,000-foot Pamir Plateau to our base camp at Achik-Tash. Sixteen days have been allotted for establishing a series of camps from base to Camp IV on the Lipkin Route on the northeast ridge of Peak Lenin.

OPTIONAL SILK ROAD TOUR: After the climb, a five-day tour is offered of the historic Silk Road cities of Samarkand, Bukhara and Tashkent. Additional cost: $345.

The goal of our expedition is an ascent of Peak Lenin (23,406'), the most frequently climbed high peak in the world.

ITINERARY:
DAY 1 and 2: Leave U.S. Arrive Moscow. Transfer to hotel.
DAY 3: Fly to Osh and Daraut Kurgan. Continue by truck to Achik Tash.
DAY 4 to 10: Time for organizing equipment and making acclimatization ascents.
DAY 11 to 25: Ascent of Peak Lenin.
DAY 26 and 27: Return to Daraut Kurgan and Osh.
DAY 28: Fly to Moscow.
DAY 29: Sightseeing in Moscow.
DAY 30: Depart Moscow and connect with homeward-bound flights.

U.S.S.R. INTERNATIONAL MOUNTAINEERING CAMPS

The U.S.S.R. Sports Committee hosts an important series of International Mountaineering Camps open to climbers, skiers and hikers. The camps are truly international and are attended by people from dozens of nations. This program has been on-going since 1974.

Mountain Travel, Inc., acts as the agent for participants from the U.S. and Canada. The camps can be booked for individuals or small groups.

For 1984, the programs will take place in four mountain regions:

THE CAUCASUS: 24-day climbing/hiking program in the Mt. Elbrus region (two July camps); 17-day alpine skiing program (three camps in February/March).

THE PAMIRS: 30-day program of expedition mountaineering with climbs of either Peak Lenin (23,406') or Peak Communism (24,590'). Two July camps. Minimum four in party.

THE WESTERN TIEN SHAN: 15-day program of skiing and climbing in the Chimgan region. One camp is offered in March.

THE ALTAI: 24-day climbing/hiking program with an ascent of Mt. Belukha (14,800'), highest peak in the range. One July camp is planned.

Participants must supply their own personal camping, climbing and/or skiing equipment. Cost includes all expenses within the U.S.S.R. The Soviet staff provides assistance in planning your activities at the camps, but there is no pre-planned itinerary; each individual must arrange his/her own activities. No change is allowed from the set program dates. Mountain Travel will provide some written material and maps.

At the time of writing (May, 1983), the exact dates and prices for 1984 are not known. As soon as they are, we will print an Information Sheet on the 1984 U.S.S.R. International Mountaineering Camps.

Write for details.

A Polish highlanders/Edward Mroz
B Rafting the Dunajec River/Edward Mroz

A

IT4PA1SFMT11

THE POLISH COUNTRYSIDE

DATES: Aug 11–Aug 25 (15 days)
LEADER: Frank Mora
GRADE: A-2
LAND COST: $1190 (6–12 members)

The main focus of this trip is southern Poland's mountain country, the High Tatras, where we'll get acquainted with the "Gorale" (Polish highlanders).

We begin in Warsaw, the bustling capital city, then head south to Krakow, with a stop en route at the village of Zelazowa Wola, where Chopin lived and created his music.

After sightseeing in Krakow, the medieval capital of Poland (and possibly the oldest intact city in Europe, with its cobblestone market place and ancient churches), we continue on to Zakopane, the main resort town of the Polish Tatras.

With our hotel in Zakopane as a base, we make leisurely hiking excursions into the Tatras, visiting remote villages and shepherds' hamlets where people still conduct their lives much as their ancestors did centuries ago. If we are lucky, we may witness a wedding or other local highland festivity.

After a half-day trip by wooden raft on the scenic Dunajec River, we drive back to Warsaw via the national park at Polomnice.

ITINERARY:
DAY 1 and 2: Leave U.S. Arrive Warsaw. Overnight at hotel.
DAY 3: Sightseeing in Warsaw's "Old City." Overnight at a country inn.
DAY 4: Drive to Zelazowa Wola, birthplace of Chopin. Continue to Krakow. Overnight at hotel.
DAY 5: Sightseeing in Krakow. Dinner at King's Inn, Wierzynek.
DAY 6: Short trip to an underground salt mine in Wieliczka then drive to Zakopane, in the Tatras Mountains. Our base for the next five nights will be the Kasprowy Hotel, from which we'll make daily excursions.

DAY 7: By aerial railway up to Gubalowka for a High Tatras panorama. Lunch on top and leisurely descent on foot back to the hotel.
DAY 8: Drive to Morskie Oko Lake, and hike to Black Pond. Return to hotel.
DAY 9: By aerial tramway to Kasprowy Wierch. Lunch at the tram's Top Station and an afternoon hike in an alpine setting above treeline. Descend by gondola and return to hotel.
DAY 10: Morning hike. Afternoon visit to a very old church at Jaszczurowka.

> We begin in Warsaw, the bustling capital city and then head south to Krakow, with a stop en route at the village of Zelazowa Wola, where Chopin lived and created his music.

DAY 11: Leaving the Tatras, we drive to Czorsztyn and visit the ruins of a medieval castle, then make a half-day trip by raft down the Dunajec River through Pieniny Gorge. We'll travel the river on a typical wooden raft guided by an oarsman. Continue by road to the resort village of Krynica, where the pre-war aristocracy spent its holidays. Overnight in hotel.
DAY 12: Morning visit by cable car to Parkowa Gora, with its Tatras views, then continue to the national park at Polomnice, where there is a herd of the last remaining European bison. Continue to Krakow.
DAY 13: Afternoon drive to Warsaw.
DAY 14: In Warsaw, sightseeing and shopping for wood carvings and other hand-made crafts. Farewell dinner.
DAY 15: Depart Warsaw and connect with homeward-bound flight.

B

IT4PA1SFMT10

THE HILLS OF CZECHOSLOVAKIA

DATES: #1 Jun 16–Jun 30 (15 days)
#2 Sep 8–Sep 22 (15 days)
LEADER: to be announced
GRADE: *B-1
LAND COST: *$950 (7–15 members)
*Note change from 1984 Trip Schedule.

This walking tour encompasses Czechoslovakian hill country at its finest—both in the alpine High Tatras and the romantic valleys of northern Bohemia.

The peaks of the High Tatras, astride the Polish-Czech border, are the highest portion of the long Carpathian chain. A compact and spectacular mountain range, the Tatras are somewhat like a scaled-down version of the Alps, a scene of fine granite pinnacles, arretes and rock walls rising as much as 4,000 feet above timberline. The highest peak in the Tatras is Gerlach (8,710'). The region's residents are farmers and shepherds who are far removed from the mainstream of modern Czechoslovakian life and still retain their traditional costumes in everyday life. Most of the Tatras is now a national park, harboring wildlife such as chamonis and European lynx.

This is fine hiking country, with its gentle meadows and beech forests, and we'll spend four days based in a mountain lodge with a beautiful Tatras panorama. Time is set aside for a variety of hikes and climbs to suit individual tastes.

Before visiting the Tatras, we journey to northern Bohemia, another area where ancient dress is still worn and folk traditions are cherished. The history of Bohemia dates to medieval times when the Hussites defeated the 70,000-strong armies of the Crusaders. Today it is a land of rich orchards and cultivated fields, a rural landscape dotted with castles and churches of Gothic and Baroque architecture, and beautiful old villages of stone and half-timber folk architecture.

In Bohemia, we will make a leisurely three-day trek in the Krkonose Mountains (rugged hills known as the "Giant Mountains"), hiking from village to village and spending nights in small hotels.

The trip begins and ends in Prague, the graceful capital city built on the shores of the Vltava River, and full of well-preserved buildings and monuments dating from the 13th to 19th century.

ITINERARY:
DAY 1 and 2: Leave U.S. Arrive Prague and transfer to hotel. Afternoon free and dinner at hotel.
DAY 3: Half-day sightseeing in Prague. Overnight at hotel.
DAY 4: Full-day excursion visiting Karlstejn Castle, Koneprusy Caves, and Konopiste Castle. Return to Prague.
DAY 5: Begin three-day trip into northern Bohemia. By bus to Harrachov in Krkonose, 135 kms. north of Prague. Afternoon hiking in the surrounding forests. Overnight at inn.

> The history of Bohemia dates to medieval times when the Hussites defeated the 70,000-strong armies of the Crusaders.

DAY 6: A whole day of hiking (about 12 miles) through the western part of Giant Mountains National Park, overnight at the village of Spindleruv Mlyn.
DAY 7: Hike about 11 miles to the village of Pec Pod Snezkou. Overnight at local htoel.
DAY 8: Hike in the area around Pec Pod Snezkou, with a possible walk up Snezka (5,255), the highest peak in the Giant Mountains.
DAY 9: Morning free. Afternoon depart by local bus for Prague. Arrive and transfer to railway station. Board overnight train for Poprad in the High Tatras.
DAY 10: Arrive in Poprad then take the electric train to Strbske Pleso (4,445') in the High Tatras. Balance of day for hiking in the area. Overnight at hotel.
DAY 11: Leave Strbske Pleso for Sliezky Dom Mountain Hotel (6,560'), seeing a beautiful panorama of the High Tatras National Park on the way. Overnight in hotel.
DAY 12 and 13: Based at the Sliezsky Dom Mountain Hotel, there are many possibilities for hikes and climbs, including Gerlach, highest peak in the Tatras.
DAY 14: In the late morning, leave for Tatranska Poljanka and take the electric train back to Poprad. Board the overnight train to Prague.
DAY 15: Arrive in Prague. Morning free. Transfer to airport and connect with homeward-bound flights.

Skogarfoss Falls, Iceland/Alla Schmitz
Dogsledding, Greenlander style/
Mike Banks

NATURAL HISTORY OF ICELAND

DATES: Jul 7–Jul 20 (14 days)
LEADER: Helgi Benediktsson
GRADE: B-2
LAND COST: $1490 (8–12 members)

Iceland, that peculiar environment of fire and ice, is a living laboratory for geologists. Natural cataclysms are constantly shaping and reshaping the land with major volcanic eruptions on the average of every five years.

We will travel in southern Iceland by four-wheel drive vehicle, camping en route and visiting some of its most interesting spots, including Great Geyser (a famous thermal spout from which the international word geyser was derived) and Gullfoss, one of Europe's highest waterfalls. We'll hike up Mt. Hekla (4,927'), Iceland's best known volcano, and (for those who are fit) climb Iceland's highest peak, Mt. Oraefajokull (6,952')

In contrast to the creaking glaciers, spouting geysers and steaming lava fields, we'll find that Iceland's landscape can also be very serene. In mid-summer (the time of our visit), there will be almost continuous daylight illuminating a pleasant and pristine landscape of deep fjords, glittering lakes, green valleys and coastal farm country which has been inhabited by Icelanders for more than 1100 years. The climate is mild (tempered by the Gulf Stream) and the air is probably the clearest and cleanest in the inhabited world.

Ornithologists take an interest in Iceland, too, since most of Iceland's wildlife (except for arctic fox and reindeer) is winged; more than 240 species of migrant birds visit Iceland, with 76 species nesting here regularly.

GREENLAND OPTION: After the trip, we can arrange an optional four or five-day tour to Angmagssalik, an Eskimo fishing and seal-hunting settlement on the eastern coast of Greenland. Cost: $500 to $540 including round trip air fare from Iceland to Greenland.

ITINERARY:
DAY 1 and 2: Leave U.S. Arrive Reykjavik, Iceland. Meet with trip leader and drive to Pingvellir National Park. Short hike in the area and overnight at hotel.
DAY 3: From Pingvellir, drive to Þjorsardalur at the foot of Mt. Hekla, and camp. En route visit the Great Geyser and Gullfoss ("the golden waterfall").
DAY 4: Easy hike to Mt. Hekla, Iceland's most famous volcano, then drive to Thorsmork, a breathtakingly beautiful valley surrounded by glaciers, massive mountains and glacial rivers on all sides. Camp.
DAY 5: Hiking in Thorsmork area.
DAY 6: Hike down to Skogar and

drive to Hjorleifshofoi. Good bird-watching opportunities from our campsite.
DAY 7: From Hjorleifshofoi, we drive to Skaftafell National Park and camp.
DAY 8: Optional hike up Mt. Oraefajokull, Iceland's highest mountain and third largest volcano in Europe. This is a strenuous hike, and those not wishing to participate can take other local walks.
DAY 9: Visit Breioamerkurlon, an iceberg-strewn glacial lake. Hike in the afternoon and return to camp.
DAY 10: Drive from Skaftafell to Eldgja.
DAY 11: Drive to Landmannalaugar and soak in a natural hot spring.
DAY 12: Drive to Reykjavik. Overnight in hotel.
DAY 13: Free day in Reykjavik.
DAY 14: Depart Reykjavik and connect with homeward-bound flights.

IT3SK1MTDS

DOGSLEDDING IN GREENLAND

DATES: Mar 29–Apr 12 (15 days)
LEADER: Mike Banks
GRADE: B-2
LAND COST: $2390 (8 members)

This is an opportunity to enter the spectacular world of the polar explorer. With Mike Banks, one of Britain's most experienced arctic explorers, we will travel the breathtaking coast of west Greenland by husky dogsled in the company of Eskimo hunters.

We must emphasize that this is not a "tourist" trip where one observes the splendor of the arctic from a cruise ship. This is a real arctic adventure using traditional and proven Eskimo methods of mushing. Dogsleds here have remained a vital form of transport outside the villages, and this is a chance to experience the last of a quickly vanishing way of life. Dogsledding is a stimulating, boisterous affair for which you should be fit and robust. It is not for anyone who is frail or out of condition.

We will travel at an ideal time of year, just before the arctic spring, when temperatures should be no colder than at a typical ski resort.

From a small village above the Arctic Circle, we undertake a five-day dogsled and camping journey with the Eskimos (one person to a sled with driver), roaming as far along the coast as conditions permit, with snow-covered frozen fjords as our grand highways.

After the trip, we visit Copenhagen, one of Europe's most charming capitals, home of Hans Christian Anderson.

ITINERARY:
DAY 1 and 2: Leave U.S. Arrive Copenhagen. Overnight at hotel.
DAY 3: Fly to Sondre Stromfjord, inside the Arctic Circle. Continue by helicopter to Christianhaab, 125 miles to the north, a Greenlander (Eskimo or Inuit) community of some 3000 people and rather more husky dogs.
DAY 4: In Christianhaab, collecting the special equipment we will need on our journey. Overnight at hotel.
DAY 5: Spend the day dogsledding to familiarize ourselves with the techniques we will need for our journey. Each member will be allocated a sled which will be driven by a Greenlander with his own dog team. We sit on the sled while traveling much of the time. However, when going steeply uphill, we walk, easing the strain

on the dogs. On steep snowbanks, we pitch in and help push the sleds over any obstacles.
DAY 6: Another day preparing for the journey, checking food, tents, equipment and personal items.
DAY 7 to 11: On a five-day dog sled journey, Eskimo style. Our exact itinerary will be governed by the weather and particularly by the condition of the sea ice, which varies each year. We will certainly approach the "ice fjord" into which the famous Jakobshavn Glacier discharges millions of tons of ice a day and moves at the extraordinary speed of three feet an hour—the fastest in the world. From time to time, we will see the dome of the immense inland icecap.
DAY 12: In Christianhaab. Optional ski tour.
DAY 13: By helicopter back to Sondre Stromfjord and continue by jet to Copenhagen. Overnight at hotel.

> **We must emphasize that this is not a "tourist" trip where one observes the splendor of the arctic from a cruise ship. This is a real arctic adventure using traditional and proven Eskimo methods of mushing.**

DAY 14: At leisure in Copenhagen.
DAY 15: Depart Copenhagen and connect with homeward-bound flights.

IT3SKIMTT

NORWAY: THE TROLL TOUR

DATES: Jun 29–Jul 13 (15 days)
LEADER: to be announced
GRADE: B-2
LAND COST: *$1215 (6–15 members)
*Note decrease from 1984 Trip Schedule.

This is a ten-day summer hiking ramble through the forests and fells along the Norwegian/Swedish border, gentle rolling country which is a good blend of old Norwegian farm country and deep woods, and legendary haunt of trolls, the mythical creatures of Scandinavian folklore.

On our hike, we pass Stone Age settlements, Lapp reindeer herders, and numerous active summer farms. The flowers of summer will be in full bloom in the marshes and meadows, and we have a chance to see fine wild-. life, including reindeer and other paleoarctic species.

The long, light summer evenings are spent with Norwegian hikers at charming mountain lodges. The lodges supply all meals and accommodations, so we only need to carry a small daypack while walking. The terrain is moderate and this is an excellent tour for families who want to enjoy a European hike together.

ITINERARY:
DAY 1 and 2: Leave U.S. Arrive Oslo. Transfer to hotel.

DAY 3: By train to Tynset and continue by bus to Rausjodalseter. Overnight at an old "seter" (summer farm) that serves as a hikers' lodge.

DAY 4: Hike from Rausjodalseter up to Rausjo Peak (4,281'), then down into the forest to Ellefsplass on the Hola River.

DAY 5: Hike across glens and marshes, past tarns and becks to the old summer farm at Saether.

DAY 6 and 7: A three-hour walk, then a boat journey across Lake Femund into Femund National Park, ending with a one-hour stroll through the pine woods to Svukurset Lodge. Layover day to look for reindeer and perhaps meet some Sami people, the Lapps who herd reindeer in the borderlands.

CROSS COUNTRY SKIING IN
FINLAND & NORWAY

Norwegian Sea

Jotunheimen + Finse
Bergen • Hamer
• OSLO • STOCKHOLM
HELSINKI
Lahti

Baltic Sea

300 Miles

A

DAY 8 and 9: Hike along cairned paths to the barren and boulder-strewn country around Roveltjorn Lakes. Much of Femund National Park is strewn with glacial debris from the last Ice Age; there are numerous small tarns and rivers. Continue to Stromrasen Hill and the River Mugga. There is time here for an easy ascent of Mt. Svuken (4,400') for panoramic views of the Norwegian/Swedish border country.

DAY 10 and 11: Easy hike from Ljosnavollen down through the forest to the village of Langen. Layover day for exploring the countryside.

DAY 12 and 13: Scenic walk to Marenvollen Hut, followed by an easy walk to Roros, a small mining town with a long history. It was an important source of copper and falcons for trade in the 18th century. Overnight at hotel in Roros.

DAY 14: By train to Oslo. Afternoon sightseeing. Overnight in hotel.

DAY 15: Depart Oslo and connect with homeward-bound flights.

B

IT3SKIMTTT

THE JOTUNHEIMEN HIKE

DATES: Aug 17–Sep 2 (17 days)
LEADER: to be announced
GRADE: B-3
LAND COST: *$1350 (6–15 members)
*Note change from 1984 Trip Schedule

The Jotunheimen tour is ten days of hiking and scrambling through the highest peaks in Scandinavia, the spectacular Jotunheimen Mountains, glaciated peaks rising out of the fjords to heights of 3,000 to 8,000 feet.

At night we'll stay in mountain lodges, and by day we'll hike through a magnificent setting of glaciers, deep valleys, waterfalls and fjords, and make non-technical ascents of the two highest peaks in Norway.

Visits are also included to Oslo and Bergen.

ITINERARY:
DAY 1 and 2: Leave U.S. Arrive Oslo and transfer to hotel.

DAY 3: Day free for visiting the Viking Museum and Oslo Fjord.

DAY 4: By train and bus to Krossbu in the Jotunheimen Mountains. The train passes through some of Norway's loveliest farm country.

DAY 5 and 6: Cross Smorstabb Glacier to Leirvassbu, then an easy hike down a deep valley to Spiterstulen, at the foot of Galdhogpiggen.

DAY 7: Ascent of Galdhogpiggen (8,100'), a strenuous climb with a vertical rise of 4,000 feet—non-technical but demanding.

DAY 8: Hike from Spiterstulen past Glittertind, second highest peak in Norway. At Glittertind there is an isolated lodge surrounded by glaciers and barren peaks.

DAY 9: Hike over several ridges to Gjendesheim, one of the oldest lodges in the Jotunheimen, situated in the mountains immortalized by Ibsen in *Peer Gynt*.

DAY 10: Ascent the "Peer Gynt" ridges above Lake Gjende and hike down to a lodge at Memurubu.

DAY 11: Scenic hike with good views of the central Jotunheimen to Gjendebu, situated at the far western end of Lake Gjende. Continue to Olavsbu, a self-service hut where everyone helps with fire-making and cooking.

> At night we'll stay in mountain lodges, and by day we'll hike through a magnificent setting of glaciers, deep valleys, waterfalls and fjords, and make non-technical ascents of the two highest peaks in Norway.

DAY 12: Hike to one of the most idyllic spots in the Norwegian mountains at Skogadalsboen, surrounded by glaciers and high peaks.

DAY 13: Ascent of Fannaraken (6,758'), from the summit of which the clear-weather views extend from the North Sea to Sweden. This is a good day's scramble, a strenuous but non-technical ascent.

DAY 14: Hike down to Vetti, passing Vetti Falls. Overnight at a summer farm.

DAY 15: Hike to Hjelle, bus to Ardalstangen, ferry through picturesque Sognfjord, then by train to Voss. Overnight in hotel.

DAY 16: By train to Bergen. Afternoon stroll around this old Hanseatic North Sea port. Overnight in hotel.

DAY 17: Depart Bergen and connect with homeward-bound flights.

IT3SKIMTTT

SKI TOURING IN NORWAY

DATES: Mar 10–Mar 25 (16 days)
LEADER: Dave Parker
GRADE: B-3
LAND COST: *$1250
 (12–15 members)
 $1350 (8–11)
*Note change from 1984 Trip Schedule.

Norway's national parks and wilderness mountains are the birthplace of nordic skiing. They offer unparalleled back-country touring and comfortable ski lodges situated in remote areas where skis are the only form of transportation.

There are marked routes throughout the rolling plateaus, frozen lakes and high slopes, as well as unlimited open wilderness for cross-country tours.

We visit three areas which offer differing experiences: Jotunheimen Park is known for deep glacial valleys and jagged peaks; Rondane Park contains rounded mountains and gentle, open foothills with dry snow; the Finse Plateau, located high in the treeless plains, has wide open skiing mixed with flat glaciers.

The comfortable lodges, all in remote areas and built just for nordic skiers, have hearty food and offer perfect access to skiing. The skiing is suitable for most skiers who enjoy off-track touring. Beginners are welcome if they are in good physical condition and want to learn and experience ski touring in the best possible conditions.

OPTIONAL HUT-TO-HUT TRIP: At the end of the trip at Finse, we can arrange an optional eight-day hut-to-hut trip through Hardangervidda, accompanied by a dogsled. For strong intermediate skiers. $575.

ITINERARY:
DAY 1 and 2: Depart U.S. Arrive Oslo. Transfer to hotel.

DAY 3: Morning train up the long Gudbrandsdalen Valley, an area of forests, farms and long river gorges. By van from Otta to our trailhead lodge at Lake Gjende.

A   Jotunheimen Mountains/Dave Parker
B   Ski Hut, Rondane Park/Dave Parker
C   The trails at Finse/Dave Parker
D   Jotunheimen National Park/Dave Parker

FINLAND/NORWAY • 23

A

DAY 4 to 6: Marked routes extend from our lodge out into the glacial mountains and frozen lakes of Norway's highest mountains The routes vary from flat, to moderate, to steep slopes for telemark turns. There is a variety of terrain, so all levels of skiers can find suitable terrain. The lodge has double rooms with bunks, good food and hot showers.

DAY 7: By van to the trailhead for Rondane National Park, a three-hour ride through some of the oldest farmland in Norway, where log barns and wooded churches are still common. Ski from the trailhead to Rondvassbu Lodge.

DAY 8 to 10: Our rustic lodge is located in the middle of Rondane Park, below rounded peaks that tower several thousand feet above. The entire countryside is higher than treeline and there are unlimited tours down and across the undulating ridges and moraines nearby.

DAY 11: Ski out of the park and catch the train to Oslo, then up to Finse in the mountains of southwest Norway.

Beginners are welcome if they are in good physical condition and want to learn and experience ski touring in the best possible conditions.

DAY 12 to 14: Finse is accessible only by train, and although it is not a national park, the surrounding glaciers and mountains are unspoiled. The skiing is easy but there are also challenging ascents of the Hardanger Glacier and local ridges.

DAY 15: Afternoon train to Oslo and evening free in town.

DAY 16: Depart Oslo and connect with homeward-bound flights.

C

IT3AY1SF01

CROSS COUNTRY SKIING IN FINLAND & NORWAY

DATES: Feb 24–Mar 11 (17 days)
LEADER: Dave Parker
GRADE: B-2
LAND COST: $1450 (12-15 members)
$1590 (8-11)

Ski touring originated in the mountains of Norway and forests of Finland, the best terrain in the world for this sport.

We begin in Finland, skiing on the forest trails at Lahti, where hundreds of kilometers of ski tracks wind through stands of birch and spruce. February is the ideal month to ski at Lahti: the snow is at its best and the days begin to lengthen. After skiing there's time for an authentic sauna with the Fins.

In Norway, we ski on the vast trail system outside Oslo, then continue on to Lillehammer, with its rolling forests and low treeless peaks, which contrast with the flatter Finnish routes. Lillehammer's trails include the famous Birkebeiner run, site of the classic citizens race of the same name.

We travel from Finland to Norway by ferry across the Baltic and train across Sweden, with time to visit Helsinki, Stockholm and Oslo.

This trip is open to skiers of all levels and is an excellent chance to sample the world's best ski tracks and trails.

ITINERARY:

DAY 1 and 2: Leave U.S. Arrive Helsinki and continue by train to Lahti. Overnight at hotel.

DAY 3 and 4: Ski the trails winding from Messila (where our hotel is located) into Lahti, ski capital of Finland. The trails are easy and this is an excellent place to brush up on ski skills. Lahti, with its perfect tracks and ski stadium

B

with five jumps, draws the elite racers of nordic skiing, and we'll have a chance to watch them training.

DAY 5: By train to Helsinki. Afternoon sightseeing in this attractive Baltic port, then an evening sail on the overnight ferry to Stockholm.

DAY 6: Arrive Stockholm in the morning, half a day to sightsee in the historic section of the city, then by afternoon train to Oslo.

DAY 7: Ski the city trails ringing Norway's capital. The trails are accessible by trolley from our hotel.

DAY 8: Morning free for skiing or sightseeing. Afternoon train through heavily forested valleys north to Lillehammer and Sjusjoen.

DAY 9 to 15: Skiing right from the hotel door, we have perfect access to Lillehammer's famous trail system. The network includes maintained tracks like the famous Birkebeiner run that winds ten miles downhill to town, as well as marked routes to the small mountains above treeline. Our hotel was once a summer farm and has a warm, nordic atmosphere and excellent food.

DAY 16: Morning train to Oslo. Day free for sightseeing.

DAY 17: Depart Oslo and connect with homeward-bound flights.

D

We travel from Finland to Norway by ferry across the Baltic and train across Sweden, with time to visit Helsinki, Stockholm and Oslo.

IT4TW14O53

MOUNTAINS OF THE BALKANS

DATES: Sep 10–Oct 1 (22-days)
LEADERS: Maki Idosidis &
Allen Steck
GRADE: B-2
LAND COST: *\$1790 (8–14 members)
*Note change from 1984 Trip Schedule.

Visiting Greece, Yugoslavia, Romania and Bulgaria, this unusual journey combines hikes in beautiful mountain regions with visits to historic cities and villages. Needless to say, this is one of the least "touristed" parts of Europe.

We start with a hike up Mt. Olympus (9,570'), highest summit in Greece, then drive up to Yugoslavia's mountainous southern tip, called Macedonia in ancient times. Driving past medieval monasteries and through orchards and vineyards along the Vardar River, we devote two days to exploring and hiking in the snow-capped Jakupica Mountains.

After visiting Belgrade, Yugoslavia's capital, we cross into Romania. Here our destination is the Transylvanian Alps, wooded hills known for their abundant wildlife and feudal-era castles (including Castle Bran, renowned haunt of Count Dracula, which we'll visit). Our hiking itinerary will take us up Negoiu (8,359'), second highest peat in Romania, after which we tour Bucharest, the 500-year-old capital.

Our last lap brings us to Bulgaria, in the heart of the Balkan Peninsula. Bordered on the north by the Blue Danube and on the east by the Black Sea, Bulgaria traces its historical roots back to the Thracians (1,500 B.C.). It was part of the Turkish Ottoman Empire until 1878. We'll visit Sofia, the capital, then journey through countryside sprinkled with villages which have changed little since the days of Tsar Alexander II, who liberated Bulgaria from the Turks 100 years ago. In the pine-forested Tila Planina Mountains, where there are a hundred peaks of 9,000 feet or higher, we hike up Mt. Musala (9,596').

Accommodations will be in inns, farmhouses and mountain huts. Travel will be by van or mini-bus.

Part of the itinerary in this little-visited region may be "unscouted," so expect the unexpected.

ITINERARY:
DAY 1 and 2: Depart U.S. Arrive Athens and continue by air to Salonika. Transfer to hotel.
DAY 3: Drive to Litochoron. Overnight at beach inn.
DAY 4: Drive to roadhead and hike to a hut below Mt. Olympus.
DAY 5: Hike to the summit of Mt. Olympus (9,750'). Descend and hike to Litochoron.
DAY 6: Drive across the border into Yugoslavia and proceed to the town of Titov Veles.
DAY 7 and 8: Hikes in the Jakupica mountain area. Ascend Jakupica (8,333').

DAY 9 and 10: Drive to Belgrade.
DAY 11: Drive into Romania and proceed to the town of Sibiu.
DAY 12 and 13: Hikes in the Transylvanian Alps. Ascent of Negoiu (8,359'), highest summit in Romania.
DAY 14: Drive to Bucharest.

> **Our destination is the Transylvanian Alps, wooded hills known for their abundant wildlife and feudal-era castles (including Castle Bran, renowned haunt of Count Dracula, which we'll visit).**

DAY 15: In Bucharest
DAY 16: Drive to Sofia, Bulgaria.
DAY 17: In Sofia.
DAY 18 to 20: Hikes in the Rila Planina mountains, with an ascent of Musala (9,596').
DAY 21: Return drive to Salonika.
DAY 22: Fly to Athens. Depart Athens and connect with homeward-bound flights.

IT4TW14O51

MT. OLYMPUS & NORTHERN GREECE

DATES: #1 Jun 2–Jun 17 (16 days)
#2 Aug 12–Aug 27 (16 days)
LEADER: Maki Idosidis or
Allen Steck
GRADE: B-2
LAND COST: \$1175 (6–12 members)

The rugged Pindos Mountains on Greece's northern border are among the most spectacular yet least traveled mountains in the whole country. On our four-day trek in these remote reaches, we hike through the dry river bed of the Vikos Gorge. Perhaps the most beautiful of all canyons in Greece, it is flanked by immense, jagged limestone cliffs and filled with wildflowers. We venture high up through forested terrain, then alpine pastureland, descending to the Zagorian village of Tsepelovon.

Traveling to Mt. Olympus (9,750'), the many-ridged home of Zeus, we make a four-day traverse beginning in the hill village of Ellasona on the west, crossing the summit and ending in Litochoron in the east. Athough less than 10,000 feet high, Olympus has impressive rock walls and snow which lasts most of the year.

In between treks, we visit the famed medieval monasteries built on the rock towers of Meteora, and after our Olympus hike, we relax on the sunny beach at Stomion.

ITINERARY:
DAY 1 and 2: Leave U.S. Arrive

Athens. Drive to the small seaside community of Varasova. Overnight at local inn.
DAY 3: Continue by bus to Ioannina, capital of Epiros, then onto Monodendri, a small hamlet located high above Vikos Gorge. Overnight at local inn.
DAY 4: Begin four-day trek with an all-day hike to Papingo. From Monodendri, an indistinct trail leads down through lush forested terrain to the dry riverbed of the Vikos Gorge. Continue to the Viodomatis, a full-size mountain river that gushes out of the dry riverbed from underground channels. Hike up an old trail system to the hill town of Megalo Papingo. Overnight at a local inn.
DAY 5: Continue hiking through forested terrain, then alpine pastures to the Astraka Refuge, maintained by the Greek Alpine Club.
DAY 6: Fee day for short hikes or ascents of the nearby peaks.
DAY 7: Mid-morning departure for a hike to the Zagoria village of Tsepelovo, descending through a limestone gorge. Meet our bus and drive to the Mt. Olympus region.
DAY 8: Drive to the lovely mountain village of Metsovon. Overnight at local inn.
DAY 9: Drive to Kalambaka, where we will visit the famed medieval monasteries built on the rock towers of Meteora. Overnight at a local inn.
DAY 10: Drive on to Ellasona, a hillside village near the roadhead on the western approach to Mt. Olympus. Overnight at inn.
DAY 11: Hike up to Vryssopoules Refuge (6,233') on Mt. Olympus.
DAY 12: Ascent of Mt. Olympus main summit, which is called Mytikas (9,750'), snow conditions permitting. Descend to the Spilios Agapitos Refuge (6,889') on the eastern side of the peak.
DAY 13: Rest day.
DAY 14: Descend along lovely forested path to Litochoron, and meet our bus for the drive to Stomion Beach, an ideal place to relax fater the traverse of Mt. Olympus. Overnight at local inn.
DAY 15: A long day's drive back to Athens. Overnight at hotel.
DAY 16: Depart Athens and connect with homeward-bound flights.

A Greek dancing practice/Allen Steck
B Lunch on the boat, Greece/Allen Steck
C Village of Loutro, Greece/Allen Steck

A

IT4TW14050

TREKKING IN GREECE

DATES: Sep 10–Sep 25 (16 days)
LEADER: to be announced
GRADE: B-2
LAND COST: $1660 (11–12 members)
$1790 (8–10)

Greece is a country of enchanting rural villages with a populace known for its hospitality. The rugged mountains and coasts of Greece and Crete present an exquisite Mediterranean panorama of wooded mountains, barren rock summits, silvery-green olive groves, golden beaches and a deep blue sea.

The focus of our trekking journey is to get out into back-country Greece and come in close contact with the local people.

We trek for three days through the Taiyetos Mountains, which rise above Sparta and form the spine of the central Peleponnesus. Our journey follows Spartan warrior paths through dense forests of chestnut and oak and into rugged river gorges.

On Crete, largest and most mountainous of the Greek islands, we trek for three days in the Levka Ori ("White Mountains"), a tremendous range from whose peaks we can see almost the entire western half of Crete.

Besides trekking, we visit some of the most famous Mycenean and classic sites of Greece, and the mysterious sites of the Minoan civilization on Santorini, the most beautiful island in the Cyclades.

Most of our camp gear is transferred by vehicle while we walk, so we only need to carry day packs. Our accommodations are in mountain huts, in tents or in very simple pensions.

ITINERARY:

DAY 1 and 2: Leave U.S. Arrive Athens. Transfer to Piraeus harbor and continue by ferry to Hydra. Overnight in pension in the fishing village of Kaminia.

DAY 3: By ferry to Hermione and continue to Epidavros, site of the Temple of Aesclepius and his holy snakes. Drive to Nafplion, first capital of modern Greece. Camp nearby.

DAY 4: Drive to Mycene, Agamemnon's capital, and continue across the Tayetos Range to Sparta. Camp near the beautiful monastery of Phaneronamy.

DAY 5: Hike to the village of Parury with excellent views of the valley of Sparta, the Parnon Range and the Aegean Sea. Continue hiking up to Mistas, the well-preserved Byzantine "ghost town" that was the capital of the Peleponnesus during the Middle Ages. Drive to Anoya and continue by bus and tractor to Krionerion. Begin four-day trek in the Tayetos Range. Hike to a mountain hut maintained by the Greek Alpine Club.

DAY 6: Hike over Pilgrim's Pass to the summit of Prophitis Elias, highest peak in the Tayetos Range. A small chapel consecrated to the prophet Elijah is at the summit. Descend and camp by a shepherds' colony in the valley of Ayo Dimitrio.

DAY 7: Descend on an ancient Spartan path along a spectacular canyon to the village of Exochorion. End trek and drive to the seaside village of Kardamili, an ancient site mentioned in Homer's writings. Overnight at pension.

DAY 8: In Khardamili to rest, swim and wander in the village.

DAY 9: Drive southward along the steep coast to Githion and board an overnight ferry to Crete.

DAY 10: Morning arrival in Kastely in northwestern Crete. Drive to Hania, picturesque capital of the island. Overnight in hotel.

DAY 11: Drive southward across the western part of Crete. Visit the ancient site of Lyssos and continue driving to the Omalas plain. Begin Levka Ori trek with a walk to the alpine hut of Kalergy atop a tremendous cliff which dominates the Gorge of Samaria.

DAY 12: Optional rest day or climb of Gingilos, second highest peak in the Volakias Range.

DAY 13: Descend the Gorge of Samaria, one of the largest canyons in Europe. A clear, cool stream flows along its entire length.

> **An exquisite Mediterranean panorama of wooded mountains, barren rock summits, silvery-green olive groves, golden beaches and a deep blue sea.**

DAY 14: Drive along the wild southern coast toward central northern Crete, where most of the Minoan sites are found. Visit Knossos and Fesstos and continue to Heraklion. Overnight in hotel.

DAY 15: Free day in Heraklion. Board overnight ferry to Athens.

DAY 16: Arrive in Athens. Afternoon depart Athens and connect with homeward-bound flights.

IT4TW14049

THE GREEK ISLANDS

DATES: #1 Jun 20–Jul 3 (14 days)
#2 Jul 7–Jul 20 (14 days)
#3 Jul 24–Aug 6 (14 days)
LEADER: Maki Idosidis or Allen Steck
GRADE: A-1
LAND COST: $1790 (9–10 members)
$1990 (8)

For this free-form journey, we charter a *kaiki* and cruise to several of the most interesting and remote islands in the western Cyclades.

We travel island to island, avoiding the tourist areas, to explore remote fishing villages where the old Greek way of life still exists. This trip will have a very flexible itinerary and a few surprises.

We also plan to do some beach hiking, swimming, snorkeling, and spend many evenings dancing in small tavernas.

Our boat will be a motor-sailer, called a *kaiki*, a term which refers to a variety of hull shapes and boat designs. It will be a very comfortable and livable boat. There will be a crew of two.

A typical day on the boat may go like this: up early for a light breakfast on board, then leave port (usually by motor) for the next island. We stop around noon on most days for a swim at a secluded beach followed by a Greek salad-style lunch on board. Continuing to the next port, we might go ashore for coffee, perhaps some ouzo and octopus, then walk to a nearby village. The evening meal will be taken in a taverna, where we hope to do some Greek dancing.

Much of the emphasis of the trip is on enjoying the scene in the local tavernas and outdoor cafes, where we spend a lot of our time. Greece is one of the few places where the national dances are not just relegated to the performing stage, but are part of everyday life. Every joyous occasion calls for music and dancing, and we will dance with the Greeks in their tavernas and cafes, or sometimes by ourselves on isolated beaches... wherever the spirit moves us! Nightly accommodations will be four-bunk cabins on the boat.

> **Every joyous occasion calls for music and dancing, and we will dance with the Greeks in their tavernas and cafes, or sometimes by ourselves on isolated beaches...wherever the spirit moves us!**

ITINERARY:

DAY 1 and 2: Leave U.S. Arrive Athens. Transfer to hotel.

DAY 3: Day free in Athens. Evening visit to our favorite dancing spot in the Plaka.

DAY 4: Drive to Pireaus or Porto Rafti and board the boat.

DAY 5 to 13: For the next nine days, we will motor (or occasionally sail when winds and currents are favorable) among the following islands: Kithnos, Sifnos, Sikinos, Thera, Skinoussa, Antiparos, Tinos, Delos, Kea and back to Pireaus and Athens. We will keep the sea itinerary flexible according to weather conditions.

DAY 14: Depart Athens and connect with homeward-bound flights.

C

IT4TW14O52

ACROSS CORSICA

DATES: #1 Jul 21–Aug 5 (16 days)
       #2 Aug 4–Aug 19 (16 days)
LEADER: to be announced
GRADE: B-3
LAND COST: $790 (6–12 members)

Corsica is primarily a mountain rising out of the sea. Almost the whole length, coastal cliffs and headlands surge out of the blue sea to heights of 3,000 feet or more. Monte Cinto, highest peak on the island is 8,881 feet high; dozens of needle-like smaller peaks surround it. Terraced gardens, small cultivated fields, olive groves and vineyards spread out below the peaks.

Our ten-day trek across Corsica follows a portion of the "Grand Randonee 20," a marked trail linking 177 miles of ancient shepherds' trails that wind across the mountainous interior of the island. The route crosses only three roads and one village during its entire length. The hiking is challenging, but the scenery is truly impressive and the herbal fragrance of the *maquis* scrub softens the harshness of the mountains.

There are two three-day stages of the trek on which we carry backpacks weighing about 25 lbs. Our accommodations will be a mixture of bivouacs, hut nights and camping. Average walking time is about six hours a day.

After the trek, we have two days to relax on the beaches at Calvia.

ITINERARY:

DAY 1 and 2: Leave U.S. Arrive Ajaccio, Corsica via Paris. Continue by bus to Bastelica, where we establish our first camp. "Welcome to Corsica" dinner at Pension Chez Paul.

DAY 3 and 4: Carrying packs for a one-night, two-day hike, we ascend through woods of beech

and silver birch up to the Scaldasoli Ridge and the "bergeries" (shepherds' huts) at Possi and on to Capanelle, with a side trip to climb Monte Renoso (7,716').

> Our ten-day trek across Corsica follows a portion of the "Grand Randonee 20," a marked trail linking 177 miles of ancient shepherds' trails that wind across the mountainous interior of the island.

DAY 5: Day's walk contouring around the Punta de Zorpi, descending through forest to Vissavona, the only village on the Grand Randonee 20. Camp on the banks of the Ronde Manganello.

DAY 6 and 7: With backpacks (carrying supplies for a two-night, three-day hike), hike to the Refuge Pietra Piana (6,043') and traverse out to climb Corsica's second highest peak, Monte Retondo (8,602'), descending to Refuge de Manganu, enjoying spectacular views along the way.

DAY 8 and 9: Hike from Col De Vergio to Berg Ballone, skirting the impressive peaks of Paglia Orba and Capu Tafonatu, and reach the summit of Monte Cinto (8,877'), Corsica's highest peak. Descend to Haute Asco and dine at a local hotel.

DAY 10: Hike from Haute Asco up to the Sommet de Muvrella (7,047') and descend into the Spasimata Valley.

DAY 11: End trek at Calenzia.

DAY 12: By bus to the beach resort at Calvi.

DAY 13: At leisure in Calvi.

DAY 14: By train to Ajaccio (a six-hour ride) on Corsica's funicular mountain railway. Overnight at hotel.

DAY 15: Depart Ajaccio and connect with homeward-bound flights via Paris.

IT3PA1SFMT12

THE BLUE CRUISE & WESTERN ANATOLIA

DATES: Jun 16–Jul 4 (19 days)
LEADER: to be announced
GRADE: A-2
LAND COST: $1690 (10–15 members)
            $1950 (8–9)

On a relaxing seven-day cruise, we explore a remote section of the Mediterranean Coast with delightful villages and fascinating ruins from the Lycian Age (not yet on the tourist route!).

Our boat, a small converted fishing vessel, will cruise for a few hours each day and give us ample time to wander the beautiful surroundings on shore. At night we camp at little secluded beaches and bays.

Before the "Blue Cruise," we spend a week visiting some of Turkey's finest sites of antiquity, including Troy, which recalls the epic struggle of the Iliad, and the ancient city of Ephesus. We also visit Pergamum, with its Acropolis, and the town of Antalya, founded in the 2nd century B.C. at one of the prettiest settings on the Mediterranean, where the crescent of Konyalti Beach sweeps away to the precipitous Lycian mountains in the west.

ITINERARY:

DAY 1 and 2: Leave U.S. Arrive Istanbul. Transfer to hotel.

DAY 3: Drive to Pergamum, with a visit to the ruins of the ancient city of Troy. Overnight in hotel.

DAY 4: Visit Pergamum's Acropolis and Asclepion, one of the earliest medical centers of classical times. Drive to Kusadasi for overnight.

> Our boat, a small converted fishing vessel will cruise for a few hours each day and give us ample time to wander the beautiful surroundings on shore. At night we camp at little secluded beaches and bays.

DAY 5: Excursion to the ancient city of Ephesus and Basilica of St. John the Baptist.

DAY 6: Drive to Dinizli, visiting the ruins of Hierapolis and Aphrodisia and the petrified gardens en route.

A   High pass in the Kachkar Mountains, Turkey/Leo Le Bon
B   Remote Taurus mountain village/Leo Le Bon
C   Village women/Leo Le Bon
D   Mt. Ararat

TURKEY • 27

A

DAY 7: Drive to Bodrum, ancient Halicarnassus, dominated by a castle built by the Crusader Knights of St. John. Overnight in hotel.

DAY 8 to 14: Seven-day Blue Cruise from Bodrum to Fethiye. We will stop at most of the following places: Cnidus, Ciftlik, Serce, Marmaris, Dalyan, Manastir, Fethiye, Kikova, Kas, and Kale. Our boat itinerary will remain flexible according to the wishes of the trip members.

DAY 15: Arrive in Fethiye and drive to Kemer to visit ruins of ancient Phaselis. Overnight in hotel in Antalya.

DAY 16: Morning visit to Atalya and afternoon flight to Istanbul. Overnight at hotel.

DAY 17 and 18: Tour Istanbul.

DAY 19: Depart Istanbul and connect with homeward-bound flights.

IT3PAISFMT13

THE TAURUS MOUNTAINS TREK

DATES: Jul 8–Jul 29 (22 days)
LEADER: to be announced
GRADE: B-2
LAND COST: $1590 (10–15 members)
$1975 (6–9)

Turkey has some very rugged mountain country, including the Taurus Range, a limestone group on the southern coast which has a complex system of spires, peaks and ridges of almost mystical beauty.

We trek for eight days in these mountains, crossing a high plateau beneath the rocky 12,000-foot summits of the Aladag group, highest portion of the Taurus Mountains.

Visits are included to Cappadocia, with its rock-hewn chapels and remarkable underground cities of Derinkuyu, Kaymakli, and Silifke, site of the Byzantine Cennet Cehennen Caves ("Caves of Hell and Heaven") as well as Tarsus, birthplace of St. Paul.

ITINERARY:

DAY 1 and 2: Leave U.S. Arrive Istanbul. Transfer to hotel.

DAY 3: Fly to Ankara. Overnight at hotel.

DAY 4: Visit Mausoleum of Ataturk and Hittite Museum, then drive to Aksaray, passing by Tuz Golu (Salt Lake). Continue to Ihlara Valley, a unique place with its man-made cave dwellings and chapels on both sides of a deep canyon. Two extinct volcanoes, Mt. Hasan (10,662') and Mt. Melendiz (11,318') are located in the southwest part of the valley. Overnight at hotel.

DAY 5: Drive to Urgup and visit the rock churches of Goreme and Avanos. Overnight at hotel.

DAY 6: Excursion to Cappadocia, visiting Avcilar, Ortahisar and Uchisar.

DAY 7: Drive to Nigde and visit the remarkable underground cities at Derinkuyu and Kaymakli en route. Begin Taurus trek with a hike to the foot of Mt. Demirkazik.

DAY 8: Trek to the remote Cimbar Valley, with its views of the impressive north face of Mt. Demirkazik. Those who wish can climb up Mt. Demirkazik (12,322').

DAY 9 and 10: Trek to Celikbuyduran Pass (11,318') at the foot of Mt. Kizilkaya (12,214'), and on to Seven Lakes Valley. Optional climb of Mt. Embler (11,886') or Mt. Kizilkaya.

DAY 11 to 15: Trek to Sogukpinar (5,900'), visit some spectacular waterfalls, then continue to the Acimand highlands at about 7,000 feet.

DAY 16: By jeep to Karsanti over a rough road with spectacular views of the Taurus Range.

DAY 17: Drive to Adana. Tour city and have lunch at a seaside restaurant in Mersin. Overnight in hotel.

DAY 18: Excursion to Silifke, visiting the Cennet Cehennen Caves and Kizkalesi (Maiden Castle). Free time for swimming. Overnight at hotel.

DAY 19: Visit Tarsus, birthplace of St. Paul. Fly to Istanbul. Overnight in hotel.

DAY 20 and 21: Tour Istanbul.

DAY 22: Depart Istanbul and connect with homeward-bound flights.

IT3PAISFMT14

MT. ARARAT & THE KACHKAR MOUNTAINS

DATES: Jul 29–Aug 19 (22 days)
LEADER: to be announced
GRADE: C-3
LAND COST: $1450 (10–15 members)
$1790 (6–9)

Mt. Ararat (16,916'), steeped in the mysterious Biblical lore of Noah's Ark, is one of the world's more impressive volcanoes. It rises 14,000 feet above the plain of the Aras, a river which forms the Russian—Turkish border about 20 miles northeast. Ararat stands in complete isolation and is visible for about 100 miles in all directions.

We plan to make a five-day trek up Mt. Ararat, with our highest camp at 14,800 feet, and an optional non-technical ascent to the summit.

Before climbing Ararat, we'll trek in the Kachkar Mountains, an alpine range which runs parallel to the Black Sea coastline in northeast Turkey. From the village of Machka, site of the 14th century Sumela Monastery, an eight-day trek takes us among green meadows, shepherds' pastures and the rugged Kachkar foothills.

ITINERARY:

DAY 1 and 2: Leave U.S. Arrive Istanbul. Fly to Ankara. Transfer to hotel.

DAY 3: Tour Ankara, visit the Mausoleum of Ataturk and the citadel. Seven-hour drive to Samsun by bus, visiting the Hittite sites of Bogazkale and Yazilikaya. Overnight at hotel.

DAY 4: Drive to Trabzon (Byzantine Trebizond). Overnight at hotel.

DAY 5: Drive to Macka to visit the 14th century Sumele Monastery, carved into the rock face of a deep canyon. Continue to Cat. Overnight at small mountain hotel.

DAY 6: By jeep to Elevit and begin trek. Walk to Tirevit, a summer shepherd settlement. Possible dance performance and bagpipe concert in the village.

DAY 7 and 8: Trek to Polovit (6,700'), then over Kavronasidi Pass (9,514'), where there are views of all the peaks of the Kachkar Range, including Kachkar (12,906'), Altiparmak (10,938'), and Varos (11,318').

DAY 9 to 11: Trek to Ashagi Kavron and continue by jeep to Ayder. Time for swimming at a thermal bath. Hike over a steep ridge with fantastic scenery and continue to Yaylaler. Time to explore the ruins of some churches and monasteries from the early Christian era.

DAY 12: Drive to Tortum Lake, visit waterfalls and old Georgian churches. Continue drive to Erzurum. Overnight in hotel.

DAY 13: Tour Erzurum and continue to Dogu Beyazit, starting point for the Ararat hike.

DAY 14 to 16: Drive to Eli and hike up to a camp at 10,500 feet, then up to higher camps at 13,800 and 14,800 feet.

DAY 17: Climb to the summit and descend to Camp II. The upper third of this giant dormant volcano is covered with snow all year and the last hundred meters to the summit is ice. It is not a technically difficult climb but does require stamina. Below the snowline, the slopes are covered with great blocks of black basalt.

DAY 18 and 19: Descend to Dogu Beyazit and drive to Van, which was once the center of an Armenian kingdom founded by Tigranes the Great in the first century B.C. Overnight at hotel.

DAY 20: Fly or drive to Istanbul.

DAY 21: Tour Istanbul

DAY 22: Depart Istanbul and connect with homeward bound flights.

D

B

C

Summer wildflowers in the Dolomites, Italy/Beppe Tenti

PERU

SOUTH & CENTRAL AMERICA

In Peru, a lofty Andean wilderness where 100 or more peaks top 18,000 feet, the legacy of the Inca Empire is everywhere. It is at its most astounding in the massive stone monuments of Cuzco and Machu Picchu, and still impressive in little-known mountain valleys where today's paths follow Inca-built trails and viaducts.

For 1984, we offer fifteen different Peruvian journeys, some for touring and cultural exploration, some for mountain trekking.

We trek to Machu Picchu via a spectacular 15,000-foot pass below Mt. Salcantay (20,564'), we follow a llama traders' trail to Paucartambo to attend the once-a-year Indian "Fiesta del Carmen" and we climb the snowy ridges of the Cordillera Blanca, highest tropical mountain range on earth.

Our South American journeys are not only in Peru; we also sail the world-famous wildlife habitat of the Galapagos (Darwin's Islands), explore the fjords and pampas of Patagonia at the tip of the continent, and ascend Ecuador's tropical yet ice-covered volcanoes and Argentina's Mt. Aconcagua, highest peak in the Western Hemisphere.

In Central America, we search the wildlife-rich national parks of Costa Rica, and climb up three of Mexico's highest mountains.

Mountain Travel offers the most comprehensive adventure travel program on the continent, with imaginative itineraries designed for very small groups and led by expert guides.

1984 CALENDAR INDEX

Most of our 1984 trips will be repeated in 1985 on approximately the same dates.

LEADERSHIP

Our South American trip leaders each have unique backgrounds, an individual blend of cultural expertise and wilderness knowledge. They are capable guides whose experience will enhance the special delights of South American travel.

TERRY BRIAN, 32, is an experienced wilderness guide with expertise in the ethnology and natural history of South America. An avid river-runner, he is a senior guide on the Colorado River and has made many first descents of South American rivers. Fluent in Spanish, with a knowledge of various Indian dialects, he has explored most of South America and has led Mountain Travel treks for seven years.

JAMES DIRKS, 36, a Canadian, was born in Peru and raised in the Peruvian jungle among the Campa Indians. He has traveled throughout South America (and once walked from Bolivia to Chile for three months, crossing much of the Atacama Desert). He lives on a farm in Curahuasi, Peru, and guides our "Peru Festival Trek."

Peguche weaver, Otavalo/Lynn Meisch

Terry Brian

James Dirks

Front cover left to right:

Galapagos giant tortoise/Alla Schmitz
Volcano climbing in Mexico/Sergio Watkins
Patagonian sunset/Bruce Klepinger
Setting up camp, C. Huayhuash/Leo Le Bon
Indian guide loading M.T. bus/Leo Le Bon
Rafting in Costa Rica/Tracy Lynch
Hiking in northern Peru/Leo Le Bon
Peruvian Indian musician/Allen Bechky
Jungle flora/Lawrence Carpenter
Colorado Indians/Alla Schmitz
Breakfast in camp, Inca Trail/Sara Steck
Galapagos flora & fauna/Alla Schmitz
Moreno Glacier, Patagonia/Bruce Klepinger
Peruvian weaving/Leo Le Bon
Hiking to Mt. Ausangate/Pam Shandrick
Sailing in the Galapagos/Alla Schmitz

Galapagos giant tortoises

Jungle flora/Lawrence Carpenter

Toucan

Amazon parrot

BRUCE KLEPINGER, 42, has led more than 50 Mountain Travel treks in Asia and South America. His mountaineering background includes over 1,000 climbs, and he has led expeditions on Aconcagua (highest peak in the Western Hemisphere), Huascaran (highest peak in Peru), and several peaks in Nepal and India. Bruce also has ten years experience as a boatman on the Grand Canyon of the Colorado River and on several South American rivers. He speaks fluent Spanish.

JIM LEWIS, 42, formerly of Smithsonian Institute and Point Reyes Bird Observatory, is a professional biologist with over six years field experience in the national parks of Costa Rica.

LYNN MEISCH, 33, is author of the acclaimed *Traveler's Guide to El Dorado and the Inca Empire.* She has an M.A. in Latin American humanities and studied weaving in Ecuador on a Fulbright fellowship. Fluent in Spanish and familiar with Quechua (the Indian language), she leads treks in Peru and Ecuador and is writing a book on the Indian weavers of Otavalo.

SARA STECK, 29, is Mountain Travel's South American operations manager. She has lived in Central America, speaks fluent Spanish, and spends six months of the year leading treks in Peru, Ecuador and the Galapagos.

CARLOS VELAOCHAGA, 43, of Peru, has a degree in cultural anthropology and has lived in Cuzco for the last seven years, where he continues his studies of both Quechua and Inca cultures and leads trekking expeditions.

SERGIO FITCH WATKINS, 32, of Mexico, is a professional climbing guide with experience in the U.S., the Alps, Spain and the Himalayas. He leads our climbing expeditions on the volcanoes of Mexico and Ecuador as well as on Aconcagua, highest peak in the Western Hemisphere.

Jim Lewis

Sara Steck

Bruce Klepinger

Lynn Meisch

Sergio Fitch Watkins

Rockhopper penguin

IT3EAIMTO2

DISCOVER PERU

DATES: #6 Dec 20, 1983–Jan 3, 1984
(15 days)
#1 Jan 7–Jan 21 (15 days)
#2 Mar 3–Mar 17 (15 days)
#3 May 26–Jun 9 (15 days)
#4 Sep 15–Sep 29 (15 days)
#5 Nov 10–Nov 24 (15 days)
#6 Dec 22, 1984–Jan 5, 1985
(15 days)
LEADER: Carlos Velaochaga
GRADE: A-2
LAND COST: $1850 (4–16 members)

This non-trekking trip explores many facets of Peru's natural history and Inca heritage, including the Nazca lines, Paracas Wildlife Park, the Arequipa volcanoes, plus Lake Titicaca, and the Inca ruins at Machu Picchu and Cuzco.

All the hikes on the trip are non-strenuous and largely optional. Accommodations are in hotels.

ITINERARY:

DAY 1: Leave U.S. Arrive Lima and transfer to hotel. Afternoon city tour of Lima and visit to the city's well-known archaeological museums.

DAY 2: Drive south along the Pacific Coast to Paracas, visiting the Pachacamac ruins (circa 500 B.C.) en route.

DAY 3: Boat trip to Islas Ballestas, islands off the shores of Paracas Wildlife Park with large colonies of flamingos and sea lions. Return to mainland and drive south to Nazca.

DAY 4: Morning tour and scenic overflight above the famous archaeological site of the Nazca Lines, enormous mysterious markings cut into the coastal desert during Nazca Civilization (800 B.C.). Maria Reiche, the German expert who has studied the Nazca lines for over 25 years, maintains that the lines represent a vast astronomical pre-Inca calendar.

Lake Titicaca is a huge "inland sea," the highest navigable body of water on earth.

DAY 5: Drive south along the coast, turning inland to the town of Arequipa (8000').

DAY 6: Half-day tour of Arequipa, a lovely white stone city built in the colonial era and set in an arid highland environment. The big peaks of the Cordillera Volcanica can be seen from town—snow-capped El Misti (19,200') and Chachani (20,000').

DAY 7: Drive to Nacional Aguada Blanca Vicuna Reserve, a sanctuary for vicunas, which have become an endangered species. The road goes through high desert terrain and over a pass between the volcanoes of Misti and Chachani. Continue driving higher up on the altiplano ("high plains") to Puno, a town on the shores of Lake Titicaca (12,500'). Lake Titicaca is a huge "inland

PERU
ABOUT TREKKING IN THE ANDES

A

To make your Peru trek as comfortable as possible, all camping gear is carried by pack animals and/or porters. You will only need to carry a light day-pack for your jacket, camera, and water bottle.

In addition to the Mountain Travel leader, there will be a camp manager, camp staff and cook. Breakfast and dinner are hot meals served in a dining tent; a cold lunch (with hot tea) is served picnic-style each day.

All water used for drinking and cooking is filtered and boiled; we maintain a high standard of camp hygiene. The staff does all camp chores.

Most of our Peru treks take place in sparsely populated highland regions, often at 10,000 feet or higher. Campsites are chosen for their scenic beauty as well as their proximity to available sources of water and fodder for the pack animals.

sea," the highest navigable body of water on earth.

DAY 8: All-day excursion out onto the lake to visit Takili Island, with its population of Aymara Indians. We'll also pass by the floating

reed islands of the Uros Indians, with their hand-made reed boats that are still the main form of transport on the lake.

DAY 9: By train from Puno to Cuzco (11,204'), the Inca capital,

arriving in the afternoon.

DAY 10: Early morning train to Machu Picchu, a scenic four-hour ride through the beautiful Urubamba Valley. Arrive at Machu Picchu station and proceed up to the ruins by bus. Afternoon to explore the vine-covered stone buildings of this "lost city" of the Incas. Overnight at the Machu Picchu Hotel.

DAY 11: More exploration at Machu Picchu and a chance to climb Huayna Picchu (9000'), the small peak above the ruins. Catch the afternoon train to Urubamba and check into a small country inn.

DAY 12: Morning walks in the very beautiful Inca ruins at Pisac and Ollantaytambo, then continue by bus through the Urubamba Valley to Cuzco.

DAY 13: In Cuzco. Day free for sightseeing and shopping.

DAY 14: Fly to Lima. Day free in Lima. Depart on evening flight.

DAY 15: Arrive Miami and connec with homeward-bound flights.

Maria Reiche, the German expert who has studied the Nazca lines for over 25 years, maintains that the lines represent a vast astronomical pre-Inca calendar.

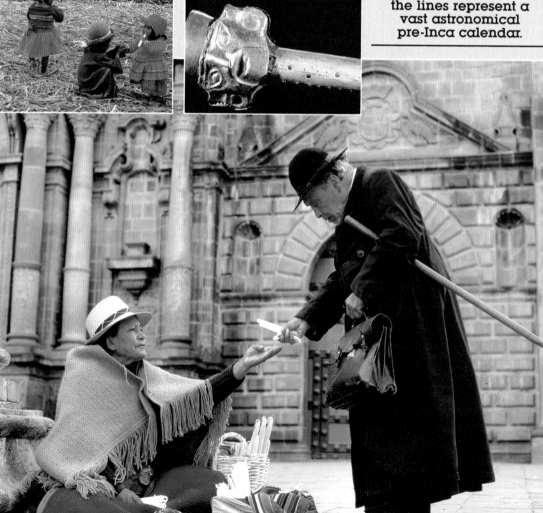
B

C

D

Ruins of Sayacmarca, Inca Trail/Sara Steck
Machu Picchu stonework/Sara Steck
Urubamba rafting/Alfredo Ferreyros
Peruvian street vendor/Pam Shandrick

PERU • 5

3EA1MTO2

THE PERU ADVENTURE

DATES: #1 Mar 17–Mar 31 (15 days)
#2 Apr 14–Apr 28 (15 days)
#3 May 12–May 26 (15 days)
#4 Jun 2–Jun 16 (15 days)
#5 Jul 7–Jul 21 (15 days)
#6 Aug 4–Aug 18 (15 days)
#7 Sep 1–Sep 15 (15 days)
LEADER: to be announced
GRADE: B-2
LAND COST: $1350 (4–16 members)

Sampling the best of wilderness Peru, our "Peru Adventure" includes a five-day trek on the Inca Trail to Machu Picchu, a two-day whitewater trip on the Urubamba River, visits to Cuzco and the Inca ruins of the Urubamba Valley, and an Amazon visit with a chance to explore jungle rivers by canoe.

ITINERARY:

DAY 1: Leave U.S. Arrive Lima. Continue by air to Cuzco. Transfer to hotel.

DAY 2 and 3: Drive to the Urubamba Valley, the "sacred valley of the Incas," for a leisurely two-day raft trip on the Urubamba River, floating through a rich, green mountain valley walled by

the ridges of the Cordillera Urubamba and dotted with spectacular Inca ruins. Visit the ruins at Pisac en route, overnight at inn, and continue raft trip. Visit the Ollantaytambo ruins, known for their exceptional stonework. Overnight at inn.

> **A leisurely two-day raft trip on the Urubamba River, floating through a rich, green mountain valley walled by the ridges of the Cordillera Urubamba and dotted with spectacular Inca ruins.**

DAY 4: Leaving our rafts and donning our hiking boots, we begin a five-day trek on the Inca Trail to Machu Picchu, walking on Inca-built steep stone stairs and over green ridges. Today's walk takes us from Chilca (8,000') near the banks of the Urubamba River up to the village of Huayllabamba (9,700'). Walk along the upper banks of the river with a view of the ruins at Llactapata.

DAY 5: Hike over the Warmi-wanusqa Pass ("Pass of the Dead

Woman"—13,776'), longest and steepest part of the trek, and highest point on the Inca Trail. Descend and camp below the ruins of Runkuraqay (11,800').

DAY 6: Over Runkuraqay Pass (12,494') to Sayacmarca. Stop to visit the ruin, and continue on to camp near Phuyupatamarca ("Town in the Clouds") at 11,906 feet.

DAY 7: A three hour walk, passing the ruins of Winaywayna ("forever young") to Intipunku at 8,900 feet, the original entrance to Machu Picchu, through which we will enter the ruins.

DAY 8: All morning to explore the ruins and hike up Huayna Picchu (9,000'). Catch the late afternoon train and arrive in Cuzco in early evening.

DAY 9: Morning free in Cuzco. Afternoon city tour, including the major ruins at Sacsayhuaman and Kenko.

DAY 10: Day free in Cuzco.

DAY 11: Fly to Puerto Maldonado, and proceed by motorized dugout canoe to a lodge on the tributary of the Amazon River.

DAY 12: Time for walks in the jungle, visits to a nearby Indian village, or exploring the river environment by dugout canoe.

DAY 13: Transfer to airport for morning flight to Lima. Afternoon free. Overnight in hotel.

DAY 14: Morning tour of Lima. Afternoon free. Late evening transfer to airport and depart Lima.

DAY 15: Arrive Miami and continue on homeward-bound flights.

IT3EA1MT12

FAMILY TREK IN PERU

DATES: #1 Jun 16–Jun 30 (15 days)
#2 Aug 18–Sep 1 (15 days)
LEADER: #1 to be announced
#2 Jan Tiura &
Joe Brennan
GRADE: B-2
LAND COST: adults: $1350
(6–15 members)
*children age 10–14: $990
age 2–9: $790

*Note: Children's rates are not representative of operational cost and are only offered on this special trip.

A Peruvian wilderness adventure for parents and children, this trip has the same itinerary as our "Peru Adventure." Certain special amenities will be added, such as extra porters to carry younger children on trek days when necessary.

D

A

B

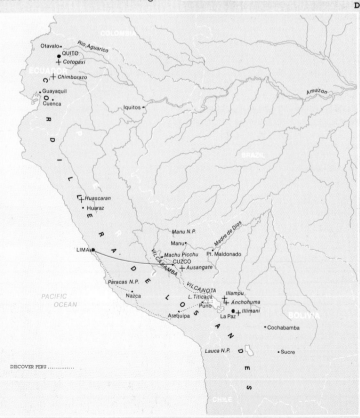

DISCOVER PERU ....

C

A Machu Picchu/Pam Shandrick
B Lunch stop, Cordillera Vilcanota/Pam Shandrick
C Victoria Pass, Trans Andean Trek/William Boehm
D Chincheros market/Pam Shandrick
E Inca ruins at Choquequirao/Terry Brian

A

IT3EA1MT03

THE PERUVIAN HIGHLANDS

DATES: #1 Apr 28–May 19 (22 days)
#2 Jun 9–Jun 30 (22 days)
#3 Jul 14–Aug 4 (22 days)
#4 Aug 18–Sep 8 (22 days)
LEADER: #1 Lynn Meisch
#2 Bruce Klepinger
#3 & #4 Terry Brian
GRADE: C-2
LAND COST: $1850 (13–16 members)
$2150 (10–12)

Exploring two of southern Peru's mountain regions, we first trek for six days to Machu Picchu through the Cordillera Vilcabamba, a range which juts out of the lowlands and has glaciers feeding the Amazon. We begin walking in a remote section of the range and cross a spectacular 15,000-foot pass in the shadow of magnificent Mt. Salcantay (20,574') and Mt. Palcay (18,645'). Our route eventually links with the Inca Trail leading to Machu Picchu.

The second section of the trip is a seven-day trek in the Cordillera Vilcanota, a mountain range of stunning, isolated ice peaks which rise from the rolling grasslands of the "altiplano." Our route completely circles glacier-covered Mt. Ausangate (20,945'), and our camps are in splendid meadows at 14,000 feet where we may meet Indian shepherds and see herds of llamas and alpacas.

In between treks, we'll relax at a comfortable country inn for two days in Urubamba, visiting the superb ruins at Ollantaytambo.

ITINERARY:
DAY 1: Leave U.S. Arrive Lima and continue by air to Cuzco. Transfer to hotel. Afternoon free.

DAY 2: Morning excursion by bus to Indian market at Chincheros.

DAY 3: By bus to the hilltop ruins of Pisac in the Urubamba Valley. Return to Cuzco.

DAY 4: All-morning drive to a rustic hacienda at Mollepata (8,500').

DAY 5: Begin six-day trek to Machu Picchu, with a long, gradual uphill hike to a high meadow at Soray (10,000'), just beneath the spectacular southwest face of Salcantay.

DAY 6: Steep push up over the Incachilaska Pass (about 15,000'), then descend a long, flat valley to a camp at about 12,000 feet.

DAY 7: Following the remnants of Inca terraces, hike over another 15,000-foot pass. Camp at 11,000 feet.

DAY 8: Hike past remnants of Inca irrigation canals to a camp at about 10,000 feet, where we join the "regular" Inca Trail.

DAY 9: Continue along the Inca Trail, crossing over the Warmiwanusqa Pass (13,776'), highest point on the Inca Trail. Camp at a meadow at about 11,000 feet.

DAY 10: Hike to Phuyupatamarca, descend about 2,000 feet to Inti-

punku ("Door of the Sun"), and arrive at Machu Picchu.

DAY 11: All day at Machu Picchu. Optional hike up Huayna Picchu (9,000'). Afternoon train to the town of Urubamba. Overnight at inn.

DAY 12: Visit the town of Ollantaytambo and its beautiful Inca ruins.

DAY 13: Six-hour drive to the highland village of Tinki (13,000'), crossing over a rugged 14,000-foot pass.

DAY 14: Begin five-day Vilcanota trek, walking across an expanse of golden pampas from which the peak of Mt. Ausangate, highest mountain in the Cordillera Vilcanota, rises. Camp at Upis (13,500') near some hot springs.

Hike over the sand-colored slopes of the Incapampa Pass (15,400') and then alongside a deep glacial lake called Pucacocha, above which towers Mt. Ausangate.

DAY 15: Hike over the sand-colored slopes of the Incapampa Pass (15,400') and then alongside a deep glacial lake called Pucacocha, above which towers Mt. Ausangate. Camp by the lake at about 14,000 feet and hear Ausangate's glaciers drop huge blocks of ice into the lake.

DAY 16: Over a 15,750-foot pass and down to Lake Ausangatecocha, then over Palomani Pass (16,900') with views of Ausangate and neighboring Mariposa. Camp at 15,000 feet.

DAY 17: Trek along the Rio Jampamaya and above Lake Ticllacocha, with views of the

19,000-foot ice peaks of Jatunjampa and Collque Cruz. Cross Pacchanta Pass (16,725') and camp.

DAY 18: Meander down the Pacchanta Valley and camp near Pacchanta hot springs at about 14,000 feet.

DAY 19: Hike to Tinki where we started our trek, and board a bus for a five-hour drive to Cuzco.

DAY 20: In Cuzco for last-minute shopping and sightseeing.

DAY 21: Fly to Lima. Day free. Evening transfer to airport.

DAY 22: Depart Lima, arrive Miami and connect with homeward-bound flights.

B

IT3EA1MT06

THE TRANS ANDEAN TREK

DATES: Jun 14–Jul 14 (31 days)
LEADER: Terry Brian
GRADE: C-3
LAND COST: $2475 (13–16 members)
$2785 (10–12)

An exceptional Andean odyssey, this 23-day trek seeks out extremely remote Inca ruins which are accessible only on foot. It begins in the Cordillera Urubamba, with its well-known Inca sites, and circles up through the Cordillera Vilcabamba to Machu Picchu, the most famous Inca ruin of them all. On route we'll visit many of Hiram Bingham's Inca discoveries and most of the classic Inca sites of the Vilcabamba—some of the least known and most remote ruins of all Inca civilization—including Nusta Hispana and exquisite Vitcos, the last Inca capital, where the Inca Manco the Second was murdered at the end of the Spanish conquest. At mid-point in the trek, there is an opportunity to make a four-day round trip hike to the extremely remote Inca ruins at Choquequirao. This section of the hike is very strenuous, so we have made it optional.

ITINERARY:
DAY 1: Leave U.S. Arrive Lima and continue by air to Cuzco. Transfer to hotel.

DAY 2 to 4: Excursions to Sacsayhuaman, Kenko, Pisac and Ollantaytambo and other Inca ruins of Cuzco and the Urubamba Valley.

DAY 5: By truck to Chaullay, near Mt. Veronica (20,000') in the Cordillera Vilcabamba. Begin 23-day trek with a hike to Yupanca (11,000').

D

C

E

A

DAY 6: Morning visit to the ruins at Vitcos and Nusta Hispana. Hike up to the base of Chucuito Pass (14,500'). Camp at 13,000 feet.

DAY 7 to 9: Cross Chucuito Pass and descend into the valley of Chilliluapampa; hike up to a valley beneath the hanging glaciers of the beautiful ice peak called Panta (18,593'); optional hike to 17,500 feet for incredible views of Panta and the Cordillera Vilcabamba.

On route we'll visit many of Hiram Bingham's Inca discoveries and most of the classic Inca sites of the Vilcabamba—some of the least known and most remote ruins of all Inca civilization.

DAY 10 to 12: Skirt the headwaters of Quebrada Arma; ascend through a glacier-carved valley surrounded by ice and granite over an unmarked pass of about 15,000 feet; descend into rain forest then ascend a 14,000-foot pass with views of the canyon of Quebrada Yanama.

DAY 13 and 14: Traverse the hanging valley of Paccha with views of Pumasillo (19,915'), known as "the puma's claw"; optional hike up to Lake Yanama Cocha via an ancient Inca aqueduct.

DAY 15 to 18: Four-day round trip hike to the very remote Inca ruins at Choquequirao, with many steep ascents and descents in a high jungle environment called the "selva" ("eyebrow of the jungle"). This is a rugged journey and those who don't want to undertake it can stay in Yanama on these days.

DAY 19 and 20: Follow the pampa north of the Rio Apurimac toward the Salcantay massif, with superb views of Panta and Pumasillo to the north. To the south we look into the tremendous gorge of the Rio Apurimac. Cross Yanama Pass (15,100').

DAY 21 and 22: Cross Salcantay Pass (15,000 feet) below the peak of Salcantay (20,574'), then over the Incachilaska Pass (16,500'). Descend a long, flat valley to a camp at about 12,000 feet.

DAY 23: Cross Tocto Pass to Cruz Q'uasa with views of Salcantay and the distant Cordillera Vilcanota. Camp at Millpu beneath the snows of Caracruz.

DAY 24 to 26: Cross the Incaraqay Pass (15,000'), descend to Huayllabamba (9,700'), passing the ruins of Colca and Paucarcancha, and join the Inca Trail. Cross the Warmiwanusqa Pass (13,776') to Sayacmarca.

DAY 27: Continue along the Inca Trail past Phuyupatamarca to Intipunku and descend to Machu Picchu.

DAY 28: Explore Machu Picchu, hike up Huayna Picchu (9,000'), catch the afternoon train to Cuzco, arriving in early evening.

DAY 29: In Cuzco for last-minute shopping and sightseeing.

DAY 30: Fly to Lima. Day free. Late night transfer to airport.

DAY 31: Arrive Miami and connect with homeward-bound flights.

IT3EA1MT13

THE FESTIVAL TREK

DATES: June 30–July 19 (20 days)
LEADER: James Dirks
GRADE: C-3
LAND COST: $1575 (13–16 members)
$1780 (10–12)

This 15-day trek through the Cordillera Urubamba is timed to coincide with the lively Indian "Fiesta del Carmen" at the village of Paucartambo.

Villagers come from all around to attend this once-a-year celebration and festival. It is a joyous "dance parody" of life, complete with hundreds of dancers in brilliant costumes and masks. The dances parody certain occupations—from herders and traders to doctors and lawyers—and many aspects of daily life from Inca and colonial times.

The trekking route to Paucartambo is strenuous, following a major trade route used by alpaca and llama herders. On the way we'll pass many villages and remnants of Inca terracing and Inca irrigation canals. There will be long days and much "up and down" walking on steep ridges, but this trek is a special opportunity to glimpse into a mysterious, ancient culture before "progress" and paved roads change it forever.

ITINERARY:

DAY 1: Leave U.S. Arrive Lima, and continue by air to Cuzco. Transfer to hotel.

DAY 2: Afternoon tour of Inca ruins.

DAY 3: All-day excursion to the "Sacred Valley of the Incas," for visits to Pisac and Ollantaytambo ruins. Overnight at Urubamba.

DAY 4: Begin trek, hiking along the Patacancha River, a major trade route from Urubamba to

Lares, where we may see alpaca herds and Inca terracing. Camp at Huilloc.

DAY 5: Walk to Queunaococha on high and rocky terrain through rare *quenual* tree groves. On clear days there is a view of Salcantay (20,574').

DAY 6: Cross a high pass under Colque Cruz snow peak, hiking past the beautiful village of Huacahuasi to the Inca-built Lares Hot Baths.

DAY 7: Hike past the town of Lares to the Lares River.

DAY 8: Hike over a rolling pampa ridge to the Inca village of Choquecancha. Two sides of the main plaza of this town are Inca walls, a third is now a colonial church.

DAY 9 and 10: Continue to Ampares, cross the main pass on the trip and descend on a long downhill stretch to Chimor and the Chimor Hot Baths.

DAY 11: A short hike today to the Mapacho River; in the evening enjoy a *Pachamanca*, or Peruvian barbeque.

DAY 12: Hike up 4,000 feet today on a llama trail and camp by a lake in the high grasslands with views down to the jungle to the east.

DAY 13: Hike along rolling country, past numerous lakes, with jungle views and views of Pitusiray, a peak above Calca. Mt. Ausangate (20,945') comes into view on a clear day.

DAY 14: Hike along a ridge and arrive at Tres Cruces, once the site of two large Inca roads that descend to the tropics and an area called "paititi," where in 1980 the remains of an Inca-built turquoise mosaic road were found.

DAY 15: Long day down the Mapacho River.

DAY 16: Hike to Paucartambo for the beginning of the Fiesta del Carmen. Camp outside of town.

DAY 17: At the Fiesta del Carmen. Watch hundreds of dancers in brilliant costumes performing traditional, ancient ritual dances.

There will be long days and much "up and down" walking on steep ridges, but this trek is a special opportunity to glimpse into a mysterious, ancient culture before "progress" and paved roads change it forever.

DAY 18: Morning drive to Cuzco, arriving in the afternoon.

DAY 19: Fly to Lima. Day free. Late evening transfer to the airport. Depart Lima.

DAY 20: Arrive Miami and connect with homeward-bound flights.

B

IT3EA1MTO5

THE ANDES, INCAS & AMAZON

DATES: #1 Jun 2–Jun 23 (22 days)
#2 Jul 21–Aug 11 (22 days)
LEADER: #1 To be announced.
#2 Sara Stek
GRADE: C-2
LAND COST: $1990 (13–16 members)
$2250 (10–12)

An in-depth Peruvian odyssey, this trip features a nine-day trek in the wilds of the Cordillera Vilcanota, an excursion by dugout canoe on the quiet streams of the upper Amazon, plus visits to colonial Arequipa, Lake Titicaca, Cuzco and Machu Picchu.

The Cordillera Vilcanota is one of southern Peru's least traveled yet most spectacular mountain ranges. Our trekking route starts in cultivated valleys and ascends to the golden altiplano and windswept 15,000-foot-high Lake Sibinacocha (where we may see flocks of pink flamingos), and past the flanks of Mt. Ausangate (20,945').

ITINERARY:

DAY 1: Leave U.S. Arrive Lima. Transfer to hotel.

DAY 2: Fly to Arequipa (8,000'). Afternoon free for exploring the Spanish colonial environment of this pretty town, with views of the volcanoes of Misti (19,200') and Chachani (20,000').

DAY 3: Fly to Juliaca and drive to Puno on the shores of Lake Titicaca (12,500'), visiting the "chull-pas" (tomb-towers) at Sillustani en route.

DAY 4: Boat out to the island of Takili on Lake Titicaca, passing by the "floating islands" of the Uros Indians, returning to Puno in the afternoon.

DAY 5: Early morning train ride to Sicuani, arriving in the afternoon.

DAY 6: Drive to Pitumarca (11,800'), via the ruins at Racchi, and camp.

DAY 7: Begin nine-day trek in the Cordillera Vilcanota. Hike up the Pitumarca River passing the small village of Ucchuyucllu and camp at 13,500 feet.

DAY 8: Continue up Pitumarca Canyon, with views of Ausangate (20,945'), highest peak in the Vilcanota, and camp at 15,000 feet in the high, barren "altiplano."

DAY 9: Cross a pass at 16,200 feet and walk the high and fairly level grasslands of the altiplano to camp near the foot of Laguna Sibinacocha.

DAY 10: Hike over a small ridge to Lake Sibinacocha (15,000'), and continue along the shores to camp at the north end.

DAY 11: Cross two passes today (at 16,500' and 16,800') and camp at Ojepampa, a beautiful meadow at 15,800 feet where sheep and llamas graze.

DAY 12: Walk down to the Rio Chillcamaya then camp at 15,200 feet on the shoulders of Mt. Ausangate.

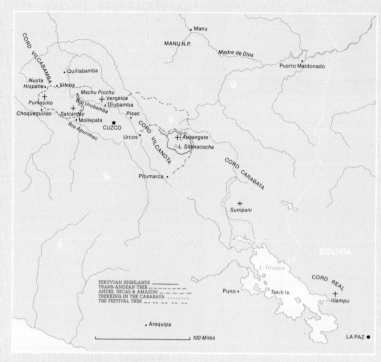

DAY 13: Cross over Mariposa Pass (17,000') below the fluted ice peak of Mariposa (19,800'). Descend to Ausangatecocha, a lake just below Ausangate, and walk further to a spectacular campsite at Lake Pucacocha (14,600').

DAY 14: Trek over a couple of small passes and down a valley to the hot springs at Upis.

DAY 15: Trek to the village of Tinki (13,000'), and drive by bus to Cuzco (11,204'), arriving in the evening.

DAY 16: Half-day tour of Cuzco and nearby Inca ruins. Afternoon free.

DAY 17: Morning train to Machu Picchu, arriving about 11 a.m. Afternoon to explore the ruins, and return to Cuzco on the late afternoon train, arriving in early evening.

DAY 18: Free day in Cuzco.

DAY 19: Fly to Puerto Maldonado and transfer by motorized canoe to a lodge on a tributary of the Amazon River. Afternoon walk

and overnight at lodge.

DAY 20: By motorized dugout canoe to an Indian village passing gold seekers on the banks of the river or natural history walk to observe Amazon plants and birdlife.

> Our trekking route starts in cultivated valleys and ascends to the golden altiplano and windswept 15,000-foot-high Lake Sibinacocha (where we may see flocks of pink flamingos), and past the flanks of Mt. Ausangate (20,945').

DAY 21: Fly to Lima. Afternoon free. Depart on late night flight to U.S.

DAY 22: Arrive Miami and connect with homeward-bound flights.

IT3EA1MT14

MANU JUNGLE EXPLORATORY

DATES: Sep 1–Sep 13 (13 days)
LEADER: to be announced
GRADE: B-2
LAND COST: $1290 (10–16 members)

Join a wildlife expedition in Manu National Park, the largest national park in the entire Amazon.

This very special four-million-acre park is one of the most beautiful and most untouched natural areas on the entire continent of 'South America. Its isolation on the eastern slope of Peru's southern Andes has helped keep its ecological integrity. In 1977, Manu was declared a Biosphere Reserve by UNESCO, joining a select group of reserves whose scientific value is internationally recognized.

The impenetrable forest of Manu National Park gives shelter to jaguars, pumas, 13 species of monkeys, Andean deer, and rare spectacled bear. A dazzling abundance of birds (more than 500 species) flutter in the high canopy of orchid and vine-laden trees. The rivers and lakes are home to caimans, turtles, piranhas, anacondas and very rare giant otters.

The "highways" which allow us to penetrate the green walls of the Amazon are the reddish waters of the Manu River and the clear-flowing Madre de Dios River. Each day, we'll glide on the rivers observing wildlife from our motorized dugout canoes. Each evening, we'll set up a tent camp on sandbars along the shores and listen to the haunting night sounds of the jungle.

The trip also visits the beautiful highland town of Cuzco (11,200'), ancient capital of the Incas, with its many Inca ruins.

ITINERARY

DAY 1: Leave U.S. Arrive Lima. Transfer to hotel.

DAY 2: Fly to Cuzco. Afternoon tour of Inca ruins at Sacsayhuaman and Kenko.

DAY 3: Drive to the Paucartambo Valley, an important trading center in colonial and republican times. Overnight at farmhouse.

DAY 4: Early morning drive to Tres Cruces de Oro to witness dawn

B

C

A Piranha
B Alpaca and ice peaks in the Carabaya/Bruce Klepinger
C Town of Asiento/Bruce Klepinger
D Local architecture of the Carabaya/Bruce Klepinger
E Weaver at village of Ayapata/Bruce Klepinger

over the jungle, and continue to camp at Manu National Park.

DAY 5: By canoe to upper Madre de Dios, leaving the jungled hill country and entering the flood plains. At confluence with Manu River, head upstream to Playa Romero.

DAY 6: Continue upstream deep into the jungle and see water birds, perhaps red deer, tapirs and monkeys. Camp by a lake at Cochas Kashun.

In 1977, Manu was declared a Biosphere Reserve by UNESCO, joining a select group of reserves whose scientific value is internationally recognized

DAY 7: Take wildlife walks around Cochas Kashun Lake.

DAY 8: Morning walks, afternoon drift downstream to the park's personnel camp at Pakitza.

DAY 9 and 10: Float downstream to Boca Manu and return to Rio Alto Madre de Dios, making slower time against the current.

DAY 11: Drive back to Cuzco, arriving in the afternoon.

DAY 12: Fly to Lima. Day free.

DAY 13: Depart Lima, arrive Miami and connect with homeward-bound flights.

IT3EA1MTO8
TREKKING IN THE CARABAYA

DATES: May 12–Jun 2 (22 days)
LEADER: Bruce Klepinger
GRADE: C-3
LAND COST: $1990 (13–16 members)
$2275 (10–12)

In the easternmost reaches of Peru's altiplano, just north of Lake Titicaca (12,500'), is a mountain range called the Cordillera Carabaya.

The Carabaya is little-traveled by outsiders and has fantastic mountain scenery, colonial-era Inca ruins and some of the most beautiful pampas in the Andes. It also has a fine share of Andean wildlife, including condor, vicuna and flamingos. At its western end, it links with the impressive Cordillera Vilcanota, and both ranges together stretch nearly 100 miles across the highlands from Lake Titicaca to Cuzco.

Our 14-day Cordillera Carabaya trek begins near Lake Titicaca's northern shore. Our route follows trails through moderately high altitudes with surprising subtropical vegetation, hot springs and waterfalls. Views extend upwards to the Carabaya's carved and fluted 18,000-foot ice peaks and down thousands of feet to the mists of the Amazon Basin.

At mid-point in the trek, we cross a 16,500-foot pass with views of the Andean ice cap and a 360-degree panorama of ice peaks. This summit is the line where the Carabaya changes names and

becomes the Cordillera Vilcanota. From here we descend to Lake Sibinacocha (15,000'), pass along the ramparts of Mt. Ausangate (20,945'), and end the trek at the highland village of Tinki (13,000').

The trip also visits Lake Titicaca, Cuzco and Lima.

ITINERARY:
DAY 1: Leave U.S.

DAY 2: Arrive Lima. Continue by air to Juliaca. Drive to Puno on the shores of Lake Titicaca (12,500'), visiting pre-Inca tomb towers at Sillustani en route. Overnight at hotel.

DAY 3: By boat across the lake, passing the floating island-villages of the Uros Indians and visit the island of Takili. Continue to the northern shore and camp at Taraco.

DAY 4 and 5: Drive to Macusani, crossing a high pass, and camp. From camp, take a day hike around Lake Chungara and descend by bus to the remote village of Ayapata to visit a native market.

DAY 6: Begin trek, hiking into a valley with many lakes and Inca ruins. Camp at one of the lakes.

DAY 7: Cross a 13,500-foot pass with extensive views north toward the Yungas (the deep valleys which lead to the Amazon) and southward toward the Carabaya. Descend to Olleachea and relax in public hot springs.

DAY 8: Ascend from Olleachea, past the town of Asiento, to the crest above Rio Corani. Cross a pass and camp near a small mountain lake surrounded by grassy meadows.

DAY 9: Over two passes with splendid views of open pampas, flanks of steep carved mountains and the deep gorge of the Rio Corani.

DAY 10: Trek west through immense pampas, approaching snow-capped peaks. Camp at about 14,000 feet.

DAY 11 and 12: Rest day and optional hike to the head of the Rio Corani valley, where the peaks of the western Carabaya are at their most magnificent. The Peruvian icecap is seen to the south and many jagged ice peaks to the northwest.

DAY 13 and 14: Cross a 17,000-foot pass, entering the "Departmento de Cuzco" and the mountain range called the Cordillera Vilcanota. Descend past a large cirque of 20,000-foot peaks and camp at the pueblo of Finaya. Rest day or optional hikes to the base of the ice cap or to Lake Sibinacocha (15,000').

At mid-point in the trek, we cross a 16,500-foot pass with views of the Andean ice cap and a 360-degree panorama of ice peaks.

DAY 15 and 16: Trek along the banks of Lake Sibinacocha with incredible views of lakes and towering ice peaks and cross a 17,500-foot pass to Jampa.

DAY 17 and 18: Cross two more passes and descend into Ticllacocha, then cross Pacchanta Pass (16,900') and camp near the hot springs at Pacchanta.

DAY 19: Walk to the highland village of Tinki (13,000') and drive to Cuzco.

DAY 20: Free day in Cuzco.

DAY 21: Fly to Lima. Day free.

DAY 22: Depart Lima, arrive Miami and connect with homeward-bound flights.

A Fluted ridge of Chacraraju, Cordillera Blanca/Leo Le Bon
B Below Santa Cruz/Jan Parker

IT3EAIMTO4

THE INCA-BLANCA TREK

DATES: #1 May 19–Jun 9 (22 days)
#2 Jun 30–Jul 21 (22 days)
#3 Sep 15–Oct 6 (22 days)
LEADER: #1 & #2 Lynn Meisch
#3 Terry Brian
GRADE: C-2
LAND COST: $2190 (10-16 members)

This is our only Peru itinerary which features treks in both northern and southern Peru.

In southern Peru, a seven-day trek takes us to Machu Picchu via a seldom-traveled route in the Cordillera Vilcabamba, following long, high altitude valleys below Mt. Palcay (18,645'). Joining the Inca Trail at mid-trek, we descend to the misty ruins of Machu Picchu.

In northern Peru, we will trek for six days in the Cordillera Blanca, highest tropical mountain range in the world. We'll walk through a variety of environments from subtropical to alpine, enjoying great panoramas of the Cordillera Blanca's well-known "skyline" of 20,000-footers, including Huascaran (22,204'), highest peak in Peru.

ITINERARY:

DAY 1: Leave U.S. Arrive Lima and continue by air to Cuzco. Transfer to hotel.

DAY 2: Excursion by bus to Sacsayhuaman and other Inca ruins nearby.

DAY 3: Early morning bus ride to the Urubamba Valley, the sacred valley of the Incas, for an all-day float trip on the Urubamba River and a visit to the Inca ruins at Pisac on route.

DAY 4: Visit the Inca site at Ollantaytambo, then continue on to Chilca (8,000') to begin our seven-day trek to Machu Picchu.

DAY 5 and 6: Hike up into the Silque Valley to a meadow below the Ancascocha Pass (13,950'); cross the pass with views of the peaks of Huayanay and Palcay (18,645') in the distance.

DAY 7 and 8: Hike down toward the valley of Sisaypampa below Mt. Salcantay (20,574'); continue downhill past the ruins of Incaraqay to the village of Huayllabamba (9,700').

DAY 9: Hike through Llulluchapampa, cross a pass at 13,300 feet and descend to the Pacamayo River.

DAY 10: Up to the second pass past the ruins of Rukuraqay to Sayacmarca ("The Waiting Town") and Phuyupatamarca (11,900'). Enter Machu Picchu via Intipunku at 8,000 feet.

DAY 11: Explore Machu Picchu, hike up Huayna Picchu (9,000') and return to Cuzco on the afternoon train, arriving early evening.

DAY 12: Day free in Cuzco.

DAY 13: Fly to Lima and continue by bus on a seven-hour drive to northern Peru and the highland town of Huaraz (10,200'). On

route, visit the pre-Inca ruins of Paramonga.

DAY 14: By truck to the roadhead at Vaqueria, stopping en route to visit Llanganuco Lakes, and drive over Portachuelo de Llanganuco, a pass at 15,740 feet with a great panorama of the major peaks of the Cordillera Blanca, including Huascaran (22,204'), Huandoy (20,980'), Pisco (18,898'), Chopicalqui (20,816'), and Chakraraju (20,052'). Descend to the east side of the range and camp at Vaqueria.

In northern Peru, we will trek for six days in the Cordillera Blanca, highest tropical mountain range in the world.

DAY 15: Begin trek with a hike up the canyon of the Quebrada Huaripampa and camp at Quebrada Paria.

DAY 16: Trek to Tuctubamba and camp. Optional hike up the Alto de Pucaruri (15,150') for exceptional views of the Cordillera Blanca, including Alpamayo (19,511'), a peak known for its almost perfectly symmetrical pyramid shape.

DAY 17: Hike over Punta Union, a 15,580-foot pass, and camp on the western side. Optional hike for views of Quitaraju (19,816').

DAY 18: Hike down the Santa Cruz Valley and camp at Llama Corral, passing beautiful meadows and a lake.

DAY 19: Hike out to Cashapampa and return to Huaraz by truck.

DAY 20: Seven-hour drive to Lima.

DAY 21: Visit Anthropological Museum in the morning, afternoon free to shop or visit Lima's other famous museums. Late night transfer to the airport.

DAY 22: Depart Lima, arrive Miami and connect with homeward-bound flights.

IT3EAIMT10

TREKKING IN THE CORDILLERA BLANCA

DATES: #1 Jun 16–Jun 30 (15 days)
#2 Jun 30–Jul 21 (22 days)
#3 Aug 4–Aug 18 (15 days)
LEADER: #1 Lynn Meisch
#2 Sara Steck
#3 Terry Brian
GRADE: #1 & #3: C-2; #2: C-3
LAND COST: #1 & #3:
$1450 (10-16 members)
$1690 (7-9)
#2: $1875 (13-16)
$1980 (10-12)

Delicate corniced snow ridges and fluted ice faces make the mountains of the Cordillera Blanca ("White Mountains") among the most beautiful in the world.

In this great ice range, most of which is now protected within "Parque Nacional Huascaran," eleven major summits top 20,000 feet and more than 70 peaks top 18,000 feet.

Because these peaks are so close to the equator, snow conditions here are quite different from those of mountains in higher latitudes. Above snowline, even the steepest slopes are draped with ice, while the summits often consist of incredible overhanging cornices.

Perhaps no other mountain range with peaks so high is of such easy access. The glaciers (the longest in the tropics) can almost be reached by road in some places. Our treks here are high altitude adventures, with campsites at about 13,000 to 14,000 feet.

Trip #2 is a 16-day trek which crosses nine passes of 15,000 feet or higher. Views en route include most of the Blanca's famed northern peaks, including Santa Cruz (20,534'), Huascaran (22,204'), Huandoy (20,980'), Chacraraju (20,052'), the "perfect" pyramid of Alpamayo (19,511'), and the glacial slopes of Copa (20,252') and Toqllaraju (19,790'). As we continue walking, often along neatly cultivated fields and past lakes and waterfalls, we also see peaks much farther south, as we encircle the massifs of Contrahierbas, Hualcan and Copa.

Treks #1 and #3 feature nine-day treks, which cover slightly more than half of the same route covered on the longer trek, only starting in the opposite direction. We'll be circling three major massifs, Alpamayo, Santa Cruz and Pukajirca, and crossing six passes over 15,000 feet, the highest of which is Cullicocha Pass (16,240'). The views are of the northern Cordillera Blanca with beautiful glacial-blue lakes of Azulcocha, Kullicocha and Jankarurish, the immense glaciers of Pukajirca and Santa Cruz, the cultivated fields of the eastern valleys and finally, views of the giant peaks of the Llanganuco Valley: Huascaran, Huandoy and Chakraraju.

ITINERARY: SIXTEEN-DAY TREK (Trip #2)

DAY 1: Leave U.S. Arrive Lima. Transfer to hotel.

DAY 2: Seven-hour drive to the highland town of Huaraz (10,200'), with a visit to the pre-Inca Paramonga ruins and views of the southern peaks of the Cordillera Blanca en route. Overnight at hotel.

DAY 3: Visit market and town of Huaraz and day hike in the Rio Santa Valley.

DAY 4: By truck from Huaraz to the roadhead at Caranca in Quebrada Ragranco, with good views of Huascaran, Santa Cruz and Copa en route. Camp at 13,000 feet.

DAY 5 and 6: Trek through a gentle valley cultivated with potatoes, Pass Inca ruins en route. Splendid views of the Cordillera Negra to the west. Enter the Quebrada Los Cedros with views of the classic pyramid of Alpamayo.

DAY 7 and 8: Cross Huilca Pass (15,800') with sweeping views of the northern reaches of the Cordillera Blanca and up to the base of a pass leading to Quebrada Yanajanka. Camp at 13,500 feet.

DAY 9 to 11: Trek through wooded groves, grassy meadows and the steep glaciated cliffs of the eastern foothills of the Cordillera Blanca. Views include the formidable glaciers of the eastern face of Pukajirca. One day to be used as a rest day if necessary.

DAY 12 to 14: Cross Pucaraju Pass (15,345') with views of Piramide and Chakraraju. Hike down the canyon of Quebrada Huaripampa. Side trip to the summit of Portachuelo de Llanganuco (15,740'), with its famous panorama including Huascaran, Huandoy, Pisco (17,900'), Chopikalqui (20,100') and Chakraraju.

DAY 15 to 17: Hike into lower farmlands above Yanama then

Panorama of the Northern Cordillera Blanca/Leo Le Bon
Pukajirca/Bruce Klepinger
Huascaran/Bruce Klepinger
Peruvian guide with Rima plant/Leo Le Bon
Highland farmlands/Leo Le Bon

scend the canyon of Quebrada anayacu and cross Yanayacu ass. (16,170'). Views include the outhern flanks of Huascaran and ontrahierbas (19,550'). Cross Ulta ass with extensive views to the orth including Artesonraju and e peaks of Quebrada Paron, as ell as Huascaran and peaks far the south.

AY 18 and 19: Hike down Que- ada Putaca, pass the village of ompeii and on into Quebrada uitish. Cross Portachuelo Honda nd camp at Rinconada.

In this great ice range, most of which is now protected within "Parque Nacional Huascaran," eleven major summits top 20,000 feet and more than 70 peaks top 18,000 feet.

AY 20: Long descent down uebrada Honda through culti- ated fields to Ruripaccha. Meet uck for late return to Huaraz.

AY 21: Drive to Lima.

DAY 22: Depart Lima, arrive Miami and connect with homeward-bound flights.

ITINERARY: NINE-DAY TREK (Trips #1 & #3)

DAY 1: Leave U.S. Arrive Lima. Transfer to hotel.

DAY 2: Seven-hour drive to the mountain town of Huaraz, visiting the Paramonga ruins on route.

DAY 3: Visit Wilcahuain ruins and take a short acclimatization hike.

DAY 4: Drive over the Portachuelo Llanganuco, with its impressive panorama of the Cordillera Blanca, to a roadhead and camp.

DAY 5 to 8: Trek to Huaripampa, cross Pucaraju Pass, and pass a lake called Huecrococha to Jancapampa.

DAY 9 to 11: Cross Huilca Pass (15,800') to Quebrada Tayapampa and cross a 15,842-foot pass to Quebrada Alpamayo.

DAY 12 and 13: Cross Cuillicocha Pass (16,240'), end trek at Caranca and drive to Huaraz.

DAY 14: All-day bus ride to Lima.

DAY 15: Depart Lima, arrive Miami and connect with homeward-bound flights.

IT3EAIMT09

CORDILLERA BLANCA EXPEDITION: HUASCARAN

DATES: Jul 14–Aug 9 (27 days)
LEADER: Sergio Fitch Watkins
GRADE: E-1
LAND COST: $2590 (7–12 members)

The goal of this expedition is an ascent of Huascaran (22,204'), highest peak in the Peruvian Andes and one of the highest in the Americas.

A huge massif, Huascaran was first climbed in 1932 (Huascaran Sur, the highest of its twin summits)

by the landmark Austrian-German expedition of Kinzl and Schneider, who also made the first survey of the Cordillera Blanca.

Snow conditions have changed on Huascaran in the last few years, increasing the technical difficulties of an ascent. Participants should be experienced in snow and ice climbing.

Before the ascent, we will freshen up our climbing and glacier travel techniques with climbs in the vicinity of Nevado Kayesh (18,800') and Nevado Chinchey (20,532'). Visits are included to Huaraz and Lima.

ITINERARY:

DAY 1: Leave U.S. Arrive Lima. Transfer to hotel.

DAY 2: All day drive to Huaraz (10,200'), the main town in northern Peru. Expedition briefing. Overnight at hotel.

DAY 3: Day hike along the crest of the Cordillera Negra and walk back to Huaraz through small colorful villages.

DAY 4: Afternoon hike to a view-point above the Rio Santa at Monterrey.

DAY 5: Drive to Pitec and hike up the canyon called Quebrada Quelquehuanca. Views of Puka-ranra (20,281'), Tullparaju (18,836') and Chinchey (20,532'). Establish base camp at about 13,500 feet.

DAY 6: Practice and review climbing techniques.

DAY 7 to 10: Ascents in the area of Nevado Kayesh.

DAY 11 to 14: Climb Nevado Chinchey (20,532'). (Note: depending on the skills and acclimatization of the party, another peak may be substituted). We'll have views of the entire Cordillera Blanca from Copa (20,420') in the north as far south as Nevado Huantsan (20,980').

DAY 15: Hike out and truck back to Huaraz.

DAY 16: By truck down the Rio Santa Valley. Hike to lower base camp of Huascaran.

DAY 17 to 19: Shuttle loads to our higher camps on the granite slabs of the western side of Huascaran and past Camp I to high camp below Gargantua, the saddle between Huascaran's two summits.

The goal of this expedition is an ascent of Huascaran (22,204'), highest peak in the Peruvian Andes and one of the highest in the Americas.

DAY 20 to 22: Summit attempts on Huascaran Sur (22,204'), and extra days to allow for bad weather.

DAY 23 and 24: Return to lower camps and return to Huaraz.

DAY 25: Drive to Lima.

DAY 26: Day free in Lima.

DAY 27: Depart Lima, arrive Miami and connect with homeward-bound flights.

IT3EA1MT07

SOURCE OF THE AMAZON

DATES: May 5–May 22 (18 days)
LEADER: Sara Steck
GRADE: C-2
LAND COST: $1775 (13–16 members)
$2050 (10–12)

This unusual ten-day trek has as its goal a small, azure lake at 15,700 feet in the heart of the Peruvian Andes. This glacier-ringed pool, called Ninacocha ("Lake of the Child"), was determined in 1951 to be the actual source of the Amazon, the longest river in the world.

We begin our trek to the source of the Amazon traveling up and over several passes in the spectacular Cordillera Huayhuash, second highest of Peru's great ice-ranges. Views here will include the imposing fang of Jirishanca (20,099') and Yerupaja (21,759'), the 2nd highest mountain in Peru and locally known as El Carnicero ("The Butcher").

Continuing across a 15,000-foot pass, we enter the virtually unknown Cordillera Raura, hiking along rocky ridges and grassy slopes at 14,000 feet with turquoise lakes and astounding views of Yurupac and Matador, the two big peaks of the Cordillera Raura. Our goal, the glacier-fed tarn of Ninacocha at 15,700 feet, is reached on the last day of the trek.

Transport will meet us below the lake for a drive back to Lima.

ITINERARY:

DAY 1: Leave U.S. Arrive Lima and transfer to hotel.

DAY 2: Seven-hour drive to Huaraz. Overnight in hotel.

DAY 3: Morning visit to Huaraz (10,000') and afternoon hike.

DAY 4: Day trip by bus to Porta-chuelo de Llanganuco (14,470') for breathtaking views of the Cordillera Blanca.

DAY 5: Drive to Chiquian (10,560'), main village of the Cordillera Huayhuash.

DAY 6: Begin trek, ascending for about four hours along the Llamac River to a pass at Pitec (10,900') then on to the village of Llamac (10,560').

DAY 7: Hike over Punta Llamac Pass (13,860'), then to a beautiful lake called Jahuacocha (13,200'),

our first major viewpoint of the Cordillera Huayhuash, including Nevado Yerupaja (21,759'), the second highest peak in Peru, towering 8,000 feet above the Punta Llamac Pass.

DAY 8: Rest day.

DAY 9: Over 15,345-foot Rondoy Pass, with views of Lake Soltero-cocha, the Yerupaja icefall, and the limestone face of Nevado Rondoy. Descend a beautiful valley to the main trail to Pocpa.

DAY 10: Hike over Cacanampunta Pass (14,890') on the Continental Divide. Descend to Queropalca Valley and camp at Mitucocha Lake below the peaks of Rondoy and Ninashanca.

DAY 11: Hike up a valley to the pass of Punta Carhuac (14,950'), with views of Yerupaja and Jirishanca (20,099'). Arrive at the large lake called Carhuacocha.

DAY 12: Rest day.

DAY 13: Cross the river on horseback, hike over Punta Camicero Pass with fine views of the peaks of Siula, Sarapa and Siria, camp at 13,200 feet.

DAY 14: Leaving behind the Cordillera Huayhuash, we cross a 14,850-foot pass with great views of Yurapac and Matador, two big peaks in the Cordillera Raura. Camp amid a string of glacial lakes.

DAY 15: Slow ascent past Lake Patarcocha, and two more lakes with views of the whole of the Cordillera Raura in the background. Camp below Lake Tinquicocha.

DAY 16: Walk to Ninacocha, the source of the Amazon at 15,700 feet, fed by glaciers in the Cordillera Raura. At a nearby silver mine, we board transport back to Lima.

DAY 17: Free day in Lima for sightseeing.

DAY 18: Depart Lima, arrive Miami and connect with homeward-bound flights.

IT3EA1MT07

ANDEAN CLIMBING SEMINAR

DATES: Jun 28–Jul 15 (18 days)
LEADER: To be announced
GRADE: C-3/D-1
LAND COST: $1990 (7–12 members)

The 20,000-foot peaks of the Peruvian Andes attract expert mountaineers from all over the world.

Our climbing seminar takes place in the high altitude valleys of the Cordillera Raura, a beautiful range with a multitude of gentle peaks as well as precipitous ice faces—all in all, a great variety of high altitude terrain on which to learn and practice snow and ice climbing techniques.

To get to our Cordillera Raura base camp, we hike up and over the eastern flanks of the stunningly beautiful Cordillera Huayhuash, a compact range with six summits topping 20,000 feet. Two of its better known peaks are Yerupaja (at 21,759 feet, Peru's second highest peak) and the imposing ice fang of Jirishanca (20,099'), the "Matterhorn of Peru."

Crossing the Continental Divide into the Cordillera Raura, we'll establish a camp at about 15,000 feet and spend three days in an intensive climbing course. We will review rope handling, snow and

glacier travel, ice climbing and crevasse rescue, and spend four days on ascents of two or more 18,000 to 19,000-foot peaks in the region. The course will be geared to the varying abilities of the participants.

ITINERARY:

DAY 1: Leave U.S. Arrive Lima. Transfer to hotel.

DAY 2: Drive to Cajatambo (11,100') and camp.

DAY 3: Trek up a gentle valley to Laguna Viconga (14,200'). Great views of the peaks of the Cordillera Huayhuash.

DAY 4: Walk around the northern end of the Cordillera Raura to camp at Aguascocha (14,200'). Establish base camp.

DAY 5 to 7: Instruction, practice and review of mountaineering techniques.

DAY 8 to 11: Cross a 16,500-foot pass and camp and descend to Laguna Checchi or Yuracocha (about 14,850'). Proposed ascents of Nevado Leon Yuaccanan (about 16,500') and Quesillojanca (17,500'), a slightly more difficult peak.

DAY 12 to 14: Additional days for climbs in the area. The choice of peaks will depend on party strength and weather.

DAY 15: Hike out to roadhead and drive to Lima. Overnight in hotel.

DAY 16: Morning free, afternoon city tour.

DAY 17: Day free in Lima. Evening transfer to the airport and depart Lima.

DAY 18: Arrive Miami and connect with homeward-bound flights.

> **We will review rope handling, snow and glacier travel, ice climbing and crevasse rescue, and spend four days on ascents of two or more 18,000 to 19,000-foot peaks in the region.**

A Villager of Cordillera Raura/Leo Le Bon
B Lake Titicaca/Bruce Klepinger
C Alpaca herd, Cordillera Real/Bruce Klepinger

BOLIVIA • 13

PERU OPTIONS

Whether you plan to visit Peru on one of our trips or on your own, we can arrange a variety of outdoor adventures for you, on foot, on horseback, by raft or dugout canoe.

For private treks, we can provide a full range of services such as bilingual guides, pack animals, camp staff and cooks, camp equipment and transport. Contact Mountain Travel for rates and further details.

Among our most popular "after the trek" excursions are:

IQUITOS AMAZON EXPLORATION

From a remote lodge on the banks of the Amazon River, hike the trails of the jungle, swim in secluded lagoons, and explore the Amazon's tributaries by boat. Time: three days.

URUBAMBA RIVER RAFTING

Whitewater rafting on the lively Urubamba River as it tumbles through the "sacred valley of the Incas." Also visit the fine Inca sites at Pisac or Ollantaytambo. Time: One or two days.

PUNO/LAKE TITICACA EXCURSION

From the red-roofed village of Puno on the shores of Lake Titicaca, journey by boat to visit Indian weavers on Takili Island and watch sunset over the highest navigable body of water on earth. Time: Three days.

CUZCO/MACHU PICCHU

Tour the mountain town of Cuzco and its famed Inca fortress-ruins, such as Sacsayhuaman, Kenko and Tambomachay, plus take an unforgettable journey by train to the superb jungle citadel of the Incas, Machu Picchu. Time: Three days.

A

IT3EA1MT17

HIGHLANDS OF BOLIVIA

DATES: May 31–Jun 22 (23 days)
LEADER: Sara Steck
GRADE: C-2
LAND COST: $1890 (11-15 members)
$2190 (6-10)

The main range of the Bolivian Andes is the Cordillera Real ("Royal Mountains"), a superb wilderness where massive blue-white glaciers tumble from 20,000-foot peaks. The high valleys of the Cordillera Real descend thousands of feet into the cloudy forests of the upper Amazon.

Our 16-day trek begins at Sorata, in the shadows of some of the highest peaks of the Cordillera Real, including Ancohuma (21,082') and Illampu (20,873'). En route, we'll hike 100 miles through remote Indian villages and llama pastures. We cross several 14,000-foot mountain passes, and meet Indian descendants of the Incas and Aymaras who seldom see "outsiders."

Visits are also included to the high city of La Paz (12,000') and enormous Lake Titicaca (12,500'), legend-filled birthplace of the first Inca king.

ITINERARY:

DAY 1: Leave U.S. Arrive La Paz and transfer to hotel.

DAY 2: Morning city tour of La Paz.

DAY 3: Drive to Lake Titicaca (12,500'), visiting the colonial village of Laja, ruins at Tiahuanaco and Puma Kunku en route. Camp at Taraco Beach on the shores of Lake Titicaca.

DAY 4: By motor launch, visit Inca tombs and monuments on the

> En route, we'll hike 100 miles through remote Indian villages and llama pastures, cross several 14,000-foot mountain passes, and meet Indian descendants of the Incas and Aymaras who seldom see "outsiders."

island of Kalahuta. Continue to eastern side of the lake and drive to Sorata over San Francisco Pass (14,200') where the snow peak of Illampu comes into view.

DAY 5: Drive by truck to the picturesque village of Oncoma.

DAY 6: Begin trek with pack mules and/or llamas to carry equipment. Trek to Cocoo (12,250') over Kalamutuni Pass (14,600'), passing silver mines en route.

DAY 7: Rest day and optional hikes.

B

DAY 8: Hike past numerous waterfalls and the hanging glaciers on Chearoco. Cross Sarani Pass (15,050') and descend to the valley of Chacolpaya.

DAY 9 and 10: Trek past the flanks of the Chacocomanis massif. Splendid views of glaciers and ice-covered peaks.

DAY 11 and 12: Cross Taipipata Pass (16,100'), with stunning views including Vinohuara and Chacocomanis, and another pass with views eastward toward more tropical regions.

DAY 13 and 14: Ascend the Ancolacaya Valley to a 15,650-foot pass between Cerro Wila Llojeta and Cerro Jankho Hoya. Great views across the entire width of the altiplano as far as Sajama, 150 miles away. Rest day in area.

DAY 15: Walk to roadhead and drive to Lago Tuni (14,050').

DAY 16: Walk from Lago Tuni to a lake at the base of Cerro Condiriri.

DAY 17 and 18: Explore around Cerro Condiriri, then cross two passes and descend into the upper Livinosa Drainage (15,800'), continuing down to camp at Chacapampa (12,800').

DAY 19 to 21: Walk across a very deserted section of the southern Cordillera Real on an old, well-preserved Inca highway. Arrive at the roadhead and drive to Chiquilini.

DAY 22: Drive to La Paz by bus, crossing valleys with impressive tropical canyons covered with abundant vegetation. Transfer to airport; depart La Paz.

DAY 23: Arrive Miami and connect with homeward-bound flights.

C

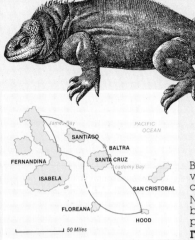

THE GALAPAGOS ISLANDS

DATES: #1 Apr 8–Apr 18 (11 days)
#2 Jun 17–Jul 4 (18 days)
#3 Dec 16–Dec 26 (11 days)
LEADER: #1 Peter Ourusoff
#2 to be announced
#3 Sara Steck
GRADE: A-1
LAND COST:
#1 & #3: $1490 (9 members)
$1690 (8)
#2: $2290 (13–15 members)
$2390 (6–12)
all trips: +chtr. $312

The Galapagos Islands, situated in quiet isolation some 600 miles off Ecuador's coast, contain animal and plant life of a most unusual nature. Some Galapagos birds and shorefish, many of the plants, and nearly all of the giant Galapagos reptiles are found nowhere else on earth. Charles Darwin visited the islands aboard the H.M.S. Beagle in 1835, and today the Galapagos' unique habitat is the subject of constant scientific study.

The islands are a haven for naturalists. Huge land tortoises inhabit the inner valleys. Large dragon-like marine iguanas roam the shores on sea-drenched black lava cliffs, giving one the feeling of a glimpse into the historic past. The much-studied Galapagos bird-

life includes the flightless cormorant, the albatross, blue-footed boobies, the Galapagos penguin and Darwin's famous finches. Galapagos wildlife has no fear of human presence and can be approached closely, making this place a photographer's dream!

> **Galapagos wildlife has no fear of human presence and can be approached closely, making this place a photographer's dream!**

Trips #1 and #3 include 8-day Galapagos yacht cruises. Trip #2 includes 15-day cruise. We will travel island to island on a small sailing vessel with an experienced naturalist guide and skilled crew.

Before and after the cruise, we visit Quito (9,350'), the Ecuadorian capital.

NOTE: The cruise on Trip #2 can be booked for one week only for a part-trip cost of $1490.

ITINERARY:

DAY 1: Leave U.S. Arrive Quito. Transfer to hotel.

DAY 2: Half-day city tour. Afternoon free.

DAY 3: Fly to Guayaquil and by charter flight to the Galapagos Islands. Board boat.

DAY 4 to 9 (8-day cruise) or DAY 4 to 16 (15-day cruise): The cruise itinerary varies according to weather, but most trips will visit Plazas Island, Academy Bay and the highlands of Santa Cruz Island, Caleta Tortuga, James Island, Bartolome Island, and either Tower Island or Floreana Island and Hood Island.

DAY 10 (8-day cruise) or DAY 17 (15-day cruise): Motor to Baltra. Fly to Quito. Overnight in hotel.

DAY 11 (8-day cruise) or DAY 18 (15-day cruise): Depart Quito and connect with homeward-bound flight.

IT3EA1MT16

ECUADOR NATURAL HISTORY

DATES: #1 May 3–May 27 (25 days)
#2 Nov 22–Dec 16 (25 days)
LEADER: #1 Terry Brian
#2 Sara Steck
GRADE: B-2
LAND COST:
$2550+chtr. $312 (13–15 members)
$2690+chtr. $312 (6–8)

Within its relatively small boundaries, Ecuador encompasses most of the world's climatic and vegetation zones.

In the Ecuadorian jungle, we'll travel by canoe on the Rio Aguarico and Rio Aguanegro, visiting Secoya and Sinoa Indian villages. We'll have time to fish, bird-watch, swim with fresh-water dolphins and hike in the jungle.

In the mountains, we'll visit the famed Indian market at Otavalo, then make a four-day hike through highland villages beneath Cotopaxi (19,347'), the giant snow-capped volcano which rises from the sparkling green highland farmlands. One of our camps will be near the rim of Volcano Quilatoa.

Finally, we fly 600 miles out into the Pacific to the Galapagos Islands, the unique wildlife habitat where Darwin compiled much of

B

C

D

E

he evidence for his theory of evolution. We cruise from island to island for seven days in a small vessel with a naturalist guide and crew.

ITINERARY:

DAY 1: Leave U.S. Arrive Quito, Ecuador. Transfer to hotel.

DAY 2: Morning tour of Quito. Afternoon free.

DAY 3: Drive to Taraboa, swim in hot springs, visit the Cataratas de San Rafael; continue to Rio Agua Negra and camp.

DAY 4: Paddle your own dugout canoe down the Rio Agua Negra. Camp near a village of Siona Indians.

DAY 5 and 6: By motorized boat upstream to the Lagunas of Cuyabeno and camp. Time for hiking, fishing and night wildlife viewing by canoe.

DAY 7: Drive to the rough and tumble "frontier" jungle town of Lago Agrio.

DAY 8: Fly to Quito. Drive to the mountain village of Otavalo. Overnight at hacienda.

DAY 9: Visit the Indian market, San Francisco de Ibarra, and Laguna Cuicocha. Afternoon return to Quito.

DAY 10: Drive to Latacunga. Begin the three-and-a-half-day mountain trek.

DAY 11: Hike toward volcano Cotopaxi (19,347'), one of the world's highest active volcanoes.

DAY 12 and 13: Enter Parque Nacional de Cotopaxi; great views of the south side of Cotopaxi.

DAY 14: Drive to Ambato. Camp below volcano Chimborazo (20,561'), highest peak in the region.

DAY 15: Visit local market and drive to the refugio (mountain hut) high up on the slopes of Chimborazo for picnic lunch. Return drive to Riobamba.

DAY 16: All-day train ride to Guayaquil on the coast.

DAY 17: Fly to the Galapagos Islands. Board boat and begin 7-day wildlife cruise.

DAY 18 to 23: The cruise itinerary varies according to weather but includes Plazas Islands, Academy Bay and the highlands of Santa Cruz Island, Caleta Tortuga, James Island, Bartolome Island, and either Tower Island or Floreana Island and Hood Island.

DAY 24: Motor back to Baltra. Fly to Guayaquil.

DAY 25: Depart Guayaquil and connect with homeward-bound flights.

IT3EA1MT21

ECUADOR SPINNING AND WEAVING TOUR

DATES: Aug 8–Aug 28 (21 days)
LEADER: Lynn Meisch
GRADE: A-1
LAND COST: $1990 (7–12 members)

This is a comprehensive folk art tour of Ecuador led by Lynn Meisch, who studied Ecuadorian weaving on a Fulbright scholarship.

The tour visits the famous Otavalo and Ambato markets, and spends the balance of time in and around Cuenca, visiting the homes of several weaver families.

We will learn to spin with the distaff and hand spindle (Ecuadorian style) and observe

backstrap loom weaving, indigo dyeing, warping, tapestry weaving and Panama hat weaving. Lynn has set aside time for lectures and demonstrations. The artisans whose homes we visit are enthusiastic about teaching their age-old skills.

Our close contact with the families of Cuenca and our special look at Ecuadorian Indian culture and family life will be an additional plus on the trip.

ITINERARY:

DAY 1: Leave U.S. Arrive Quito. Transfer to hotel.

DAY 2: Drive to Otavalo Valley in the highlands. Visit homes of poncho, tapestry and wool fabric (bayeta) weavers in Peguche. Evening slide lecture.

DAY 3: Visit weaving cooperative of Miguel Andrango in Agato; and tour around Lago San Pablo and Lago Cuicocha.

DAY 4: All day visit to the famous weekly market at Otavalo.

DAY 5: Morning visit to the Songolqui market and continue by bus to Ambato.

DAY 6: All day visit to the Ambato Market.

DAY 7: Visit tapestry weavers of Salasaca; afternoon visit to the thermal hot baths at Banos.

DAY 8: By bus from Ambato to Cuenca, a city many Ecuadorians think is their most beautiful.

DAY 9: Morning visit to the Cuenca market. Evening slide lecture and demonstration on Cuenca-area textiles.

DAY 10: Visit to Cuenca spinners and weavers.

DAY 11: Visit today to the Azoguea market, the center for "Panama" hat weaving.

DAY 12: Morning visit to Canar market and weavers in the Canar jail. Afternoon visit to the nearby Inca ruins of Ingapirca.

> **Our close contact with the families of Cuenca and our special look at Ecuadorian Indian culture and family life will be an additional plus on the trip.**

DAY 13 to 18: Visit Bullcay el Carmen to see an ikat *pano* being warped, wrapped, dyed with indigo and woven on the backstrap loom; to Chordeleg to see an ikat poncho warped, wrapped, dyed with walnut bark and anilines and woven; to Chicticay to learn to spin and see a belt or *alforja* warped and woven; to Gualaceo to see the fringe on a *pano* macramed. Evening slide lectures on the various textile processes involved.

DAY 19: Visit to Paute market for handspun wool yarn and other crafts.

DAY 20: Fly to Quito. Day free.

DAY 21: Depart Quito and connect with homeward-bound flights.

IT3EA1MT18

THE MOUNTAINS OF ECUADOR

DATES: *Nov 28–Dec 15 (18 days)
LEADER: Sergio Fitch Watkins
GRADE: D-2
LAND COST: $1590 (10–12 members)
$1750 (7–9)

*Note change from 1984 Trip Schedule.

The Andes of Ecuador are actually two separate ranges, the Eastern and Western Cordillera. Running between these ranges for over 200 miles is a central valley lined with more than 30 volcanoes. On this mountaineering journey, we will attempt two of these volcanoes: Cotopaxi (19,347') and Chimborazo (20,561'), the highest peak in the region.

While not technically difficult, these climbs are physically demanding due to the altitude and snow conditions. Ample time is allowed for inclement weather and acclimatization. Basic mountaineering experience is required. The trip begins in Quito (9,350'), with time for enjoying the local culture, including the annual Fiesta de Quito, and ends with a relaxing visit to the Banos hot springs.

ITINERARY:
DAY 1: Leave U.S. Arrive Quito, drive to the village of Otavalo. Overnight at hotel.

DAY 2: Visit the Otavalo market, one of South America's oldest Indian markets.

DAY 3: Drive to Imbabura; afternoon fitness and acclimatization hike. Camp nearby.

DAY 4 to 6: Hiking, climbing and glacier practice in the area of Nevado Cayambe, an 18,996-foot mountain situated on the equator. Return to Quito.

DAY 7: Return to Quito.

> **While not technically difficult, these climbs are physically demanding due to the altitude and snow conditions.**

DAY 8: Enjoy Quito Week festivities, including bullfights and dancing in the streets!

DAY 9 to 11: Climb and descend Cotopaxi.

DAY 12: Drive to Ambato, "the city of flowers."

DAY 13 to 15: Climb and descend Chimborazo.

DAY 16: In Banos, set on the edge of the jungle.

DAY 17: Drive to Quito, arriving in the afternoon.

DAY 18: Depart Quito and connect with homeward-bound flights.

IT3EA1MT20

THE ACONCAGUA EXPEDITION

DATES: Jan 14–Feb 11 (29 days)
LEADER: Sergio Fitch Watkins
GRADE: E-2
LAND COST: $1875 (9–10 members)
$2100 (6-8)

At 22,834 feet, Aconcagua is the highest mountain in the Western Hemisphere and the highest outside Asia.

A difficult and demanding mountain to climb, it is of intense interest to mountaineers. The precipitous southern face was climbed by the French in 1954 and presents one of the most demanding routes in the Andes—close to 10,000 feet of severe technical snow and ice climbing. The normal route, which is technically quite easy, is nonetheless a formidable ascent when one considers the altitude and the possibility of sudden and furious storms. This mountain makes its own weather, and caution and wise mountaineering judgement are required for a successful ascent.

We will attempt the Polish Route, first climbed in 1934. This route involves some 1800 feet of technical ice climbing which, though low-angle, can present serious difficulties depending on weather and acclimatization. Only experienced mountaineers will be accepted for this climb.

> **At 22,834 feet, Aconcagua is the highest mountain in the Western Hemisphere and the highest outside Asia.**

ITINERARY:
DAY 1: Leave U.S. Arrive Buenos Aires, Argentina. Transfer to hotel.

DAY 2: Fly to Mendoza. Day free for organizing gear.

DAY 3: A day in Mendoza to finalize permits and have an expedition meeting and gear check

DAY 4: Bus to Punta de Vaca (7,500') and camp.

DAY 5 to 7: Approach hike to Aconcagua base camp at 13,500 feet, via Rio de Vacas and Rio Relincho.

DAY 8: At base camp.

DAY 9 to 24: Sixteen days will be devoted to the climb and descent to base camp. Establishing Camp I (15,500') and Camp II (18,000') will probably take six days (relaying loads, hacking out tent sites and acclimatizating). From Camp II to the summit and back should take about two days, with a high camp at 20,000 feet. Descent from Camp II to base camp takes one day, leaving a few spare days in case of storms and bad weather.

DAY 25 and 26: Hike out to roadhead.

DAY 27: Bus ride back to Mendoza. Afternoon free.

DAY 28: Free day in Mendoza.

DAY 29: Depart Mendoza and connect with homeward-bound flights.

Grey Glacier/Bruce Kelpinger
Guanacos/Bruce Klepinger
Cordillera del Paine/Bruce Klepinger

A

B

74PAISFMT12
PATAGONIA OVERLAND

DATES: Jan 22–Feb 10 (20 days)
LEADER: To be announced
GRADE: A-2
LAND COST: $1990 (8–15 members)

This is a camping and hiking odyssey in the southernmost tip of South America, land of golden pampas, steep granite spires which make up the southernmost end of the Andes, and Alaskan-size fjords and glaciers.

Our journey through this wild place will be over rough roads, traveling in our own "expedition" bus, camping and occasionally staying in simple inns.

First visiting Santiago, Chile, we then head for Paine National Park, a magnificent wilderness and setting of the great rock towers and "cuernos" of the Cordillera del Paine, whose compelling grandeur is an unmistakable landmark of the Patagonian Andes.

Our four days here will include a hike around the northern flank of one of these peaks for one of the most sensational views in all Patagonia. An optional overnight backpack trip to the Grey Glacier is also possible.

Our Patagonian travels continue with a drive along the wild Strait of Magellan and a motor launch ride on the Last Hope Sound to view the glaciers of Cerro Balmaceda and the rugged peaks at the southern end of the Great Patagonian icecap.

After a night of camping on the Strait of Magellan (with a possible visit to Isla Magdalena to see a penguin colony), we'll explore the scenic waterways of the fjord country of Tierra del Fuego for three days by boat.

Land of golden pampas, steep granite spires which make up the southernmost end of the Andes, and Alaskan-size fjords and glaciers.

ITINERARY:

DAY 1: Leave U.S.

DAY 2: Arrive Santiago. Transfer to hotel.

DAY 3: Half-day city tour.

DAY 4: Fly to Punta Arenas.

DAY 5: Visit Patagonian Institute and drive to Puerto Natales. Camp near Milodon Cave.

DAY 6: Drive to Parque Nacional de Paine. Set up base camp with fantastic views of the peaks of Paine Grande and Admirante Nieto.

DAY 7 to 10: The next four days will be spent hiking in and

around the Paine Massif from our base camp. Possibilities include visits to Valle Frances and Valle de Ascencio, overnights to Grey Glacier or Lago Azul, or to Rio Serrano for excellent fishing.

DAY 11: Drive to Milodon Cave and camp nearby.

DAY 12: Excursion by launch up the Seno Ultima Esperanza to Balmaceda Glacier, and return to Puerto Natales.

DAY 13: Drive to Punta Arenas and camp on the Strait of Magellan. Possible visit to Isla Magdalena to see a penguin colony.

DAY 14 to 16: Boat trip through the dramatic fjord country of Tierra Del Fuego visiting glaciers and looking for Patagonian wildlife. Camp on shore each night.

DAY 17: Drive back to Punta Arenas.

DAY 18: In Punta Arenas. Pending weather conditions, we can arrange an optional overflight of Cape Horn.

DAY 19: Fly to Santiago. Late evening transfer to airport.

DAY 20: Depart Santiago, arrive in Miami and connect with homeward-bound flights.

C

A

IT3EA1MT21

ANTARCTIC CIRCUM-NAVIGATION

DATES: Jan 15–Feb 18 (35 days)
LEADER: Leo Le Bon
GRADE: A-1
LAND COST: From $8000, not including airfare.

In the comfort afforded by the expedition ship *World Discoverer*, we will circumnavigate the Antarctic continent for 30 days, beginning at Punta Arenas, Chile, skirting along the Antarctic Peninsula and the coast of the Ross Sea, ending the journey in New Zealand.

Except on days of exploration into the pack ice, we will use the ship's fleet of Zodiac inflatable rafts to land on remote beaches, photograph and observe penguins and other wildlife we encounter. We plan to visit several scientific stations en route.

The *World Discoverer* has all the conveniences of a conventional cruise ship, including lecture room, movie theatre, two lounge/bars and observation lounge, gym, sauna, outdoor pool and sundecks. Meals are prepared by European chefs. The ship holds a maximum of 130 passengers.

As with all Antarctic expeditions, weather and ice conditions will dictate our schedule, although we will make every effort to adhere to the itinerary below.

> **We will use the ship's fleet of Zodiac inflatable rafts to land on remote beaches, photograph and observe penguins and other wildlife we encounter. We plan to visit several scientific stations en route.**

ITINERARY:
DAY 1 and 2: Fly from Miami to Punta Arenas, Chile.

DAY 3: Excursion to Fitzroy Channel, where we hope to see many unusual species of birds.

DAY 4: Board the *World Discoverer* and cruise the Strait of Magellan and Beagle Channel. .

DAY 5: Into Drake Passage, past Cape Horn, hoping for the rare ideal weather which would allow us to land.

DAY 6: Sail the Drake Passage.

DAY 7 to 11: During these days, we visit many Antarctic highlights, such as King George, Anvers, Nelson and Deception Islands, Paradise Bay and Port Lockroy. Along the route, study wildlife colonies, observing seals, penguins and other bird species.

DAY 12 to 20: Cruise the Amundsen and Bellinghausen seas and enter into the Ross Sea, an expeditionary route very few have taken. We see hundreds of beautiful icebergs and tabular ice

floes carrying seals or penguins. We may spot some whales or elusive emperor penguins as well.

DAY 21: Lost to International Dateline!

DAY 22: Ice conditions permitting, cruise along the Ross Ice Shelf.

DAY 23: Enter McMurdo Sound and land at America's McMurdo Station and New Zealand's Scott Base.

DAY 24: At Cape Evans and Cape Royds, visit the huts of fabled Antarctic explorers Scott and Shackleton.

DAY 25: At sea.

DAY 26: Ice conditions permitting, land at Cape Adere and Cape Hallett.

DAY 27: Wind conditions permitting, cruise between the Balleny Islands.

DAY 28 and 29: At sea.

DAY 30: Visit the Australian scientific station at MacQuarie Island. Photograph huge sea elephants and thousands of king, royal and rockhopper penguins.

DAY 31: At sea.

DAY 32: At the Auckland Islands, see royal albatross and yellow-eyed penguins.

DAY 33: Cruise in our Zodiac landing craft along the Snares Islands, where we have a good chance to see Snares penguins.

DAY 34 and 35: Arrive at Port Bluff New Zealand. Morning sightseeing at Invercargill and depart for Auckland and homeward-bound flights.

IT3LR4MTCR

THE WILDS OF COSTA RICA

DATES: #2 Dec 19, 1983–Jan 1, 1984 (14 days)
  #1 Mar 19–Apr 1 (14 days)
  #2 Dec 17–Dec 30 (14 days)
LEADER: Jim Lewis
GRADE: B-2
LAND COST: $1490 (11–14 members)
  $1690 (7–10)

The tiny country of Costa Rica has exceptional birdlife and unmatched flora that includes over 1,000 species of orchids alone. Its national park system is known throughout the world.

Our Costa Rican adventure includes a three-day whitewater trip on the Rio Pacuare, a hike up to the crater rim of still-active Poas Volcano, a two-day visit to the orchid-laden Monteverde Cloud Forest (where we may see the rare quetzal, sacred bird of the Mayas) and three days of beach camping in Corcovado National Park, an exceptionally beautiful beach wilderness. Horses can be rented for riding in the park.

A Quetzal, sacred bird of the Mayas
B Horseback riding in Corcovado National Park/Terry Brian
C Jungle orchids/Lawrence Carpenter
D Climbing Ixtacihuatl/Sergio Fitch Watkins
E Rafting the Rio Pacuare/Tracy Lynch

ITINERARY:

DAY 1: Leave U.S. Arrive San Jose, Costa Rica. Transfer to hotel.

DAY 2 and 3: Rafting on the Rio Pacuare, which runs from the central highlands through virgin jungle. Ample time to explore side canyon creeks, to swim and fish.

DAY 4: End river trip in mid-afternoon and drive to San Jose.

DAY 5: Drive to Poas Volcano for a day hike in a moonscape of dwarfed vegetation and volcanic rock. At the top, peer 1,000 feet down into the crater of this active volcano. Drive to Monteverde Cloud Forest.

DAY 6: Day hike in the Monteverde Cloud Forest, with its overhanging canopy of jungle vegetation. We will see many beautiful birds and, with luck, the rare and beautiful quetzal.

DAY 7: Drive to San Jose.

DAY 8: Fly to Palmar for short charter flight to Corcovado National Park.

> **Costa Rica has exceptional birdlife and unmatched flora that includes over 1,000 species of orchids alone. Its national park system is known throughout the world.**

DAY 9: With horses to carry our packs, walk ten miles along the beach to Playa Llorona. Good jungle and marine wildlife.

DAY 10 and 11: Fishing, swimming, hiking in the jungle, or riding horses along the beach.

DAY 12: Return along the beach to Park Center.

DAY 13: Fly to San Jose.

DAY 14: Depart San Jose and connect with homeward-bound flights.

VOLCANOES OF MEXICO

DATES: #3 Dec 26, 1983–Jan 8, 1984 (14 days)
*#1 Feb 19–Mar 3 (14 days)
#2 Oct 21–Nov 3 (14 days)
#3 Dec 23, 1984–Jan 5, 1985 (14 days)
LEADER: Sergio Fitch Watkins
GRADE: D-1
LAND COST: $890 (5–15 members)
*Note date change from 1984 Schedule.

On this trip we'll make climbs of Orizaba (18,851') and Popocatepetl (17,887'), the third and fifth highest mountains in North America, plus a third peak, Ixtaccihuatl (17,343').

Many now-famous mountaineers started their careers on these snowy peaks, which provide a good introduction to climbing.

We've been operating successful Mexican volcano climbs for 13 years.

The climbs require the use of ice axe and crampons, and are not technically difficult. Instruction on the necessary techniques will be given by the leader. The real criteria for reaching these high altitude summits are desire and stamina.

Looking over the lip of the gigantic crater of Popo, one wonders how Cortez' men managed to get into it and return with the sulphur they needed for their conquest of the Aztecs.

The approach to these giant volcanoes is through the Mexican countryside, where one still sees women weaving serapes of natural colored wool, farmers reaping crops with hand scythes, and

woodcutters hauling firewood to their villages on burros. Part of the charm of the trip lies in visits to small villages; there will be a one-day visit to the pretty colonial town of Puebla.

> **Looking over the lip of the gigantic crater of Popo, one wonders how Cortez' men managed to get into it and return with the sulphur they needed for gun powder in their conquest of the Aztecs.**

ITINERARY:

DAY 1: Leave U.S. Arrive Mexico City. Overnight at hotel.

DAY 2: Free day in Mexico City (7,000').

DAY 3: Drive to base camp on Ixtaccihuatl. Camp in Alcalican Canyon at 11,000 feet.

DAY 4 to 6: Climb and descend Ixta, and drive to Tlamacaz.

DAY 7: Day free in Tlamacaz.

DAY 8: Early morning start for the climb of Popocatepetl, via the Ventorrillo Route.

DAY 9: Drive to Puebla.

DAY 10: Drive to Piedra Grande Hut (13,776') on the north side of Pico de Orizaba.

DAY 11: Early morning start to climb and descend Orizaba via the Glacier de Jamapa.

DAY 12: In Puebla.

DAY 13: Drive to Mexico City.

DAY 14: Depart Mexico City and connect with homeward-bound flights.

Galapagos albatross / Alla Schmitz

ALASKA

NORTH AMERICA & HAWAII

Alaska, "the great land," is a huge wilderness encompassing four time zones, 33,000 miles of coastline and fourteen of the highest peaks in North America.

For 1984, there are fifteen Alaskan adventures to choose from, each with emphasis on a particular activity, perhaps rafting, backpacking, climbing or a combination of several outdoor pursuits.

In Southeast Alaska's waterbound wilderness, our journeys present the unique opportunity to witness nature in action, to watch tidewater glaciers shed giant icebergs into the fjords with a thunderous roar.

In central Alaska, we field treks, expeditions and mountaineering seminars on Mt. McKinley, highest peak outside the Himalayas and Andes, and one of the most spectacular mountains in the world.

In the jagged Brooks Range, south of the Arctic Slope, we travel by kayak, canoe and on foot, exploring a primal wilderness where brown bears fish in swift arctic rivers and the glow of the northern lights illuminates the sky.

The "Lower 48" still has many wilderness adventures of note. We offer backpacking, llama trekking and climbing in Washington's North Cascades (the "American Alps"), as well as a "range walk" in New Hampshire's White Mountains, and a hiking trip in Hawaii.

Our groups are very small (maximum of 12 on North America trips), our leaders are expert, and our itineraries are flexible enough to accommodate a wide variety of individual interests.

1984 CALENDAR INDEX

Most of our 1984 trips will be repeated in 1985 on approximately the same dates.

Polar bears

LEADERSHIP

Mountain Travel's Alaskan leaders are all residents of Alaska, experienced and certified members of the Alaskan Association of Wilderness and Mountain Guides. Our Pacific Northwest climbing and backpacking journeys are led by that region's top guides and mountaineers. All our North American trip leaders are adept at making your outdoor journey agreeable and memorable.

TOM BAKER, 27, teaches mountaineering, nordic and downhill skiing and guides backpacking trips in the Pacific Northwest.

JUDY BRAKEL, 43, is a research analyst for the Alaska Coastal Fisheries Commission and leader of backpacking, alpine and cross-country ski expeditions throughout Southeast Alaska.

GARY BOCARDE, 36, in his 15 years of climbing, has been involved in many difficult ascents, including the first ascent of the Shield on El Capitan, the first big wall route in Alaska (Moose's Tooth), first winter ascent of Mt. Hunter, and many other ascents throughout the Alaskan Range. He has guided for ten years on Mt. McKinley, Mt. Foraker, Mt. Hunter, and Mt. Sanford and was a member of two mountaineering expeditions in China: 1980 Gongga Shan and 1981 Everest East Face.

Tom Baker   Gary Bocarde

Judy Brakel

Walrus

Chuck Horner

ON & IDA BURROUGHS lead our White Mountains hiking trip in New Hampshire. They have spent considerable time exploring the mountains of New England as well as climbing in the American West, Alaska and Mexico. On is a former White Mountain hutman and guide.

MARY GRAYSON, 31, is a professional wilderness guide and instructor in nordic and alpine skiing. A resident of Juneau, she also teaches canoeing, snowshoeing and is knowledgeable about Alaska's natural history.

CHUCK HORNER, 53, is Chief Ranger for the Southeast District of the Alaska Division of Parks and is an active canoeist, kayaker and cross-country skier.

HAYDEN KADEN, 39, is an outdoorsman and naturalist with 14 years' experience in kayaking and camping in southeast Alaska. A lawyer turned wilderness guide, he lives on a homestead at the mouth of Glacier Bay.

BOB JACOBS, 31, is an Alaskan mountain guide and ski instructor who has climbed and backpacked extensively in the Wrangell/St. Elias Range as well as in South America, New Zealand and Canada.

DAVE KETCHER, 33, is an Alaskan river runner, bush pilot, dog team guide and wilderness enthusiast who resides in the bush community of Bettles, Alaska.

KEN LEGHORN, 28, is a mountaineer and nordic ski instructor with a strong naturalist background and extensive guiding experience in Southeast Alaska.

MIKE & DEBBIE O'CONNOR are professional wilderness guides. A high school counselor in Angoon during the school year, Mike guides backpacking and kayak trips in the summer. Debbie teaches special education and also spends the summers guiding wilderness trips.

PETER OURUSOFF, 41, leader of our Hawaii hiking trips, is a professional naturalist who was formerly with the Massachusetts Audubon Society and holds an M.A. in Teaching Natural Sciences from Harvard University.

NIC PARKER, 35, a lifelong Alaskan mountaineer, has guided on Mt. McKinley, Mt. Hunter and Mt. Illiamna and is also involved in mountain rescue, avalanche safety and emergency medical training.

ERIC SANFORD, 31, has been climbing, skiing and guiding for more than 15 years in the U.S., Canada, Alaska and Europe. He has many major climbs and first ascents to his credit and has worked with Colorado Mountain Rescue and the Yosemite Rescue Team.

JEFF SLOSS, 28, is a wilderness guide, ski instructor and naturalist who has led trips throughout much of Southeast Alaska.

JOHN SVENSON, 35, has been climbing for almost 20 years, with successful climbs in Europe, Alaska and throughout the Lower 48. He has taught climbing seminars and guided expeditions on Mt. McKinley and Mt. Sanford.

DOUG VEENHOF, 28, is a professional mountain guide and nordic ski instructor with extensive experience in the North Cascades in both summer and winter conditions.

Mary Grayson

Hayden Kaden

Ken Leghorn

Peter Ourusoff   Eric Sanford

Jeff Sloss

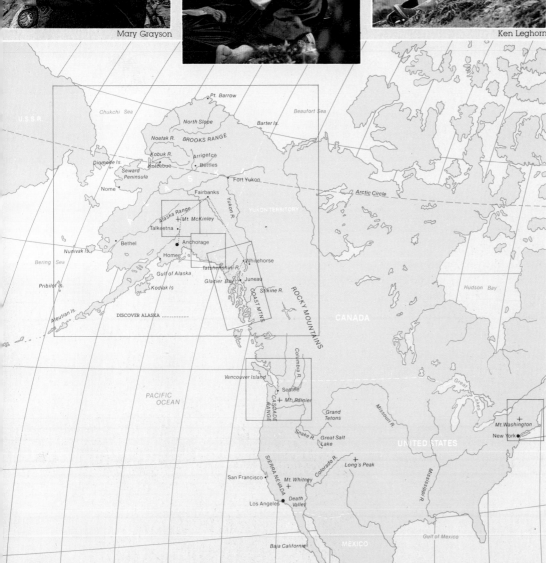

DISCOVER ALASKA

Arctic wildflowers/Dave Ketscher

DISCOVER ALASKA

DATES: *#1 Jun 16–Jun 30 (15 days)
*#2 Jul 14–Jul 28 (15 days)
*#3 Aug 11–Aug 25 (15 days)
LEADER: #1 & #3 to be announced
#2 Jeff Sloss
GRADE: A-2
LAND COST: $2190 incl. chtrs.
(10–12 members)
$2390 incl. chtrs. (8–9)
*Note date change from 1984 Trip Schedule.

Two of Alaska's most famous wilderness attractions are the iceberg-strewn fjords of Glacier Bay and the superb mountain country of Denali National Park.

In three days in the fjord-wilds of upper Glacier Bay, we'll appreciate its immensity and serenity as we hike on nearby glaciers and paddle kayaks through the still waters of the fjords. Among the drifting icebergs we'll undoubtedly see playful seals and perhaps a humpback whale in the distance. This is truly one of the most spectacular settings in all of Alaska.

Leaving Glacier Bay, we fly by charter direct to Skagway, a historic town with much Gold Rush flavor. From here, a scenic bus ride takes us over White Pass, which was crossed on foot by thousands of eager gold stampeders in 1898. Our drive parallels the route of the old narrow-gauge train to Whitehorse, capital of the Yukon, from where we fly to Fairbanks.

The Alaska Railroad will take us from Fairbanks to McKinley Station, for a one-day float trip on the Nenana River. Our final stop is Denali National Park, known for its spellbinding views of the great massif of McKinley (20,320').
In comfortable cabins at Camp Denali in the heart of the park, we'll take nature walks, fish, pan for gold and look for some of the more famous McKinley wildlife, such as grizzly bears and moose.

ITINERARY:
DAY 1: Leave hometown. Arrive Juneau. Transfer to hotel.
DAY 2: Visit Mendenhall Glacier, then fly to Gustavus, at the mouth of Glacier Bay. Time for nature walks, bicycling along country roads, fishing, or visiting the homestead community.
DAY 3: By floatplane or boat to a remote section of Glacier Bay National Monument, setting up camp near the shore. Afternoon practice kayaking in easy-to-paddle two-man Klepper kayaks, gliding silently among the icebergs, and perhaps spotting seals at play.
DAY 4: Morning hike, then pack gear into the kayaks and glide to a scenic spot for picnic lunch. Short afternoon paddle to a new campsite.
DAY 5: Optional day hike to a scenic high ridge with sweeping vistas up and down the bay.

DAY 6: By floatplane or boat to Gustavus, then on by plane to the little Gold Rush "ghost town" of Skagway.
DAY 7: Scenic drive by bus across White Pass to Whitehorse, Yukon.
DAY 8: Morning sightseeing in Whitehorse, afternoon flight to Fairbanks.
DAY 9: Morning train to McKinley Station. Local sightseeing around McKinley Village.
DAY 10: Day of rafting on the Nenana River, with afternoon drive to Camp Denali in Denali National Park.
DAY 11 to 13: From our cabins in the heart of the park, we will spend time wildlife viewing, panning for gold in a local river, or relaxing in the spectacular alpine environment. Splendid views of Mt. McKinley (20,320').
DAY 14: By train back to Anchorage, arriving in Anchorage in the late evening.
DAY 15: Leave Anchorage on homeward-bound flights.

NOTE: Commercial flights between Juneau and Gustavus, Whitehorse and Fairbanks are not included in Land Cost.

ALASKA WILDLIFE SAFARI

DATES: *#1 Jun 5–Jun 21 (17 days)
*#2 Jun 19–Jul 5 (17 days)
LEADER: Chuck Horner
GRADE: A-2
LAND COST: $1895 + chtr. $290
(10–12 members)
$2075 + chtr. $290 (8–9)
PRIBILOF OPTION: 2-night, 3-day: $675
*Note date change from 1984 Trip Schedule.

This safari begins in "ultimate wilderness park"—the 8.9-million acre Arctic National Wildlife Range in the northernmost reaches of the North American continent. In the luxury of almost 24 hours of daylight, we'll spend five days experiencing the high arctic in summer, making optional day hikes into this rugged land where caribou, moose, and wolves roam. Our trips are timed to take advantage of the caribou migration and best wildlife viewing season.

From Fairbanks, we take the train to the sub-arctic splendor of Denali (McKinley) National Park, home to 37 species of mammals and 132 species of birds. With five

days in comfortable cabins at Camp Denali, we'll have an un-regimented schedule during which we can hike, fish, photograph, or just relax and enjoy the beauty of the alpine tundra world.

At the end of the trip, we can arrange an optional visit to the very isolated Pribilof Islands in the Bering Sea, renowned as the breeding ground of the largest fu seal herd in the world and of liter ally millions of birds (more than 180 species, including kittiwakes, puffins, murres, and cormorants).

> **In the luxury of almost 24 hours of daylight, we'll spend five days experiencing the high arctic in summer, making optional day hikes into this rugged land where caribou, moose, and wolves roam.**

ITINERARY:
DAY 1: Leave hometown. Arrive Fairbanks. Transfer to hotel.

AY 2: Fly to Barter Island in the
eaufort Sea.

AY 3 to 7: By charter flight
om Barter Island to a very
mote part of the Arctic National
ildlife Range. Here in America's
rgest wildlife refuge, a place of
iiet beauty, the great caribou
erds will migrate from near
arter Island southeastward
ward the Yukon. We hope to see
part of the migration, and there
also a chance to see bear,
eep, wolves and waterfowl.
ghts are spent at a lake camp
om which we will take daily
kes.

AY 8: Return by charter flight to
arter Island.

AY 9: Fly to Fairbanks.

AY 10: Day free in Fairbanks, or
adjust itinerary if weather has
elayed flights.

AY 11 to 15: By train to Denali,
en continue by bus about 90
les to Denali National Park. At
amp Denali, we will have four
ays for wildlife viewing, panning
r gold, and enjoying the beauty
the surroundings. The cabin
imp is set in tundra and spruce
oods with splendid views of Mt.
cKinley (20,320').

AY 16: By bus and train to
nchorage.

AY 17: Depart Anchorage on
omeward-bound flights.

OTE: Commercial flights between Fairbanks
d Barter Island are not included in Land
st.

HIKING IN THE WRANGELLS

DATES: Jul 21–Aug 3 (14 days)
LEADER: Bob Jacobs
GRADE: B-3
LAND COST: $1275 + chtrs. $140
(8–10 members)
$1425 + chtrs. $140
(6–7)

Wrangell/St. Elias National Park
is one of the most beautiful and
intriguing regions in Alaska. In the
gorge of the Chitistone Canyon, in
the very heart of the Wrangells,
we'll make a ten-day backpacking journey, partly following the
famous "Goat Trail," a natural
path through the Wrangell Mountains that was used as far back as
the Athabascan Indian hunting
days and more recently by the
miners traveling to the Chisani
gold fields during the stampede
of 1912.

We'll follow this narrow trail up
to views of Chitistone Falls, where
the river plunges 300 feet, and
hike further on to Chitistone Pass,
one of the most scenic spots imaginable, with its views of the vast
St. Elias Range and Russell Glacier
to the east, and unclimbed Mt.
Frederica to the north, Hole-In-The-
Wall Glacer to the west, and the
20-mile-long Chitistone Canyon
to the south.

We fly in and out of Chitistone
by bush flight, which will not only
give us great views of the Wran-
gell/St. Elias Range but a chance
to spend a little time in a small
Alaskan bush community and
get a taste of a bush pilot's way
of life.

ITINERARY:

DAY 1: Leave hometown. Arrive
Anchorage. Transfer to hotel.

DAY 2: Fly to McCarthy. Trek briefing and preparation of gear.

DAY 3: Fly by bush plane to a
small airstrip at the junction of
Glacier Creek and the Chitistone
River. Set up camp and explore
the river bar for wildflowers and
animal tracks.

DAY 4: Explore old miners' cabins
and mines and hike up Glacier
Creek to view the Twa Harpies
Glacier, with magnificent vistas of
the 15,000-foot Twa Harpies peaks
and the University Range.

This is an area very unique in Alaska, similar to the canyonlands of the American southwest, only with glaciers!

DAY 5: Begin backpacking today,
heading along the "Goat Trail"
near the Chitistone River,
meandering through meadows
and white spruce to Toby Creek.

DAY 6: Cross Toby Creek and continue along the Goat Trail, through
alder groves and out onto river
bars in the afternoon.

DAY 7: Hike large gravel bars
along the Chitistone River to the
old lateral moraines of the Chitistone Glacier. Camp in a moonscape of rock piles and clear
water pools alongside the glacier.

DAY 8: Day hike across the
Chitistone Glacier, up steep
hillsides, through mud and water
to Chitistone Gorge for a close

view of Chitistone Falls. We see
from here why our trail is called
"Goat Trail" as it becomes a thin
line traversing the sides of steep
mountains to gain the upper Chitistone Valley. Return to camp.

DAY 9: Learn river crossing techniques as we ford the Chitistone
Falls River to our next camp at
5,000 feet.

DAY 10 and 11: Hike the narrow
Goat Trail along scree slopes. This
is an area very unique in Alaska,
similar to the canyonlands of the
American southwest, only with
glaciers!

DAY 12: We reach the high point
of the trek, both physically and
scenically on our crossing of
Chitistone Pass, truly one of the
most beautiful places in Alaska.
Continue to camp at Skolai
Creek.

DAY 13: From the Skolai Creek strip
we will fly back to McCarthy
following Skolai Creek and the
Nizina Glacier, giving us a
chance to make the circle by air
of the Nizima/Chitistone drain-
ages and view Mt. Regal, Mt.
Frederika and over Nikolai Pass.
Arrive in McCarthy.

DAY 14: Fly to Anchorage and
connect with homeward-bound
flights.

HIKING IN THE WRANGELLS ....

D

NATURAL HISTORY OF SOUTHEAST ALASKA

DATES: #1 Jul 7–Jul 18 (12 days)
#2 Aug 4–Aug 15 (12 days)
#3 Aug 18–Aug 29 (12 days)
LEADER: #1 Chuck Horner
#2 to be announced.
#3 Judy Brakel
GRADE: A-2
LAND COST: *$1490 + chtrs. $400
(8–12 members)
*Note change from 1984 Trip Schedule.

Southeast Alaska has a wealth of beautiful scenery and wildlife, and a unique blend of native American and Russian heritage. On this tour, we'll see quite a bit of Southeast Alaska, traveling by floatplane and boat, with time set aside for optional canoeing, fishing and hiking.

Accommodations will be in cabins and lodges (and tents in Glacier Bay). All meals are included except in Juneau.

We begin with a visit to historic Sitka, once the headquarters for the Russian fur trading monopoly. It was in Alexander Baranof's castle above Sitka that Alaska changed hands in October, 1867, to become U.S. territory. We'll spend a day studying southeast Alaska's Tlingit and Haida Indian cultures, and boat out to the wildlife refuge at St. Lazaria.

Flying by floatplane to Baranof Island, we'll stay in rustic cabins in the tiny fishing community of Baranof Warm Springs, with time for optional hiking, fishing, canoeing and skiff touring around this isolated island.

Continuing by floatplane to Admiralty Island, we'll explore its unique rain forest vegetation and visit the Tlingit Indian community of Angoon, then fly into a remote section of Glacier Bay for two days of exploring by easy-to-paddle Klepper kayaks, a great opportunity for close-up views of this region's spectacular glaciers, icebergs and marine wildlife.

ITINERARY:
DAY 1: Leave hometown. Arrive Sitka and transfer to hotel. Visit St. Michael's Russian Orthodox Cathedral, focal point of Sitka's Russian heritage.

DAY 2: Day trip by charter boat across Sitka Sound, cruising in the shadow of Mt. Edgecumbe (3,200'), a snow-capped volcano. Visit St. Lazaria, a birdwatchers' paradise where we'll see jaegers, petrals, gulls, cormorants, kitty-wakes, puffins and murrs.

DAY 3: Although the Russian past is evident, so is Sitka's native heritage. Visit Sheldon Jackson Museum, with its fine native crafts, and walk in Sitka National Historical Park to Tlingit Fort, destroyed in 1804 in the last major stand of Tlingits against Russian settlers. Afternoon flight over the 5,000-foot snow-capped peaks to Baranof Island. Overnight in a rustic cabin by the shore.

DAY 4: Explore the forested trails and lakes of Baranof Island. Fishing, optional canoeing, skiff touring. Evening dip in the cabin's hot tub, which is fed by the warm mineral springs which have made Baranof famous.

DAY 5: Visit with the local fishing fleet—trollers for salmon and halibut—at Baranof's general store, stroll along the shores and pick blueberries and salmonberries. Afternoon flight to Angoon on Admiralty Island.

DAY 6: Explore the shores of Kootznahoo Inlet, observing the powerful tidal surges, and visit Angoon, one of the most traditional of southeast Alaskan Indian villages. Afternoon by boat across the inlet to Killisnoo Island.

DAY 7: On Killisnoo Island, brown bears outnumber men and there is at least one eagle nest per square mile. As we explore this remote area, we can try our hand at canoeing or fishing from the shores. Optional charter fishing boats are available for forays deeper into Mitchell Bay.

It was in Alexander Baranof's castle above Sitka that Alaska changed hands in October, 1867, to become U.S. territory.

DAY 8: Explore the inter-tidal zones of Admiralty Island, look for old Indian graves and other archaeological sites. Afternoon flight to Glacier Bay National Park. Set up our tents and camp within sight and sound of the active, thundering Riggs Glacier.

DAY 9: A day for exploring the barren but beautiful shores of Glacier Bay, an area only recently—in geological terms—exposed by the retreating ice. From our vantage point along the outwash, we may be able to see seals sunning on icebergs, and even an occasional porpoise or killer whale. In the afternoon, we'll load our camp gear into Klepper kayaks and move camp a couple of miles down the bay.

DAY 10: Morning exploring in kayaks among the floating icebergs, and return by the M.V. Thunder Bay to Bartlett Cove. Overnight at Gustavus Inn.

DAY 11: Explore the homestead community of Gustavus and walk along the sandy beaches of Icy Straits. Optional fishing charters available. Afternoon flight to Juneau.

DAY 12: Depart Juneau and connect with homeward-bound flights.

GLACIER BAY & ADMIRALTY ISLAND

DATES: #1 Jun 23–Jul 6 (14 days)
#2 Jul 14–Jul 27 (14 days)
#3 Aug 11–Aug 24 (14 days)
LEADER: #1 Mary Grayson
#2 & #3 Hayden Kaden
GRADE: B-2
LAND COST: *$1390 + chtrs. $330
(8–12 members)
*Note change from 1984 Trip Schedule.

This two-week adventure takes place in the water wilderness of Southeast Alaska, a wonderful place to learn how to explore by kayak and canoe.

We start on the east shore of Admiralty Island National Monument, the "fortress of the bears," connecting five blue wilderness lakes by canoe with short portages. Enjoying great salmon fishing (and salmon feasts) along the way, we'll end up at the Indian village of Angoon, where hunting and fishing are still the main occupations.

From here we fly by floatplane to John Muir's beloved Glacier Bay, where snow-covered 15,000-foot mountains rise above ice-choked fjords. Glacier Bay's mountains are habitat for brown and black bear, coyotes, wolves, and mountain goats; the waters are home to seal, sea lion, humpback and killer whales, salmon and trout. There is an abundance of waterfowl, including guillemots, puffins, murrelets, cormorants and kittiwakes.

From a very remote inlet, we'll have five days of easy kayaking in the turquoise waters amidst ice floes and tiny coves. There will be time for hiking on shore to explore several glaciers. Our inflatable two-man Klepper kayaks are simple and fun to use, allowing easy access to remote coves and inlets.

ITINERARY:
DAY 1: Leave hometown. Arrive Juneau. Transfer to hotel.

DAY 2: By charter flight from Juneau to Mole Harbor on the east side of Admiralty Island. Organize gear and hike 2.5 miles to Alexander Lake, one of the most beautiful lakes along the Admiralty Island Trail System.

We fly by floatplane to John Muir's beloved Glacier Bay, where snow covered 15,000-foot mountains rise above ice-choked fjords.

DAY 3: To Beaver Lake, setting up camp on the outlet of Beaver Creek. Time for sightseeing on Hasselborg Lake or fishing for cutthroat trout.

DAY 4: Paddle across Hasselborg Lake, short portage into Guerin Lake and paddle to the creek flowing from Distin Lake. Camp near an old Civilian Conservation Corps shelter.

Chilkoot Trail
Exploring serene fjords of Glacier Bay by kayak/Hayden Kaden
Canoeing the lakes of Admiralty/Hayden Kaden
Camp at Wolf Bay/Leo Le Bon

ALASKA • 7

AY 5: Paddle through a slough
reated by beaver dams in
avidson Lake. Portage between
avidson and Distin Lakes, then
ake a 3-mile backpack trip to
alt Lake, where we pick up
nother set of canoes.

AY 6: Layover day at Salt Lake,
great campsite for wildlife view-
g, fishing and laying about.

AY 7: Paddle through Mitchell
ay and the island complex be-
veen Mitchell Bay and the
llage of Angoon. Good tide
ools and, with luck, a chance to
e eagles, martin, deer, porpoise,
ter, humpback whales and an
ccasional bear. Arrive in
ngoon, a native village where
e old traditions still survive. Over-
ght at hotel.

AY 8 to 12: By charter flight from
ngoon directly into Reid Inlet, a
mote region of Glacier Bay.
om different campsites each
ght, we'll have five days to
avel to inlets and nearby
aciers by kayak and on foot.
e waters are home to seals, sea
ons, porpoises, and whales and
n abundance of fascinating
rds. On shore, we may see
gles, brown and black bears,
oyotes, and mountain goats.

AY 13: Pack up gear for pickup
y charter flight to Gustavus.

AY 14: Leave Gustavus and con-
ect with homeward-bound
ghts.

GLACIER BAY & CHILKOOT TRAIL

DATES: #1 Jul 7–Jul 18 (12 days)
#2 Aug 4–Aug 15 (12 days)
LEADER: Judy Brakel
GRADE: B-2
LAND COST: $1080+chtrs. *$225
(6–12 members)
*Note change from 1984 Trip Schedule.

This trip combines a four-day
kayaking/camping journey in
the heart of Glacier Bay National
Monument and a four-day backpack trip across the historic
Chilkoot Trail of the 1898 Gold
Rush.

In Glacier Bay, we'll travel from
camp to camp in Klepper kayaks,
paddling near the faces of the
Riggs and McBride glaciers,
witnessing the dramatic spectacle
of huge chunks of ice "calving"
off the glaciers into the serene
blue waters of the bay.

In Gold Rush country, a four-day
backpack trip takes us from Skagway to Lake Bennett over the
Chilkoot Trail, "the meanest 32
miles in history," or so the gold
stampeders called it, since they
were required to carry a year's
worth of supplies over it in the
dead of winter! The trail has
splendid mountain scenery and
many remnants of the Gold Rush.

ITINERARY:
DAY 1: Leave hometown. Arrive

A

Juneau. Transfer to hotel.
DAY 2: Visit Mendenhall Glacier
then fly to Gustavus, near Glacier
Bay National Park headquarters.
DAY 3: Board M.V. Thunder Bay for
a cruise through the Muir Arm of
Glacier Bay, disembarking at
Riggs Glacier. Assemble the Klepper kayaks and paddle toward
the face of Muir Glacier, with a
good chance of observing seals
and marine birds such as kitty-
wakes, cormorants, puffins, gulls
and eagles. Camp near Muir
Glacier.
DAY 4: By kayak towards Riggs
Glacier, passing sculpted icebergs

and the active face of Muir
Glacier, camping on the high
limestone ledges south of Riggs
Glacier. Beautiful view of upper
Muir Inlet.
DAY 5: By kayak to McBride
Glacier, then on across the Muir
Arm to Wolf Point. Evening camp
at Wolf Point.
DAY 6: Walk up to White Thunder
Ridge, or hike along a remnant of
the Muir Glacier. Late afternoon
pickup by floatplane for a scenic
flight through Endicott Gap, over
the mountains and down to the
little town of Skagway.

**A four-day backpack trip
takes us from Skagway
to Lake Bennett over
the Chilkoot Trail,
"the meanest 32 miles
in history," or so the
gold stampeders called it.**

DAY 7: Travel by van to the
abandoned mining site of Dyea.
Explore the historical site and
old avalanche graveyard. Then
begin the Chilkoot Trail hike,
walking along an abandoned
logging road through mature
spruce rainforest.
DAY 8 and 9: Continue hiking
through deep forest, exploring old
gold mining camps; enter alpine
country and scramble over the
steep Chilkoot Pass.
DAY 10: Once we have crossed
the pass, we are in Canada. Hike
along through high alpine country to the shores of Lake
Lindeman.
DAY 11: Hike to Lake Bennett and
the junction of the old cog railway. Return to Skagway by highway and continue by charter
flight to Juneau. Overnight at
hotel.
DAY 12: Depart Juneau and connect with homeward-bound flights.

C

D

EXPLORING MISTY FJORDS & TRACY ARM

DATES: Jul 28–Aug 10 (14 days
LEADER: to be announced
GRADE: A-2
LAND COST: *$1735 (8-10 members)
*Note change from 1984 Trip Schedule.

This trip makes an in-depth exploration of the sea-and-mountain wilderness of Southeast Alaska, traveling by comfortable motorized Zodiac raft, which allows easy access to the maze of channels, bays, and deep fjords of this grand wilderness.

Starting from Ketchikan, one of Alaska's major fishing ports, we'll spend the first half of the trip on a 100-mile circuit around Misty Fjords National Monument. This is one of the most impressive fjordlands in Alaska, where huge granite walls rise from the water's edge and spectacular waterfalls break the wilderness silence.

After a visit to Juneau, we set off with our Zodiac rafts for Tracy Arm/Ford's Terror Wilderness, a magnificent region of active tidewater glaciers and surprising wildlife. On our journey through the fjords, we'll have lots of time for fishing, beachcombing, hiking, and enjoying the marine wildlife of Southeast Alaska.

ITINERARY:

DAY 1: Leave hometown. Arrive Ketchikan, Alaska. Transfer to hotel.

DAY 2: By Zodiac raft to the Naha River and Salt Lagoon. We may see black bear feeding on salmon along the river.

DAY 3: To Yes Bay, a deep fjord which runs from the mouth of the beautiful McDonald River into the Behm Canal. Excellent fishing for red, pink and silver salmon, and cutthroat and Dolly Varden trout.

DAY 4: Enjoy the Bell Island Hot Springs, and continue to the wild Unuk River, one of the largest which flows out of Canada into the Behm Canal.

DAY 5: Travel to Rudyerd Bay in the heart of the Misty Fjords National Monument. This is a classically beautiful area with granite cliffs rising 3,000 feet directly from the sea.

DAY 6: Cruise Rudyerd Bay and hike to Nooya or Punchbowl Lake, which have extensive views of the fjords.

DAY 7: Return to Ketchikan and take the afternoon ferry to Juneau. Overnight on ferry.

DAY 8: In Juneau.

DAY 9: Cruise on the M.V. Riviera through Gastineau Channel, across Taku Inlet and down Stephens Passage. Disembark inside beautiful Tracy Arm Fjord and board our Zodiac rafts. Tracy Arm is a narrow 40-mile fjord where granite walls rise 3,000 feet from the crystalline waters. As we approach the North and South Sawyer Glaciers, massive

ALASKA
ABOUT RAFT, KAYAK & CANOE TRIPS

On our adventures on the wilderness waterways of Alaska, all camping supplies are transported from camp to camp by raft, canoe or kayak (depending on the particular trip). Trip members will be expected to help pack and unpack group camping gear from the boats, pitch their own tents (which we provide), and help as necessary with the camp chores. Breakfast and dinner will be hearty, hot gourmet meals made with fresh food supplies whenever possible. Lunch will be prepared picnic-style. Previous camping experience is recommended but certainly not necessary. All boat gear (including life jackets) is provided, and the boats are stable, easy-to-handle and fun to use, so it isn't necessary to have previous experience with kayaks, canoes or rafts. Our Alaskan leaders (all members of the Alaskan Association of Mountain and Wilderness Guides) are experts at making your wilderness experience a pleasant and safe one.

building-size icebergs drift in the tides. We have seen what the glaciers did long ago to the landscape in Misty Fjords; now we will see active tidewater glaciers still at work.

> **This is one of the most impressive fjordlands in Alaska, where huge granite walls rise from the water's edge and spectacular waterfalls break the wilderness silence.**

DAY 10: Leisurely Zodiac run down the fjord, passing icebergs, towering waterfalls, maybe even a brown or black bear lumbering along the steep shore or mountain goats perched precariously on the cliffs.

DAY 11: On to the majesty of Endicott Arm, cruising this 30-mile-long fjord towards the Dawes Glacier in the farthest reaches of the arm.

DAY 12: Catch the high tide into Ford's Terror (so named for a navy crewman who rowed into the entrance at slack water and was caught in the surging tidal currents for six hours when the tide changed!) Rock cliffs rise to 4,000 feet above this dramatic estuary. Rushing tides and icebergs combine to create an exciting ride into and out of the area.

DAY 13: Catch the tide out of Ford's Terror and back to Endicott. We explore Holkum Bay, venture out to a sea lion hauling area in Stephens Passage or spend some time trout fishing or beach combing.

DAY 14: Pick up by the M.V. Riviera and return to Juneau. Connect with homeward-bound flights.

TATSHENSHINI/ ALSEK RAFTING

DATES: Aug 4–Aug 15 (12 days)
LEADER: to be announced
GRADE: A-2
LAND COST: *$1350 incl. chtrs.
(8-18 members)
*Note change from 1984 Trip Schedule.

Known by seasoned river runner the world over, the Tatshenshini/Alsek is one of the world's premie wilderness raft trips. From the lush green hills at the start to the glaciated mountains near the end, this journey reveals nature in its most pristine state. As we approach the coast, the horizon seems to shrink as the great St. Elias Mountains rise from the river's edge. Wildlife abounds, including grizzlies, big-horn, Dall sheep, and bald eagle. But the single most impressive thing about this river trip is the immense blue-white glaciers we'll see on route.

Once the Tatshenshini joins the Alsek, glaciers flow right down to the river banks. The sights and sounds of the seven-mile-wide Alsek Glacier are an experience not to be missed. Huge icebergs will accompany our rafts downstream. Coming ever closer to the Gulf of Alaska, we'll be able to feel and smell the sea.

We return to civilization on a scenic bush flight over the Fairweather Range and the immense Brady Glacier before touching down in Gustavus, gateway to Glacier Bay National Park.

We travel five to a raft with an experienced oarsman. No previous rafting experience is necessary.

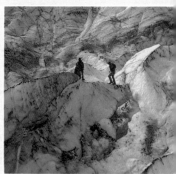

B

Stikine rafting/Fred Faye-Hiltner
Organizing camp/Fred Faye-Hiltner
Upper Tatshenshini River/Bruce Kelpinger

A

ITINERARY:

DAY 1: Leave hometown. Arrive Juneau. Transfer to hotel.

DAY 2: By Alaska State Ferry to Haines. Arrive late afternoon and continue by car about 100 miles to the put-in point near Dalton Post, Canada.

DAY 3: On the upper Tatshenshini, we enjoy a solid half-day of exhilarating rapids in the Tatshenshini Gorge. Emerge from the gorge into more placid waters.

DAY 4 and 5: The river slowly builds momentum as we wind our way towards the beautiful Alsek and Noisey Ranges. There are many good short hikes to take in this area.

DAY 6: The river gets increasingly broad as the huge unnamed tributary creeks add their silted water. This is prime country for moose, bear and wolf. Rounding one last fast bend in the river, we camp in the immense valley of the Tat's confluence with the Alsek.

Huge icebergs will accompany our rafts downstream. Coming ever closer to the Gulf of Alaska, we'll be able to feel and smell the sea.

DAY 7: A day of hiking and exploring the vast meadows, glacier deltas and ridges of the Alsek Valley.

DAY 8: A short but dramatic day on the Alsek brings us to the Walker Glacier, so named by rafters because of the ease of walking onto this moraine-covered glacier right off the shore. Hike onto the glacier and explore the base of the spectacular icefall from the upper glacier.

DAY 9: The Alsek quickly carries us through terrain where high peaks rise steeply from the river. This is ice age country, and dozens of large and small glaciers fill every vista, dwarfing our tiny rafts.

DAY 10: Enter Alsek Bay, a spectacularly beautiful place. At the foot of the St. Elias Range, Mt. Fairweather looms 15,000 feet above us across the bay. We'll hear icebergs the size of ships calving off the face of Alsek Glacier, while smaller sculpted icebergs drift slowly by. Hike up to an overlook on Gateway Knob, then paddle the rafts amidst the icy giants of Alsek Bay.

DAY 11: Fly by floatplane over Brady Icefield, along the Fairweather Range, over Glacier Bay to Gustavus. Overnight at lodge.

DAY 12: Fly to Juneau and connect with homeward-bound flights on Alaska Airlines or Alaska State Ferry.

STIKINE RIVER RAFTING

DATES: Jun 28–Jul 6 (9 days)
LEADER: Ken Leghorn
GRADE: A-1
LAND COST: $975 incl. chtrs.
(8–18 members)

The Stikine, meaning "Great River" in the language of the Tlingit Indians, served as a migration and trading route for the Indians who traveled from the interior of Canada to coastal Alaska. Gold Rush fever in the late 1800's also lured people to the area.

But for us, the Stikine's great attraction is its scenery. John Muir, on a visit to the Stikine in 1879, described it as "a Yosemite 100 miles long." Flying to the one-time gold settlement of Telegraph Creek, B.C., we will raft the historic Stikine River for 160 miles to Wrangell, Alaska.

We'll drift at a brisk pace, basking in the dry interior weather and occasionally glimpsing the 5,000 to 10,000-foot boundary peaks. Day by day, the scene changes: low river banks become mountains, vegetation and weather patterns shift, and hanging glaciers are seen along the river.

B

Even the names of the glaciers are memorable: we pass the Mud, the Scud, the Flood, and the Great, and take time for a soak in Chief Shakes Hot Spring.

Fishing is good, with all five species of Pacific salmon spawning in the tributaries. We may also catch trout along the way.

Wildlife abounds, from black bear to harbor seal, land otter to eagles. The Stikine Delta is the resting place for more than half a million migrating birds each fall and spring.

Our rafts hold four people plus an experienced oarsman. No previous rafting experience is necessary.

ITINERARY:

DAY 1: Leave hometown. Arrive Juneau. Transfer to hotel.

DAY 2: Fly to Telegraph Creek, Canada, with a scenic view of the Stikine Icefield and Stikine River. Begin raft trip with a float to Glenora Flats, where there was a camp of 10,000 miners during the 1870's Gold Rush to the Cassiar District of upper British Columbia.

DAY 3: Leave Mt. Glenora behind and head downriver towards the larger peaks. Approach the confluence of the Chutine and Stikine rivers, behind which rise the Sawback Mountains.

DAY 4: Today we pass through Klootchman's Canyon and come ever closer to the heart of the Coast Range. Camp tonight at Vekops Creek, which offers a bit of hiking and time to explore an old trapper's cabin.

DAY 5: Little Canyon truly marks the beginning of the Coast Range. The pine and aspen forests are left behind and we are surrounded by stands of virgin spruce forest.

DAY 6: As we pass the Scud River, we can look east and see Kate's Needle, one of the boundary peaks between the U.S. and Canada. There are many active glaciers here, the most prominent being the Flood Glacier, the Mud Glacier, and finally, the Great Glacier, our destination.

John Muir, on a visit to the Stikine in 1879, described it as "a Yosemite 100 miles long."

DAY 7: A day for rest, photography or hiking on the Great Glacier, climbed by John Muir on his first trip to Alaska. A mile walk from our campsite brings us right to the snout of the glacier.

DAY 8: Enter the Lower River, characterized by numerous channels and sloughs. Depending on the tides, we float to our pickup by riverboat to Wrangell. Clear customs.

DAY 9: Depart Wrangell and connect with homeward-bound flights on Alaska Airlines or Alaska State Ferry.

KOBUK RIVER KAYAKING

DATES: Aug 12–Aug 25 (14 days)
LEADER: Larry Fitzwater
GRADE: B-2
LAND COST: $1490 incl. chtr.
(8–10 members)
$1690 incl. chtr.
(5–7)

This trip features a week-long journey down the swift Kobuk River by kayak, through a region recently designated as Kobuk Valley National Park. En route, we'll stop often to enjoy the sunny, sandy beaches and, on the lower river, try our hand at fishing for migratory salmon and sheefish. We'll also visit some Eskimo fish camps and see remnants of abandoned gold mining operations. The beaches are a rock hound's paradise since the area is highly mineralized—jasper and jade are especially common.

The Kobuk is one of the richest rivers in all the arctic for fishing and it supports an amazing abundance of birdlife, including bald and golden eagles, osprey, kingfishers, ravens, arctic terns, and many varieties of gulls and predatory birds. Grizzly and black bears, moose, fox and wolves are also common.

No previous kayaking experience is necessary for this trip. We'll be paddling stable, easy to use, two-man Folboat kayaks.

ITINERARY:
DAY 1: Leave hometown and arrive Fairbanks. Transfer to hotel.

DAY 2: Fly to Bettles, north of the Arctic Circle. Continue by chartered floatplane to beautiful 16-mile-long Walker Lake. Barbecue dinner at camp.

DAY 3: Free day for exploring around Walker Lake or fishing for lake trout, arctic char, arctic grayling and northern pike.

DAY 4: Begin kayak trip with a short paddle through some easy and fun rapids on an outlet river which joins with the Kobuk River about four miles from Walker Lake.

DAY 5: Continue float trip down river through rolling hills and prime arctic wildlife habitat. The river picks up speed as we pass through the upper Kobuk canyon, with its 200-foot rock bluffs.

A

DAY 6: Enter lower Kobuk Canyon, with its exciting but safe whitewater, the last rapids on the Kobuk.

DAY 7 to 12: Continue float trip on the now-placid Kobuk. Salmon will be spawning up small creeks and bears are commonly seen. At the Pah River confluence, we will spend half a day on the sandy beaches and try our luck at catching arctic sheefish, a tarpon-like fish distantly related to salmon and whitefish. There is an abandoned gold mining operation nearby, and also some Eskimo archaeological sites in the area. We will have an extra day here to adjust the itinerary as desired, depending on water conditions. Arriving at the village of Kobuk.

> **En route, we'll stop often to enjoy the sunny, sandy beaches and, on the lower river, try our hand at fishing for migratory salmon and sheefish.**

DAY 13: Visit with Eskimos of Kobuk, watching them cutting and drying fish. Fly by scheduled charter to Kotzebue.

DAY 14: Fly to Anchorage and connect with homeward-bound flights.

NOTE: Commercial flight from Fairbanks to Bettles is not included in Land Cost.

NOATAK RIVER BY CANOE

DATES: Jun 16–Jun 29 (14 days)
LEADER: Tamara Ketscher
GRADE: A-2
LAND COST: $1450 incl. chtrs.
(10–12 members)
$1590 incl. chtrs. (5–9)

Born in the melting snows of the Brooks Range and emptying 400 miles later into Kotzebue Sound, the Noatak is a majestic wilderness river, all of it above the Arctic Circle. It is now protected as a national park, called Noatak National Preserve.

This trip features a leisurely week-long float trip by canoe on the Noatak's headwaters where the peaks of the Brooks Range rise on both sides of the river. There will be time for day hikes on tributary creeks and fishing. Wildlife is abundant here: we'll see caribou, Dall sheep, grizzly bear, and possibly bald eagles. No previous canoe experience is necessary.

ITINERARY
DAY 1: Leave hometown. Arrive Fairbanks. Transfer to hotel.

DAY 2: Fly to Bettles, continue by chartered float plane to the headwaters of the Noatak. The flight will be spectacular, with views of the distant Arrigetch Peaks and Mt. Igikpak, highest peak in the central and western Brooks Range. Land at the farthest upstream lake where the river is still navigable. Camp on smooth tundra.

DAY 3: Today we'll hike most of the day, looking for Dall sheep and caribou.

DAY 4: Portage gear and canoes to the Noatak and begin leisurely float by canoe, stopping along

the way to photograph and explore.

DAY 5: Hike up the gravel beache along Kugruk Creek to visit secluded hot springs. Excellent fishing for grayling and arctic char.

DAY 6: By canoe to camp at Igning Creek confluence, a very scenic area with many grizzly bears. Excellent grayling and pik fishing.

DAY 7: Free day to explore Igning Creek, fish, hike or look over old gold mining claims.

DAY 8 to 11: On our final day canoeing on the Noatak, we will pass by a denning area for wolves, which are easily seen by the careful observer. Numerous ground squirrels live here, too (un willing food for the growing wolf families). Our last two days will be spent canoeing and exploring Matcharak Lake. There is excellent fishing for lake trout. Often, the weather is warm enough for swimming.

DAY 12: Charter flight back to Bettles.

DAY 13: Commercial flight to Fairbanks.

DAY 14: Leave Fairbanks and con nect with homeward-bound flights

NOTE: Commercial flights between Fairbank and Bettles are not included in Land Cost.

D

C

NOATAK KAYAKING

DATES: Jul 29–Aug 18 (21 days)
LEADER: Mike & Debbie O'Connor
GRADE: B-3
LAND COST: $1790 incl. chtrs.
 (8-12 members)
 $1950 incl. chtrs. (5-7)

In a fascinating geological display, the Noatak pours from the jagged Brooks Range, over broad tundra plains, between steep, carved canyon walls and finally through deep spruce forest and out into the Bering Sea. There is only one permanent human settlement on its entire 400-mile length. Otherwise its inhabitants are moose, bear, caribou, wolves, hawks, and eagles.

Using two-man "Folboat" kayaks, we will journey for fifteen days on the Noatak from its headwaters all the way to the Eskimo village of Noatak near Kotzebue Sound. Along the way, we will fish for delicious arctic char, grayling and salmon, and hike along tributary streams.

No previous kayak experience is necessary.

ITINERARY

DAY 1: Leave hometown. Arrive Fairbanks. Transfer to hotel.

DAY 2: Fly Bettles, continue by spectacular chartered float plane to the headwaters of the Noatak.

DAY 3: Hike to the top of the mountains to look for Dall sheep and caribou.

DAY 4: Portage to the Noatak River and float to the confluence of the Noatak and Kugruk Creeks.

DAY 5: Hike up Kugruk Creek and visit hot springs.

DAY 6: Continue float to Lake Matcharak, passing a wolf denning area and prime grizzly bear country. Careful observers will probably see some wildlife.

DAY 7: Layover day for exploring Lake Matcharak, a transition area where the mountains give way to wide rolling tundra vistas.

DAY 8: Float from Lake Matcharak past Class II rapids below Douglas Creek. Caribou are commonly seen in the Aniuk Lowland area.

DAY 9: The Noatak waters pick up speed in the Aniuk lowland and Class II rapids make the day's travel exciting. This is a good opportunity to learn the art of "reading the water."

DAY 10 and 11: Float to Aniuk Creek and Cutler River, one of the larger tributaries of the Noatak.

Here the river becomes at least 100 yards wide.

DAY 12: Float beyond Okak Bend, where there are several Eskimo archaeological sites. Sometimes whalebone sleds and old hunting camps are seen.

In a fascinating geological display, the river pours from the jagged Brooks Range, over broad tundra plains, between steep, carved canyon walls and finally through deep spruce forest and out into the Bering Sea.

A

DAY 13: Now the flat, rolling terrain gives way to rugged hills. Small groves of cottonwood trees grow along the river—the first trees we've seen since Bettles.

DAY 14: Enter "Grand Canyon of the Noatak," a beautiful broad valley with strata of various types of vegetation on the hillsides which give it tremendous depth and color.

DAY 15 and 16: Float to Sisiak Creek and an area where the farthest extension of spruce forest in North America meets the river.

DAY 17: In the "grand canyon" section of the river, where colorful vertical-walled cliffs rise from either side of the river.

DAY 18 and 19: To the Kelly River, one of the finest spots in Alaska for arctic char, and continue to Noatak Village. Visit Eskimo settlement.

DAY 20: Fly by charter to Kotzebue. Continue by commercial flight to Anchorage.

DAY 21: Leave Anchorage on homeward-bound flights.

NOTE: Commercial flights between Fairbanks and Bettles and from Kotzbue to Anchorage are not included in the Land Cost.

THE McKINLEY TREK

DATES: *#1 Jun 8–Jun 21 (14 days)
         *#2 Aug 3–Aug 16 (14 days)
LEADER: #1 to be announced
         #2 Gary Bocarde
GRADE: B-3
LAND COST: $1290 (7–10 members)
            $1450 (6–9)
*Note date change from 1984 Trip Schedule.

This is a fantastic trek which takes advantage of McKinley's full 17,000-foot rise above the Alaskan plains. It leads right up onto the glaciers of Mt. McKinley, North America's highest peak, known in the native language as Denali—"the great one."

Starting near Wonder Lake in Denali National Park, the eight-day trek begins at the mile-wide McKinley River and proceeds up Cache Creek to the alpine meadows of McGonagall Canyon. Crossing McGonagall Pass, we'll stop for a day of instruction on safe glacier travel and use of ice axe and crampons.

We then ascend the Muldrow Glacier (from which the pioneer ascent was made in 1913) to a point near the lower icefall beneath McKinley's great northern flanks. From a central camp, we'll make day hikes near the Tralieka and Brooks glaciers and optional climbs of several easy peaks before retracing our route over McGonagall Pass to Wonder Lake.

This will be a very spectacular trek involving simple glacier travel, vigorous hiking and a few difficult river crossings.

ITINERARY:

DAY 1: Leave hometown. Arrive Anchorage. Transfer to hotel.

DAY 2: By Alaska Railroad to Denali National Park. Camp at Park Headquarters.

DAY 3: Scenic bus ride to Wonder Lake Camp nearby.

DAY 4: Begin trek. Cross the mile-wide McKinley River and hike the trail to Clearwater (Camp I) Creek. We'll carry all our own supplies in backpacks; however, our loads will be reduced somewhat by supplies we have cached in advance.

DAY 5 and 6: Hike up to Cache Creek drainage, McGonagall Canyon and cross McGonagall Pass.

DAY 7: Ascend the Muldrow Glacier to the base of the Lower Icefall and Gunsight Pass.

DAY 8: Ascend Gunsight Mountain; spectacular views of the north side of McKinley.

DAY 9: Day trek up the Tralieka Glacier, with possible ascents of small peaks.

DAY 10 and 11: Walk out to Clearwater Creek.

DAY 12: Bus to Park Headquarters.

DAY 13: Train to Anchorage.

DAY 14: Leave Anchorage and connect with homeward-bound flights.

McKINLEY CLIMBING SEMINAR

DATES: Jun 18–Jul 1 (14 days)
LEADER: Gary Bocarde
GRADE: B-3/D-1
LAND COST: $1090+chtrs. $275
            (8–12 members)

This climbing seminar takes plac in a spectacular mountain setting surrounded by the big peaks of the Alaska Range including McKinley (20,320'), Foraker (17,402') and Hunter (14,573').

We will fly to the southeast fork o the Kahiltna Glacier, the starting point for most McKinley ascents. From here, we ski or snowshoe to the base of Control Tower Peak (8,060'). From this base camp, we begin instruction in rope handling glissading and snow climbing techniques.

After a few days of instruction, we make a night ascent of Control Tower Peak. The seminar continues with instruction in technica rock and ice climbing technique and the final few days are spent climbing Radar Peak (8,670') and Mt. Francis (10,450').

The seminar is suitable for strong backpackers (capable of heavy load carrying) who want to learn a full range of mountaineering techniques.

ITINERARY:

DAY 1: Leave hometown. Arrive Anchorage. Transfer to hotel.

DAY 2: Drive or take the train to Talkeetna. Continue by spectacular charter to the Kahiltna Glacier at the base of Mt. McKinley.

DAY 3: By ski or snowshoe for 1½ hours to the western base of Peak 8060 (Control Tower Peak). Establish a base camp, learning winter camping techniques.

DAY 4 and 5: Begin the seminar: basic knots, belaying, basic rope handling, self arrest, glissading, snow climbing techniques, rappelling, use of ice axe and crampon.

DAY 6: Continue seminar: glacier travel techniques, crevasse rescue avalanche rescue procedures, discussion of mountain safety and first aid. Night climb of Control Tower Peak.

DAY 7 and 8: Technical ice climbing instruction and practice using modern techniques and equipment.

C

A   Crossing Kahiltna Glacier/Gary Bocarde
B   At 16,200 feet on the West Buttress/Gary Bocarde
C   View of Mt. Foraker from 15,000 feet on McKinley/Gary Bocarde

ALASKA • 13

A

AY 9 and 10: Basic rock climbing
nstruction: climbing techniques,
se of pitons and chocks, setting
p belay anchors, rappelling.

AY 11: Move camp to north of the
nding site, set up camp. Night
me ascent of Mt. Francis
0,450').

**The seminar is suitable
for strong backpackers
(capable of heavy load
carrying) who want to
learn a full range
of mountaineering
techniques.**

AY 12: Night ascent of Radar
eak (8,670').

AY 13: Fly out to Talkeetna, and
eturn to Anchorage.

AY 14: Depart Anchorage and
onnect with homeward-bound
ights.

MT. McKINLEY
EXPEDITION

DATES: #1 May 4–May 25 (22 days)
#2 Jun 1–Jun 22 (22 days)
LEADER: #1 John Svenson
#2 Nic Parker
GRADE: E-2
LAND COST: $1390 + chtrs. $275
(8–10 members)

Mt. McKinley (20,320') is the
highest point on the North
American continent. It is a
beautiful and impressive mountain by any standards, soaring a
dazzling 17,000 feet above the
plains—one of the greatest base-
to-summit rises of any mountain on
earth. It was first climbed in 1913;
subsequent ascents were few until
the 1950's.

The West Buttress route, first
climbed in 1951, has become the

B

standard approach to the summit,
and will be our route of ascent,
beginning at a base camp on the
Kahiltna Glacier at 7,000 feet.

A climb of McKinley is a physically demanding ascent requiring a
range of mountaineering skills.
Technically, it is of moderate dif-
ficulty; weather and altitude make
it a true mountaineering challenge. The duration of the ascent
can take as little as ten days, but
can require 15 or more because of
frequent and prolonged storms
which hit the peak.

Members must be very fit, and
capable of carrying loads of 75 lbs.
or more at high altitudes and
assisting with expedition chores.
All community equipment will be
provided. The party will be flown
in by charter from Talkeetna.

ITINERARY:

DAY 1: Leave hometown. Arrive
Anchorage. Transfer to hotel.

DAY 2: Drive to Talkeetna. Prepare
expedition gear for tomorrow's
flight onto the Kahiltna Glacier.

DAY 3: By charter flight to the
7,000-foot level on the southeast
fork of the Kahiltna Glacier. Establish base camp. Note: weather
conditions may delay the departure of this mountain flight.

DAY 4 to 7: Carry loads from 7,000
feet to 10,000 feet at Kahiltna
Pass. Conditioning and acclimatization during this period.

DAY 8 to 10: Move camp from
11,000 feet to 14,200 feet in a basin
below the West Buttress, in accordance with weather conditions,
acclimatization and strength of
party.

**It is a beautiful and
impressive mountain by
any standards, soaring a
dazzling 17,000 feet above
the plains—one of the
greatest base-to-summit
rises of any mountain
on earth.**

DAY 11 to 14: Load carrying up fixed
lines to 16,400 feet on the West Buttress. Establish high camp.

DAY 15 and 16: Move to high camp
at 17,200 feet.

DAY 17 and 18: Summit attempts,
depending on weather conditions,
acclimatization.

DAY 19 and 20: Descend and
return to Kahiltna Glacier pick-up
point.

DAY 21 and 22: Charter flight from
the Kahiltna Glacier to Talkeetna.
Return to Anchorage by bus or
train and connect with homeward-bound flights.

Note on itinerary: The daily schedule
listed above is a guideline only, and
will vary in accordance with conditions
on the mountain.

C

A   Grizzly bea
B   The Alatna River/Jim Stua
C   Hiking towards the Arrigetch/Dave Ketsche

A

THE ARRIGETCH WILDERNESS

DATES: #1 Jul 16–Jul 29 (14 days)
#2 Aug 1–Aug 14 (14 days)
LEADER: To·be announced
GRADE: B-3
LAND COST: $1450 incl. chtr.
(8–12 members)
$1590 incl. chtr. (5–7)

The impressive granite spires of the Arrigetch Peaks, now part of "Gates of the Arctic National Park," are perhaps the most spectcular part of the entire Brooks Range. The name Arrigetch in the native language means "fingers of the hand outstretched," and these peaks seem to reach up toward the sky, rising out of delicate alpine valleys.

To reach the Arrigetch wilderness, we fly to Bettles (above the Arctic Circle) and continue by floatplane to Circle Lake. From here, a two-day backpack trip takes us to our base camp in the heart of the Arrigetch Peaks, where we'll spend a few days hiking and photographing among the peaks. Dall sheep, black and grizzly bears are often found in the remote valleys. The hike into the Arrigetch is strenuous but the spectacular scenery makes it worth the effort.

We then hike out to the Alatna River for a float trip on a gentle arctic river which meanders through scenic bluffs and mountains. Moose, wolves, beaver and waterfowl are seen along the river. We will set aside ample time for hiking to nearby lakes to fish for lake trout and northern pike.

ITINERARY

DAY 1: Leave hometown. Arrive Fairbanks. Transfer to hotel.

DAY 2: Fly to Bettles, north of the Arctic Circle. Continue by chartered floatplane to Circle Lake and camp nearby.

DAY 3: Today's hike, although only about 3 miles, is a difficult and strenuous one through bogs and terrain with tricky footing. Camp on flat bluffs overlooking Arrigetch Creek in Gates of the Arctic National Park.

DAY 4: Six miles to our base camp in the Arrigetch Valley, a little easier than yesterday's hike, but with some bushwacking and fording icy streams.

DAY 5 and 6: From our base camp we will explore and hike up to the spires, past emerald glacial tarns. We carry only day packs on the walks during these two days, and return to base camp each night.

DAY 7: Break camp and retrace our route back to Arrigetch Creek

DAY 8: Hike along Arrigetch Cree down to the Alatna River.

DAY 9: Begin float trip on the gen tle Alatna River, a nice change o pace after our strenuous back-pack trip. We'll drift slowly down river, observing wildlife along the river.

DAY 10: Continue float trip and arrive at Takahula Lake. Portage the gear to the lake and camp on the lakeshore.

DAY 11: Free day at Takahula, a scenic lake nestled below majestic mountains. Time for fishing for lake trout and northern pike.

DAY 12: Afternoon pickup for charter flight back to Bettles. Barbecue on the Koyukuk River.

DAY 13: Fly to Fairbanks.

DAY 14: Depart Fairbanks on homeward-bound flights.

NOTE: Commercial flight from Fairbanks to Bettles is not included in Land Cost.

B

> The name Arrigetch in the native language means "fingers of the hand outstretched," and these peaks seem to reach up toward the sky, rising out of delicate alpine valleys.

On Mt. Rainier/Eric Sanford
Rock climbing in the North Cascades/Eric Sanford
The Grand Teton/Eric Sanford
Mt. Whitney/Diane Yates

CLASSIC CLIMBS IN AMERICA • 15

CLASSIC CLIMBS IN AMERICA

DATES: #1 Jun 24–Jul 14 (21 days)
#2 Jul 21–Aug 10 (21 days)
LEADER: To be announced
GRADE: D-3
LAND COST: $1950 (9–10 members)
$2100 (6–8)

This expedition combines ascents of four of the highest mountains in the Lower 48: majestic Mt. Rainier (14,410') in wilderness Washington, the shapely Grand Teton (13,776') in Wyoming, Longs Peak (14,256') in Colorado's Rocky Mountain National Park, and finally, Mt. Whitney (14,494'), highest peak in the U.S. outside Alaska.

This is a physically demanding trip requiring stamina, endurance and basic mountaineering skills. Routes will be chosen according to weather conditions and party strength. There will be a guide ratio of one per four members.

Trip #1 begins with the Rainier climb in Seattle and ends in San Francisco after the Whitney climb. Trip #2 operates in the reverse order.

Our driving itinerary is quite scenic and includes the following (based on the Seattle to San Francisco itinerary): from Mt. Rainier we head southeast through the rolling prairies of Oregon and Idaho, stopping near Boise for the night. Then straight east towards the dramatic Tetons, crossing into Wyoming via Teton Pass (8,400'). From Jackson Hole, we drive into the Wyoming plains, through the well-known cowboy towns of Rawlins and Laramie, to Estes Park, the entrance to Rocky Mountain National Park. The long, flat desert highways through Utah and Nevada are broken up by many scenic and interesting spots along the way. On the way to Mt. Whitney, we will pass through the Wasatch and Uinta Mountains, across the great Salt Flats, and right by Wheeler Peak, jutting over 13,000 feet out of the Nevada desert. Our return takes us over the Sierra Nevada to San Francisco.

TRIP #1: SEATTLE TO SAN FRANCISCO
DAY 1: Meet group and leader in Seattle and drive to Mt. Rainier National Park. Camp.
DAY 2: Practice snow and ice climbing.
DAY 3 and 4: Climb Mt. Rainier (14,410').
DAY 5 and 6: Drive to Grand Teton National Park, Wyoming.

> **Routes will be chosen according to weather conditions and party strength. There will be a guide ratio of one per four members.**

DAY 7: Rest day. Pack up for Grand Teton climb.
DAY 8 to 10: Climb the Grand Teton (13,776').
DAY 11: Drive to Rocky Mountain National Park.
DAY 12: Rest day. Pack up for Longs Peak climb.

DAY 13 and 14: Climb Longs Peak (14,256').
DAY 15 and 16: Drive to Mt. Whitney, highest peak in the U.S. outside Alaska.
DAY 17: Rest day. Pack up for Mt. Whitney climb.
DAY 18 to 20: Climb Mt. Whitney (14,494').
DAY 21: Drive to San Francisco and connect with homeward-bound flights.

TRIP #2: SAN FRANCISCO TO SEATTLE
DAY 1: Meet group and leader in San Francisco. Drive to Mt. Whitney. Camp.
DAY 2 to 4: Climb Mt. Whitney (14,494').
DAY 5 and 6: Drive to Rocky Mountain National Park.
DAY 7: Rest day. Pack up for Longs Peak climb.
DAY 8 and 9: Climb Longs Peak (14,256').
DAY 10: Drive to Grand Teton National Park.
DAY 11: Rest day. Pack up for Grand Teton climb.
DAY 12 to 14: Climb the Grand Teton (13,776').
DAY 15 and 16: Drive to Mt. Rainier National Park.
DAY 17: Rest day. Pack up for Mt. Rainier climb.
DAY 18 to 20: Climb Mt. Rainier (14,410').
DAY 21: Drive to Seattle and connect with homeward-bound flights.

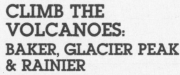

NORTH CASCADES SEMINAR & CLIMB

DATES: *#1 Jun 17–Jun 30 (14 days)
*#2 Jul 8–Jul 21 (14 days)
LEADER: Eric Sanford
GRADE: B-3
LAND COST: $1050 (5–10 members)
*Note change from 1984 Trip Schedule.

This two-week course is designed to teach all the basics for safe and efficient mountain travel. While little or no previous mountaineering experience is required, it is advised that members be in top physical shape and well broken in to the rigors of extended back-country travel. Trip members will learn belaying, knots and rope work, rock, snow and ice climbing techniques, route selection and safety, crevasse rescue and glacier travel, mountain first aid, safety and rescue, use of ice axe, crampons and other climbing equipment, and rapelling and descending techniques. The seminar will take place in several locations in the Cascades depending on weather and climbing conditions. Several major Cascade peaks, including Mt. Baker (10,750') will be climbed during the course.

ITINERARY:

DAY 1: Meet group and leader in Seattle. Drive to Mazama and camp.

DAY 2 to 4: Hike into Wing Lake (5 miles) and camp. Climb Black Peak (8,970'). Instruction will include basic rock climbing, knots, rapelling and some basic snow climbing skills.

DAY 5: Hike out from Wing Lake and drive back to Mazama and camp nearby. Afternoon rock climbing practice and re-pack for the next trip.

DAY 6 to 8: Hike up to Blue Lake and our high camp in the Liberty Bell basin. Very close to our camp are a number of fine rock peaks and spires which provide excellent practice. These include Blue Peak and the Liberty Bell and Early Winter spires. Camp at the lake.

> **Trip members will learn belaying, knots and rope work, rock, snow and ice climbing techniques, route selection and safety, crevasse rescue and glacier travel, mountain first aid, safety and rescue, use of ice axe, crampons and other climbing equipment, and rapelling and descending techniques.**

DAY 9: Drive to Mt. Baker and hike into Kulshan Cabin.

DAY 10 to 12: Establish a high camp on the Coleman Glacier and practice snow and ice climbing and crevasse rescue.

DAY 13: Climb Mt. Baker (10,750') and return to high camp.

DAY 14: Hike out, drive to Seattle, and connect with homeward-bound flights.

CLIMB THE VOLCANOES: BAKER, GLACIER PEAK & RAINIER

DATES: #1 Jul 1–Jul 14 (14 days)
#2 Jul 29–Aug 11 (14 days)
LEADER: Tom Baker
GRADE: D-3
LAND COST: *$1050 (6–10 members)
*Note change from 1984 Trip Schedule.

This is a mountaineering seminar with ascents of Washington's major glaciated volcanoes: Mt. Baker (10,750'), Glacier Peak (10,541') and Rainier (14,410').

Mt. Baker is a beautifully proportioned peak which soars a full 7,000 feet above a green skirt of forest in the North Cascades. The whitest of the Cascade volcanoes, it has one of the heaviest snowfalls in the state and has twelve active glaciers.

Ice-mantled Glacier Peak, in the heart of the Cascade Range, is an eroded volcanic cone which is prominently etched into the Cascade skyline.

Mt. Rainier, highest peak in Washington, rises 8,000 feet above surrounding ridges and lesser peaks, and has been called "an arctic palace floating on a sea of green trees." This massive volcano has a circumference of 20 miles and 26 named glaciers.

Members must have basic mountaineering skills, but the climbs are more physically demanding than technically difficult. Backpacking is required on the approach to the peaks. There will be one guide for every four members.

ITINERARY:

DAY 1: Meet group and leader in Seattle, drive to Mt. Baker National Forest and camp.

DAY 2 and 3: Hike to Kulshan Cabin on the slopes of Mt. Baker. Spend day on Coleman Glacier learning or brushing up on snow and ice climbing and crevasse rescue.

DAY 4: Climb Mt. Baker (10,750') via the Coleman Glacier route. Descend to Kulshan Cabin.

DAY 5: Hike out, drive to Darrington and camp nearby.

DAY 6: Drive to trailhead. Hike to Kennedy Hot Springs (3,300') and camp.

DAY 7: Hike to base of Sitkum Glacier (7,000') and practice ice climbing.

DAY 8: Climb Glacier Peak (10,541') and descend to Kennedy Hot Springs.

DAY 9: Hike out, drive to Darrington for rest and relaxation.

DAY 10: Drive to south side of Mt. Rainier and camp.

DAY 11: Hike to Camp Hazard (11,300').

> **Mt. Rainier, highest peak in Washington, rises 8,000 feet above surrounding ridges and lesser peaks, and has been called "an arctic palace floating on a sea of green trees."**

DAY 12: Climb Mt. Rainier (14,410') via Kautz Glacier and return to Camp Hazard.

DAY 13: Descend to Paradise. Farewell dinner in Mt. Rainier National Park.

DAY 14: Drive to Seattle and connect with homeward-bound flights.

THE PTARMIGAN TRAVERSE

DATES: *Aug 11–Aug 24 (14 days)
LEADER: Tom Baker
GRADE: D-3
LAND COST: $1050 (4–7 members)
*Note change from 1984 Trip Schedule.

If you're ready for a challenge and are up to the demands, these are the "American Alps" at their finest.

This is the classic North Cascades high mountain traverse, known for its superb scenery as well as challenging and varied climbing. First traveled in the 1940's, the route has drawn some of the nation's finest climbers to test themselves on many of the rugged peaks along the way. Participants should be prepared for changing climbing conditions. Cold, wet mountain weather may be encountered on the crossing of several major glaciers and high mountain passes. Time permitting, we will make ascents of several of the Cascades' finest peaks along the way. The trip begins with a three-day practice session to hone your mountaineering skills for the trip ahead, since once you begin, there's no turning back. If you're ready for a challenge and are up to the demands, these are the "American Alps" at their finest.

ITINERARY:
DAY 1: Meet group and leader in Seattle. Drive to Marblemount and pack up for practice course. Camp at trailhead.

DAY 2 to 4: Three days of shakedown training before the actual traverse. Practice climbing in Boston Basin and Eldorado Peak.

DAY 5: Rest day and pack up for Ptarmigan Traverse.

DAY 6: Hike over Cascade Pass (5,400') to Cache Col (7,000').

DAY 7 and 8: To Cool-Aid Lake. Climb Hurry-Up Peak (7,800'); to Yang-Yang Lakes via Spider-Formidable Col (7,400') and Middle Cascade Glacier.

DAY 9 and 10: Climb La Conte Mountain via La Conte Glacier; climb Sentinel or Old Guard Peak (8,200') and descend to White Rocks Lakes (6,200').

DAY 11 and 12: Traverse to Dana Glacier and climb Spire Point; climb Dome Peak (8,800') and return to Spire Camp.

DAY 13: Descend to Cub Lake and continue down Bachelor Creek and Downey Creek.

DAY 14: Hike out, drive to Seattle and connect with homeward-bound flights.

*NORTH CASCADES LLAMA TREK

DATES: Aug 12–Aug 25 (14 days)
LEADER: Doug Veenhof
GRADE: B-2
LAND COST: $1200 (5–8 members)
*This replaces the CASCADES BACKPACKING trip listed in the 1984 Trip Schedule.

One of the most spectacular parts of the North Cascades is the northern border of the Pasayten Wilderness which stretches along the Canadian border in Washington.

We'll undertake a 12-day trek through this region, using llamas for pack animals. These delightful, furry beasts can carry a lot of weight (so we don't have to), and their antics and personalities will

keep us entertained for hours. We'll hike the entire Pasayten Wilderness from east to west, connecting sections of the Pacific Crest and Cascade Crest Trails,

crossing high, hidden mountain passes and skirting alpine lakes. The total distance covered is just over 100 miles.

Trip members will share in camp chores. There are optional rest days or side trips along the way, great wildlife viewing and wildflowers galore.

ITINERARY:
DAY 1: Meet group and leader in Seattle, drive to Mazama and camp.

DAY 2: Drive to Thirtymile Campground, meet with llamas and begin hiking on easy terrain along the Chewack River for eight miles to a camp on Tungston Creek.

DAY 3: Hike eight miles on easy terrain to Remmel Lake.

DAY 4: Day hikes to Cathedral Lakes, Cathedral Peak and Amphitheatre Mountain. Fishing and easy climbing.

DAY 5 and 6: Hike a moderate ten miles to Ramon Lake; 11 miles to Dean Creek via Park Pass, Peeve Pass and around Sheep Mountain and Quartz Mountain.

These delightful, furry beasts can carry a lot of weight (so we don't have to), and their antics and personalities will keep us entertained for hours.

DAY 7 and 8: Hike an easy 11 miles to Hidden Lakes; hike to camp on the Middle Fork of the Pasayten River via Tatoosh Buttes, 12 moderate and spectacular miles.

DAY 9 and 10: Gradually uphill along the West Fork of the Pasayten River to Holman Pass, an easy 13 miles; along Cascade Crest Trail over Sky Pilot Pass, Deception Pass and enjoy magnificent views along the way to Devil's Pass. Eight moderate miles.

DAY 11: Day hike to Devil's Dome. Easy climbing, great wildlife viewing and many flowers.

DAY 12 and 13: Hike six miles to Devil's Park via Anacortes Crossing; downhill to the North Cascades Highway via Macmillian Park. Drive back to Mazama.

DAY 14: Drive to Seattle and connect with homeward-bound flights.

NEW ENGLAND: THE WHITE MOUNTAINS OF NEW HAMPSHIRE

DATES: #1 Jul 13–Jul 22 (10 days)
      #2 Aug 31–Sep 9 (10 days)
LEADER: #1 Jon Burroughs
       #2 Ida Burroughs
GRADE: B-3
LAND COST: $590 (10–15 members)

This is one of New England's classic treks—a nine-day, 60-mile "range walk" from Franconia Notch to Pinkham Notch by way of Mt. Washington (6,288'), highest peak in the northeastern U.S.

Although these mountains are not high, they are extremely rugged and demand a high level of fitness. Despite the many steep "ups and downs" of this walk, it is a popular one for its scenic beauty. Trip #2 takes advantage of New England's glorious display of autumn colors.

The White Mountains have a well organized system of huts, maintained by the Appalachian Mountain Club. Bunks and blankets are provided, as are homestyle breakfasts and dinners. Each hut has a distinctive New England ambience—rustic, friendly, alpine and wholesome. The Hutmasters and their assistants are generally young men and women from eastern colleges who are energetic and more than willing to share their knowledge of these mountains.

ITINERARY:

DAY 1: Leave hometown. Arrive Boston. Meet with trip leader and transfer to bus for three-hour ride to Franconia, New Hampshire. Hike six miles to Lonesome Lake hut.

DAY 2: Descend the Lonesome Lake Trail, ascend Falling Waters Trail past three sets of waterfalls to Mt. Little Haystack (4,800'). Continue over Mts. Lincoln and Lafayette (5,249') to Greenleaf Hut (4,200'). 7.1 miles.

DAY 3: Ascend over the summits of Mt. Lafayette and Mt. Garfield (4,488') to Galehead Hut (3,800'), a strenuous 7.6 miles.

DAY 4: Steep ascent of Mt. South Twin (4,926') and descend to Zealand Falls Hut. 7 miles.

Trip #2 takes advantage of New England's glorious display of autumn colors.

DAY 5: Either a demanding but spectacular 14.2-mile hike up to Mt. Webster (3,910'), with views into Crawford Notch, site of the Willey House (immortalized by Nathaniel Hawthorne) and over Mt. Jackson (4,052') to Mizpah Spring Hut, or take the moderate Avalon-Zealand Trail to Mizpah Spring Hut, a considerably easier 7.7 miles.

DAY 6: An easier (5.1 miles) but no less spectacular day over the Southern Presidential Range to Lake Of The Clouds Hut, located on the shoulder of Mt. Washington near three alpine lakes.

DAY 7: Along famed Crawford Path to the summit of Mt. Washington (6,288'), highest peak east of the Mississippi and north of the Carolinas, and crowded with a cog railway, auto road, museum, and observatory/weather station. From here, we traverse the beautiful Northern Presidential Range with optional side trips over the summits of Mt. Clay (5,532'), Mt. Jefferson (5,715') and Mt. Adams (5,798'). Descend to Madison Spring Hut (4,825'). Total hiking distance 7.7 miles.

DAY 8: Down the precipitous Madison Gulf Trail to the Glen House and a gentle ascent up to the beautiful Carter Notch Hut with its two sparkling lakes and numerous caves. Hiking distance 7.9 miles.

DAY 9: A rugged 6.8 miles over the summits of the Wildcat Ridge with its beautiful views of the Northern Presidential Range and Mt. Washington. Down to Pinkham Notch and the Pinkham Notch Camp, summer headquarters of Appalachian Mountain Club activities.

DAY 10: Return by bus to Boston to connect with homeward-bound flights.

A Summit of Mauna Kea/Sara Steck
B Taro fields of Waipio Valley/Jan Tiura
C Haleakala crater/Sara Steck
D Beach at Pololu Valley/Sara Steck

HAWAII • 19

THE OTHER HAWAII

DATES: #1 Apr 7–Apr 21 (15 days)
#2 Oct 6–Oct 20 (15 days)
#3 Dec 19, 1984–Jan 2, 1985

LEADER: #1 Sara Steck
#2 Peter Ourusoff
#3 to be announced

GRADE: B-2

LAND COST: $890 (11-14 members)
$990 (6-10)

During our sojourn in the other Hawaii, we will hike, camp and explore the exotic natural beauty of the Hawaii of old, as it still exists on the outer islands.

With ten days on the "big island" of Hawaii, we will hike the Waipio Valley, swim and snorkel in the warm waters of Hapuna Beach, then make a summit hike on Mauna Kea (13,796'), highest peak in the Pacific.

Driving down the beautiful Kona Coast, we stop at Hawaii Volcanoes National Park to hike across the still-steaming Kilauea Caldera to explore Mauna Ulu, a very active volcano.

Our five-day sojourn on Maui includes a memorable sunrise from the summit of Haleakala (10,023'), followed by a two-day backpack trip across the moonscape of craters which form the volcano's floor. Our accommodations will be in beach camps and state park cabins, with our last night spent at an inn in the picturesque whaling port of Lahaina.

A

D

ITINERARY:

DAY 1: Leave hometown. Arrive Hilo, Hawaii. Transfer to hotel.

DAY 2: Early morning drive up Hamakua Coast for a walk in the Waipio Valley, a six-mile long valley bounded by 2,000-foot high walls. Swim under a beautiful waterfall and camp at Keokea.

DAY 3: A day's hike on the Pololu Trail, with its fantastic seascapes and profusion of native plants. Overnight at Hapuna Beach.

B

DAY 4: Morning swimming at the white sand beach of Hapuna, the best beach on the island of Hawaii. Afternoon drive to cabins at 6,000 feet in the saddle between Mauna Kea and Mauna Loa.

DAY 5: On our way before sunrise for a round trip day hike, we drive to the trailhead and begin hiking, reaching the summit of Mauna Kea (13,796') by noon. From here, there are grand views of the "Big Island" below us and distant views (if it's clear) of Haleakala Volcano on the island of Maui.

DAY 6: Morning visit to the town of Kamuela, afternoon of body-surfing or snorkeling on Hapuna Beach. Sunset barbecue.

DAY 7: Drive along the Kona Coast, stopping at Kailua, the Place of Refuge, and Captain Cook's monument. Camp at a beach park.

DAY 8: At the southernmost point on the island, we'll walk along the coast and see canoe moorings which were part of an ancient Hawaiian civilization. Overnight at cabins.

DAY 9: Spend the day at Hawaii Volcanoes National Park, walking across the crater of Kilauea, with its active fumaroles.

DAY 10: Visit the bird park and hike to Mauna Ulu, a recently active volcano. Drive down to the rugged southern coast for a short walk and a freshwater swim in a natural pool.

DAY 11: Drive to Hilo and fly to Kahului on the island of Maui. Drive to the slopes of Haleakala Volcano and camp at Hosmer Grove, a beautiful hardwood forest at 8,000 feet.

> **We will hike the Waipio Valley, swim and snorkel in the warm waters of Hapuna Beach, then make a summit hike on Mauna Kea (13,796'), highest peak in the Pacific.**

DAY 12: Very early start for a drive to the summit of Haleakala (10,023'). Watch the magnificent sunrise from the summit, then don 30-35 lb. backpacks for a long day's hike down and across the huge seven-mile-long crater. Walk on Sliding Sands Trail in a landscape of colorful cinder cones and rare silversword plants. Overnight at cabins or camp.

DAY 13: Hike the Halemauu Trail back through the crater to camp at Hosmer Grove.

DAY 14: Enjoy a last morning on the beach, then drive to Lahaina. Overnight at Pioneer Inn.

DAY 15: Transfer to airport to connect with homeward-bound flights.

C

Mt. McKinley from Wonder Lake/Alla Schmitz

Buddhist monks in Ladakh, India/Leo Le Bon

ACKNOWLEDGMENTS

Our dream book is the combined effort of many people. Many thanks to Managing Editor, Pam Shandrick, for writing and editing the text, and to Art Director, Ken Scott, for the book's design. Thanks also to Hugh Swift for proofreading and map preparation, and to Linda Davis of Ann Flanagan Typography for typesetting. Thanks must also go to the Mountain Travel staff, all of our trip leaders as well as our overseas agents and outfitters, our "extended family" of friends, numbering in the hundreds, who contributed their leadership, their advice and a vast array of original photographs for this book.

Above all, I'd like to express my gratitude and thanks to our members, those intrepid travelers who have participated in our adventures in the last seventeen years. Without their interest and support, Mountain Travel would not exist. It is the sharing of some small and unique adventure somewhere on our planet with these special people that has made it all worthwhile.

LLB

Created by INPRINT International Promotions in in Travel   Printed in Japan

HEALTH MATTERS

As our experience continues to grow, we find that we are able to pass on to our trip members more and more hints and suggestions concerning preparations for the trips they are about to take.

IMMUNIZATIONS

Only a few immunizations are LEGALLY REQUIRED for entry to certain countries, but it is very unwise to take only those shots needed to travel legally. Mountain Travel trips are by definition designed to get you away from the "usual tourist routes" and into what U.S. Public Health Service calls "rural or remote sections." While every effort is made to ensure proper sanitation, there is always the chance of disease exposure.

These suggestions should be used **only as a guideline.** Requirements are subject to change and travelers should check with their local Health Department, the Center for Disease Control and/or your personal physician.

YOU MUST START EARLY (at least two months before leaving) so that the shots can be sensibly spaced for maximum protection and minimum discomfort. All immunizations must be entered on your yellow "International Certificate of Vaccination" form which you should keep with your passport while traveling.

Diptheria-Tetanus Booster
Normally needed every 8 years, unless you are injured. BUT almost everyone on a walking trip will get a minor scrape or cut and we do often share trails with the local livestock. Get a booster!

Oral Polio
Regulations change periodically; check with your Health Department. If you have had the original 3 doses, a single oral booster is all that is needed. This is still a real disease in much of the world. Get a booster!

Smallpox
The disease no longer exists and vaccine is no longer available or required.

Typhoid
This is desirable for anyone traveling and camping in rural areas—even in the U.S. It is essential for Mexico, South America, Asia, Africa and the Middle East. A booster is good for 3 years and gives about 60% protection. The Typhoid-Paratyphoid combination is no longer recommended since paratyphoid protection is minimal and the combination often causes reactions (i.e. fever, aches).

Gamma Globulin
An injection of 2 cc. (varies with weight) given as close to departure time as possible is for protection against hepatitis. The immunity is passive and does subside within a few months. Some trip members report their physicians are reluctant to give Gamma Globulin, but it is no longer controversial. The U.S. Public Health Service recommends it for travelers to "tropical areas," "developing countries," and those who "bypass the ordinary tourist routes." Get it.

Typhus
Its value is debatable and it is generally not recommended.

Yellow Fever
This is a legal requirement for travel to many countries that either have the disease or fear its introduction. The yellow fever zone covers central and the northern half of South America and a band across Africa. Yellow fever immunization is mandatory for travel in the areas above, and is strongly recommended for all travel in Africa or South America. A few Asian countries fear its introduction and MAY require it.

Cholera
Often required by local authorities and subject to change on short notice. All travelers to Africa, the Middle East and Asia should have a current cholera shot. This immunization is only valid for 6 months, but a booster is all that is ever needed once the primary series has been completed. Get it even though its value is questionable, since at least you'll get it with a clean needle in the U.S.

Malaria
Malaria pills (Chloroquine Phosphate) are recommended for anyone traveling and camping in tropical areas. In some areas where malaria is prevalent and exposure cannot be avoided, some physicians recommend taking Primaquine during the six-week follow-up. In addition some areas require other medication for Chloroquine-resistant strains. Consult your physician in this matter.

FOOD AND DRINK

On Mountain Travel trips, food is prepared by experienced cooks using the highest possible degree of sanitation. The water we use for cooking and drinking is boiled and/or filtered. However, in hotels, restaurants and on your own, **take the following precautions seriously:**

Drinking tap water or brushing your teeth with it is dangerous. Use the bottled water which is available in most hotels, preferably after adding your own disinfectant. Ice cubes are generally made from the local water supply, which may be contaminated. Streams may look enticing, but germs are invisible.

Eat no food which is uncooked or which is bought from sidewalk vendors. Thoroughly cooked food which is still hot from a hotel kitchen is generally safe. Beware of salads! Custards, ice cream and creams in pastries and desserts are not safe in areas where refrigeration is primitive. Unboiled milk is suspect.

In order to stay well hydrated, which is essential to good health, you must keep up your fluid intake. Fill your water bottle with boiled water at night.

Water Purification
For purifying questionable water sources, we recommend iodine tablets (available from camping stores) or iodine crystal solution (available by prescription from your physician. Iodine in crystal form should be used with care, as it is poisonous if ingested). Consult your physician and/or druggist.

PERSONAL FIRST AID SUPPLIES

The following suggestions are based on past trekking experience. Your own experience and preferences will, of course, influence your choice. Do not forget to bring medications used for individual conditions, since these are not generally available overseas. **This list is a guideline only, to be used as a basis for discussion with your physician.**

Mild pain, Headache, Fever
Aspirin, 5 gr. or Tylenol, if allergic to Asprin.

Pain, Cough, Diarrhea
Aspirin w/Codine 1/2 gr. (Ascodeen-30 or Tylenol w/Codine, 1/2 gr.

Antacid, Upset Stomach, Ulcers
Maalox, Gelusil M, or Mylanta antacid tabs. Donnatal tabs are good for stomach cramps, mild diarrhea, and are a mild sedative.

Diarrhea (symptomatic relief)
Codeine compounds listed above. Avoid Lomotil which has been reported to prolong illness with some types of dysentery. Some people find Peptobismal effective.

Diarrhea (prevention)
Small daily doses of tetracycline, or its long-acting relative, doxycycline, have been shown to decrease the incidence of "traveler's diarrhea." This is certainly desirable when one has limited time and has invested a lot of money in a trip. This treatment is still somewhat controversial. Some people become sun sensitized by the drugs and can acquire a truly disabling sunburn. Also there is at least theoretical reason to fear that these drugs, while protecting against minor (albeit annoying) diarrheas, may be limiting the normal flora in the intestine and making one more susceptible to the more virulent organisms responsible for truly life-threatening dysenteries. **Please discuss the pros and cons carefully with your own physician before taking these medications.**

Colds, Allergies (symptomatic relief)
Chlorpheniramine Maleate tabs., 4 mg. Actifed tabs (good for 4 hours) or Tuss-Ornade Spansule caps. (12-hour relief).

Topical Antibiotic
Most antibiotic ointments contain one or more of the following in about the following proportions: Neomycin (3.5 mg.)/Bacitracin (400 units)/Polymyxin (5,000 units). Neosporin is typical.

Sun Protection
The sun can be fierce! PABA preparations such as Pre Sun (applied often because of perspiration) are usually okay to about 10,000 feet. At higher altitudes, the only sun protection that works for many is a total mechanical blocking agent—a hat, bandana around the back of the neck, etc. Don't forget reflected sun on areas such as under the chin and nose—especially when on snow. A-Fil Sun Sticks (Texas Pharmaceutical) are good for lips, and inside of nose.

Skin
Mycolog ointment is very useful for itching, chafing and irritation in moist areas (especially after diarrhea).

Miscellaneous
Band-Aids, Moleskin, foot powder, spare glasses, personal drugs, etc.